The Seven [illegible] of Modern Cinema

A Philosophy of The Cinematic Image

Paul E Hill

Roger
With Best Wishes
Paul

Published 2022 by Abramis academic publishing

www.abramis.co.uk

ISBN 978 1 84549 798 9

Abramis is an imprint of arima publishing.

arima publishing
ASK House, Northgate Avenue
Bury St Edmunds, Suffolk IP32 6BB
t: (+44) 01284 700321

www.arimapublishing.com

Acknowledgements

Over the decades there have been far too many influences to mention. Some early examples of people who fed my interest in - at that time for me, unfamiliar cinema, usually the foreign-language jobs - were the more mature and more knowledgeable members of the committee of the now long defunct Grimsby Film Society. I was the youngest member and still a novice. From that same era I must add the tutors from both the WEA and The University of Hull who taught annual local 'night-school' courses on film appreciation. Classy cinema, and thought about just what it was that made it classy, began to flow through my veins and any further analysis would still test positive. In more recent years there have been countless discussions with my colleagues on the committee of the Louth Film Club – Heather Jenkins, Pete Hickman, Alan John and Professor Richard Keeble. I would like very much to thank Richard also for reading through and checking my draft manuscript. His knowledge and experience with such matters is much appreciated. My attempts to justify the placing of various films on the programme has constantly sharpened up my capacity for argument. I would like to single out for individual mention three other members – Steve Mansfield and Neil Ward, and especially the founder chair, Alex McMullen. The conversations (and sometimes debates) questions and conflicting views of all these people have challenged me to clarify my own thoughts and strengthen my own arguments. A more recent addition to the influences and motivation is my companion Pat Kelly. She lets me get away with nothing – except writing this book – as I endlessly air my views on films we've seen together, though she has rewarded me by becoming herself a lover of more challenging cinema – a fit business for one of such impressive intelligence. My brother, Andrew – a cineaste, actor and writer – has also given me a great deal to think about in observations made over many decades. I say a big thank you to them all. Important, too, was my own dear late wife, the Reverend Bridget Hill, who, once I had retired from full-time teaching, tolerated my frequent absences from home as I took myself off to 'Cinema City' in Norwich, an 'art house' cinema not far from our then-home in Norfolk. Without them *all* one way or another, I doubt this book would have ever been written, even though its faults, including the fault of its very existence, are all mine.

Dedication

To the late Alex McMullen, a dear friend, the founder-chair of Louth Film Club, and a dedicated fellow hunter of good cinema.

About the Author

For a living, Paul has spent his professional days as a primary school teacher in Grimsby, UK. He has had a serious interest in cinema since the age of 15 when he saw the film *Ben-Hur* (William Wyler, US, 1959) – a film he found to be both inspirational and noble. (Rare!) Shortly after this he joined the committee of the then 'Grimsby Film Society' and opened himself to the best in non-English language cinema. In those far off days, names like Antonioni, Bergman (Ingmar, that is) and even Ozu were the directors whose latest offerings were the ones to look out for. The interest remained and for the last few years he has had the honour of being chair of Louth Film Club' in Lincolnshire. Looking for good films takes up much of his time nowadays. He enjoys what he likes to call "the thrill of the hunt" and "bagging one for the club". He has written several books on his other main interest – philosophy – a couple of which have been accepted for publication. This is his first book on cinema. He holds a BA, MA and PhD in Philosophy and a BEd and MEd in Education, including History and Psychology. He has taught Philosophy with the WEA and with the Continuing Education Department of the University of Hull. One of the most exciting things in his life, though, was being married to Bridget, one of the pioneering new women priests in the Church of England. He trained as a Lay Reader in the church where he still serves. He counts himself as a Philosopher *for* Christ and a Philosopher *of* Cinema. Apart from a good film, Paul enjoys music, art, wine, gin, dining, reading and playing Ingress on his smartphone. (Level 9)

Referencing Films

I follow a simple system. For example: *Pain and Glory* (Pedro Almodóvar, Spain, 2020)

The title comes first, written in italics. Inside the parenthesis comes, in order, the name of the director, the country of origin and the year. If I cite the film again soon after an initial mention, I give only the title.

Films these days, for reasons tied to securing sufficient finance, are often funded from sources in multiple countries. I usually cite the one given first mention on the Internet Movie Database (IMDb). Often this reflects the culture and setting of the given country – as it does in the above example. But these days that may not always be the case. To say of today's films that they are French, German, Africa, American, and so on is sadly ambiguous. I have seen films which are foreign by (main) country of origin in which nearly every word was spoken in English (by the actors, not dubbed). So, make no assumptions. I will give extra details (of setting in time and place, culture and personnel, and anything else) where I consider it important enough so to do.

The year I give is the year of production. The year of initial theatrical release may be later, especially in countries other than its own. *In extremis* this may be several years. 'Foreign' films may often take quite a while to secure a UK distributor.

The details (title, director, country and year) I take from a fairly standard source: the IMDb.

Table of Contents

Introduction

This book is a reasoned complaint about a fundamental aesthetic failure, one that I believe plagues too much modern cinema. It is the failure to exploit, enlarge and intensify to the full, the visual, psychological and narrative power and potential of what I call the *cinematic image*. It is a wilful turning away from a special kind of artifice that essentially constitutes cinema. Even good directors seem to fall for the rhetoric, though thankfully ignore it in practice. For example, director Alan Parker once said, "Too many young filmmakers are interested in the technique of film. It's a red herring. What matters is what you have to say. When I started, Ken Loach told me, (when it comes to making a film) 'Don't ask how, just ask why'". In like manner, director Lindsay Anderson said, "No art is worth much which doesn't aim to change the world".[1] At least that message is simple, if arguable. My complaint, though, is also simple: just *that* way of thinking about the issue is the real mistake. Thank goodness that the three directors I cite here never altogether fell for their own misbegotten advice. (Perhaps Loach has more recently but, on the whole, I think them guilty more of confused thinking than poor filmmaking.)

I will now be equally plain: if you've got something to say, and it's important, then *how* you say it – in terms of story structure and technique - is crucial. The need for a proper authenticity in treating your subject matter does not entail a *lack* of technique or artifice – it *demands* it – and the 'how', so breezily dismissed by Loach, will depend upon the fundamental nature of the medium one is using – in our case, cinema. My case is also, at bottom, simple: bland naturalism (which I define later) is just not up to the job real authenticity so desperately needs. Expanding on Anderson, we may say that no art that isn't great art stands much chance of changing the world. Thank goodness also, then, that the great artists of the mediaeval church and Renaissance humanism did not fall for the increasing error of downplaying technique and style when you've got an issue to put across. In short, the strength of the message to be conveyed is dependent on the powers of the medium. If the latter is weak, the former will be diluted rather than appear in all its strength. This book is largely an attempt to demonstrate this thesis.

If there is just one major point at play here 'in a nutshell' here it is this: that what makes a film a great film, is its fittingness - aesthetic and moral. It must have fitting scale, fitting shape, fitting composition, fitting colour, fitting sound, fitting narrative structure and fitting points to make. Bad cinema would be then understood as cinema that lacks such fittingness. In a nutshell again, this is the main thesis of the present book. But one can only know whether something is fitting by, so to speak, knowing the nature of the beast. Hence, my opening, and very big question concerns the medium itself: What *is* a cinematic image? What is its fundamental nature? Questions of what turns it into art come later. Do not take the word 'art' too narrowly, though. The safest definition is that art is whatever sufficient numbers of people say it is. This used to be restricted to members of the authoritarian 'art establishment' but we are far more egalitarian these days. I am aware that this is not helpful. However, I am sufficiently familiar with the dangers of rushing into any alternative definition of 'art', to do so carelessly.[2] In any case, I think cinema is *both* art and entertainment under fairly ordinary and broad understandings of both terms. Also, it seems to me that the sins I isolate apply whether film is regarded as art *or* entertainment. My focus is primarily on the nature and potential of the cinematic image as a 'medium' and a medium is not necessarily an art form (in any very serious way, at least). I may use the medium of the email to send you a message, but I am hardly engaging in art – at least not under the usual understanding of things. The medium of the pencil can be used to make sketches (an art form) but it can be used also to construct diagrams or make shopping lists (not art forms). The cinematic image is likewise a medium but whether it becomes art or not is always a further question.[3]

To ask, 'What is the nature of a cinematic image?' is to ask a philosophical question and what characterises such questions is a sense of wonder, as Plato pointed out. But what begins with innocent wonder can soon end up with some head hurting arguments in support of different positions. I make no apology for the fact that the reader will face such argument at various points in the present book. It's just the nature of the beast. The fact is that inadequate argument establishes nothing. In this deep philosophical vein, I ask further questions: What exactly does one *see* when one looks at a cinematic image? How and where is motion involved? Can moral and aesthetic properties can be pulled apart? – and more. We need to understand what a cinematic image *is*, and have answers to the further questions, in order to see why, how and just what can be good or bad about it.

This should not be surprising. One simply cannot say what the misuse of *anything* at all may be, even say an everyday object like a teapot, unless one first understands its proper function, and one can only understand a thing's proper function if one knows just what the thing *is*. What a teapot is (in Britain, at least) may be obvious; what a cinematic image is, in contrast, is far from obvious – as we shall soon see. Some philosophy, therefore, is simply inevitable.[4] My first chapter will address these fascinating, necessary, initial and deeply philosophical questions, so I make no apologies for the philosophy. We are, amongst other things, doing 'philosophy of film' in this book.

I attempt to make things as clear as I can, but I will do the decent thing and signal here certain places in which the philosophising may seem a little too heavy-duty for readers unfamiliar with this kind of thinking. I hope you will give them a try, but you may avoid if you wish the sections – 'In Defence of Transparency', 'The Problems with Transparency' and perhaps 'The Concept of Vision' – all from Chapter 1 and the sections from Chapter 9 from 'Ethicism: A Defence' onwards. The section in Chapter 5 on music and emotional manipulation can get philosophically demanding at times, too. Missing out these sections certainly means missing out some important thinking. They wouldn't be there if I thought otherwise, but the reader may skip them without the main ideas falling completely apart. One will simply be left without the deeper level of reasoning behind them. Nonetheless, this book is a 'philosophical analysis' – complete with a framework of argument, and no matter how unfamiliar this kind of discourse may be, it will be helpful to show some willingness to engage with it. Full engagement with the themes of this book would be pretty well impossible without it. I make no apologies for the length of the first chapter, either. Failure to get right the issue of just what a cinematic image *is* would threaten the whole project of the book. Instead of my estimations of what is and is not sinful being rationally based, the book would amount to nothing more than a rather self-indulgent rant expressing my personal taste.

To ask what a cinematic image is also leads us inevitably to the technology of cinema. However, just as this book is not directly concerned with whatever we want to call 'art', it is not directly concerned with the technological aspects of filmmaking, either. Nevertheless, it simply cannot be denied that cinema is one of the most technologically complex of art forms (or entertainment forms). Moreover, what goes on technically in the making of a film affects both what we see and how we see it. Some discussion of the technology involved, therefore, is simply essential. The discussion will always be governed, though, by the book's more philosophical concerns.

Why are the sins 'modern'?

Not only that, but what do I even *mean* by 'modern' in this context? Besides, were there no sins at earlier times? In one sense, of course, *all* cinema is modern. It's pretty well the archetypal modern medium. However, cinema has a history, and this can be carved up into various stages: the so-called 'silent' era, the beginnings of sound, the battle with television and the coming of the wide screen, the digital age – and so on. (One can carve up matters even finer than that.) Styles have definitely changed during its existence – in the way films are shot, cut, acted, directed, and in, well, the very way they generally *look* and *sound*. What I am saying is simply this: in recent times, now moving into decades, some of the stylistic changes have not been particularly good ones. This book arises from my feeling moved to give serious justifications for this view.

Were there sins before my 'modern' ones? Of course! Cinema was born into its own world of sin. For example, if films now are made with cameras that move about too much, as I will argue they are, the earliest of films suffered because the cameras never moved at all. Watching a film was like being seated in a theatre, looking at a fixed stage. Although camera movement was sometimes well exploited in the later silent era, at the beginning of the sound era, the cumbersome apparatus and tricky technical demands of successful recording restricted the dynamic flow of the camera once again. Indeed, sound almost brought about the total destruction of decent cinema. Compare the flowing cinematic qualities of any really good silent film from the mid-20s with almost any 'talky' just a few years later. The latter seem primitive in comparison. (See *Singin' In The Rain*, Stanley Donen, US, 1952, for a wonderful mocking take of this troubled time.) Then came 3D in the early 50s, offered to combat TV's effect of dwindling cinema audiences. "A lion in your lap", became the go-to expression in the evaluation of that technique. One can list others, though films can be bad for various reasons, not just because they commit a sin of the sort I have identified as such.

Note, though, my use of the phrases 'earliest of films', and 'of *this* troubled time'. I can use them because they were *temporary* setbacks. They were *overcome* – even in the case of 3D. (See Hitchcock's, *Dial M for Murder*, US, 1954, for an example of improved use of this technique.) In short, filmmakers learned to do better. Moreover, they were not exactly widely lauded as 'good' in their own initial time. The sin was to be eradicated as soon as possible. Inventive technical people got to work on the problem and the 'artists' then got to work with the improvements. Much of the bad time I have with the 'modern' sins is precisely the fact that they are not (often enough, at least) thought of as sins in the first place. Quite the contrary, many seem to think of them as advancements which break free from earlier restrictions. Nor are they taken as being mere growing pains, as was the case with early sound. They've been around for a sizeable portion of the history of cinema already and show no signs of disappearing. All we can be thankful for is that the infection at least seems self-limiting. Let me say it: at least *some* directors know about cinema. This would be my justification for focusing on the 'modern' sins, and even my calling them 'sins' in the first place. Sin, in theology, is a particular kind of failure – missing the mark, falling short of the good life. (The English word 'sin' comes from Anglo-Saxon archery, where it meant missing the bull's eye.) This is frequently accompanied by the assumption that the failure has not even happened. Much modern cinema, I say, follows suit – just substitute 'good film' for 'good life'.

One may ask why all this is important. Why is it all worth an entire book, especially a long one? I can but quote John Updike, an influential 20th century American novelist, poet and critic:

"The cinema has done more for my spiritual life than the church. My ideas of fame, success and beauty all originate from the big screen. Whereas Christian religion is retreating everywhere and losing more and more influence; film has filled the vacuum and supports us with myths and action-controlling images."[5]

"Action controlling images"! Gosh! Filmmaker Alejandro Gonzalez Inarritu has similarly said, "Cinema is a mirror by which we often see ourselves."[6] *That* is why it's important - it influences our lives and our attitudes.

Do not take my title too heavily. I am not against progress, nor anything at all, on the sole grounds that it is new, or because I am not use to it, or because – being old – I have trouble adapting to innovation. Despite the all but impossible difficulties faced by even (perhaps one should say 'especially') the very best of modern filmmakers in getting the 'green light' to make their films, some excellent cinema still somehow gets made and I revel in it. Though years vary quite considerably in the quality of their offerings, there have been released during the twenty-four months prior to my writing this very sentence quite an impressive list of films. I would not have wanted to miss any of them. They come from around the world, too. One good-making feature they all have in common, though, is that they do not commit, either wilfully or by default, any of the seven deadly sins I identify.

I should add here, of course, that while avoiding the sins is a necessary condition for a film's being good cinema, it is far from being sufficient – a film needs a virtue or two as well. Sinners and saints exist in cinema, ancient and modern. This book is not simply negative, though. I will be giving some examples of saintliness in films alongside naming and shaming some of the sinners. After all, the notion of 'bad practice' is rather vacuous unless one knows what good practice is supposed to be. (And don't suggest that one could just as easily say that one needs to know what bad practice is before one can tell that something constitutes good practice. Good and bad, in my view, are not equal and symmetrical opposites. Good always comes first.) Another initial point: despite my title, one thing will be obvious as you read the book: there are many more than merely seven sins. My title is meant to have a rather teasing religious allusion. Besides, the title *The Umpteen Deadly Sins of Modern Cinema* didn't quite ring as well. The sins do however, tend, rather conveniently, to group themselves under seven broad headings.

However, do not take my title too lightly, either. I *mean* what I say. Though the word 'sin' may seem overly religious and old-fashioned, I think it fits. The defects of much modern cinema trouble my very soul, and they are deadly at least in the metaphorical sense that they set me too much against an art medium I have loved most of my life – at any rate since first seeing *Bambi* (Walt Disney, US, 1942). Yes! I use the word 'art' in this context unabashedly, not thinking art to be remotely inconsistent with entertainment. Good art of any sort never really has been. I often think that what we need is not (or not *just*) an increased focus on 'arty' cinema but a richer conception of entertainment. O dear, how our facile categories can so easily put some off so many from coming to appreciate what is valuable and make others too snooty about it all. Still, the word 'sin' seems neither too quaint and outdated nor too heavy-duty to express the effects had on me by certain kinds of defects that I find in modern cinema. The job I give myself in this book is to convince you, as best I can, just how serious and fundamental these defects are, or perhaps just to convince you that they *are* defects.

However, it is worth making clear at the outset that it is no part of my contention that the characteristics I list are sins *in themselves*. None could be in any sense outlawed without qualification. (Here, the word 'sin' deviates from its religious origins.) How can it always be a *sin* to move one's camera or to use colour? Such restriction would be clear nonsense. Look well enough and one can easily see that (nearly) all the 'sins' have, on occasion, been used to brilliant effect. The sin lies in either their inappropriate use or their use by sheer unthinking default when the employment of alternative techniques would have been far better. This makes the fundamental underlying sin something far more familiar – sheer thoughtlessness. Lest I be thought an oppressive old fuddy-duddy, though, I will be giving examples of both times when a given technique succeeds and when it doesn't.

In play here, of course, is the biggest question of all: just what it is that makes a good piece of cinema? There is no single way of answering that question because lots of factors are involved. I will thus allow my own views on the matter to emerge during the course of the discussion. In fact, I find it useful to grade films on two distinct scales. The first concerns the seriousness and real depth of the subject matter; the second, the quality and richness of the cinematic image. Thus, *Napoleon* (Abel Gance, France, 1927) would score high on both, most (though by no means all) modern 'feel good' films would score low-ish on both, and *Gigi* (Vincente Minnelli, US, 1958) would score low-ish on the first scale (despite the more serious intent of its literary origin) but fairly high on the second. (It's a pretty dashing piece of musical cinema.) Almost any recent Ken Loach film would score very highly on the first but low-ish on the second. (A pity, because *Kes* (UK, 1969) scored high on both and still made its point, even more powerfully.) I commend this method of dual classification, for one often wants to praise the one aspect of a film and criticise something about the other, though one can, of course, enjoy a well enough made piece of trivia. It's called relaxation. It gets even more complicated, though. Although distinct enough, these parameters are, nevertheless, closely related. The quality of what I call the 'cinematic image' can very much impact upon the depth, meaning and psychology of the film. One will meet such examples in the book.

In one sense there is really only *one* sin of modern cinema, though an overriding one. Throughout this book one will find references to how much like dreaming film-watching is. This is a constant, underlying theme. The overriding sin is that too many serious (and other) filmmakers these days ignore this key feature of our gaze towards the cinematic image and go in for a kind of bland naturalism instead, thinking this better and more realistic. My case will frequently be centred on the thesis that it is, paradoxically, *less* realistic. This lies at the bottom of pretty well all of the more specific sins. In my books, the more naturalistic approach simply deadens the cinematic impact of the reality it is attempting to convey.

My plan then is as follows. I first list the key theses of this book in a nutshell. Moving on to the detailed case, in Chapter 1, I examine just what a cinematic image is and introduce the 'oneiric theory' – the dream thesis of the cinematic image. This will be key in much of what follows. Armed with the necessary concepts involved in understanding the cinematic image, I move on in Chapter 2 to deal with a raft of sins that fall under appearance, with what can go wrong with the way a film just *looks*. In Chapter 3, I examine the very idea of motion in cinema and its associated sins – a key task given that the book is about 'motion pictures'. In Chapter 4, I come to the sins of colour – a rather specialised aspect of appearance that deserves separate attention. In Chapter 5, I shift modalities and deal with the problems of sound and music. It is here that I get to grips with the nature of emotion and its proper role in cinema. In Chapter 6, I deal with the unique aspect of performance in film, and in Chapter 7, I move on to the roles of space and time, which focusses on the sins of editing. In Chapter 8, I examine the various sins of storytelling. Chapter 9 covers issues connected with beauty and goodness in cinema and tackles the question of whether they can really be considered in grand separation. Finally, in Chapter 10, I look at the issue of genre. The issues in both Chapters 9 and 10 fall under the broader heading of sins of storytelling but their distinctive concerns call, I think, for chapters all their own. The reader will throughout discover that my overarching complaint is what I call an over emphasis on 'naturalism' in too much serious cinema. My key task is to provide a rational case against this tendency.

The Key Theses of This Book in a Nutshell

1. Too much cinema, especially serious cinema, downgrades itself by committing a variety of key cinematic sins that seem often presented as virtues. These sins are the subject of this book. A great film is a *fitting* film – aesthetically, morally and narratively.
2. Realism must always be distinguished from naturalism – then placed at opposite ends of the spectrum. Realism *expresses* reality through the artifice of cinema, but naturalism, in turning away from artifice, merely photocopies reality and ignores the fact that our experience of cinema is crucially like our experience of dreaming.
3. The artificial is almost always more real than the naturalistic.
4. All good cinema is, in the end, morally decent cinema.
5. Black and White (and, of course, the various shades of grey) should be the default colours.
6. There should be no camera movement beyond cinematic necessity. Motion should, by default, be *in* the frame.
7. Aesthetic values cannot survive moral ugliness.
8. The telling of grim life must be done with utmost cinematic style and grace together with consummate story-telling skill. Merely thumping the issues is never enough.
9. Default aspect ratios should be narrower.
10. Music is a near essential in conveying emotional depth.

Defending these deep theses requires careful and thorough (and, alas, often intellectually challenging) philosophical thought, but there is no alternative.

If this book goes a decent way towards providing this defence, it will be successful.

Before we move on to the sins directly, though, we have our initial big question to address: Just what *is* a cinematic image? I now turn to this epic task.

Chapter 1: What is a Cinematic Image?

"A film is never really good unless the camera is an eye in the head of a poet."
Orson Welles

As I have made clear, the first task is to think about the nature of the cinematic image and lay clear its more general features. This discussion is a key preliminary, for the general features I uncover in this chapter will have important implications for what I say later. Indeed, alleged sins against the cinematic image can only be understood as such if we know exactly what such an image is in the first place.

There are two kinds of question lurking hereabouts and they must be distinguished: metaphysical and aesthetic. I am concerned in this chapter with the first. This is simply to enquire what *kind of thing* a cinematic image is. Aesthetic evaluation is no more required in answering this question than it is in answering the question, 'What kind of thing is a teapot?' Of course, the adjective 'cinematic' is often meant as a term of aesthetic evaluation: cinematic films are often held in higher value. That issue is key also, of course, but that is covered in our discussion of the sins.

However, before one can evaluate something one has to know what sort of thing one is talking about. Remember, one could hardly evaluate the effectiveness of a teapot if one has no idea of what a teapot is or what it is supposed to do. The nature of a thing determines, at any rate in part, the aesthetic features and values it is supposed to exemplify. Well! Ditto for cinematic images. If I am to evaluate cinematic imagery in the aesthetic sense – which I will come to do – I must first know exactly *what* a cinematic image is (as opposed to an image of some other kind – a painting, a rough sketch or a still photograph, for example). Without understanding this, agreement and disagreement in aesthetic evaluation would be groundless. It would be rather like debating the value of a widget without knowing what a widget is or what it's supposed to do. That is why the metaphysical question comes first – and we will soon see that the answer to it is by no means obvious.

I do not think we can appeal to science here. Science tells us about the physical mechanics and structures of things. In that sense, a cinematic image is, at most, just the little picture on a strip of cinematographic film (or its digital equivalent) – the bit that gets projected. That isn't what I mean *here* by 'cinematic image'. The image on the strip of film is not itself a cinematic image. It cannot be, it doesn't even move (save through the projector). It is merely (part of) the mechanical means of *producing* the cinematic image, an item in the chain of cause and effect that terminates with the appearance of a cinematic image.

The cinematic image is a brand of photographic image and, like others in the same family, it has its strangeness, a strangeness perhaps of which we are standardly unaware, at least without further reflection. This is doubtless because of its huge degree of familiarity. It, and related imagery, have become so much a part of our lives that we take them for granted. This was not so in cinema's very earliest days, with reports of its first viewers ducking from motion-picture images of approaching trains. These days we may flinch just a bit only when viewing the most advanced stereoscopic image of something being thrown in our faces.

But let us reflect for a moment, for there is a deep and very odd tension in the structure of the cinematic image. On the one hand, it has a deep reality, wrought by its essentially photographic nature. (I deal with exceptions, such as animation, later.) The world it shows is as solid and real as the 'real' world because, well, it just is an image *of* the real world, a kind of photo-accurate simulacrum of reality. This distinguishes it from, say, paintings and sketches, however full of detail they may sometimes be. (I will return to this distinction, too.) It even moves about like reality. (Yes! It really does move about. I believe the idea that the motion is an illusion is a scientific conceit – something else to which I return in due course.)

On the other hand, this simulacrum has a kind of ghostly aspect. Space in a cinematic image in certain ways still looks like the space of ordinary worldly perception but it also has a detached strangeness. It just hangs before the viewer on a now invisible screen, gleaming down as if an apparition. It seems (to the eye alone) to come from nowhere, at least nowhere knowable by or accessible to the viewer. It's just *there* and it seems to occupy a space all its own. Although it is before our very eyes and we can point to it, its space is not *altogether* part of our shared public space, the space in which we move about and do things. It's a kind of non-physical space that looms strangely before us. Of course, we know that in some sense it comes from a projector but this apparatus is not part of our fundamental visual experience of the image. The physical causes are not built into what may be called the 'phenomenology' of the cinematic image. This is quite unlike ordinary perception in which one readily understands the things one sees as material objects and embodied persons who move around in accordance with what we call the laws of nature and which we can approach and interact with, even, in some cases, talk to.

I am not remotely suggesting that the perceived space of ordinary worldly perception carries no psychological power at all. Of course it does. An enemy remaining in the distant background seems less threatening than one rapidly approaching, and a physically close friend can be more psychologically comforting. Even physical space, as perceived, can never be fully understood in wholly objective terms. However, the distanced strangeness of space in the cinematic image has greater malleability and thus modifies the psychological potential at play.

Lens, focus, camera position and movement and the surrounding context of the editing change the significance of the photographed physical space and can give the latter meanings that just aren't a feature of ordinary worldly perception.

In such ways, the cinematic image has an insistent reality in that it demands, even *commands*, our attention, it's just that the reality it conveys is not there materially in front of us. The image is only *in a sense* 'there'; the reality it conveys is not there *at all*, and may not even any longer exist – a film set, for example, may been taken down long before we see the film. Though the reality it *presents* is certainly tangible, there is nothing tangible about what is directly *visible* to us – the image itself. The only tangible thing in our field of view is the screen, yet the screen disappears, replaced inexorably by the image. This, in broad brushstroke terms, is the nature of the cinematic image, and even when it comes in forms that are not all that terribly impressive aesthetically (and it is the sad thesis of the present book that this is all too common, and its task to argue why and how) it is still *strange*. If there is one sensibility I would like a reader to hold on to as they read the book it would be just this strangeness. Take a hint here: watch a few really boring films. One will be much freer to reflect on the nature of the cinematic image while one is watching such a film than one is as one watches a good one, for one's attention will be less diverted.

Just what, then *is* a cinematic image? What ingredients must an image have in order to count as cinematic? Remember, I am not in this chapter asking what an image needs in order to be aesthetically pleasing – that's an extra – just what it needs to count as a cinematic image *at all*. I am concerned here with the structure, the very nature, of the cinematic image, with what a cinematic image *is*.

To start off, we may note that the cinematic image seems to occupy that tricky-to-get-a-grip-on territory somewhere midway between *percepts* (the experience of seeing things before one's eyes in the course of ordinary perception[7]) and experiences like dreams, hallucinations and mental images (something we often call 'seeing with the *mind's* eye'). Indeed, that the cinematic image is, *by its very nature* (if not always *aesthetically*) at least a bit dreamlike is a fundamental aspect of the case I make in this book and I return to it below.

My claim is that an image is cinematic in the full sense if and only if it satisfies all of the following conditions:

i) It must involve sight and sound.
ii) It must be photographically realistic.
iii) It must have motion
iv) It must be temporal (it changes with time)
v) It must have 'intentionality' (be *about* something)
vi) It must be technology dependent upon photographic equipment.

The above lay out the properties an image has by which it can count as cinematic in the first place – at least fully. They distinguish the cinematic image from other kinds of image, such as still photography, computer graphic images, painting and drawing. There are further properties that arise in varying ways and to varying degrees from these more basic properties. How imaginatively they are put to use will determine how cinematic the imagery is in the aesthetic sense of the word. The reader will find this point surfacing at various places herein. This should hardly be surprising, for it underlies many a sin. The resultant properties are as follows.

vii) a potential for psychological unity

viii) being a *way* of seeing rather than *what* one sees – in which lay its aesthetic potential

ix) aesthetic, spatial, temporal and aesthetic distance

x) framing, composition and its own distinctive space

xi) a dream-like presence.

I shall be giving further elucidation and defence of these below. The first six properties constitute what has been called a form of 'medium essentialism' – the view that unless an image strictly satisfies some precisely defined list of criteria, it could not possibly constitute cinema. This is not a particularly 'cool' view these days. It seems rather prescriptive and can be accused of ruling out too much. If you feel that way, fair enough. My job is to try to argue you round to accepting my thesis. I think that some form of medium essentialism is worth sticking to, though, because images with these properties have an important distinctiveness. Each of these conditions, I would contend, contributes to what we have learned to accept as cinema. They are all crucial one way or another. To some extent they are a matter of how cinema has evolved. What's wrong with that? It is hardly irrelevant, at the very least. After all evolution and history partly determine what many kinds of things are. Besides, if nothing is to be counted as essential, then it is hard to see how cinema can be anything at all, certainly anything distinctive. There must be some boundaries if there is to be cinema at all. Some things seem audio-visually inappropriate in films. We can aesthetically *evaluate* cinema.

Yet, it is hard to see how we could do this if nothing in particular constituted a cinematic image in the first place. I think that the cinematic image is there to do something for us, that it has a *purpose* - to use a piece of philosophical jargon, that it is 'teleological'. I think it can do things well or badly. I would suggest that most film lovers feel that way. It's part of the reason why one becomes a film *lover* in the first place. This would seem impossible from an '(almost) anything goes' perspective. At the very least it seems essential to rational discourse about film – and to rational argument about it. Disagreement would otherwise amount to little more than throwing things at each other. Yet lovers of film just do seek rationally to persuade one another.

Perhaps another available option would be the 'family resemblance' view. This view would eschew the need for a set of rigid, strictly-to-be-observed criteria such as I have just put forward in favour of something at least a bit more flexible. This would allow various forms of image to count as cinematic just so long as they possess sufficient resemblance to others that *are* so countable. I'm sure that such a view may attract many but I still worry. How *much* resemblance is needed? And resemblance to *what* exactly? Such a view all too easily seems to disintegrate into 'anything goes', though a very modest version of it may accommodate abstract and animated images, which can surely be cinematic in some strong enough sense. Indeed, the position I adopt in this book could be set out as follows: there are paradigmatic cinematic images (ones that satisfy the criteria I put forward) and other cases (such as animation) that only satisfy some of them.

Arguably, the final five properties (save perhaps vii) are always there to some degree (though they may also typify other kinds of imagery as well – to varying extents) but are not always well exploited by those who make films. How well or badly they are exploited determines, so I claim, how aesthetically good a cinematic image is. This, as we shall see, lies at the bottom of many a sin. I explore each of these conditions in turn.

Sight and Sound

It seems uncontroversial to say that a cinematic image is a medium of sight. That is, it must give an audience something to look at other than a naked cinema screen, so I continue my answer to the metaphysical question, in somewhat jesting mode, by offering what I call my 'acid test'. Although this is primarily an aesthetic test of good cinema, it will also suggest part of the answer to the metaphysical question. Choose a film you haven't already seen, and about which you know nothing, and 'watch' it with your eyes *closed.* If you can still make good sense of it you'll know that it isn't a very good piece of cinema and would have better been produced as a play for the radio, for nothing of importance, in terms of meaning or value, will have been lost – or, at any rate not much. It might be thought that this is because the cinematic image is primarily a *visual* item. What one sees should certainly be central to the experience of cinema, never merely a visual accompaniment to what one hears. However, this I contend, is only part of the story. What one hears also counts – and this should never be a mere aural accompaniment to what one sees, either. So, now conduct a second amusing experiment on another film, only this time bung up your ears. You *still* shouldn't be able to make total sense of it. But this isn't because the cinematic image is primarily an aural item either.

It is because the cinematic image is a medium of *both* sight and sound. Both are key and they should work together, almost mystically, as if being essentially *one*. The so-called 'silent' era, by the way, a source of some of the greatest pieces of cinema in the catalogue, is not a counter-example to this. The term 'silent film' is a retronym. Sound was typically both demanded and provided, and sometimes music was specially provided for films, it just wasn't precisely synchronised with the picture. It depended purely on the inventiveness and alertness of a talented cinema pianist (or full orchestra in the plusher and more expensive 'picture palaces'). I suppose so-called 'experimental' so-called cinema exists in which there is no sound at all. No absurdity surprises me these days but, frankly, I would judge this to be no less crazy than a piano concerto in which the piano is not played and I am not prepared to let something that seems close to clinical insanity parading as art run counter to a perfectly good thesis. I do not care how beautiful a film *looks*, there seems always something missing about it if there is *never* any sound.

These evaluative experiments suggest that both picture and sound, as a fundamental unity, are what essentially *comprise* the cinematic image. They tell us (alongside the other criteria) pretty much what sort of thing a cinematic image *is* and show that there just *is* no cinematic image without *both* sound and picture acting in unity. In short, it's just not true that cinema is primarily a visual medium. I realise, of course, that there are times in films in which there is a picture without sound, sometimes without even the incidental sounds of, say, a street, yet one may still have a cinematic image. Equally there can be times in films in which there is sound but no picture (though this is much rarer). My favourite candidate here is *It's A Wonderful Life* (Frank Capra, US, 1946). Near the beginning of the film two senior angels are discussing the fate of a junior angel who has yet to earn his wings and who may do so by coming to the aid of the film's main character. As their dialogue continues, the screen goes more or less a uniform grey – and it all continues to be (a very effective) cinematic image. However, these episodes tend to be *phases* of a longer cinematic image and, I suggest would not remotely work if considered in total isolation. In any case, I will show that 'cinematic image' is not just synonymous with 'shot'. Sight and sound, though, are at work in other kinds of motion picture, too, so we must press on to complete our analysis of the uniquely cinematic image.

Photographic Realism

We must ask what 'realism' is supposed to mean in this context. The pivotal question here is just what it is one *sees* as one watches a film. I begin with one form of realism, often called 'transparency'. I then move on to consider other forms of realism.

Photographic realism proclaims that photographs reveal or show the world in a unique way. But exactly what way is that? Let us first isolate the options regarding just what one sees as one looks towards a photograph or a cinema screen.

1. We literally see *only* the photographic image, this representing reality.
2. We literally see *only* what the picture is a picture *of* (i.e., the persons, objects, scenery, etc that was photographed by the camera). What is on the screen is only part of the causal chain by which we come to see such things.
3. We literally see both photograph and subject but *in different senses.*

Option 1 may seem intuitively correct. After all, the image seems to be what my eyes are directed on. Option 2 may sound initially silly but it can be defended. After all, we often talk of having seen this or that in a photograph not of having seen an *image* of this or that. The question would then be whether such talk is meant to be taken literally or intended just as meaning that looking at a photograph is, in some respects, *like* seeing the things, places or persons themselves. Secondly, there are images on our retinas but these images are not what we *see.* We see the world around us. Our retinal images are merely part of the causal chain by which we *come* to see the world. Option 2 says this is the way it is with photography. Still, there is a dis-analogy. In the case of photography my eyes are directed towards the image, but my eyes can hardly be directed on to their own retinal images. However, I shall not defend this view. Option 3 is the one I will defend: we see *both* image and world but in different senses of the word 'see': the image is seen *directly*; the world, *indirectly* – but it is still seen. Option 3 is often called 'The Transparency Thesis'.[8] This is because it claims that we see the world, in some sense, *through* the photographic image. As the French filmmaker Jean-Luc Godard famously quipped, "The cinema is truth twenty-four times per second". The cinematic image is, to use a remark from Colin McGinn, "consciousness transplanted"[9]. The image is a way of seeing the world.

McGinn's description puts me in mind of Emerson's celebrated metaphor of the 'transparent eyeball'. The idea is that in a special perceptual experience of nature one sloughs off one's embodiment and sees things in a greater purity, merging with what one sees as one is unencumbered with the usual presumptions of daily perception. Emerson sees a special spiritual and religious oneness in all this. While one could critique how far one can literally eliminate embodiment from one's daily perceptual experience of the world, I think that there is a sense in which it captures one's experience of a photograph, and especially of the cinematic image. One is both *there* (a hidden observer in the environment of the story world) and *not there* (because one is seeing it all from a distant and darkened chamber – perhaps the closest thing to being disembodied that one can get and still remain alive. If one does not exactly see the story world with a cleansed spiritual purity, one certainly seems to see it from a special, intimate and privileged position.[10]

Still, should we regard such talk of seeing the world through the image as literal talk?[11] Yes! I thus offer a defence of the Transparency Thesis.

The defence of transparency[12]

The transparency idea may seem odd but its oddity may be lightened a bit by considering an older medium, that of the camera obscura. Normally we would say that we still see the world through its strangely projected image. But what is a photographic and indeed a cinematographic image if not the image from a different kind of camera, an image fixed to last? Cinema is a photographic medium, and photography is a mechanical process. I mean by this that the final result is produced by mechanical (broadly speaking 'physical') processes. This contrasts with painting and drawing, in which the final result is produced by the *intentional* movement of a human hand, relying on perception, acuity, memory and imagination – all the human stuff. Likewise, when you just look at the things around you, you do not produce what you see as the artist does, you just get to the final result – your perception of something – by purely mechanical means: light is reflected from the objects around you, enters your eyes and strikes your retinas. Electrical signals are sent to your brain, then, *voila*, you see those things.[13] Of course, in the processes behind our ordinary, daily perceptions, these physical processes (the light travel, the neural signalling and so on) happen very quickly, so much so that they are effectively instantaneous. (Unless one is looking at an object at astronomical distance.)

Now think of photographs. How do they come about? Light is likewise reflected from the objects around the camera, is focused by the lens and strikes the film (or digital sensor). This is then subject to some sort of physical processing which terminates in a photograph (or cinematograph or video). Next, the mechanical processes of perception come into play again and we end up seeing the photograph. This obvious similarity between how we get our perceptions and how we get our photographs and then see them invites the thought that one just as much literally *sees* the things in the image when one's eyes focus on a photograph of those things as one does when our eyes focus on those things themselves, when they are physically in front of us. In the case of the photograph, all that's happened is that we have a somewhat longer, more complicated, chain of purely mechanical cause and effect. Of course, someone might start being creative with the photograph, giving some sort of form all its own that the original objects did not have, but while this is important in other ways (as we shall later see) it does not, all by itself, seem to refute the idea of transparency.

So, let's have a recap to keep on track. Say you look at a photograph of Churchill, who has been long gone. The idea at play here is that you literally see both the photographic image of Churchill *and* Churchill himself, but that you see the photograph *directly*, and Churchill *indirectly*. For all that, Churchill is standardly the final object of your vision. The photograph all but drops out of things unless it has its own distinctive features. If someone has been creative with the photograph you may, for example, see Churchill sepia toned, but that doesn't mean that you do not see (indirectly) Churchill, only that you see him in a somewhat visually distorted way. After all, I could look at *you* now through sepia tinted lenses but it would still be you I see. All this contrasts with a painting or drawing of Churchill. In these cases you see *only* an image of the man, no matter how convincing an image it may be or how well you can *imagine* it as seeing him. Thus, unlike photographic images, paintings and drawings are *opaque* to the world itself rather than *transparent* to it.

Still, there is a difference at play. In a photograph, you don't see a thing as it is *now*, of course, for it may have been destroyed by the time you come to look at the photograph. Even so, according to the idea of transparency, you do still, quite literally, *see* it. This is no problem for the transparency thesis, for time delay is involved in ordinary perception, too. Though the processes involved in vision are as good as instantaneous, they are not literally so. Light still takes time to get from the object to your eye, as does the subsequent neural signalling. More dramatically, if one looks at an astronomical object, a star say, it is possible that it may have disappeared many years before as a supernova, but you still see the star, you just see it as it *was*, not as it (now) *is* – just like Churchill.[14] Let me ram home the point. When we look at a photograph of Churchill and say that we literally see the man, there is no *as-if-ness* at play in our language here. Rather, we *actually do literally have* genuine, though considerably delayed perceptual access to Churchill.

This is not to say that photographic media are as good a guide to reality in *all* ways as ordinary perception. For example, a subject looking at a photograph or film of Paris has no way of locating themselves in relation to the place. The subject couldn't say, "Paris is here" or "there" or "all around me" on the basis of seeing Paris through the photograph. Nor could they reliably *point* to Paris on this basis. On the other hand, the photograph does still give us some realistic information about what we see. Given that Paris looks a certain way then it will look that way in standardly produced photographs. Had Paris looked differently to the eye, the photograph would be correspondingly different. Photographs can be tampered with of course. How many times has Photoshop been used to make a model look even more beautiful? We will come to these and other kinds distortion in due course, for now, we can just say that transparency applies to standard, unadulterated photography. This makes photography quite distinct from painting and drawing. In those cases there is no merely mechanical guarantee that the artist has got things right, even if that was the intention.

Films in particular also give us the same basic range of ways for interpreting the thoughts and feelings of characters as we would get by looking at them (if we could) in the normal way: seeing expressions, gestures, movements, and so on, and the cinematic image gives us such perceptual clues by purely mechanical means. These are what the philosopher Paul Grice calls "natural meanings". These can be found when one thing reliably indicates (is a sign of) something else.[15] Photography also gives us perception levels of accuracy about the physical environment in front of the camera. If it *looks* like a crowded room in the photograph, it doubtless was. Thus, straight photography fits this bill as does ordinary perception but it is quite unlike, say, painting or drawing. An artist may add anything they like (or can get away with). Of course, today's filmmakers have digital manipulation to work with but remember the thesis is that photography is transparent to the extent that it just *is* photography. Digital manipulation comes closer to painting.[16] I will discuss these kinds of distortion under The Sins of Appearance. (Though my thesis is not that distortion, *per se* is a sin. If it were, *Citizen Kane* itself would be down the drain.)

None of this is to deny that plenty of interpretation is going on in seeing photographs. However, interpretation happens all the time in matters of straight perception, too. We interpret (usually quite subconsciously) what we see as being this or that. For example, I interpret what I see around me now as solid objects placed around a room, even though only some of their surfaces are strictly visible to me. Seeing is a thing that has to be learned but once learned, interpretation is usually quite automatic and habitual. As I walk down a residential street, for example, I standardly take myself to be seeing three-dimensional houses, with hidden surfaces, inside rooms, and so on. (This is opposed to traditional Hollywood sets which are just frontages buttressed from behind, though it is only because we have already learned certain kinds of interpretation in the course of ordinary perception that we see the sets in the way we do.) This is the case even though only certain surfaces are visible to me from the street. In short, my perception comes *always and already* interpreted. It is because of the gap between what is strictly visible at any given time (certain surfaces) and what we take ourselves to see (proper houses) that interpretation is required. It is the same gap that opens up the possibility of our being fooled. If some of the structures I saw were not houses but just sufficient lookalikes to houses from the street position (say they lacked a back wall) I would be fooled, as I am with those film sets. That is, my habitual interpretation of seeing a house would be defeated by the reality. All this extends to our perception through the photographic image, though this has to be learned, too. One can find reports from the early days of cinema of people from cultures not already accustomed to painted portraits being frightened by close-ups, interpreting what they saw as, unaccountably still talking, decapitated heads. Perception is always learned. The new-born baby seems to have only buzzing, booming, chaotic confusion, even though baby quickly gets to know who is mum. Of course, perceptual interpretation can come in more refined levels.

The idea, then, is this: the photographic (and thus cinematic) image is a *way* of seeing or perceiving things, a *mode* of vision rather than simply or solely an *object* of perception. The final objects of perception are whatever has been photographed. Cinematic images, insofar as they are straightforwardly photographic in nature, are ways of perceiving the world that was in front of the camera. The director Andrei Tarkovsky once said, "Relating a person to the whole world: that is the meaning of cinema." That is why they are so important and why sins against them matter. This, then, is essentially what is meant by the photographic realism of cinema. Thus, cinematic images do not *depict*, in the way that paintings and drawing do. In seeing anything purely photographically, one is no more seeing a pure depiction than one is seeing depicted the scene outside as one peers through a window. One sees the things outside the window. In this sense, the photographic image *is* a kind of window.

I do not mean that images cannot distort reality. Any window, though, might do that. One has selection for a start and the image can draw one's attention to some things more than others or induce you to see things in a particular way. I say only that this isn't depiction in the sense used in connection with, say, painting.[17] I do not mean by all this either that one's visual attention cannot be drawn to the cinematic image, only that what one is being drawn to is one's *way* of seeing. I may attend to areas of light and dark, for instance or to an arrangement of colour. I may describe such features. I shall be doing precisely that throughout the book. It's just that what I am describing, I contend, are *ways* of seeing the world before the camera, ways of seeing that are photographic rather than, as it were, *live*. Nor, as we shall see later, does it imply that a cinematic image cannot have aesthetic qualities which come from what can be called the 'form' of the image. It's just that what has these qualities – the ones that constitute the form - are our *ways* of seeing things through the cinematic image.

More Serious Problems with Transparency

Critics of transparency often focus on one idea crucial to transparency thesis. They then try to show that this cannot support the conclusion the transparency theorist needs. These criticisms take the form of thought experiments. I deal with two of them. The crucial notion here is what philosophers call 'counterfactual dependence'. One thing, call it Y, is counterfactually dependent on another thing, call it X, if, as X changes, Y tracks that change accordingly. For example, I happen to see a red rug on the floor before me. This is because it *is* red. However, were it of a different colour, blue, say, I would see a blue rug instead. Were it to change colour, my vision would track that change as I look at the rug. It happens (unsurprisingly) to remain red (the factual) but had it been blue (the 'counter-factual') I would see it as blue. Thus, ordinary vision is said to be counterfactually dependent upon reality with respect to colour: if the colour changed, so would my perception of that colour (standardly, at least). Note, no change actually *has* to take place, it's just that *if* it did, our perception would change correspondingly. Nor does it mean that vision cannot go wrong, as in forms of colour blindness, for example. It is just that vision is paradigmatically counterfactually dependent on reality with respect to colour. It doesn't mean that vision is counterfactually dependent upon other properties of things, either. If, for example, the rug suddenly gained weight but managed to look the same as it did before, my eyes would not track *that* change. Vision, unsurprisingly, has counterfactual dependence only upon the visual properties of things. That's what eyes are for, after all. 'Putting on a bit of weight', as it is delicately called, is not in itself a visual change – it's a mass change – even though it may have longer term consequences that are all too visible, as I, alas, know.

Very well, if vision is counterfactually dependent upon and tracks changes in, the visual properties of things seen, then any other medium that is said to be a case of seeing the world – as is the case in photography according to transparency theory – should also be counterfactually dependent on the visual properties of things. So far, so good, of course, because it *is*. Just as in vision, if I took a photograph of the aforementioned rug it would come out looking red, and had it been blue, it would have been blue in the photograph. Photography (and hence standard cinema) passes this test of counterfactual dependency on the things photographed, with respect to their visual properties.

Now, though, an awkward question, even granting counterfactual dependency to photography, is this sufficient to make photography a kind of seeing things in the world, as claimed by transparency theorist? The two following thought experiments attempt to show that counterfactual dependency, all by itself, is not sufficient. Before I dive in, though, I should issue a word of warning: when first encountering a philosophical thought experiment many people, especially non-philosophers, become quickly tired out by what they think is some impractical or just plain silly proposal that they find posited in the experiment. (I know this from years of experience in teaching philosophy.) Well! We *know* that. What is proposed in the experiment does not have to be practical or even technically possible at all – it just has to be *thinkable*. That's what makes them *thought* experiments. They are not intended as practical possibilities, they are intended to tease out whether some philosophical proposal is intelligible or justified – in this case, whether something's having counterfactual dependence upon on the visual properties of the world is sufficient to make it a case of vision.[18]

First thought experiment: the counterfactually dependent model of a jungle

Imagine a model of some part of an actual jungle, complete with all its wildlife. The exceptional thing about this model it is that by some mechanism one can scarcely imagine, the visual features and the movements taking place in it are counterfactually dependent upon the exact visual features and changes that take place in the real jungle of which it is the model – just as, say, a streamed wildlife video would be. The model tracks the reality in the same way. The charge against the transparency thesis is this: though this model was counterfactually dependent upon the real jungle, in the exact same ways as a streamed video would be, we would not judge it as a case of *seeing* the jungle, not even as an *indirect* seeing of the jungle. It would, indeed, be a remarkable model and no doubt a technological impossibility, but that is all. But if (relevant) counterfactual dependence is not sufficient to make *this* a case of seeing (even indirect seeing) why should we allow photography to so count? Mere counterfactual dependency, in other words, would be insufficient to establish the case for transparency. (I hope you now see the purpose of a philosophical thought experiment.)

Second thought experiment: counterfactually dependent mechanically generated descriptions of things and situations

One can go further than the model. Imagine that a remarkable writing machine is equally counterfactually dependent upon some visible real-world situation. It describes all the visual features of this situation and, when changes occur to these, it reports them – features and actions are described, as fully and exhaustively as is required, as they occur. (Or, as in photography, they could be delayed.) The charge, again, is that despite the counterfactual dependence, this would not count as a case of seeing the real-world situation, even indirectly.

How can the transparency theorist respond to these two thought experiments? Remember, it doesn't matter here how preposterously impractical or unlikely such models and machines are, they just have to be *thinkable* or imaginable. This alone allows us to cast serious doubt on the truth of the proposed thesis.

Critics of the transparency thesis may point out that if such things were advertised as 'See a Real Jungle', or some such, the 'audience' would demand its money back. So they might but people may well have the same response to cinema owners if jungle films were similarly advertised. However, this seems only to show that in our normal use of the word 'see', we refer to and think only of things that are directly in front of our eyes. This hardly shows that there cannot be extended but still literal cases of seeing, cases of *indirect* seeing, as proposed by transparency theory. Kania also thinks, and I concur, that there is a failure of imagination at play in these criticisms. Should such a model jungle as is being proposed (as opposed to some merely clunky animatronics) *really* to exist, we can ask whether it is so obvious that we would so readily discount it as a way of seeing.[19] Much would depend on exactly how the machine worked, but, if machine it was, the workings would be purely mechanical (in some sense) as is the case in photography.

How about the writing machine, though? The obvious difference here is that descriptions of visual features and changes, no matter how exhaustively accurate they may be, do not visually *resemble* the objects they describe: the word 'red' need not itself *be* red. Photographic images, of course, do have this resemblance. We have not so far explicitly mentioned resemblance but transparency theory can easily (and non-arbitrarily) accommodate it as a fairly obvious necessary condition. Altogether we have to appeal here to the notions of necessary and sufficient conditions: both visual resemblance and counterfactual dependency are *necessary* for something contentious counting as an instance of perception (in some extended sense of the term) but neither alone is *sufficient*. I thus dismiss these two thought experiments. They fail to show that counter-factual dependency, when combined with visual resemblance, is insufficient for something to count as a case of indirect seeing.

Two further problems: interruption of the light beam & a cessation in causality

In ordinary vision there is just one light beam – straight from object to eye, one light beam from the red rug to my eye. In photography there are at least two: one from object to camera and a second from photographic image to the eye. Is this sufficient to show that we do not see the world through photographic images. I do not think so. Light is simply a mechanical progression and there are plenty of other mechanical causal chains between camera and final image. It is not clear why the presence of one single uninterrupted beam of light should be a decisive criterion.

What goes on during the delay between the time at which the camera took the image and our seeing it – it could be years – might seem more worrying. Isn't there a break in the chain of cause and effect altogether? If this were the case, then so much the worse for the idea that we literally see the world through photography. But this is not the case. As a photograph, say, lies for years in an album, untouched, or a film lies in a vault, there are still continuing chains of cause and effect going on. Indeed, sometimes such chains of cause and effect have all too obvious visual consequences, as when images fade or deteriorate. If we do not want that to happen, then photographic images have to kept in conditions that keep in operation chains of cause and effect that keep the image in existence. At no time at all is there really any cessation of (relevant) causal chains – and they matter to the final experience. I conclude that transparency can still be ascribed to photography – that is, photography can be understood as a way of genuinely, though also indirectly, seeing the world. In any case, it is not clear that intermediate chains of cause and effect need exist at all. Could there not be a case of 'miraculous seeing'? If I went blind and God wanted me to see again, couldn't he simply miraculously restore my visual experience of the world and make it counterfactually dependent upon the world's visual properties – all without cause and effect between the two at all?

The concept of vision

The transparency theorist can, it seems to me, rest on the fact that the concept of vision – which determines what features should be present in order for something to count as a case of seeing – is not a tight, unitary concept. That is, there is no final, absolute, list of conditions all of which a visual experience has unambiguously to meet in order to count as a case of seeing. Some features may be necessary but not sufficient all by themselves. Counterfactual dependence on visual properties is one such. If something does not exhibit this dependence *at all* it cannot be a case of seeing, but having it does not, all by itself ensure that something can be counted as a case of seeing. Resemblance, as we have just identified, is another. There has to be a visual resemblance between my photograph of the red rug and the rug itself – and there is. If how you see things does not, in some systematic way, retain the visual properties of ordinary vision, then it cannot count as a case of vision. Resemblance all by itself, though is insufficient. A painting of the rug would also visually resemble the rug (unless it was a Picasso) but looking at this painting would not be a way of seeing the rug.

Some features may be present in some cases of vision and not in others while all remain cases of seeing. For example, coloured glass in a window to some extent compromises the counterfactual dependency of our vision, but we would still say that we were seeing the world through it. As a child I used occasionally to amuse myself by looking at the room through a crinkled, transparent, nicely coloured toffee paper. Yet even through this distorting filter, I still saw the room. What else? The filter contains no image. (I can still amuse myself this way. I have looked at many a boring film through a toffee paper in a desperate attempt to improve them. Nor is this an entirely futile exercise, for it certainly improves the experience.) Another piece of fun came from distorting mirrors at a fairground. (Do such simple amusements still fascinate or are we too busy looking at our smartphones and tablets?) I loved the way I could see myself as extra wide through a distorting mirror. (Nowadays, alas, ordinary flat mirrors do the same trick.) The crucial point though is that I still *see* myself through them. Cataracts may compromise our ordinary vision, too, but they do not necessarily do so to the extent that they remove all counterfactual dependency. Distortion counts as such precisely because it compromises reality by reducing counterfactual dependency not because it removes it entirely. To do that would be effectively to bring about blindness, even if one was still left with some kind of visual experience.

Another kind of example: if a thing is too far away or too small to be seen by the naked eye, one can employ an arrangement of lenses to help, as in telescopes or microscopes. In ordinary vision the only lenses we need are the ones in our own eyes but that doesn't mean that we don't genuinely see things through optical instruments. I wear spectacles but I still see the world beyond them. In fact, I see it *better*. That's rather the point. Why should a few extra lenses make the difference between a case of seeing or not seeing? I use a mirror when brushing my hair. Does the necessary presence of a mirror mean that this is not seeing oneself simply on the grounds that mirrors are not involved in more straightforward ordinary perception? Of course not. Of course, there are some tricky cases. Do *electron* microscopes, give us aided *vision*, as light microscopes do, so that we can say that *see* through them, or are we to conceive what they do differently? The images they produce are not, of course, literally *photo*graphs, because light was not (relevantly) used in the making of them. Such microscopes do not reveal hidden *visual* properties of things, strictly speaking. If vision they give, it will be a kind of vision very different from anything produced by simple optics. Nonetheless, they seem to offer something analogous to vision. The point here is that our concept of vision is insufficiently refined decisively to rule out or rule in as genuine vision certain kinds of case. Should straightforward photography count, then? Some conditions (counterfactual dependence and resemblance) are met to a very high degree; other conditions are not met (there is no one single light beam involved, we cannot spatially orientate ourselves to the objects presented to us). That seems to leave us in a kind of conceptual space in which we can say that photography, and thus cinema, is genuinely a case of seeing the world, even if in a somewhat extended sense. The camera, then, can legitimately be regarded as a kind of visual prosthetic.

Other kinds of realism

So far we have been focussing exclusively on *photographic* realism, construed transparently, but 'realism' is a word of many aspects and we can soon find ourselves speaking at cross purposes without making further distinctions. A problem is that there is no universally accepted set of 'jargon' terms one can employ. We must nonetheless acknowledge that what I have said already is only one of a number of different senses in which cinema can be regarded as realistic. Here, I draw upon Hopkins. He helpfully identifies five kinds of realism associated with three levels involved in filmmaking. I share much of what he has to say but add my own thinking here and there and reduce the number of 'realisms' to three.[20]

The three levels are:

THE MOVING ('cinematic') IMAGE >

THE THINGS FILMED >

THE STORY TOLD

THE STORY TOLD indicates the story told by the film but it can be widened to include what the film is about (its *intentionality*).

THINGS FILMED includes all that happens before the camera as it 'rolls' – the actor's performing, the sets and so on. Only some of these, of course, make it through to the final film. One way of understanding these is as *representations* of the fictions in the story. For example, the actor's performance represents the doings of the character. (Hopkins uses the term 'the events filmed' for this level but my term is wider. Depending on the degree of control the film makers have over the filmed environment, THE THINGS FILMED will include things, people and events more or less relevant to THE STORY TOLD. Relevance matters because one doesn't want the audience diverted by mere incidentals, but it is a matter of degree and judgement. (In historical dramas, for example, it has been known for modern road markings to be removed.)

THE CINEMATIC IMAGE (Hopkins calls it the 'moving' image but I prefer 'cinematic' because the word conveys more about the image than the fact that it moves.) This is, of course, what the present chapter is about.

So, it's like this: one sees, *in imaginary fashion*, THE STORY TOLD by means of THE THINGS FILMED and one sees THE THINGS FILMED through THE CINEMATIC IMAGE. Thus, in some sense, one sees THE STORY TOLD by means of, or through, one's experience of THE CINEMATIC IMAGE. The word 'Realism' can be used to describe what is going on at all three levels, though, as we shall see, issues can get subtle. I distinguish three kinds of Realism[21]

Photographic Realism (The Photographic Image as a way of seeing the world)

This applies at the level of THE CINEMATIC IMAGE. The 'Transparency Thesis' is a position one can adopt within photographic realism. It says that one perceives THE THINGS FILMED quite literally, though indirectly. I shall assume the truth of transparency throughout the book but it is not clear that the sins of which I speak depend exclusively on its truth. Even if we literally see only the photograph, or cinematic image (Option 1, recall) photography would still be realistic in that it at least *conveys* what was in front of the camera in a realistic way. That is, photography would still be a way of looking at the world that did not apply to other visual arts, even though it would not be literal indirect perception of the world. In other words, photography would remain realistic in some strong sense no matter how one may plausibly understand its deeper nature. This could still be strong enough to render certain matters *sins*. I have already dealt with this form of realism, however, so I will move on to the other two types of realism, though in short order just for the moment.

Appearance Realism (Naturalism) Photo-copy-ism

I shall defer discussion of this until the chapter on *The Sins of Appearance*. It is related to but not entirely the same as photographic realism if only because arts like painting can have it.

Human Realism (Authenticity – Carbon-Copying Human Beings and situations)

This is generally concerned with matters of narrative, psychological, political plausibility and I shall discuss this in the chapter on *The Sins of Storytelling*. We come now, then, to the other ingredients of the cinematic image itself.

Motion

I discuss the matter of motion more fully in the next chapter. Here I take it as obvious that some kind of motion must be involved in cinema in order for it to be distinguished from 'still' photography or even from looking at the images on a strip of cinematographic film one by one as separate acts of vision, as a film restorer may do when looking for scratches.

Temporality

This brings in a next element to join picture and sound – *time*. Time is implied already, of course, but it is a necessary ingredient to something's being a cinematic image, in a special sense that does not apply to still photography. What is this 'special' sense? It is simply that motion is a necessary part of the experience that the cinematic image produces – and that motion is temporal (it is *in* or *takes* time). A slogan: 'No experienced motion - no cinematic image'. In the example of the angels above, the continuing dialogue, even in the absence of a picture, still ensures a sense of progression. It gets more extreme than that. When one scene fades out and another appears, even the *absence* of both picture *and* sound are experienced as motion in that they convey the passage of time.

Time is important in another way, too. It has been well argued that there are three levels of time: objective, immanent and internal. Objective (or 'transcendent') time is the time that goes beyond human interest or the involvement of consciousness. It is the time measured by clocks and investigated by physics. Immanent time involves consciousness. It is the stream that is only roughly correlated with objective time, as when five minutes waiting for a bus (or watching a boring film) can seem like an hour and fifteen minutes drinking a gin and tonic can seem over in a flash - unfortunately. Then there is 'internal time', a special form of awareness of time. This is the time of perception, remembering and imagining – all the more deeply personal stuff.[22]

Time at all three levels is involved in watching a film, and in various ways. The 'running time' of a film (or cinematic image) is perhaps the most obvious case of whatever objective time is involved but it's involved in what we see also. Mostly, as we watch a shot, action takes place in what is often called '*real* time' In films that are made in one long continuous shot, this applies to the whole film. But we have selection, too. Thank goodness! A 'biopic', covering a large period of a subject's life would take up far too much of ours if done in real time. (On a slightly smaller time scale, this has been done by experimental filmmaker and artist Andy Warhol in his film *Sleep* (US, 1964). Apart from being a five-and-a-half-hour-long psychological endurance test in which we see a man sleeping, it is hard to see what value this has. I cite it only because it is an example.) The (thankfully more typical) strategy of selection, though, means that we see only certain stretches of objective time. This has implications connected with just *how* one should select. We will be discussing this in the chapter on editing but here we may note that we should make the further distinction between real time in the sense of running time and real time *within* the story. This matters, for the latter impacts on how well the film flows. Despite the gaps in real time *on the screen*, there is still real time *in the story*, and despite the gaps in the former, the latter stretches standardly come across as seamless. Matters can get very 'bitty' otherwise.

Immanent time enters film in its capacity to be compressed and expanded in various ways (through judicious editing) relative to objective time. Years can pass in a mere second. Quite often, at moments of danger in a film, times can be compressed and / or expanded for purely dramatic impact. Slow motion does this.

Selection, though, suggests that we also have in film the equivalent of internal time, rather in the fashion of memory and dream. As memory and dream select, so does film. Yet with selection must go coherence, even though it will be more the coherence of dream and memory than of our waking perception of objective time. Thus, if film is an instance of photographic realism and the transparency that goes with it, it is so in the extended sense of coming in the manner of memory and dream. Memory and dream are, after all, part of our human relatedness to the world and they can capture reality as well as (though in a different way to) waking experience. I think that internal time trumps other kinds of time where films are concerned, just as it does in memory and dream. It most directly moves our perception of a film. It is one of a film's most fundamental psychological drivers. We cannot, of course, literally see another's dreams and memories as we can their bodies and physical movements, but cinema can bring them out into the light *as if* they were visible. It does so using photographic realism. Thus, photographic realism is never quite abandoned. The dream-likeness in films I come to later.

There is something deeper than this to cinema, though. Film makes all its times present to us in a way that is similar but not *identical* to memory and dream. (Memory and dreams are similar, even though in dreams we are more deeply taken in. We *know* when we are remembering something (standardly, at least) but (standardly again) do not know we are dreaming.) The similarity is that all three bring past events *into* the present – with varying degrees of distortion. Further, a film brings disconnected stretches of objective time together into a unified flow (though the flow can jar as well as smooth over) whereas memory and dream are less well disciplined. Both similarity and difference are important. Like memory and dream, film is selective in its choice of the stretches it encompasses. In film the selection is in accordance with the will of the filmmaker who, one hopes, is serving the needs of the story; in memory the selection is controlled by the various aspects of the psychology of the person whose memory it is, and in dream – well the controlling forces are richer and deeper still. But it is important that film be more disciplined than the other two because film heads towards a kind of psychological unity that just isn't there (necessarily at any rate) in the other two. Moreover, its story has predetermined needs.

There have been occasions when filmmakers have eschewed too tight a selection and made films in one continuous take or at any rate what *looks* like one continuous take: examples include *Rope* (Alfred Hitchcock, US, 1948), *Russian Ark* (Aleksandr Sokurov, Russia, 2002), *1917* (Sam Mendes, US, 2019), and one half of *Long Day's Journey Into Night* (Gan Bi, China, 2018). This can be effective for special purposes but the standard for a cinematic image is time-selection and the degree of distance from daily reality it brings. This means that the cinematic image is a medium of selective concentration – as are dream and memory. We are told things on a need to know basis. This, in turn, aids focus and reflection on what matters. We do not need to see *all* the actions of the characters. We can just assume certain things. Further, it suggests that the cinematic image should contain no irrelevant elements, or at the very least, that every attempt should be made to exclude them. The cinematic image, then, is also a medium of *focus* – again as are dream and memory. This is to say, a cinematic image has something it is specialising in.

Temporal flow in cinema is curious in another way, too. It has been said that cinema is a medium of *moments*. In a sense, I agree. Without extra effort, of sorts, it is the moments that are the best remembered aspects of a good film. Moments matter. They are replete with meaning, ring bells and reverberate for years in our souls. But being a medium of moments does not stop cinema from being essentially a medium of motion, for there are no *lone* moments. Moments are necessarily embedded in time, they are part of the *flow* of time. The moments alone would mean nothing. Another slogan: no flow, no moments either. In any case, the word 'moment' in this context just means 'very short periods of time that can be remembered *all at once*'.

Here is an example of a moment mattering, one of the most famous. It comes from the wartime film *In Which We Serve* (David Lean, UK, 1942). Celia Johnson plays the wife of a Royal Navy captain played by Noel Coward. It is Christmas, and family and various officers are enjoying a meal together. She toasts the ship on which the men are shortly going to war, a vessel she calls her "implacable enemy" because it competes with her for her husband's time – and, of course, inexorably wins. The entire image is remarkable but its power lies in the moment in which Johnson moves only her eyes. It is what one remembers. We will all have our own favourites, of course, but I think, that there is more thoughtful emotion to this dinner table moment than in anything I have ever seen. It was once remarked that Celia could read the Yellow Pages and make you cry. Be that as it may, the connection of moments to motion is the take-home point here. One could almost say that the moments are what do the moving.

Thus, while cinema may not be primarily a medium of vision (or sound) taken separately, it *is* primarily, indeed *essentially*, a medium of motion. I shall be saying more about motion in the next chapter. Even the very word 'cinema' is related to 'kinematics', the physics of moving objects. The buildings in which films are shown were once alternatively called *kinemas*. (They can still be found. The delightful Lincolnshire market town of Woodhall Spa, not far from my home, has a fascinating place called 'The Kinema in the Woods'. Forsake the multiplexes, I implore you. Go to where the magic still prevails, places that positively *invite* one to imagine that Dorothy squashed the wicked witch as her house landed on Oz.) However, we move on.

Intentionality

A cinematic image has *intentionality*, that is, it is *about* something in the world beyond itself or points to something about its world. (This is a philosophical use of the word. 'Intentionality' here does not mean 'intentional' in the ordinary sense of doing something intentionally.) Intentionality gives the image focus. This should not be surprising given transparency. Our perception has intentionality – it points us to things. Thus, if photographic imagery is a form of perceiving the world, intentionality will be transferred to it. Moreover, it is hard to see how one could maintain anything like a standard interest in a feature film that was, quite literally, about nothing at all. (Though it is worrying how often this strategy seems to have been tried out.) The difference between a cinematic image and an ordinary perception in this context is that the intentionality will have a more intensified focus. It comes undiluted, uncontaminated and uninvaded by extraneous things – in the way dreams do.

Technological dependence

The cinematic image is also technology dependent. Of course, one can appreciate the beauty and meaning of an image without knowing how it was achieved but one will not have a full appreciation of its achievement. This subtly nuances one's perception of its beauty. Take the well-known low-light scene in *Barry Lyndon* (Stanley Kubrick, UK, 1975). This was lit only with candles. Lens expert Ed DiGuilio had to adapt an f/0.7 glass for this scene to get enough light on to the film. Kubrick, "wanted to preserve the natural patina and feeling of these old castles at night as they actually were".[23] The point is this: understanding the technicality here – essentially and crudely, that one needs a lens with a big enough hole behind it to let in enough light, and knowing that this, especially in cinematography, is breath-taking, helps lead us more into the sheer beauty of the scene. As Gaut puts it, "Appreciating a cinematic artwork depends in part on understanding the technology that the cinematic artwork incorporates."[24] There is an analogy here with music. It is often, and quite rightly, observed that one needs no understanding of the technicalities of music in order just to enjoy it, even to enjoy it profoundly. Nonetheless, there are times when aspects of its beauty are strengthened by such understanding. One can always *learn* to see extra levels of beauty in things.

Psychological unity: telling cinematic images apart

I would suggest that psychological unity is involved in how one *individuates* cinematic images – that is, how one can tell one from another? When, in any given film, does one cinematic image end and the next one begin? What would be the average cinematic image count be for, say, a typical two-hour feature film? I think the answer to such questions must necessarily remain vague. Nothing too important rests upon this vagueness, though, for although a cinematic image, being temporal, is stretched out in time, it does not have to last for this or that *amount* of time. It has to be a matter of judgement. Cinematic images do not have to be *precisely* distinguishable. One crucial distinction, though, I think is in order. 'Cinematic image', at least as I use the term in the present book, is not merely a synonym for 'shot', since a shot may contain neither sound nor visual motion (as when a shot shows us a still picture). Motion, though, is essential to an image's being cinematic. I think we have to say that cinematic images are individuated (told apart) by their contributory psychological significance to a scene. That is, they are distinguished by some sufficiently significant point that feeds into the whole film. Often it will consist of a single shot, just not necessarily. A quick sequence of related shots, as in a montage for instance, may comprise a single cinematic image. This is because the entire montage, rather than any of its constituent shots alone, presents the viewer with a psychologically unified audio-visual temporal whole - in this case, one that conveys the passage of time during which some important psychological or narrative motion takes place. (The technique is hardly used now, jump cuts are almost ubiquitous – and this, as we shall see, *can* be a sin.)

The cinematic image, then, is an aesthetically and psychologically unified temporal combination of sound and motion picture. Merleau-Ponty, a philosopher of perception, wrote, ". . . a film is not a sum total of images [the individual image as projected on the screen] but a temporal Gestalt" – (i.e., whole).[25] We experience a unified structure. It seems to me that this definition fits what I am calling the 'cinematic image'. This fits in with their being intentional (being about or pointing towards something). It cannot be understood in any purely technical way, though how a cinematic image plays into one's experience of a film is crucial, and such things as camera and lens choice, size, shape, film type, and cinematography play into that experience, including the meaning and psychology one gets out of it. It matters just as much as script, direction, performance, and so on – as we shall come to see. The sins considered in this book are, at bottom, sins against the cinematic image because they fail in some way to exploit well enough the natural potential of the cinematic image.

Ways of seeing

For all its transparency, the cinematic image still has something of a nature that ordinary perception of the world does not. We see the world *through* the image but, in so doing, we experience also the image itself (as we earlier argued). Our ordinary perception involves images, too, of course – the ones on our retinas. In that case, however, the images are simply an essential physical *causal* component of our seeing the world beyond our eyes, we do not literally *see* them at all – not even in some special sense. Access to the world by perception is thus direct and visually unmediated.[26] In contrast, access to the world through the photographic image is most decidedly visually mediated. Keep in mind, the thesis is not that we see two things, full stop, but that we see the photographed scene *through* seeing the image. Seeing the image on the screen becomes our *means* of seeing the world – but, unlike retinal images, they are a *phenomenological* means. That is, the process involves a kind of perceptual fusing of image and world. Phenomenologically, they become (a kind of) *oneness*. The object we see is, say, the actor performing a role, but we see that person, in turn, *as* the character in the story. However, we see these further things by *means* of, in some sense, seeing the image.

This very mediating nature of the photographic image, though, brings about further qualities. Such qualities contribute to what can be called the *form* of the image. These are the *formal* qualities of the cinematic image, qualities that the image has all by itself, rather than qualities possessed by the photographed object. (Though in various ways or to various extents this applies also to the qualities we have analysed already.) Thus, the image is not simply a necessary causal component in our seeing the world beyond, as our retinal images are.

The formal qualities of the image are welded to the way a film *looks*. Some of the formal qualities possessed by the photographic image are shared, in some degree, with other kinds of imagery; others are unique to the photographic image. The first four I take from the entry in *Encyclopaedia Britannica* online[27] with my own added gloss in places, though they are widely accepted as qualities of cinema. They all play into how a cinematic image is a way of seeing.

Intensity, intimacy, ubiquity

A cinematic image focusses on whatever point of interest the filmmaker wants. In ordinary daily perception as we, for example, walk down a street, our focus could turn to random happenings – a screech of tyres, a loud noise, someone playing music, and so on. Much of the rest of the time it's up to us what we pay attention to, hopefully guided by the needs of the moment, but we may be lost in our thoughts and pay attention to them instead. There is no particular order or single governing purpose to this process. In a film, though, there *is* such order and purpose to what we see and hear. This has been described as intensity because our focus is *forced*. We have to see *this* face or *that* event. We may still avert our eyes from something horrific, of course, but that is just to cease engaging with the film, even if only momentarily.

The time allowed for each act of focussing is also not of our own choosing. A long close-up forces attention on certain kinds of physical or emotional detail. A long shot may focus attention on a character in their environment. Nor can we choose what *literally* to focus our eyes on. The camera lens decides what is in focus and what isn't. At the moment of writing this, for example, I can if I wish turn my eyes on to something else in the room and ask, "What is that?" My eyes re-focus to find out that, say, a carpet needs the vacuum cleaner. I can similarly allow my eyes to wander over different parts of a cinematic image and look around the environment of some character, but if it is hidden from view or out of focus it remains that way. One's perception is under alien control when it comes to an image and the only available options are a willingness to be carried away by it or ceasing to engage. I like this experience, for it is a relatively benign kind of alien control. In watching a film we are relieved for an hour or so of seeing the need to be control freaks. What could be more a blessing?

This applies to any kind of image, of course, but given the photographic nature of cinema, this forced seeing seems all the more intense, for it is an especially intensified way of seeing the world itself. The motion of the world is also seen in a more intensified way. But it also carries with it another intensification. As film theorist Charles Barr put it, "It [the image] suggests inner reality with the greatest possible intensity."[28] Aesthetically good cinematic images squeeze out of this intensity what is appropriate and bad ones do not, as we shall see when we revisit this quality in *The Sins of Appearance.*

Intimacy arises from the fact that the camera and microphone can convey to the viewer greater detail about something than the eye can normally take in. It can join a character in situations that would not be allowable or possible in daily life. Again, other kinds of image can do this in their own way but, as with the quality of intensity, the photographic realism and motion of the cinematic image gives the intimacy a more realistic force. Both qualities, and much else about cinema leaves little time, if any at all, for immediate reflection as we watch the film. Reflection has to wait until afterwards. In a film something is *always* happening to keep you busy – yes, even in a hugely elongated Bela Tarr job.

A single cinematic image, given its standard total occupancy of the screen, is hardly ubiquitous but collections of them are. We can be in one place and one time now and a different place and time after a single cut. Here the psychology of editing comes into play so we will be revisiting this feature when we deal with this area of cinema.

Particularity

The word 'man' is general – it applies to all men. In contrast, a photographic image of a man is always particular – it is a photograph of *a* man. In a film, the focus is always on the individual, though not necessarily, of course, on the very same individual throughout the film. It can be on groups or even crowds, of course, but even then it is always on this or that *particular* group or crowd. No one *sees* man, we see either *a* man or men – particulars or groups of particulars. We do not, in a film, see man's cruelty to men, we see *this* man's cruelty to *that* man, or ditto for particular groups. This has implications for the ways in which films get across their point. We will revisit this under *The Sins of Storytelling.*

Neutrality – truth-telling

There is a sense in which the camera doesn't lie. Photographs are better evidence than verbal reports. One realises, of course, that tampering can go on – in our digital Photoshop-age more readily than ever. But given that nothing has been tampered with, we see what was before the camera. One may say that accuracy in visual representation is what photography is largely *for*. This raises the question as to how far cinema can deviate from straight photography, and in what ways, and still remain cinema as it has been traditionally known. I revisit this under *The Sins of Appearance*.

Luminosity

Any image can have luminosity – one of Turner's sea pictures, for example. However, a cinematic image shines down on us from a screen (hopefully a larger than life one) – standardly in a suitably darkened environment. (A film really should not be seen in other kinds of circumstance, even at home. Give it a chance of doing its job.) It takes up our attention because of this. How far luminosity is important to the cinematic image, therefore, needs some exploration and this we will focus on again in *The Sins of Appearance*.[29]

Distance

Under transparency, we have some kind of indirect but genuinely perceptual access to the objects photographed but we are also at a distance from them – spatial, temporal, psychological and aesthetic. We have seen how the idea of transparency can accommodate spatial and temporal distance. The other two do not seem to pose any obvious problem either but we do have to lay clear just what they are.

Spatial distance

Everything we look at is at a spatial distance from our eyes, of course, some – such as astronomical objects – at a considerable distance, but photographic images have a special kind of spatial distance. The objects presented are not literally in front of our eyes at all, even though we have seen how that does not refute the idea that we are still enjoying genuine perceptual access to them – of a kind. This, of course is always present in TV images. In fact, the word 'television' means 'distant vision'.

Temporal distance

Again, as we have seen, everything we look at is at a temporal distance from our eyes for the simple reason that light takes time to get to us. But, again, photographic imagery has a special kind of temporal distance that is not due solely to the finite speed of light. There are other causal chains involved. The events seen are not part of one's objective temporal present even in the sense that some distant astronomical event would be. For example, say you were out star gazing and noticed an exploding star. Even though the event will have happened perhaps many years before you see it (because it has taken light such a long time to get to us) there is a sense in which it is still happening not only in one's own *personal* present but even in our collective *objective* present. One may say, "Look what's going on *now*! A star *is* exploding". This does not apply in films. There is no exactly similar sense in which the events in the film (understood either as the goings on that were literally happening in front of the camera or as story events) are happening in our collective objective present. (That is different in 'live' TV.)

These two kinds of distance, however, seem to open up two other forms of distance for the photographic image that simply do not exist, at least in the same way, in ordinary perception.

Psychological distance

We do not psychologically relate to events we see by means of a cinema screen in exactly the same way as we do to events in our daily perception of 'real life'. If we did, we would either freeze in fear or flee at high speed to the exit door as a cinematic monster approached us. But, of course, in cinema, the monster isn't really approaching us. We may have some of the same *physiological* responses in each case but overall the psychology is different.

All this puts paid to a theory about the nature of cinema called 'Cognitive Illusion Theory'. This involves an alleged false belief. The false belief is supposed to be that in watching a film we believe that the events in the story are real. Clearly we do not, and our behaviour reveals this. We do in some sense go along with it *as though* it was real but this is a legitimate act of imagination not a deluded act of entertaining a false belief. (I return to this important distinction later on.) Psychological distance is important precisely because what we value about a film may well include the fact that it provides us with an opportunity to engage in a different set of reactions.

This distinction is important to story-telling in general. Seeing a heated argument in front of one's eyes, for example, may provoke a sense of keeping well out of the way but in a film one may just get even more involved, though in a special way. In the first case the argument may just be none of our business, but what one sees on a screen is decidedly *made* our business. If we were really present at, say, a real murder, our reactions may be strongly affected by the concern that we may be the next victim, but in watching a film murder we are freed from such fear and can bring into play other emotions. Even if one does get involved in a 'real-life' case, it will be a different kind of involvement. In real life one's involvement is always as an *agent* (participatory or otherwise) and one's simple presence can make a difference, but in films one's involvement is always that of a distanced and therefore detached viewer. We are not agents but reactors. We do not participate in the events of the story as we do in the events of things happening in our physical presence. Being freed from agency and *real* fear is hugely important. In general, our psychological involvement with events in the film is not identical to our psychological involvement with events taking place before our eyes, even though the two are still strongly related. Thus, a psychological distance always opens up in the case of the film that cannot open up in real life, however much one may otherwise keep one's distance in the latter case. Trying to reduce this distance and go for something usually called 'immediacy' goes against the grain of the thing we are dealing with – the cinematic image. I deal with this matter further, too.

Aesthetic distance

The Encyclopaedia Britannica defines aesthetic distance as 'the frame of reference that an artist creates by the use of technical devices in and around the work of art to differentiate it psychologically from reality'.[30] Like the other forms of distance, aesthetic distance is a kind of gap between our experience (in our case of a cinematic image) and the reality of the story that the image tells. It suggests also that aesthetic distance is a kind of psychological distance. Here is an example. Most directors would film a punch-up in excited, wobbling, hand-held close- up, in which one can hardly discern which fist belongs to which combatant. This may be the point, as one might expect, in *Raging Bull* (Martin Scorsese, US, 1980). In contrast, in the epic western *The Big Country* (US, 1958) director William Wyler (an old Hollywood craftsman) filmed most of a key fight in extreme long shot. The two combatants were seen as tiny little characters settling their differences violently against a background of a literally big country that was quite indifferent to their squabble and could have swallowed them up without a single thought. Quite beautiful, yet how effectively it conveyed something very real about a common human failing. Indeed, aesthetic distance is whatever allows the word 'beautiful' to be appropriately used.

This does not, of course, rule out the opposite technique. *Raging Bull*'s images are beautiful also because the poetry of the visual movement in the scene affords the aesthetic distance. In this case, the in-yer-face scene is also in one's soul. Rare! Note, I am not saying that aesthetic distance *guarantees* actual beauty, it simply provides a gap in which beauty can emerge given that the filmmaker is imaginative enough in relevant ways. To the extent that filmmakers have no idea how to exploit the opportunities offered by this gap they are obviously missing a potentially powerful trick and should preferably be employed in a different line of work. (I would suggest sweeping up the studio after the real artists have gone home.) This issue will also surface in other places in the book.

An oddity emerges from all this distancing. On the one hand, the essential photographic nature of the cinematic image ensures that cinema is *more* realistic (in the sense of *looks*) than many other visual media but many of the resultant qualities generated by its photographic nature, including the resultant forms of distance, render it *less* realistic (in other senses of the word that we discussed briefly earlier). We see what is before the camera (realism) but the *way* we see it may be far from the way we see the world with our raw, unaided eyes. Cinema, thus, can be regarded as a fundamental paradox: it is *an unreal seeing of reality*. (Or, more accurately but less pithily, *in a sense* a less real seeing of reality.)

Another thing that seems to follow here is that the cinematic image is also necessarily and quite literally superficial. It doesn't even go skin deep. Materially it conveys only the surface – of things, places and people. This is due to a combination of its very photographic nature and the physical absence of the things it presents. We must be careful here, though. This unreal *way* of seeing doesn't have to lead us *away* from reality. Indeed, we can be led closer to it and go deeper into some aspect of reality precisely because the cinematic image can give us experiences of reality that our unaided eyes cannot. It's another aspect of the paradox – the superficiality of cinema can be very profound. But it can be so only by artifice, that is, by exploiting the unrealistic components of the imagery - intensity, luminosity, distance, particularity in the extreme, selection, and so on – in short, the form. These are characteristics that direct, unmediated experiences of life either do not have at all or do have only in a completely different sense. I come to explore this whole issue of artifice (form) more under *The Sins of Appearance*.

Many other qualities of the cinematic image also matter to psychological and dramatic effect. I describe them below and return to them for a discussion and give examples of their sins and virtues at appropriate places in the book. They are all a part of the poetic structure of cinema. Indeed, one way of understanding the whole present book is to see it as an investigation into the poetic structure of cinema. The viewer takes in most of the remaining qualities at a barely conscious level, yet they all have their effect on the poetics of a film.

Framing, Composition, Space and scale

The Frame and Composition

This relates to a film's use of space. In our ordinary perception of the world we are surrounded by the context of what we directly and immediately see. We can turn our heads to check out this and that, but in cinema all that matters is in the space of the frame. (Even noises coming off frame items have significance only because they affect what is going on *in* the frame.) An image is spatially confined in a way that perception is not, even though there remains a rather ill-defined limit to the visual field. The existence of a definite frame means that what is within it is composed, either by accident or design. In the very earliest of cinema composition was minimal. One watched a film as one would see a live play on the stage from a position somewhere in the theatre. I do not think it an exaggeration to say that film only became art when composition and a more conscious use of framing came into being. Wide angle images made the spectacle bigger, close ups gave actors a means of nuancing performance in a new way, and a composition full of angles and points could become the stuff of dreams and nightmares.

What is in the frame *orders* what we look at and gives additional meaning and weight to it. In ordinary perception we just *see*; in a film we *see for the purpose of the story being told.* In ordinary perception we see part of *the* world; in cinema we see wholly *a* constructed world – the world of the cinematic image. Thus its intensity. The framing and composition must make clear what we need to know. There is no independent checking up, so what and who are 'in the frame' is clearly important.

But *how* items are in the frame is crucial, too. Framing and composition (the general placement of items within the frame) should be expressive, for it determines *how* we see what we see. This is because it gives meaning to a shot and tells us what is important. It shapes the way we feel. It gives what we see a deliberate dynamic (of purpose and power and direction). Watching a character get bigger on the screen as the figure approaches the camera gives them increasing domination; seeing them recede is to see them as leaving a dominant position. We say goodbye to 'Uncle Ethan' (John Wayne) in the final scene in John Ford's *The Searchers* (US, 1956) as he famously walks away from the open door and away from the homestead. We see him heading into solitude. On the other hand, in one shot in Orson Welles' *Citizen Kane* (US, 1941) we see Kane at first on the opposite side of a room looking as though he doesn't matter very much, as other characters dominate in the foreground. Then he walks towards the camera and by the close of the shot, we know who is really in the commanding position – and we know it from the framing and composition. Sometimes we have to take all but the main subject out of the frame to focus on what matters and get the right feel. At the end of Hitchcock's *Psycho* (US, 1960) we see young Bates give the audience a disturbing, psychotic smile, made all the more disturbing by a completely grey background.

A good example of how composition affects power dynamics concerns how conversations are filmed. The standard way of shooting a conversation is as follows. We first see a shot containing the two conversing characters. This is usually important and it is a good standard default because the viewer then knows that a conversation has begun and who its participants are. This is standardly followed by alternate closer shots of each character as they speak or react. But things feel different when a conversation is filmed so that the faces of both characters are visible all the time. In *Pulp Fiction* (Quentin Tarantino, US, 1994) we see in profile a large part of a conversation between two key characters who are facing each other directly. This visual directness is important psychologically because each character is competing for some kind of supremacy. Again, the composition matches the psychological needs of the story. If this doesn't happen, something is wrong and the storytelling is weakened. (For a quite different approach to conversation, and a masterclass in the art, watch pretty well any film from the Japanese director Yasujiro Ozu.)

Scale

The *scale* of the cinematic image concerns the relative sizes of things as they are on the screen. It is a further expression of a film's use of space. In ordinary perception, we have a sense of depth and can tell the distances between things. Something small but close to us is not seen as bigger than something much larger but further away. (This does not seem entirely due to having stereoscopic vision – though that may refine things – because we still retain this sense even with one eye closed.) When some item is more dominant on the screen, though, it *means* something. The example from Orson Welles above is a matter of scale as well as composition. In fact, scale and composition are intimately related.

We can be tricked by scale. A normal sized human can seem small against supersized furniture – as in *The Incredible Shrinking Man* (Jack Arnold, US, 1957). In ordinary perception our angle of vision remains fixed but in photography lenses of different focal length offer different angles of view. There are also changes of effect and visual impact. Normally, for example, a close up will be taken with a lens of longer than 'standard' focal length because such shots taken with standard or wide-angle lenses exaggerate facial depth. Putting no too fine a point on it, noses can protrude unnaturally – useful if one wants to create a rather intimidating effect but otherwise undesirable. On the other hand, very long focal length lenses can flatten things out a great deal, and one may not want that to happen, either. At the other extreme, wide angle lenses can help with landscapes. Choice of close up, medium shot or long shot is crucial in making a film. Filmmakers should be aware of the dramatic opportunities of choice of lens, sticking to the obvious only if one wants to keep the image without stark effect. The sins that occur in this department are dealt with later.

Aspect Ratio

This is the ratio of the width of the image to its height – another way in which a photographic image differs from ordinary perception. Thus a ratio of 2:1 (read, 'two to one') means that the image is twice as wide as it is high. Aspect ratio is another important feature of scale. For decades after the coming of cinema the ratio was standardised at 1.33:1 – not quite square. This suited the 35mm film gauge using a picture four perforations high – also a global standardised parameter.

This settled to 1.37:1 with changes that came with the introduction of sound. This is often called the 'academy ratio' because of its approval by *The Academy of Motion Picture Arts and Sciences* in America. The difference, of course, is scarcely discernible. In the early 1950's, however, cinema was under threat from a new rival – television. Audiences were dwindling rapidly and the studios had to respond to survive. One answer was more colour. At that time TV was black and white. Another was 3D. I deal with these later.) Yet another came with the idea of the wide-screen. (TVs were stuck at this time with a 4:3 screen ratio – more or less the 'academy' standard.) Older readers will remember that older films played very well on these TVs but one had fun with later 'wide-screen' films. Either they had to be played with black bars at the top and bottom of the screen or the dreadful practice of 'pan and scan' was employed. Itself a sin, because it ruined the effect of such a film, this technique involved making TV versions of wide-screen films that appeared at the academy ratio by broadcasting only a section of the original image. As the action moved from side to side, the section of image chosen for TV had to change. I recall with perfect horror the joylessness and complete cinematic imbecility of this practice. In any case, the true wide screen, something more visually encompassing, could be provided only by the cinema.

There are essentially five ways of producing a wide-screen image on film. The first and most obvious is to use wider film. Instead of the standard 35mm film negative, 65mm could be used. In suitably equipped cinemas the projector used 70mm film, the extra 5mm accommodating multiple soundtracks for a surround sound effect. Names like 'Todd-AO' and 'Super (and 'Ultra) Panavision 70' may be recalled.[31] This was a costly option (the film stock was more expensive) but it was popular at special venues from the mid-fifties and throughout the sixties for big epics and musicals. Its big negative produced a very high resolution image – as good as and sometimes better than today's 'HD'. For less fancy cinemas who could not afford the 70mm conversion, 'reduction' 35mm prints were used. The image still looked pretty good, due to the original larger camera negative. I recall, though, as a young fellow, that I would visit a special venue – usually in London – to see such films "projected in 70". The clarity and openness of the image was breath-taking and the screens were physically much bigger, too. Think of seeing *Ben-Hur* (William Wyler, US, 1959) or *Lawrence of Arabia* (David Lean, UK, 1962) this way. I can report that no other method of presentation even approaches it – no, not even high resolution 4K digital projection. It all gave the image a special open feel. Though it went out of fashion later, as 35mm film stock improved, and pretty well disappeared altogether as digital techniques evolved, it is enjoying a recent resurgence. Quentin Tarantino filmed his *The Hateful Eight* (US, 2015) and Christopher Nolan his *Dunkirk* (UK, 2017) on 65mm film. I made sure I saw both at the giant Odeon cinema in Leicester Square in London, a place still equipped to show 70mm prints. (Readers who are interested in the experience of 70mm can still find a selection of older 70mm films played periodically at the BFI Southbank and the Prince Charles Cinema and the Odeon in Leicester Square.)[32]

The second method was called 'Cinerama'. This involved three interlocked 35mm cameras arranged so that each would photograph one third of a very wide picture. A specially converted cinema would be equipped with three similarly interlocked and arranged 35mm. projectors. These produced an extremely wide picture on a wide, deeply curved screen. This proved popular (a number of mobile installations in circus-style 'big tops' came about) and most films made in this process were colourful travelogues. It was extremely expensive both to make and show films this way and only two feature fiction films were made this way – *How The West Was Won* (John Ford, Henry Hathaway and George Marshall, US, 1962) and *The Wonderful World of the Brothers Grimm* (Henry Levin and George Pal, US, 1962).[33] It could look good and had the effect of engulfing the viewer in the scene but one disadvantage was that it was difficult to hide the joins between each projected image. This could be annoying in some shots. It was also tricky to equalise the brightness coming from each projector. (These were the days of the carbon-arc lamps.)

A cheaper alternative had to be found. Thus enter the most popular and widespread of wide-screen process, using standard 35mm film and anamorphic lenses. Anamorphic lenses squeeze a wider picture on to standard 35mm film. A similar lens on a standard 35mm projector then un-squeezes the picture on to a wide screen producing an aspect ratio of approximately twice that of the 'academy ratio'. Though the process was developed in the early 20th century by a French optics professor, Henri Chretien, the lenses were bought by 20th Century Fox who then called it 'Cinemascope'. Fox went on to produce all its subsequent films in this process (for a long time). It was (relatively) cheap and even cinemas needed only a couple of extra lenses and a new, wider screen. (Cinemascope originally came with stereophonic sound but that was seen as an expensive luxury, and many exhibitors thought they could well do without it.) Many films benefited from being made in Cinemascope but the special lenses introduced distortions into the picture, particularly in closer shots (making faces seem unnaturally wide) and in bowing out what should be seen as straight lines. The Panavision company put right these drawbacks with a superior lens system and the process, known as 'Panavision' has been with us since. It is still used. Its wide images give the viewer a different kind of involvement with the picture but a modern sin definitely lies in its over use. I return to this sin later.

A fourth means of producing a wider picture is to run standard 35mm film through the camera horizontally, just as it does in still film cameras. One is not then limited by the width of the film. Paramount Pictures opted for this way of doing things with their so-called 'VistaVision' process. Like 65mm, it produced a much bigger and higher resolution image. John Ford used the process in his *The Searchers* (US, 1956) and Hitchcock seemed fond of it for some of his 1950s films. How far this was due to insistence from the studios, I am unsure but I think it works aesthetically. The system was hardly used in cinemas because special horizontally running projectors were needed – a considerable extra expense. Ordinary, vertical-run 35mm prints were used instead. It was discontinued as a production medium for entire films in most countries by the coming of the 1960s, though due to its superior negative image quality it continued to be used as a medium for filming scenes that required heavy-duty special effects. (Image quality could more happily survive several generations of the copying required in such scenes – adding this and that at each stage.)

For a time, when Fox wanted really superior image quality, they used a system called 'Cinemascope 55', which used an anamorphic image on 55mm film that was eight perforations high. Only two films were made that way: *The King and I* (Walter Lang, US, 1956) and *Carousel* (Henry King, US 1956). Neither film was shown using this system but with either standard 35mm Cinemascope prints or 70mm copies. Both of the films though were big, lush, romantic Rogers and Hammerstein musicals – highly popular at the time – and benefitted from the deep, highly saturated and detailed colour image produced in the photography. (Today's 'blu-ray' transfers of such films suggest at least something of the original cinematic experience.)

Sometimes systems were hybrid. Technicolor developed a process called 'Technirama'. This was a mixture of Cinemascope and VistaVision – a horizontally squeezed image (though with a less extreme squeeze than Cinemascope) was photographed on horizontally transported 35mm film. The epic *Spartacus* (Stanley Kubrick, US, 1960) was filmed this way. Again, this type of film hugely benefitted from the high resolution image quality. All this gave added sweep, scale and gravitas to the epic, so it was a dramatically important factor. Again, audiences saw such films from either 70mm transfers or 35mm vertically run reduction prints, but both benefitted from a clear, more detailed picture.

The fifth, and cheapest way of producing a wider picture is to use vertically transported 35mm film but with each image only two perforations high. The system was called 'Techniscope'. *The Ipcress File* (Sidney J. Furie, UK, 1965) was made this way. It continues to be used today, especially on lower-budget films, as does a later system using vertically run 35mm film which has an image three perforations high. Techniscope films were never projected as such, cinema prints being converted to standard Cinemascope. Because it used a smaller negative, films made in this process tended to look quite grainy on the screen. This suited the gritty and deliberately unglamorous ambitions of *The Ipcress File* (a witty and clever reversal of the posh, glossy world of the James Bond films) but it didn't confer many favours on films that used it simply because it was cheap. (Because of improvements in 35mm film stock, today's Techniscope produces an image quality much less affected by the smaller negative.)

Though the 'origination' of films during this time used a whole raft of cinematographic processes – and this still happens, even given that things are now largely (but not exclusively) digitised - so far as cinemas were concerned the choice was reduced. One tended to see wider screen films in one of three ways: in 35mm Cinemascope, in a reduced picture-height standard 35mm form, or in 70mm for special films in special places. Although a great variety of aspect ratios was possible – from the academy ratio right up to around 2.77:1, in cinema practice only the Cinemascope and standard ratios (today being 2.39:1 and 1.85:1) were, and are, used. Very recently, though, filmmakers have become more adventurous. The academy ratio has been brought back and some films go narrower than ever. *The Lighthouse* (Robert Eggers, Canada, 2019) was filmed (on 35mm black and white film negative) in a ratio that was almost square. Although I thought the usual run of clichéd visceral horror was overdone, the ratio was used thoughtfully, capturing the tight confines of both lighthouse and island.

We discuss further the resultant virtues and sins in the next chapter but picture ratio is important in the present chapter because these systems all changed the demands of picture quality and composition. Wider pictures present aesthetic and dramatic opportunities that narrower pictures do not – though it's good to have both.[34] All these matters also show how technological innovation and choice affect the kind of image the viewer sees and the resulting dramatic impact. This stuff is important and it is crucial to get it right – especially aspect ratio.

Camera angle

To make a film one needs a camera. This presents us with several questions: What lens do we use? What format do we use? Do we shoot on film or go digital? When should it move? Where do we put it? All of these issues – and their sins and virtues – arise in this book, but there is another: from what angle do we shoot? We tend, without thinking about the issue very much, to photograph things from about eye level. People, buildings, events and scenery are seen from this viewpoint, and though when photographing a child we may bend down and take the shot from the subject's eye level, it's a good default angle – nothing much can go wrong. It's a good default angle when making films, too. It feels natural and doesn't tend to draw attention to itself and thus leaves our attention to focus on some other matter. No technique at all, though, should be used in aesthetic ignorance.

The Japanese director Yasujiro Ozu favours lowish (but not extreme) shooting angles as standard. It's a part of his 'signature style' of cinema. It throws one's attention on to the characters and their movements in a particular but unforced way. The American director John Frankenheimer – from an age of Hollywood's 'new wave' – used various angles (and scales) for extreme dramatic effect, as did Wells before him in his *Citizen Kane* (US, 1941). In particular see Frankenheimer's *The Train* (France, 1964) and *The Manchurian Candidate* (US, 1962). Shooting down from pretty well vertically above the set has been used well, also. For examples, see Alfred Hitchcock's *Dial M for Murder* (US, 1954) and *North by North West* (US, 1959) – the latter film being particularly pointed and angular. The coming of drones fitted out with cameras has made vertical shots from much higher up cheaper and easier to obtain. I discuss the virtues and sins of drone use in the chapter on motion.

Notice how all this exemplifies the central truth of the cinematic image – its capacity to give us *ways* of seeing a reality unavailable to ordinary perception because the latter is usually too accidental, incidental and / or just too plain messy and restricted to do the job. It is why the cinematic image is art and life is, well, just *life*.

The Cinematic Image as a Form of Dreaming

David Lean once said,

> "I realise more and more that reality on the screen . . . is a sort of bore. I don't mean that the audience should sit there and say, "O, that's unreal", but movies are a kind of dream . . . I think they should have an unreal edge to them."[35]

Federico Fellini similarly makes the point, "Talking about dreams is like talking about movies, since the cinema uses the language of dreams; years can pass in a second, and you can hop from one place to another. It's a language made of image. And in the real cinema, every object and every light means something, as in a dream". Orson Welles said, "A film is a ribbon of dreams. The camera is much more than a recording apparatus; it is a medium via which messages reach us from another world that is not ours and that brings us to the heart of a great secret. Here magic begins". Steven Spielberg has put it more simply" "I don't dream at night, I dream at day, I dream *all* day; I'm dreaming for a living."

"Not just a recording apparatus" could well have been the title of my book. My point here is simple but two-fold: firstly, watching a film is like having a dream in some ways because of the very nature of the cinematic image, and secondly, when this is acknowledged and a film is overtly given a dream-like edge - whatever its aim or genre – it is a better and far *more* real film. It makes the film's point and conveys the realism more powerfully, as does a dream. When the camera records in a purely naturalistic way, it is an inferior film whatever its other merits may be. One way of achieving Lean's 'unreal edge' is to make sure that movements within the frame are carefully choreographed, the whole thing looking like a kind of dance. This was beautifully achieved in *West Side Story* (Robert Wise & Jerome Robbins, US, 1961). The characters seemed choreographed all the way through, not just during the actual dance numbers. The colours, the costume and art direction, too had a touch of the unreal, too, and it all added to the reality of the fury and barely controlled energy at play, something lacking too much, I thought in the 2021 Spielberg version which reduced it all to naturalism, despite the director's claim of "dreaming for a living".

This may sound curious. How can an appearance of unreality convey better some reality? This is related to what I have called 'The Paradox of Cinema' – the fact that cinema combines stark photographic realism (it's strongly like seeing things in 'real life') with 'form' – the qualities that the image itself has. The image has both reality and unreality built in – thus the dream thesis. This is a profound paradox indeed. The touch of unreality enables us to focus more on the aspects of reality that matter in the film. Irrelevant reality is supressed. When it isn't, too much reality is let in and the whole thing is dulled. Cinema should be a medium of focus, I think, on what matters. Its very nature points to this. Mentions of dream-likeness involved in cinema occur in various places in this book. Here I wish to discuss the background of this aspect of cinema in more detail.

We in some sense 'see' (take in through vision) the unreality, the form, of a film just as much as we see the reality it conveys. For instance, we take in the black and whiteness or the out of focus aspects of an image just as much as we do the persons and scenery photographed. Notice that I put the word 'see' in inverted commas, for we do not see these things as we see the items that were in front of the camera. Rather, they are *ways* of seeing these items. Just those ways of seeing, remember, constitute the form. The philosopher Colin McGinn makes what seems to be a similar point by saying that we see the image but do not look at it. What we look at, at least attend to most of the time, are the photographed people and objects.[36] McGinn likens the experience to listening to someone speaking. One does not attend to individual sounds as "acoustic signals" but to what is signified by the words. This does not imply either that our attention cannot be switched over to form or that form has no effect – of course.

All this matters and seems unique to cinema. Television and the computer screens are not quite there: firstly, their images are not projected from afar, secondly, one can see their screens in a way that we do not see the cinema screen when it is being projected upon, and finally, one generally sees them in an illuminated room. This difference, though, is not just dependent upon the merely contingent circumstances of viewing, they are intrinsic to the images themselves. All round, one is not "absorbed", as McGinn, puts it in the TV image in the way one can be in the cinematic image. "The penetration of the psyche goes nothing like as deep."[37] (This matter gets blurrier round the ages as digital origination and presentation take over from cinematographic film.) Moreover, they lack the quality of being larger than life. The celebrated film editor Walter Murch says that television is a "look at" medium and film a "look into" medium.[38] This captures much of the spirit of what I want to say. I contend that TV imagery has far less aesthetic distance because it has more direct reality and less form. The latter, remember, is the bearer of aesthetic distance. To ignore this difference is therefore to ignore the powerful unique potential of film and thus can count as a major sin itself. One may think it not a sin because one has too ready a tendency to associate the film-is-like-dream idea with Hollywood style 'dream factory' product. But it is really far more profound than that. Old Hollywood dream-factory product (which I much admire) is just one special case of it.

Dreams are a kind of mental imagery ('seeing in the mind's eye' – or *soul's* eye). The difference is that (standardly, at least) we have no control over their content. But visual imagery of various kinds, together with ordinary perception have certain family resemblances, though none are entirely alike. Viewing a film is a bit like ordinary perception in that it has a photographic realist aspect, and a bit like dreaming in that one has no control over what one 'sees'. (Though, in perception, we have the limited control in that we can choose to look at something else.) Dream is like perception in that dreams seem not to come from us but unlike perception in the fact that (in another sense) they do. The cinematic image seems to come from beyond - and does. It has that ghostly detachment of a mental image but, again, there is no control over the images – the 'dream-master' (filmmaker) has taken care of that.

The likeness between dreaming and watching a film – the so-called 'oneiric' theory – has been drawn many times. Early film theorists Ricciotto Canudo (1879–1923) and Jean Epstein (1897–1953) pointed out that films had a dreamlike quality. When Freud was all the rage, psychoanalytic theory played a large part in film theory and with it came also the dream analogy. Author Robert Eberwein is reported as describing the filmic experience as the "merging of a viewer's consciousness with the projected consciousness of the screen's subject, a process whereby the viewer's prior experiences with dreaming help to create a sense of oneness with cinema, causing the gap between viewer and what is being viewed to narrow".[39] More recently, philosopher Suzanne Langer says, "Cinema is like dream in the mode of its presentation: it creates a virtual present, an order of direct apparition".[40] The philosopher Colin McGinn calls dreaming "an emotion in sensory clothes".[41] He cites the early film theorist, Hugo Munsterberg, who saw film as expressing "the action of the mind as against the mere action of the body".[42] McGinn provides the insightful example here of Fred Astaire.

> "Only a dematerialized body could treat space and gravity as he so effortlessly does. In a certain sense, then, dance is the essence of cinema – the most visible assertion of its ability to transform the human body. When Astaire starts to move, he releases the potential of the medium – he becomes what the image suggests that he might be, a shimmering incorporeality."[43]

The reference to *watching* dance (engaging in it I have always found to be all too distressingly physical) seems to reflect well the fact that in cinema, as in dreams, one seems tantalisingly less aware of being in the physical presence of things. Look, face and movement are the three kings of the (form of) the cinematic image, not physical presence. McGinn puts it this way, "This ideal of dance is what the movie image itself aspires to be – a weightless vehicle of free motion."[44]

Note though that the thesis here is that cinema is dream-*like*, but that it is so only in certain respects. We standardly know when we are watching a film but standardly do not know when we are dreaming: we take the dream for reality in ways we do not take the cinematic image to be reality. There is more distance evoked by the latter. Cinematic images come framed, dreams do not. Strangely, being framed (having a shape or aspect ratio) makes cinema more dream-like in the sense of taking it further from ordinary perception and less dream-like by coming with a frame. This does not, though, neutralise the dream-likeness. Cinema and dreams are alike also in the sense that both seem to come from nowhere. They are both caused but phenomenologically they appear before us as if simply conjured up. In both cases, the cause is behind the scenes, as it were. Ordinary perception is not that sort of thing – the object we see is the same as the object that is the direct cause of our seeing it. We see what is before our eyes.[45]

In any case, there is a strong sense in which dreams are very real. They are the places where the mind plays on association and analogy most strongly.[46] This is very much daily business for cinema, too – or should be – for it can do it so well. There is also a sense in which both film and dream are superficial. They both largely work at the level of appearance – what things, faces, places, and so on look like and sound like. This kind of superficiality, though, possesses its own kind of depth and meaning – the kind that can only be delivered when we are set adrift from the everyday solidity of ordinary perception. In the second half of the Chinese film *Long Day's Journey Into Night* (Bi Gan, 2018) we follow a man continuously through certain activities and encounters in just this detached dream-like manner. We come thus to understand him, particularly through association, at a level that would be hardly possible by physically following his life in a less dreamlike manner. Both dreams and films are like shadows of reality, on analogy (for those who know their philosophy) with Plato's famous cave, in which the philosophically uninitiated mistake the ordinary perception as delivering reality when the real, permanent reality lies behind the visible world altogether. No wonder we are taken in, as Plato argues, for appearances, strangely, have a psychological depth all their own. Isn't this how art works?

Film and dream also share a kind of immateriality, even given their material causes. You can't shake hands with the character on the screen as you could the actor on the set. Likewise, one cannot shake hands with a character in your dreams, though you may believe you are doing so at the time. This is belief only *in a sense*, though.

Some philosophers have proposed something called 'Alief' to go with Belief. In the textbook example, one may, as one walks on to a transparent glass floor, *believe* you are safe (given that you trust the builders) but nonetheless *alieve* that you are in danger of falling through. This makes me feel philosophically playful. To this pair I propose we add *celief* and *delief*, the kind of belief that one has with respect to things you see in cinema and dreams respectively. All four are associated psychological states, belief (I would say) being parent state, but each has its own characteristics and shared features. For example, celief is freely given as something the viewer is willing to go along with, in a way that the other three tend to just come along unbidden. Celief is, in short, a willingness to engage in a certain kind of make-believe. Belief is the primary concept but celief and delief emerge from it as extensions of our imaginative life.

McGinn raises the matter of light here. Both dreams and cinematic imagery depend on light (though less directly in the case of dreams, for all is *literally* dark inside the skull). We are subconsciously aware of this dependence as we watch a film. Like light, the cinematic image is weightless yet illuminating.[47] The cinematic image, like dreams, presents physical reality in a kind of spiritual translucency. McGinn draws also a likeness of cinematic image to stained glass windows.[48] Both involve intricate patterns of light and draw from the viewer a similar gaze not standardly drawn by ordinary perception. (Though I would not wish to imply that what I am calling 'ordinary' perception lacks its own depths and mysteries. It is just that it is more directly tied to the material.) Had mediaeval window makers commanded modern technology, they would, I believe, have developed the motion picture equivalent of stained glass to tell their stories. What a glorious sight that would have been.

Continuing with such playfulness, McGinn also brings up the matter of mind-body dualism of the sort proposed by the influential 17th French century philosopher Rene Descartes. Under his schema, a human being is a fundamental duality: the body is entirely material, a kind of machine, no more; the soul is entirely non-material. Yet, our souls are the real essences of us all. We *have* a body but we *are* a soul – an ego, a thinking thing.[49] The cinematic image presents persons in an analogous way. Their essence (the essence of the character, at least) is presented (though in quasi-bodily form) in the image on the screen while not being bodily present. Pretty much ditto, I say, for dreams. It seems to me that (often at any rate) in our dreams we know who the characters are – we know them through their essence - even though they may come with a distorted or disguised appearance. Soul is presented in, as McGinn puts it, "the guise of matter". Likewise, we often 'kind of' know where and when we are even though times and places may come in disguise, which in turn, enables them to have a distinctive emotional impact. Indeed, *alief*, *belief*, *celief* and *deleif*, though *belief* is in some sense primary and the others derivative, form a group whose members bare a more or less roughly hewn family resemblance. It is all a part of the mystery of the cinematic image.

A note of caution is needed here. It would be a mistake to dismiss the importance of corporeality in films altogether – and I hope I do not. As Langer notes, "the camera is not a dreamer".[50] Indeed, it is the film viewer who is the dreamer. The camera conveys the corporeal reality and the cinematic image constitutes the source material for the 'dream'. The incorporeal – and thus the dream-likeness - lies in the *form* of the cinematic image, the cinematic way in which the story is told. Nonetheless, there is still a story being told, and this involves real corporeal actors playing fictious but (pretend) real corporeal people. Real corporeal things and places (the sets) play real (or pretend) corporeal things and places – the *content* of a film. The importance of the dream analogy lies in the insights it provides about how our perception of the corporeal is transformed in our souls by the more incorporeal form. The Astaire example is a case in point.

Further, though, I suggest that what matters to the *way* in which stories of corporeality are told are to be found in appearance and motion. These are the twin transformers of our vision – and they are made three, of course, by sound. This trio keeps track of and maintains focus on the emotional drive of a story and give it much of its power, even in the most physically impressive contexts. A good example here can be found in the closing shot of John Ford's *The Searchers* (US, 1956) in which Uncle Ethan (Wayne) famously holds one of his arms as he takes leaves of the now all too cosy company of the re-established homestead.

In some sense, the corporeality *is* the story; the incorporeality *tells* it. If the dream analogy has any power – and since the more obviously dream-like films have been the most memorable - I suggest it has, this power is precisely what allows the cinematic image to have, as McGinn puts it, "emotional stirring, a sense of great themes [and] moral focussing".[51] It induces, he adds, a trance-like state. He talks of "transport" "self-forgetfulness" and a kind of "cleansing".[52] This is part of the intensity of the cinematic image that I considered earlier. Reality comes in good cinema but it is reality enchanted. This is the *real* power of cinema.

Altogether, then, the above considerations suggest very strongly that the cinematic image intrinsically has both dream-like actuality and much dream-like potential. It suggests that herein lies its real essence and power and that it is a grave error to ignore this quality of film. Alas it has been ignored in too much recent cinema. The default use of a kind of unilluminating, purely naturalistic colour is one sin, but the focus has also been too much on the sheer corporeality and viscerality of the represented reality. It has usually been disguised as a kind of authenticity – the authenticity of appearance, or what I call "appearance naturalism". Such cinema attempts to let the content, the reality alone (or, rather, its fictional substitutes) do all the talking and forcing, but the power of content alone to do this job is limited if form is supressed. I for one, quickly tire.

There are some fairly obvious objections to this whole approach to the cinematic image. We dream when we are asleep but we are awake when watching films. But remember, the thesis is not that watching films *is* having a dream, only that it is *like* having a dream in certain key respects. The dreaming mind importantly *resembles* a film-watching mind – especially at the cinema. As McGinn puts it, "The movie exerts a hypnotic effect on you".[53] He suggests that watching a film can be regarded as a "hybrid state", containing elements from both waking and sleeping states.[54] This seems true. There can be no exact tracking between a dream and a film, for dreams are more chaotic in their narrative form (though I have known chaotic films, too). In some sense, dreams are put together 'in the background' as films are, perhaps with something in mind and 'shown only when they are ready', but their message and point – if they have one – can be more obscure than those of a film. (Though watch the films of Swedish director Roy Andersson if one wants cinema that is more obscure than any dream can be.) Nonetheless, the dreamlike aspect remains. Films may be punctuated, carved up, in the manner of a dream rather than in the manner of ordinary perception – space and time have fluidity in both.

What of the differences, though? Films, of course, require screens and projectors whereas dreams do not. However, as McGinn points out, these are simply contingent background causal mechanisms. They are not part of the experience. When the film appears, the screen disappears – and vice-versa. He adds, "If there were no solid screen but just empty air magically producing the image, it would make no difference".[55] Relatedly, one may object that dreams are private but films are public. This also seems to me to be beside the point. Strictly speaking, the thesis is – or should be – not that films in themselves are dream-like (what even *are* films themselves?) but that the *experiences* of seeing them are – and, in some sense, any experience at all is private.

A seemingly more serious objection is that dreams are egocentric in a way that films are not. Putting it bluntly, a film is not about *you* and does not involve you as a character in its story the way your dreams do. We are necessarily in our dreams. We have to be in order for them to be *our* dreams. This, I think, would still allow in the hybrid model I mentioned earlier but there are some extra subtle points. We are not characters in the films we see in *exactly* the way in which we are characters in our dreams but we can, as McGinn reminds us, psychologically *identify* with one or more of the film's characters. I cannot *be* Rick in his Casablanca bar (not even in the already extended sense in which Humphrey Bogart is) but I can empathise. We should be careful to locate the psychological position of such identification. I am already a kind of extended *me* even in my dreams. It occurs to me that I play a role – albeit an enforced and perhaps unwelcome one – in my dreams, going places that are only semi-real. Further along the line, I can certainly *day*dream about being an altered self. I can quite readily delude myself into imaging myself directing a film I am watching. (The reader should be that lucky.) The psychological, even occasionally spiritual, identification we have with people in films could be regarded as a further, different kind of, extension of self. It's being oneself further out along a spectrum, perhaps involving *celief* again. Moreover, there is a sense in which the viewer *is* involved in the film. This is analogous to the way the camera is involved. I sometimes amuse myself while watching a film by imagining that I am watching the action through the camera viewfinder, even sometimes imagining myself as a conscious version of the camera itself. (O, yes! It can get me through the all too common tedious stretches.) But leaving aside this personal eccentricity, we are willy-nilly at least carried along by what the camera 'sees'. This makes us at the very least a silent character in the film, one especially and mysteriously invisible to the other characters. How often do we use the expression 'fly on the wall'? This fact seems buttressed in any case by the transparency thesis of photography. There is a sense, in other words, that I just *am* there - perceptually even if not physically. I conclude that there is nothing here damaging to the dream-theory of film.

There are other ways in which we can seemingly drive a wedge between dreaming and watching a film. When we are watching a film we believe, indeed we *know*, that this is what we are doing, whereas when we dream, we do not believe (or know) that we are dreaming. McGinn reminds us of lucid dreams here and dreams we have when half awake, and so on but I think we need to draw here on our spectrum of belief – remember our conceptual quartet: alief, belief, celief and delief. Strictly, I *celieve* that I am 'in there' with the characters in a film while I simultaneously *believe* that I am watching a film. Then I go to bed and *delieve* that I am in hell or heaven in my dreams roughly in accordance with the dream-like quality of the film I had seen that evening. Again, we have a spectrum. Celief and delief, as with alief, are distinct enough from standard belief but also related to it – and to each other, perhaps in multifarious ways that there is not the space here to explore. Once again, there seems nothing hereabouts at least that destroys the dream hypothesis.

Dreams come from oneself, from the inside out, so to speak but films do not, they come from the outside in. There is ambiguity at play here, though. There is certainly a sense in which my dreams 'come *from*' me, perhaps ultimately from multifarious and mixed up past personal experiences, but they are no more my deliberate conscious artistic productions than are the films I see. The difference is that films are the deliberate conscious artistic productions of at least *somebody*, whereas dreams are not. All sorts of mechanisms may conjure up our dreams and something (think of Freud, for example) may control their content. Moreover, they may have meaning and purpose (of sorts) and symbolic force but they are not the product of conscious processes and deliberate script conferences. I don't necessarily *want* the dreams I have in the way that film directors (sometimes at any rate) may get the films they want. (Perhaps this is just as well, for if my dreams could be directed by David Lean, I would happily spend my life asleep and never bother with cinema and its attendant sins anymore.) Dreams, however, do have a kind of free-play over our imaginations, cut off as we are from our 'real' surroundings, as films do when we are cut off psychologically from the physical place of our seeing them. Some of the best remembered moments of cinema are best remembered precisely because we had been transfixed. Here the expression "it's only a film" seems more like a blunt, ignorant put down. In any case, though dreams are not art in some fully-fledged sense, we need not suppose that dreaming cannot function as at least one progenitor of art. Again, the relationship between the two is far richer than the present objection implies. Given McGinn's hybrid proposal, therefore, I see nothing damaging here.

We have seen that the cinematic image has something called *form*. Dreams surely do not. There is no play of light in a dream, for instance, that is distinct from their content – just in a way that parallels ordinary perception. This is, I have to admit, a strong dis-analogy between cinematic and dream imagery. It is this difference furthermore that enables the cinematic image to become art in a way a dream can never be. I come below to show how form aesthetically enables and enriches a film. Here I simply want to point out that one dis-analogy hardly destroys the dream theory of the cinematic image, especially in its hybrid form anyway. My car is a hybrid, but the fact that it sometimes runs on an electric motor that many other cars simply do not have hardly makes it wrong to count it as less car-like, given that it has all the features it needs to function as a car. Again, hence, I think that the dream proposal remains untouched.[56]

Be crucially aware! In saying that the cinematic image is dreamlike, I am not talking aesthetics, at least at this point. What are often taken as dreamlike aesthetics – soft focus and sweet romantic music, and the like – are just one aspect of dream-likeness. McGinn puts it this way: the thesis is that, "it is essential for films to *be* dreamlike not that they *seem* dreamlike".[57] I am here talking, let us not be afraid of the word, *metaphysics*. In this context it means that I am theorising about the very nature, the fundamental structure and genesis of the photographic image as it arrives in our experience. I am talking, in other words, about what a cinematic image really *is*, not how *good* it is aesthetically. I am not making value judgements – just at this point.

I do, however move on to just that below, and there I go further than McGinn in that I think if a cinematic image is *really* dreamlike, it should also *seem* that way. Why? After all, a filmmaker is free to exploit, enlarge upon and intensify the real dreamlike nature of cinematic images or ignore or downplay this nature. Nonetheless, it seems to me a pity if it is ignored, or even just lies half-dormant in the background, for this would be to deny to it the kind of psychological and aesthetic power that cinematic imagery can have – the sort that McGinn seems to admire. (Like me, one of his favourite films is *Brief Encounter*, as aesthetically a dream-like film as one could imagine bar, perhaps *The Wizard of Oz*. In some sense both films were actually *about* dreams) Moreover, though like McGinn, I would be reluctant to think of the dream-theory of cinema was a *complete* theory of cinema, in that it can contain *all* one needs to know in order to have a completed understanding of cinema, I *do* think it should be a guiding theory, in thinking about what a film is, in filmmaking and in film appreciation and evaluation. With that firmly in mind, we can move on to more aesthetically important considerations at a later point.

Problematic and peripheral cases

I have described the cinematic image as a window on to the world that was in front of the camera but I also conceded that it could be a distorting mirror, analogous (in some respects) to the mirrors one can find (or used to) in fairgrounds. So the question then arises as to how much deviation from the strictest form of photographic realism a cinematic image can take and still remain a cinematic image. Here I discuss this matter and a few other issues and potentially problematic cases.

Strangeness, Animation, Magic, Fantasy & Realism

Sometimes, one has to let go to magic when watching a film. I conjecture that it is the possession of the qualities we discussed above *combined* with photographic realism that makes the magic. In what sense, though, *is* a cinematic image 'magical'? Firstly, there is a larger than life-ness to them, quite literally on a sufficiently large cinema screen or in a close up, but I don't mean that exactly. I mean in its manner of presentation, in the way the cinematic image allows us to see. The imagery of good directors is realistic, yet just sufficiently odd enough to attract one's attention and draw one into what's happening in an eye-catching and thoughtful way. Hitchcock and Lean use this slight oddity to great effect. Not all do this, Ford and the other Hollywood greats tend not to. They go in for a kind of lushness of imagery instead. In Ford, for example, the dust has to rise with the prescribed motions. Hawks follows suit in *Red River* (US, 1948). Lushness, though, like oddity, is still exaggeration, as when beautiful female stars are shot in soft focus. Thus the magical. Paradoxically, though, it is this same slight measure of unrealism or strangeness that more forcefully conveys the realism of what is happening in a story and the cinematic image must exploit this if its realism to work at its full power. Lack of it has, in my view, reduced many a modern film to the status of the ordinary.

All the best directors know this, it's a pity that too many of today's directors seem not to have the foggiest idea of it, going in for bland-looking, plain visual carbon-copying authenticity instead. 'Bring back the magic into movies' is my motto, it makes for a more convincing realism than a mere undistorted replication of the real can ever do. It directs one's attention more and exploits the deeper realism-conferring qualities the cinematic image. Yes, I think that seeing a cinematic image is an indirect seeing of what went on in front of the camera, but it is, also an *imaginative* seeing of those events of the story. It seems entirely natural that the imagination should be worked upon. We should not fear this as mere manipulation. I return to this central issue.

But can magic go too far? How about animation? How far is, say, Disney's *Pinocchio* (US, 1940) realistic – and in what sense? I take for granted that we would agree that it is fantasy and has plenty of magic in terms of its *content* – it stars a talking cricket, after all. I also take it that this kind of fantasy can be realistic in the sense that it can convey important morals about 'real' life. It can have what I call 'human realism' or 'authenticity'. Indeed, that was much of Disney's purpose is in his story telling. Here, though, I am concerned with photographic realism. How far can an animation satisfy this criterion?

The answer here is subtle. In traditional animation, a camera is used but it is used only to record the sequence of artwork pictures that have been drawn by the various artists. Transparency still applies to these but what one indirectly sees is the artwork not the world the artwork depicts. In the ordinary sense, animations display photographic realism only insofar as they are counterfactually dependent on the visual properties of the artwork of which they are photographs. In this way, we could say that animation is more like art than photography.

What we say about the motion seen on the screen requires nuancing, too. The cinematic image itself still moves (in the sense described in the next chapter) but the motion is not that of any real thing or person. It is, we might say, *semi*-illusory.

In the case of digitally originated animation, of course, no camera is used at all. The process is entirely non-photographic. The motion of the image on the screen is, again, genuine but that is all.

Looking back at the three levels, the part that animation changes, or misses out altogether in the case of digital animation, is THE THINGS FILMED. There simply are no filmed events. You do not, as in conventional cinema, see a real *performance* that visually resembles some imagined reality in THE STORY TOLD. In this sense, the images seen are not cinematic in the full sense. That is not to deny that real performances are used in the production of animations. The Disney studio, for instance, filmed real performers to do some of the movements of their animated counterparts. But this was done purely as an aid to the animators in getting the movements right. There is no sense in which the film gives one visual access to these performances. These performers are not seen in the film, even in rotoscoping – a process in which real photographed shapes and movements are traced over and subject to artwork. (Though this process can get more subtle still.)

All that said, one still (in some sense) sees an imaginary world, through the image on the screen. It's just that the middle-man (the EVENTS FILMED) is missing. What takes its place is artwork that we interpret as a story. That, however, still matters, the story its development, its motions, its emotions, its morals, its humanity, and so on, standardly develop in a way strongly analogous to those of 'real life' cinema. This is important. Even talking animals are, in a sense, imaginative substitutes for human beings and their experiences. They just have a few interesting additional capabilities. In this sense Pinocchio was a real boy even while he was still supposed to be a puppet. 'Live' puppet shows go the same way, of course. Indeed, all such fantasy addresses human concerns. That's why it appeals. That's why some exaggerations are allowable and others are not (at least standardly). For example, a cartoon character runs of the edge of a cliff. Instead of falling immediately, as any real thing would, the character remains motionless for a while and falls only when he realises what's happened. Despite the physical level unreality, there is still a strong relation to very human reality in the moments of rapid realisation of unfortunate predicaments. The animated events echo such times in an amusing fashion. Even the physics, though, cannot be exaggerated too far. Visual timing is crucial for the animator. Get it wrong and important matters of both narration and appearance begin to fall apart because the timing derives ultimately from normal, quite real kinds of human action and concern. In this sense, fantasy worlds (standardly) are just the real, human world in disguise. These observations, of course, are hardly news. I mention them in the present book because they strongly suggest that visual techniques that justifiably count as sins in 'real life' cinema will equally (or near equally) be sins in animation. For example, in

Chapter 2, I complain against the misuse of handheld camera movements. If my reasons for this complaint hold up in 'real life' cinema, they will hold up for what *looks like* such misuse in animation, even though their cause will be physically different. To the extent that similar visual and sonic sins and virtues are at play in animation, the images can be still be regarded as cinematic even though they are not photographic.

In conclusion, one can say that non-photographic and semi-photographic forms of cinema are strongly parasitic upon the norms and principles of 'live' cinema. What is not, technically, photographic realism, necessarily has to look (in some admittedly hard to pin down sort of way) *as though* it is. Motions are similarly constrained. To that extent, photographic realism is paradigmatically cinematic. To the extent that photographic realism rules the visual roost, I think we can admit the adjective 'cinematic' to describe the imagery of films that are not technically forms of photographic realism. Perhaps we can say that animation consists of cinematic images in a derived sense.

The possibility of abstract cinematic images

Abstraction in imagery I will take to be the use of colour, line, shape and sound which has no intrinsic meaning but in such a way as nonetheless conveys certain moods or suggestions and the like. This brings us headlong into a possible refutation of my thesis. Take the pattern of dashing coloured lines towards the end of Kubrick's *2001* (US, 1968) or, more extremely, Derek Jarman's *Blue* (UK, 1993) in which we encounter an unchanging blue screen throughout the entire film. There is, though, a complex soundtrack of voices, sound effects and music. It was intended as a 'portrait' of Jarman's struggles with AIDS.

Are these cinematic images? If so, do they threaten my general thesis? There are two ways of proceeding here. One would be to deny that they are cinematic images, but this seems arbitrary if only because they are at least *parts* of certain films and, the examples given have been hailed as 'good cinema'. The second way would be to show that they can be counted as cinematic images, even under my own definition. Let's take each of some of my criteria.

Temporality is clearly present. Motion is involved in the *2001* scene and, if motion can be understood as some kind of narrative and emotional development, then it is present in in *Blue*, too. There is no problem here. The images are technology dependent so the images clearly pass here. There is also transformation: one can say that both transform one's perception of something. This happens in *2001*, too. Indeed, one can take Kubrick as being playful here, using an image that is not (fully) cinematic bang in the middle of a whole film full of some of the most impressive cinematic imagery ever created, in the sense that it is cinematic aesthetically, even if only partially so metaphysically. Again, we can say that this kind of abstraction consists of cinematic images in a derived sense.

Semi-abstraction?

In *The Cabinet of Dr Caligari* (Robert Wiene, Germany, 1920) a hypnotist leads a somnambulist into committing murders. It is a wonderful example of German silent 'expressionist' cinema. Like much of this kind of cinema it uses somewhat unusual sets. Streets and rooms and the placement of things are distorted. This is to convey a sense of nightmare and abnormality. But how does such cinema match up to our criteria? Are *these* images cinematic?

The one issue here is cinematic (photographic) realism. What do we *see* in this film? Hopkins is clear: "The movie is an unrealistic rendering of normal streets not a realistic rendering of strange ones", he says.[58] But is it? It is, after all, a photographically realistic rendering of strange *sets* of streets since these were the things present before the camera. Psychologically, Hopkins is right, though. The streets are supposed to be real and the audience is supposed to be sharing the nightmarish distortions of the characters. That is the film's main *aboutness*. Shapes are, in other words, used to convey mood. Since the film satisfies all the other criteria, I conclude that its images are metaphysically cinematic – at least to a high degree. That they are cinematic aesthetically I hope goes without further ado.

Another case of what I call semi-abstraction can be found in Disney's *Fantasia* (US, 1940). In one section, an amusing aside, we see an abstract version of an old-fashioned film soundtrack. It waves, wiggles and vibrates to various sounds. I call it semi-abstract, because although it is a pattern that conveys a mood, the mood is augmented by the fact that the soundtrack is made to behave like a real character. It's not at the level of abstraction in the example from *2001* but I think it partially metaphysically counts.

Mise-en-scène and the cinematic image

"*Mise-en-scène*" is French for "placing on stage". It originated as a theatrical term but was taken over by notable French film theorists in the 1950s. It refers to ways in which the space shown by the cinematic image is articulated and what things are in it. A BFI website says the following: "It is used to describe how sets, locations, props, costume and make-up are used in film. . . . The definition can vary - some include camerawork and performance. Bordwell and Thompson define it as setting, props, costume, lighting and acting".[59]

It isn't really a production term. No director on a film set standardly says such things as, "Yes, the *mise-en-scène* is satisfactory now, so let's go for the shot". It is primarily a term of film appreciation and criticism, though most critics do not use the term in their reviews, either. One rather supposes that it sounds pretentious and todays 'reviewers' (note that the word 'critic' is no longer fashionable) seem too afraid of not coming across as cool. I suffer from no such pathological bother and will *mise-en-scene* as much as I like. (A desire to sound cool, in my view, amounts to no less than giving in to popular thought, whatever the quality of such thought.)

Mise-en-scène constitutes much of what makes an image cinematic in the sense of the present chapter, and much of the present book is about the 'elements' of *mise-en-scene.* All that said, I do not use the term in the book. This is because the cinematic image consists of more than its *mise-en-scène. Mise-en-scène* tends to cover the relatively more static elements of the image, whereas motion is, of course, also an essential element. Cutting and change tend not to be included but are important to the image. Usually, sound (including dialogue and music) is not included under the category, either, yet constitutes an important element of the cinematic image. The concept of 'cinematic image' is, in short, wider than the concept of *mise-en-scene.* Moreover, the wider concept (and the sins against it) is the subject of the present book.

As in other places in this chapter, of course, I mean the word 'cinematic' in its metaphysical sense – that is in connection with the kind of thing the image is. As ever, whether the image may count as cinematic in the aesthetic sense is a further matter. Nonetheless, as I said at the outset, one has to know what kind of thing a thing actually is (i.e., get the metaphysics of its intrinsic nature right) before it can be aesthetically evaluated.

Helping the Magic

Every decent cinema (and they take some finding) has a big pair of curtains. This is not just to protect the screen from damage when it is not in use but to protect the cinema-goer, the lover of film. It protects them from having the magic of the experience of a film downgraded. One should never be aware of the screen, only the cinematic image, and staring at an empty screen beforehand is not the best preparation. So seriously was this once taken – and rightly in my view – that my understanding is that giving the audience even so much as a glimpse of a naked, imageless screen was counted as an offence in projectionist circles. In so many cinemas nowadays, raw, entirely nude screens are thrown into one's poor, suffering face, as if to say with that all too common and entirely self-righteous, post-modern boldness, "Get a life"! I have one already, thank you, and in that life, closed curtains before a film starts and after it ends helps to preserve that illusion of magic.

Surrounding darkness is also hugely helpful. It helps the viewer to isolate the cinematic image, appreciate its fundamental unity and focus their attention on *its* world alone. It is no longer seen as being spatially continuous with the surrounding real-world furniture. The cinematic world is freed to dominate, beguile and weave its magic without distraction. Surrounding darkness pays the cinematic image the respect it deserves for the offerings that it uniquely has. I am not here to tell you that films alone contain cinematic imagery (though in the aesthetic sense other forms of motion picture –TV, videos and computer images - are sufficiently different if not inferior). I say only that if cinematic image is what you think you are looking at, turn off the lights.

Next, the place must be public, or potentially so. I have on many occasion been the only person in an auditorium. It's been a rainy afternoon. I have been in an 'arthouse' cinema. I've been the only one in to see a 'minority interest' film. It makes a difference. We should be sharing the experience. Everyone should be partaking fully in adventure, romance, thrills and other assorted dreams – and we should need no artificial aid from popcorn to keep us satisfied. But if no other person is present, still the public nature of the experience remains and, thus, the potential for sharing.

Finally, we need size. Watching a film on a smartphone screen held close to one's face and merely 'thinking big' will simply not cut the mustard. Only *being* big will do. One of the most wonderful sights of the 20th century was that of an old 'picture palace'. This would have been a single auditorium cinema built in the early twentieth century with up to two thousand seats. (Some, like the *Gaumont State* in Kilburn, London, held twice that amount.) The audience would be at pretty well full capacity on a Saturday night. Still, even in a present day, digital mini-space holding no more than around 45 one can still imagine. (Though the film may not always make the effort worthwhile.) Real, absolute size gives the action real thump. It magnifies the dream. If you're having to peer close up at a film on an iPad, you're doing it, and yourself, down.

Put these things together. Let them blend. The result is a magic that remains unsurpassed. The only cinematic image that is worth looking at is one *bigger* than you are. It transports you to places and situations you can hardly know – and it won't take "no" for an answer. If you're a control freak about your own emotions the cinema should be no place for you. Keep out, I say, and leave alone those of us who rather enjoy getting at least a bit lost.

The world's best cinematic images also *glow* down at you – or jolly well should do. It fills one's eyesight and drenches one's preoccupations. It says "Me! Me! Me!". It comes to you. It wants to swallow you up. If you're an active player in the game of cinema, you'll let it. If you're fighting what you see, get out. Its consuming nature is a gift. If you don't want it, then go away. All art, both the great and merely playful, is this way. How can you be touched or transported if *you* want to call the odds? The latter is for gamers not film-lovers. If you prefer the place you have walled in for *yourself*, again, keep out of the cinema. My greatest hope and longing as I enter a cinema is that – this time, perhaps just *this* time – I will encounter the work of a filmmaker who takes my heart and draws it into territory *I* can hardly imagine. Whether it is deep insight or passing entertainment, I want the film to be in charge. If I'm dominating *it*, it's a pitiful failure. Art, including film, and its artistry, is the one thing I *want* to look down at me. If it does not, or even *cannot*, it can give me nothing that I do not already have. I'm part of the problem. The film should be part of the solution. I'm the one with the needs. I'm the one who desires the vision. The cinematic image should occupy one's life, insinuate itself into one's eyes, ears and heart, and draw one into its way of seeing things a bit like a dream does. Putting matters politely I can only say that a film that fails in these respects is a film I will soon forget.

With the nature of the cinematic image now spelled out in some detail and with certain matters off my chest, we are in a position to tell sin from virtue. I make no apology for its having taken around a quarter of the book to get to this point. A task takes as much space and time as it needs. It's the nature of the beast that counts.

Chapter 2: The Sins of Appearance

In a sense, many of the sins I cover in this book fall under some aspect of appearance. A film, after all, just *is* an appearance – with sound. Here I will deal with those that do so more narrowly. These particular sins, and many others, arise from a curious paradox of cinema due to the tension between two facts. One fact is that, due to its photographic nature, film is visually realistic. As we have concluded – looking at a photograph of something is crucially like looking at that something itself. Add in the transparency thesis and it is quite *literally* a way of looking at that something. The other fact is that photographic images can vary in ways ordinary perception cannot. The cinematic image has what we have called 'form' – qualities all its own that our ordinary perception has not. For example, eyes cannot see in black and white; they cannot zoom in and out; their lenses cannot change their focal length – we cannot go telephoto, standard or wide angle. We can only alter the brightness of the scene before our eyes by (typically) employing sun-glasses. Our eyes are, in short, restricted in all sorts of ways that photography is not (and vice-versa, of course). The very nature of photography – the fact that it can enable us to, in some sense, 'see' what is not materially present to us – means that it can do what our eyes alone cannot do. Thus, in a photographic medium, we simultaneously look at something both realistically (as our eyes do) and *non*-realistically (as our eyes cannot). Just this is what I call the 'paradox', for it generates that strange puzzlement that characterises paradoxes. This paradox is built-in and inescapable. The essential question is therefore when, how one can exploit this paradox, for doing so exploits nothing less than the power of cinema itself. My basic starting point is that the 'how to exploit it' question should be governed by the needs of the story. If they are not used for very well thought out effects in service of the story to be told, they are going to be fundamental mistakes – 'sins', as I characteristically call them.

The Sinful Turn to Appearance Realism (naturalism & photocopy-ism)

This will surface at a number of places in this chapter and elsewhere in the book, so let's examine it and try to understand why it is to be counted as a sin. Naturalism I define as the policy of making a film look and sound too much like life itself as though cinema was just 'a slice of life', a mere peek into life, as though one was simply *there*. It is what I call mere 'photocopy-ism', a turn to a misguided authenticity. We see it also in the ways in which films tell their stories.

One may suppose that it can be justified by appeal to the principles of some kind of minimalist aesthetic – an aesthetic that supposedly does not detract from the important stuff - but in cinema I find that minimalist aesthetic is usually accompanied by maximalist anaesthetic. Bluntly, I get tired of gazing at it because it offers little visual meaning to attract one's gaze in the first place. Its sinfulness is based on one blunt and obvious fact – to watch a film is not to see life itself but to see a treatment of life *through* the cinematic image and the cinematic image just does, as we have already seen, have properties that our ordinary perceptual immersion in the world does not – that is, it has 'form'. The sin lies in ignoring this obvious difference. In doing so it ignores the formal properties of the cinematic image – all the ways of seeing, that is, that are unavailable to natural perception and all the ways of being embedded in reality (such as being told a story) that are unlike our embodied participation in actual life. The sin of appearance realism is, in short, the sin of ignoring cinema itself. Of course, it is simply impossible for a film not to have form *at all* – it has form by its very nature – but the form can be played down. Just *that* is the sin, for the attracted gaze that a sufficiently rich form can offer is precisely where meaning can be found and reinforced. Of course, it takes visual talent to do it well – always a problem. I enlarge on all this below.

Appearance Realism

Appearance realism is one of the three main kinds of realism that we can attach to cinema alongside 'photographic realism' (discussed in Chapter 1) and what I call 'human realism' (discussed in Chapter 8). Indeed, the very photographic realism of cinema brings with it a considerable degree of appearance realism – things, scenes and people look much as they do in life. This does not mean, however, that filmmakers should ignore form (what the image has that ordinary perception lacks) and try, at least, to leave only content. Appearance realism depends upon the degree to which the *formal* properties of a cinematic image are repressed and content left as all that matters. It's a kind of 'naturalism'. If form is completely recessive, I call it '*raw* naturalism'. The first task, then is to clarify these terms.

Formalism & Realism

Form

In considering photography, the philosopher Dominic McIver Lopes defends transparency theory. He writes:

> "When we look at photographs we literally see the objects that they are of. But seeing photographs as photographs engages aesthetic interests that are not engaged by seeing the objects that they are of. These claims appear incompatible. Sceptics about photography as an art form have endorsed the first claim in order to show that there is no photographic aesthetic. Proponents of photography as an art form have insisted that seeing things in photographs

is quite unlike seeing things face-to-face. . . . . nevertheless, seeing things in photographs is one way of seeing things."[60]

Lopes maintains, as do I, that the two claims are compatible. I am maintaining that this is because photographic imagery has something called 'form'. We may, therefore, ask just what *are* the formal features of any representation? Hopkins discerns two essential conditions that they must satisfy:

(i) "**they must be detectable**, in whatever form of engagement the representation is designed to support (e.g., watching a film, reading a novel, listening to a radio play); and

(ii) **they are not simply a matter of content**, of what the representation represents."[61]

Form must be detectable or it would otherwise be as irrelevant to any assessment we may make of a film as the colour of the director's clothing as the film was made. However, form can be more or less prominent in a viewer's attention. "The less prominent it is, the more realistic the representation", Hopkins says.[62] Instead of 'realistic', I use the more qualified term 'appearance realistic' because it concerns how things look. (A film may be low on appearance realism but nonetheless be highly realistic in other ways – in what it tells us, and so on.)

But what exactly are these aspects of the cinematic image? In a painting the formal properties would be such features as the brushstrokes and colour palette. In film, colour (including black and white) and the areas of light and shade would count, as would picture composition. The issue can get tricky, though, for areas of light and shade are there in the scene, not cinematic add-ons. In one way they are content, not form. Someone standing on the set would notice them as the set was lit. Nonetheless, light and shade *can* be formal properties insofar as they emphasised, repressed or manipulated in any way, say through use of certain kinds of film stock, processing or digital alteration. Hopkins also points out that the 2D image represents 3D content: the image is 2D; the world it reveals is 3D. This formal quality is thus inevitably built into the image. (I come to stereoscopic films later.)

Form is also the audio-visual part of the *way* a story gets told. It is, we might say, the audio-visual *manner* of its telling. I think that this shows the way out of an early contrast in film theoretical circles between realists and formalists in understanding the nature of cinema. As Mark de Valk puts it, "The realist films treat film as a window upon the world, and the formalists treat film as a canvas."[63] The position of this book is that it is something of both. Photographically it's a window (of sorts) but what one does with the window can be regarded as the canvas (of sorts) – and one always has to do something with it, even if only decide on framing and composition (even if carelessly). Chapter 1 gave us this, and many other types of form to be getting on with, so *total* realism must simply be false.

Content

Matters get complicated here. In one sense the content would be whatever was before the camera as it rolled – the actors, the things, the scenery, the sets, and so on. However, in our present context, the content would be what all these items *represent* – in other words it is THE STORY TOLD, and form can be seen as an important aspect of the *way* in which the story is told. Some parts of form, though, *determine* at least the rudiments of content. Light and shade do so, as do features such as the outline shape of persons, objects and parts of the scenery. If these were different, the content would be correspondingly different. It would be no use, for example (except as some kind of visual joke) having something with the outline shape of an elephant if it were supposed to represent a human being. The photographic realism of cinema usually takes care of this, of course: put a human actor before the camera and they are unlikely to look like an elephant. On the whole lens distortion would have to be extreme to lead to mistakes on such matters. Painting contains no such built-in guarantees. (I always used to show the primary school children I used to teach how to avoid making their trees look like green lollipops on brown sticks. Bless them!) Newspaper cartoonists also play about cleverly with the natural appearance of politicians.

Formalism and realism are, in effect, two interpretations of how the cinematic image can be understood and also about what is fundamental about how it looks – and how it *should* look. The formalist places emphasis on the form of the image; the realist on what the image depicts. Both have been huge forces in the history of film theory. I come now to explore this.

How exactly can we distinguish exactly what constitutes form and content?

Take the red dress worn, bang in the middle of an otherwise black and white image in *Schindler's List* (Steven Spielberg, US, 1993). Is the redness form or content? Here we must draw upon the distinction between the CINEMATIC IMAGE, THE STORY TOLD and THE THINGS FILMED. In so far as the character's dress is supposed to be red in the STORY TOLD, it can be construed as story content; if the dress *was* red as it was filmed, it is also content in connection with THE THINGS FILMED; in so far the colour was added later, it can be construed as form. Another example: the 'horse of a different colour' in *The Wizard of Oz* (Victor Fleming, US, 1939). Is it symbolic of the magic of Oz or does the horse *actually* change colour in the story world – or both (which I think more plausible, given the dialogue of the moment)? It was, as I understand it, painted and repainted to achieve the effect, there being no digital assistance in its day, so it was certainly content in connection with THE THINGS FILMED.

The plot, however, thickens. In so far as a scene is *in reality* brightly lit or in shadow, then the light and dark are part of the content (such matters may well be important to the characters) but in so far as they are features of THE CINEMATIC IMAGE alone – the way they 'come out', the way or manner of the *telling* -- they are purely formal. Because cinema is essentially and primarily photographic, most of what one sees (and hears) is as much content as it is form. Mostly, but not always. Take the recent film *The Favourite* (Yorgos Lanthimos, Ireland, 2018). Here a number of scenes are taken with extreme wide-angle lenses which have the effect of curving vertical lines at the edges of the picture. This is pure form and nothing else. No one takes Queen Anne (the film tells part of her life story) as living in a palace where the walls and pillars *actually* bow to her as she walks through its rooms. It's just a delicious example of form. It is worth pointing out the ambiguous cases, though, for they show that the distinction between form and content is not always clear cut. At the least it shows that we have to be careful exactly how we make out the distinction. This does not mean that we can make no distinction *at all*, of course. We have already given examples of features that are more clearly formal. Nor does having form work against the idea of transparency. Form – in the sense that a cinematic image has it – is to be construed, remember, as the *way* we see things not *what* we see. We detect form but not as consisting in *objects* of our perception, the actors and other items before the camera are that. Photography, therefore, can be transparent and still have formal properties even though they are not altogether the kinds of formal property that painting has.

Here we can see a problem with the worry that philosopher Roger Scruton had with the idea of photography (and, hence, cinema) being an art form.[64] Scruton, though, is but a modern representative of a sensibility that emerged in the earliest days of imagery that could remotely be regarded as photographic. Lopes cites painter Joshua Reynolds: "set a view of nature represented with all the truth of the camera obscura" next to "the same scene represented by a great artist," and "how little and mean will the one appear in comparison of the other."[65]

Scruton takes the criticism further and argues that photography cannot be a representational art at all. This is because in order for it to be such it would have to engender aesthetic appreciation *as a photograph*. Photography, he argues is disqualified from doing this. A photograph just does not have any representational qualities all its own. It merely conveys the properties had by the actual things photographed. The transparency thesis seems just to reinforce this criticism because it takes a photograph purely to be a causal result of what is recorded by the camera. This, in turn, is purely the causal result of what was in front of the camera. What's art about that purely mechanical process? If aesthetic qualities are on display in a photograph then what has them is the subject photographed not the photographic image itself. Take a photograph of beautiful scenery. Strictly (according to the idea being canvassed here) it is the scenery that has all the beauty. The photograph merely records *that* beauty, it adds none all its own. Of the photograph itself all we can strictly say is that it is a well exposed, accurate record of beautiful scenery. These are positive appraisals but not aesthetic ones. For Scruton, a photograph of X is merely a kind of surrogate for X. This can never be said of a proper art such as a painting. I think that Scruton is wrong.

First of all, what he says somewhat misconstrues the implications of the transparency thesis. That thesis says that a photographic image *is* a causal result of what is recorded by the camera, not that this is *all* that can be said about a photograph itself. That a photographic (and thus cinematic) image is a causal result, ultimately of what was before the camera, has its implications for the way cinema should be. However, that such an image cannot have its very own formal qualities is not one of them, provided that form is construed in the way I have outlined – as residing in the *way* the image has us see its objects. So, such images can have aesthetic qualities all their own.

This doesn't mean, though, that the aesthetic qualities have immunity from certain other aspects of a film, as we shall see when we consider later the moral qualities of a film. It simply means that the causal relationship between what is photographed and the photograph itself doesn't rule out the very possibility of a photographic image having formal, and thus aesthetic, qualities all its own. Matters get even more complicated than Scruton thinks. Indeed, as Dawn Phillips points out,[66] the fact that a causal relationship between a photograph and what was before the camera, just in itself, no more determines its subject than the fact that a painting was caused by the movements of a brush makes those movements the subject of the painting. The *cause of* and the *subject of* are logically independent issues, even if, as in a photograph, what was before the camera is (part of) the cause of the final image is frequently and standardly also its subject. Even then, the two may only coincide in part. Take an old photo of granny, its subject is granny, yet it will include a background – granny's old room, perhaps. These are just as much the cause of the photograph as is granny but they are not its subject, even though the background may evoke fond memories.

Indeed, as Phillips again points out, the fact that a photograph is caused by X doesn't mean that it has a subject *at all*, still less that its subject must be X. I once took a photograph of the floor in my living room. It was an accident, committed as I was playing about with the camera. The photograph was caused, ultimately, by my suitably illuminated floor but my floor was not its subject. It had no subject. It was simply a more or less accurate visual record of my floor. Even when it may *seem* that what was before the camera is the photograph's subject it may still not be.

A very badly underexposed photograph may be so dark as to reveal nothing of its subject, in which case it also has no (actual) subject, yet it was still caused by what was before the camera in combination with the photographic apparatus itself.

All this is because what determines what the subject of a photograph may be is a matter of aboutness or intentionality. My accidental photograph was caused, among other things, by my floor but my floor was not what my accidental photograph was about. It wasn't about anything. The logical principle here is that causal relations do not determine intentional (aboutness) relations. Scruton was well aware that causal relations lack intentionality. He was far too astute a philosopher not to be. His mistake was to place just too much weight on the way in which a photographic image is caused. It just isn't *all* that counts. It can never fill that role. This is because causal chains do not really have a beginning – save maybe at the cosmic 'big bang'. I have been talking loosely of the things in front of the camera being the causes, even 'ultimate' causes of the photograph but, of course, this is not strictly true. The causal chain goes way back – for the theist even as far as God! To choose a particular cause as key, reflects only our more localised human interests.

What was before the camera may also be symbolic of its real subject. The real subject of a photograph may be almost anything: emotion and other psychological states, for instance. These were not literally before then camera in the way things, people and scenery are, nor does the photograph merely accurately record them. Even if, say, a photograph is of a person who is *really* sad, the photograph has to convey that sadness not merely record it. It does this (partly at any rate) by means of its formal qualities. Another photograph of the very same person, taken at the very same time, may not capture the sadness at all. This sort of thing is what makes good photography difficult and 'point and shoot' photography chancy. The effectiveness of the way in which these psychological states are conveyed can also be reinforced by the way the photograph's formal qualities show them. So, here we go again: the photographic image is a *way* of showing not solely a causal result of what was before the camera. Therein lies the possibility of its art – its aesthetic qualities.

In the early days of cinema, thinkers were keen on separating film from theatre, showing that it could be a quite different art in its own right. This led them (the 'formalists', such as Hugo Münsterberg and Rudolph Arnheim) to stress the formal qualities of the cinematic image. Film did not just passively record reality, giving us, as McGinn puts it, "a mere rehashing of ordinary perception".[67]

There have been those who play down the importance of form – more extremist 'realists' do this. As you will now be aware, I do not think this is sustainable, but a more reasonable stance is that form *serves* purpose. This was the view of then very influential film theorists Siegfried Kracauer and André Bazin. James Monaco puts it thus:

> "As his theory develops and broadens, it becomes clear that Kracauer has no great objections to form - so long as it serves the purpose of content. And here we get to the heart of Kracauer's true contribution to film theory: film serves a purpose. It does not exist simply for itself, as a pure esthetic (*sic*) object; it exists in the context of the world around it. Since it stems from reality it must also return to it — hence the subtitle of Kracauer's book: 'The Redemption of Physical Reality'. If this sounds vaguely religious, the connotation is, I think, intended. For Kracauer, film has a human, ethical nature. Ethics must replace esthetics, thereby fulfilling Lenin's prophecy, which Jean-Luc Godard was fond of quoting, that "ethics are the esthetics of the future." Having been divorced from physical reality by both scientific and esthetic abstraction, we need the redemption film offers: we need to be brought back into communication with the physical world. Film can mediate reality for us. It can both "corroborate" and "debunk" our impressions of reality. Now more than ever before this seems an admirable goal."[68]

I certainly accept the tone of all that but where do I stand on this great divide between formalism and realism? I lean towards realism in that I take it as axiomatic of the cinematic image that it conveys reality in a special way – by photography (as described in Chapter 1) but I believe also that it has form. Yet while I further believe that form must serve reality and the resultant aesthetics must indeed serve ethics, I believe that it can do so only if the form has its own dream-like, poetic force to begin with.

The poet Robert Frost once said that poetry is untranslatable. One takes him to mean that it cannot be made altogether literal. Meaning would get lost in translation. "Poetry is an awareness of the world, a particular way of relating to reality", observed film director Andrei Tarkovsky. The same can be said of the form of the cinematic image. Try to cancel that out, as too many serious filmmakers seem to do, and you don't get a purer, less adulterated view of some reality but simply a less insightful, and certainly less forceful, view of it. But if poetry is an "awareness of the world", in cinema it is also a dream-like awareness.

The Cinematic Film – full of form

In the aesthetic sense of the word, a film can be regarded as cinematic in so far as it appropriately exploits the kinds of aspect I describe above *as* form. Here I draw up a list of what I take to be the most important characteristics of form. In them all, the cinematic qualities, as ever, are to be found in the *way* we see things, people, performances, lighting and so on not in these things themselves. So, here is what I believe makes an aesthetically good film.

C1 The medium of cinema is a central factor. The film is *all* cinema. The aesthetic potential of the cinematic image is key. *Youth* (Paolo Sorrentino, Italy, 2015) is a cinematic film; *Two Days, One Night* (Jean-Pierre & Luc Dardenne, Belgium, 2014) is a naturalistic film.

C2 Picture composition is key. *How* you see something is as important as *what* one sees. (E.g., in *Citizen Kane* one shot shows in an interior foreground the grown-ups deciding on the young Kane's future. The boy himself is seen in the further distance through a window, playing in the snow. Seeing the picture elements this way is crucial to the *meaning* of the scene. Kane's childhood is already being *seen as* something distant and lost yet also something that would remain for Kane throughout his life.

C3 The psychology of the characters is not down to the actors and script alone. Editing, areas of light and dark and visible detail in the image, and other aspects of the cinematic context are all used to control the psychology. The cinematic image is allowed to represent matters in a way that does not merely mirror or copy what a viewer would see if they were inside the fictional world.

C4 Lighting is key. It is used to emphasise emotion and meaning. It is often used to symbolise states of affairs.

C5 Editing is key. Not only is pace paramount, everything on the screen must be there because it is intended either to be seen or to contribute to how one sees things. How shots meld together and how long they are held on the screen is also crucial. There is nothing casual about an aesthetically cinematic film.

C6 Music is used fairly extensively. The emotional character of the film crucially depends upon it. (Take Bernard Hermann's score as 'Scottie' follows his prey with obsessive longing in Hitchcock's *Vertigo*.)

C7 Style (of various kinds) is key. It is used to play into emotion and meaning of the film. The speed and ways in which the elements of the picture move across the picture is important. It can often have (at least slightly) a dream-like look. Paradoxically, a cinematically pleasing film exploits the fact that an element of *un*reality can help us focus on what matters about the reality represented in the film. Cinema is essentially a hybrid medium, part naturalism (because of its photographic nature) and part dream-like and non-naturalism (because of what gives it its form).

C8 The narrative pattern can be non-literal. There can be free use of the symbolic. Action in real time (or close to it) can often be abandoned. Streams of consciousness and other techniques can be employed to reveal the inner life of the characters – all a bit dream-like. Though none of this is strictly essential, it is not to be avoided on some sort of principle.

C9. Cinematic cinema allows for emphasis to be given to an *aspect* of a character or situation. It can focus on something interesting and legitimately not reach for mere roundedness of character. Thus, in *Youth*, we are required to see the queen's emissary as a pompous, condescending, 'Worry not, your majesty, I can pull it off with eminent people' ass. We were not intended to see any other aspect of the man. Misperceived, this could well look like bad acting. It is, I would suggest, effective acting *of a part*. We will return to this issue. The point here is that cinema can very good at all this. When the characters come across in a slightly exaggerated form, as characters in a dream, their presence can be very powerful.

C10 Actors *act*: Actors do not mumble, they merely have to sound *as though* their character is mumbling. This requires much higher skill.

C11 The dream-likeness is not ignored but used to ignite, drive and keep alive the telling of the story. This dream-likeness is aided by use of lighting and music.

C12 Cinematic films draw from a wide range of cinematic elements - to contribute to the telling and psychology of the story and add to its meaning and emotional impact. Films that are too raw in their mere carbon-copying approach to authenticity and purely naturalistic are by their very nature much more limited. I return to this issue under the Sins of Storytelling.

C13 Cinematic films can convey a greater range of what is still perfectly *real*. Cinematic techniques do not compete with reality but help draw out deeper reality. So, *Youth* can be just as *authentic* as *Two Days, One Night*. It is simply less *naturalistic* – and ten times better a piece of cinema as a result.

C14 Cinematic films can be more inventive and playful – two well acknowledged values in art.

C15 Cinematic films recognise values and purposes beyond simple carbon-copying naturalism. It can focus one's attention on a single strand and enable us to reflect rather than just record what a character may (naturalistically) *do* in a certain situation. They can, hence, dig deeper. But focussing only on the *doing* of a character instead of their inner being, misses out, I would argue, just too much of what it is like to be a human being. The cinematic film can get at *experience*; the naturalistic film merely *plight*.

C16 Aesthetic distance is important. It allows a well composed and beautifully constructed piece of art to convey even more powerfully than mere copy-cat naturalism the inner reality and meaning of matters. (See Distance in Chapter 1) Dream-likeness is important here.

C17 Cinematic films reflect the fact that the medium is not the reality itself but a *representation* of reality. The beauty of the representation matters to the force of the message or point being made about reality. Would Beethoven's *Eroica* symphony be half as revolutionary sounding if its composition mattered only to the point that drums were banged and the brass sounded crude, as they might on a battlefield itself? Beauty in representation, I would argue, is a powerful means of expressing all that needs to be said of reality. Authenticity need not be *raw* naturalism, and indeed, had better not be if a film is to come across as authentically powerful as it can. Naked copying, or over naturalistic authenticity, in its abandonment of what makes cinema carry its weight, is a reduction of proper authenticity. Again, no film can be completely without form. It isn't even possible. It is the drive towards this end *as far as we can go* that I condemn as raw naturalism.

My thesis is this – in cinema, artificiality has much greater potential for realism than can be provided by naturalism. Black and white is, in a sense, more realistic than colour; studio sets are more realistic than real places; studio rain is more *realistic* than nature's own rain, and so on – they're just less *natural*. At the very least, this is almost always the case. Paradoxically, this is precisely because cinema is essentially photographic. Downplaying the artificial is always to risk a weakening of impact, intensity and luminosity. Take rain. If we venture out in heavy rain we can not only just *see* the rain, we can *feel* its intensity. Ordinary perception provides a multi-sensory experience; photography does not, so to get maximum impact it must therefore add its own force and do so by exploiting its (artificial) form. This is what artificiality does and why, in general, it comes closer to the real. Equally paradoxically, then, the naturalistic approach reduces rather than emphasises what is authentically real. The naturalistic approach forgets all this, and its result is reduced impact. Even if one *is* filming real 'stuff', it should be photographed in a way that intensifies what is needed. This is what John Ford achieves in Monument Valley, what Antonioni achieves in the park in his *Blow Up* (UK, 1966), and what the best of the post-war Italian neo-realists and the later 'new wave' directors achieved when they took their cameras outdoors. In general, the more the artificiality of form is used – at least appropriately – the more the viewer will feel themselves to be present to the events portrayed. Artificiality *really* achieves what naturalism only *pretends* to. As some of these examples show, desirable artificiality and beauty extend beyond form, it's just that form is often important, too.

….. and full of beauty

Remember, the beauty of the representation can make the ugliness of life led in a certain way seem all the more pitiful and lacking and small-souled. We too easily dismiss beauty as mere icing on the cake, something merely subjective and in the eye of the beholder. Worse, in de-stabilising traditional values, the 'post-modern turn' emerges, among other things of equal dehumanising horror, as a torch-bearer for rejecting beauty in art. The philosopher Edward Farly puts it this way:

> "In the old French tale, Beauty is initially repulsed by the Beast. By eliminating it from the discourses of interpretation, post-moderns turn Beauty into the Beast. As the Beast, beauty is idolatrous, seductive, effete, amoral, elitist, essentialist and quaint – 'an ornament on the bourgeois past', as Hans Urs Von Balthasar says."[69]

All this does more than merely bolster the almost simple-minded view that beauty lies in the mind of the beholder. I cite von Balthasar again: "We no longer dare to believe in beauty and we make of it a mere appearance in order the more easily to dispose of it".[70] We spit with a kind of jaded sophistication, in the face of ultimate value. We should turn on it with vicious anger. Of course, this spiritual negation has not won through altogether – we'd be as good as dead otherwise - but it dominates to a degree that we stand in urgent need of a reminder of the power and *real* work of beauty. For this, I turn to the philosopher Roger Scruton:

> "It [beauty]challenges us to find meaning in its object, to make critical comparisons, and to examine our own lives and emotions in the light of what we find. Art, nature and the human form all invite us to place this experience in the centre of our lives. If we do so, then it offers a place of refreshment of which we will never tire. But to imagine that we can do this, and still be free to see beauty as nothing more than a subjective preference or a source of transient pleasure, is to misunderstand the depth to which reason and value penetrate our lives. It is to fail to see that, for a free being, there is right feeling, right experience and right enjoyment just as much as right action."[71]

"It challenges us to find meaning". I want to shout this out like thunder when I'm faced with dull, tedious, loosely-structured, dim-minded pedestrianism – in cinema or elsewhere. So, I will be blunt. Ugliness, deprivation, despair, cruelty, social injustice - all grim things of all grim life – *need* beauty, some kind of poetry (in films, *cinematic* poetry) properly and fully to show them what they are – the *absence of good*, of all that we feel in our bones just plain *ought* to be. That's why Italian neo-realism is remembered. It is why John Ford is remembered. (I am thinking particularly here of his *The Grapes of Wrath*, US, 1940 – a film about a poor Mid-West family driven from the land on which they are born, work and die. Never has the absence of beauty in human life – which is what ugliness, at bottom, is – glowed with such powerful, unforgettable beauty from the cinema screen.)

Thus, the aesthetically barren, raw 'in-yer-face' approach just won't cut it. We need to be *moved* into an awareness of the ugly, not merely viscerally *shocked* into it. What is appalling about the latter approach is that it fails to have any real or lasting force. What puts our sensibilities to sleep is memorable only in the sense that mogadon is memorable. "Every experience of beauty points to [eternity]". That's von Balthasar again, and it is worth stating because it may well explain how it makes its recipients memorable. Even at best, the merely literal, pedestrian approach does no more than *show* the surface of suffering rather than *reveal* its terrible negation. In the process, it fails to pay due respect to the suffering that is represented. But the film maker needs the talent and visual imagination to pull it off, just as Beethoven needed musical genius to convey a sense of revolution through his compositions. (Recall from Chapter 1 how Wyler used distance (in every sense) in his *The Big Country* to convey an instance of pointless conflict.) It is the poet, more even than the philosopher, and certainly more than the naturalistic film maker, who gets inside the soul. Cinematic films are a visual form of poetry, I would say, and they certainly penetrate our yearning souls.

That said, worries can be raised, so I move on to them.

Some worries about a film being overly cinematic (too 'arty')

A friend of mine lauds the more naturalistic film. I reproduce below some worries he had about the more 'cinematic' film *Youth* (Paolo Sorrentino, Italy, 2015). The points made, however, can be generalised.

Worry 1: Self-Consciousness

"Is there too much 'self-consciousness' about the *Youth*?" Indeed there is – at any rate in the characters. But why should that be bad? Many of the key characters have backgrounds in which ego plays a big part in their psychological difficulties.

That indeed seems part of the films very message. And the film's own self-consciousness? I'm never, to be frank, too sure about what that even means but if it means something like, 'Comes across as a striking piece of visual art', then, well – GOOD.

Worry 2: Too much 'artiness' reduces what a film says

"Isn't the film too busy looking cinematically clever actually to say much of substance about the past and the experience of growing older or the loss of love?" No! I think it says some very substantial things in this respect even though the film was not intended to present some finished or entirely coherent thesis on these matters. Rather, it played with them and the surrounding psychological territory. It rather seemed to say that no such thesis is even possible. Instead, the film explored certain disparate moments alone. Seen this way, I would suggest that it captured very well the oddity and unsettled angst of those moments of deep worry and sadness that I think are characteristic of greater age. Certainly the truth it conveyed about these matters was conveyed ephemerally and even a tad chaotically but that fact itself to some extent characterises age as well, doesn't it? For me, the film captured very strongly a deep paradox of older age: that one often gains wisdom but only at the cost of disintegration of the platform of life upon which one has hitherto stood proud and from which one could, if it were still in decent shape, make good use of that wisdom. "From dust we come and to dust we will return." There is a real soul-fragmenting existential fear in that thought and it seemed to me that the film captured it far more deeply than would any more naturalistic film set in the very same place and given a merely documentary camera endlessly following the backs of the same pair of frightened old curmudgeons. The viewer doesn't just trace their circumstances but, in a special way, *shares* their experiences. One saw (some of) what they *were* not simply what they *did*. Only to the extent that a film is cinematic can this happen at such depth. I believe there is something deeply and mysteriously humanistic about a piece of decent, visually exciting, poetic and beautifully constructed cinematic film. If one wants a coherent, exhaustive, scientific, and thoroughgoing *analysis* of old age one should read a sufficiently advanced textbook on psychological diagnosis, not see a film. The two disciplines address different levels of truth. On the other hand, if one wants a revealing experience it is the textbook that should be abandoned in favour of a visit to the cinema.

Worry 3: Cinematic admiration and character discernment

"Can you admire a film in which one dislikes all the characters just because it is cinematic?" My answer would be a qualified "no". One may still admire the acting and everything else about the film but if you cannot get along with any of the characters *at all,* the rest of the well-deserved admiration becomes hard work. I think this is elemental. The psychology of storytelling has always depended upon it. I would nuance the opening question, though, and replace 'like' with 'have some measure of sympathy for', or better still, 'have some engagement with'. Everyone in a film may be a pretty bad lot but one may nonetheless still engage with and care about somebody's fate. A cinematic film can draw upon its power to aid this caring, as it does for the boy in *Citizen Kane.* Total absence of sympathy or engagement, though, is lethal. The whole thing is lost, no matter how otherwise clever it is.

A recent example for me was Tarantino's *The Hateful Eight.* (US, 2015). There was much that made this a 'cinematic' film as I laid out that concept earlier – though in a limited sense. The acting was certainly good. All the characters had a kind of controlled obsession. They were taking each other in. There was a fascination about the situation. There was plenty of snow – and precipitation generally is cinematic. (It's the motion involved.) For all that, I couldn't have cared tuppence who lived and who died. I responded in no deep way either to survival or death. What a damming judgement - and how effectively it spoiled the whole show. It was all far too cleverly *in*humane. (I deal later with the moral tone of films and how this can ruin the aesthetic values of a film.) However, it is no part of my thesis that cinematic qualities cannot be *mis*used or even *ab*used, only that they should be *used.*

Worry 4: Style and Humanity

"Did *Youth* dazzle and impress with technique, at the expense of its portrayal of humanity?"

This, too, would be damming, but I do not think the film guilty. Firstly, the two main characters I found interesting – and all *too* human. Without that, everything else would seem like something done for its own sake or done to show off. Is that so here? The style, though certainly dazzling, can be seen as expressing the fragmented, deluded, ephemeral incompleteness of the characters' lives. After all, being dazzled is a bit ephemeral and unfulfilling itself , so there's definitely a correspondence at play between how the film allows us to *see* its characters and the reality of their lives. Mere naturalism would not have captured this aspect of nature. I agree, though, that good cinema cannot consist only in cinematic style, whether dazzling or more subtle. It must be for the purpose of expressing something human. Style, technique and dazzle – all will be rather tiresome if the humanity is not served. It will certainly not be art.

Worry 5: Can we worry too much about the words 'cinematic' and 'naturalistic'?

Of course. In at least some ordinary sense of 'naturalism' almost every film is naturalistic in tone. Only a film which is totally abstract or symbolic will or even can be without any naturalistic elements at all – in *any* sense. Even Bunuel films have recognisably natural characters moving about in recognisably natural environments in connection with some set of recognisably natural circumstances. In that sense, nearly everything – from *Youth* to *Battleship Potemkin* (Sergei Eisenstein, USSR, 1925) is naturalistic in some general sense. Still, I do not think that the distinctions I make between what I call the 'naturalistic' and 'the cinematic' are unimportant. Quite the contrary.

Worry 6: Art, Stylishness, Craftsmanship & Naturalism

Are the style and technique in *Youth* a substitute for real craftsmanship?

I should come clean here, too. I have a hierarchy: Art, Stylishness, Craftsmanship & Naturalism. Technique isn't missing here, it's just that it is to be found at all four levels – or at least the top three. At the highest level comes Art. To qualify (I'm old-fashioned) something significant must be said or it must get at the real depth of something. Some examples are: *The Searchers* (John Ford, US, 1956), *Citizen Kane* (Orson Welles, US, 1941), *Bicycle Thieves* (Vittorio de Sica, Italy, 1948), *The Gospel According to Matthew* (Pier Paolo Pasolini, Italy, 1964). Then comes Stylishness. Here we find a playful use of cinema. It may be hugely engaging, especially if it has a good story and characters one cares about, but there's nothing particularly profound at work. Many films, I think straddle between Art and Stylishness. (Completely vacuous stylishness would hardly be a blessing.) Next down we have Craftsmanship. Stories are told with efficiency and some psychological impact but style may be minimal and one can forget them as soon as one has seen them. They pass the time nicely enough. Craftsmanship is still vital, though. Art and stylishness would be impossible without it. Examples: virtually all of the weekly, assembly-line product of old Hollywood, save the greatest.) A film at each of the top two levels will involve elements of the one or two below. Lowest of all, though, we have what I am calling 'Naturalism'. Here Stylishness and Art are shunned as getting in the way of the social message to be conveyed. Even craftsmanship seems all too often minimised. Result? Dullness. (Examples: too much of the 'art-house' stuff nowadays, I would say.) This is a framework for thinking about films that I find useful. Reality is always a good deal messier. Many films, even quite naturalistic ones may have elements of the other three. It's a question of where the emphasis lies. We return to this issue in a big way later.

Worry 7: Dream-likeness gets in the way and becomes over-emotional

It *can* do. Worse still, it may do so in unacceptable contexts. More specifically, it can reduce to sheer sentimentalism that which should not be sentimentalised. But such sin would be carelessness, thoughtlessness, indifference or focus on commercial needs on the part of a filmmaker. It in no way de-legitimises the dream thesis. Emotion as much as thought drives our lives. Thought is often saturated in emotion, anyhow – and emotion in thought. I have more to say about this later. One should not, though, dismiss as mere sentimentalism the power which cinema uniquely has of showing us emotion.

The sin of raising issues above cinematic looks

One thing's seems sure: just telling a good story with bags of style is getting rare among makers of 'serious' films about 'serious' issues. Such films should certainly be made. *I, Daniel Blake* (Ken Loach, UK, 2018) points to wholesale injustices in the UK benefits system. My years as a volunteer adviser for the Citizens Advice Bureau leaves me in no doubt that levels of sheer desperation can be high. Anyone who thinks all (or even many) such benefits seekers are idlers is living in cuckoo land. I wouldn't mind their doing so if it were not for that fact that it is others who suffer from their sheer ignorance. Loach is entirely right to make such films. Another example is, again, *Two Days, One Night* (Jean-Pierre & Luc Dardenne, Belgium, 2014). A young family woman who works in a factory is one chosen for dismissal on economic grounds while others have been tempted by a handsome bonus. The title tells us how much time she's got to persuade her workmates that the situation is not just. Many serious films are these days about the injustices of modern life. The trouble is that such films too often place the issue above the cinema and simply don't seem much to mind what it looks like or place much weight on story structure. And don't dare say, 'Whoa! It is supposed to be cinema, isn't it?'. You'll just sound quaint, old-fashioned and frankly rather bourgeois with the 'serious' crowd. No! No! No! Authenticity is what it's all about and the more neutrally naturalistic it is, the better, just forget style and even too much story, it's too artificial. Well! I will go to my death believing that elevating the issue above the cinema is a 'serious' mistake. Thank goodness that De Sica didn't think this way when he made *Bicycle Thieves* (Italy, 1948). It would by now have been long forgotten. Ken Loach's *I, Daniel* Blake, mentioned above, is an important film which certainly had some impact. However, it is his more elegiacally cinematic *Kes* (UK, 1970) that is still remembered and, indeed, loved. It is also the more powerful.

So just what are the 'sins' involved here? Firstly, it makes for sloppy, careless, ill-composed, bland looking cinema with a narrative structure that often resembles badly erected scaffolding. Weak-kneed, wobbly, cheap handheld and frequently quite irrelevant visuals abound. (Though I suspect that this is why so many filmmakers choose to do things that way. It makes filmmaking easy for those without any visual imagination.) But who cares? The 'issue', that's what counts, remember. Often, reviewers are complicit in this business because they too spend too much time analysing how the film has dealt with the issues and one is left not knowing whether one wants to go and *see* the thing.

Of course, all this lack sometimes engenders a vague sense of guilt and the director then feels compelled to show they do in fact know a little something about filmmaking. They would do better by visiting a priest but instead they atone for their sin by bringing into the show a few mandatory lyrical moments. (The hand enjoying the breeze from an open car window, or something similar, has been a popular one, never mind its frequently complete irrelevance.)

Finally, it facilitates the pretence that fearless blunt photocopy-like authenticity is all that counts. Who needs cinema when one has a 'real issue' to worry about? All that matters is that the script and the actors get it right. Well I for one still think we do need good cinema, as well as serious issues, especially when I'm in a darkened auditorium built for the job. Besides, the whole attitude of downgrading cinema is self-defeating. I can focus just as well on an issue by staying at home and reading a 'serious' paper. The whole point about making a feature film of the issue should be to let the cinema do the talking. Using the best of styles for the job actually helps with getting the issue across. It is not the enemy here. Why bother otherwise? One could probably reach a larger audience by making a rubbishy looking video for YouTube. But - and here of course is the rub – making an effective piece of cinema would take skill and visual imagination.

The sin of seeking immediacy

The drive to immediacy – as if the events are happening right in front of the viewer's eyes in real time - seems also to be part of so-called 'authenticity' and its concomitant lack of cinematic stylishness. After all, if the events were really going on in front of one's eyes cinematic stylishness would not be present, so why should it be present in a film? As we have seen, though, this completely ignores part of the very nature of the cinematic image, which has the essential feature of psychological (and aesthetic) distance. Such an approach therefore rules out the real power that cinematic images can have in displaying events in the film. Hence, the drive to immediacy makes the imagery *less* powerful than it otherwise could be.

One supposes that filmmakers are rather afraid of falling into sentimental melodrama if they make use of some of the powers I am claiming to be attached to the cinematic image, or perhaps the thought is that they all belong to cinema's past – something many directors seem so desperate to burst out of. However, the first is simple lack of confidence in the power of cinema and the second, a symptom of the need to be 'of one's own time' or even original. Is Loach's *Kes* less powerful than his *I, Daniel Blake* because it is better cinematically? I think not. It is *more* powerful – and remains more powerful. The latter film derives all its power simply from the urgency of the present day situation that its story is about. It hits hard for that reason but the pity is that it could have hit harder still.

The 'in-yer-face-ism', as I tend to call what others call 'immediacy', of too much modern cinema simply ignores the imaginative powers conferred upon the cinematic image by its essential properties of psychological and aesthetic distance. (Recall Chapter 1) One is given less space in which to appreciate the real injustice of the issues, see them for what they really involve, place them within a bigger picture, understand them as human failings. There is less space to do these things because one's eyes and ears are being too assaulted by the 'immediacy'. Of course a viewer may be all too well aware of the seriousness of the issues anyway, but where that is the case the film wouldn't be adding anything.

In talking of *The Royal Tenenbaums* (Wes Anderson, US, 2001) Sam Turner, editor of *Film Intel* says,

> "Like all of Anderson, it is smartly scripted, featuring a forked tongue when it needs it, good timing and great, playful, visual gags which often fulfil a story purpose as well as a humorous one; the final tracking shot, featuring Raleigh (Bill Murray) and a dog, and the detective on the roof are both cases in point. Anderson's aesthetics, far from being style over substance, are the very thing that allow him to tell serious stories without bludgeoning his audience over the head with throes of social realism and depression-era levels of, well, depression."[72]

Amen! Cinema is at its best when it takes a form reminiscent of opera, dance, poetry or music. This includes both films with a pacey and excited but still connected and meaningful dynamic and those with more flowing, reflective, even contemplative motions. In contrast, plodding photocopy-like authenticity and its constant but quite dull associate, 'immediacy', are cinema's worst enemy. It is lauded by directors who have just about every quality except visual imagination, but is fit only for the news. We have to remember that living life through the screen is not living life itself. It is life transfigured by the cinematic image. It is in this transfiguration that we find the insight we need from a film about someone's reality.

Bruce Isaacs puts it this way:

> "Cinema represents an obsessive tendency to experience the world in a certain way. In an engaging meditation on cinema's effect, Sean Cubitt declares: 'I want to know what cinema does. If it causes no effect . . . cinema doesn't do anything' . . . Cubitt's charge here is to return to the essence of cinema – the

> matter that makes it what it is. But what it is, for Cubitt, is determined by what kind of transformation it effects. . . . We perceive the world differently to the world we perceive screened back to us. . . The remarkable achievement of cinematic vision, from its earliest manifestation, is to render a new image of the world. This is cinema's overarching purpose: to render the world as a creative movement beyond the perception of life. "[73]

These kinds of thought are not new but they strongly suggest that any kind of cinema that does not point out or explore this difference between art and life is missing something serious. The cinematic image has its own life and this life should be respected if we are to respect the human lives it depicts. Our perception of the lives and experiences of a film's characters is deepened and enriched by the cinematic image only when we allow that image to display its own aesthetic strengths and only when the characters and events inhabit the image rather than just find themselves blandly depicted by it. Over-naturalistic cinema is, in this sense, *less* authentic cinema.

A good example of this is given by Isaacs:

> "The final sequence in *Casablanca* (1942), in which Rick (Humphrey Bogart) and Ilsa (Ingrid Bergman) part ways, is a marvel of synthetic image strategies: mechanistic shot reverse-shot relations, camera movement for emphasis, forced framing, non-diegetic musical accompaniment for emotional effect, soft focus on the woman to maintain the ephemerality and unattainability of the female image, etc. . . . Yet in spite of the highly orchestrated composition, movement and continuity inherent in the sequence, the spectator's engagement with the emotional lives of Rick and Ilsa is personal, deeply reflective, and profoundly real."[74]

The sin of confusing photography & cinematography

I am often told that a film looks cinematic. I see it myself and find that it is simply a piece of pretty photography. Cinematography involves photography, of course. Film is a photographic medium, after all, but cinematography is more than just photography that moves about on a screen. Indeed, the photography involved in a cinematic image may not always be all that great yet still be great *cinematography*. Whether it is will depend on how far it contributes to the power required by the cinematic image as it contributes its crucial part to the telling of the story. There are indeed great films in which one could take almost any individual frame, enlarge it, put it in a frame all its own and hang it on the wall as a beautiful photograph. David Lean films tend, I think, to be this way. (He was something of an accomplished photographer.) Others, perhaps most, would not lend themselves to such treatment yet remain cinematic. The reason for this should be clear from the very nature of the cinematic image. Precisely because it moves, and because it is (standardly) accompanied by sound, its power is determined by far more than what might justifiably be judged as beautiful photography. I have complained above about over-naturalism but sometimes one may legitimately complain that a cinematic image looks *too* photographically stunning in a way that is not required by the story. All the time, filmmakers should get right the order of dependency and service.

The photographic qualities of a cinematic image should always work with its other qualities and all should contribute to the total necessary psychological work to be done by the cinematic image. In its turn, the cinematic image should always have its qualities determined by the needs of the story and serve them. If a visually stunning image fits, then let's have one, but it would be a sin for an image to be that way just because it looks good. Failure means distraction from the flow of the story being told. Framing, scale, camera angle, the choice of colour or black and white, the kind of colour and camera movement are all involved, and all should serve the film's proper end – the story. Some of these elements are so important that they have their own chapter. Here I will cover the rest. All of these elements offer the filmmaker opportunities for expression in their cinematic images.

The qualities of the cinematic image *revisited* – and their sins

The sins of intensity, intimacy and neutrality.

On the grounds of their close relationship, I deal with intensity, intimacy and neutrality together. Intensity, recall, is the fact that our focus in cinema is forced. We have to see *this* face or *that* event, whatever is in front of the camera and is used in the final cut. We cannot, as we can in ordinary perception, turn away and look at something more interesting – at least while we stay within the story world of the film. This forcedness of attention means that there should be a good reason why we are presented with this rather than that. Again, the cinematic image is important, nothing on the screen should be redundant or there just for decoration. The reason must be found in the needs of the story or something else important, such as character development. Sin would consist in being presented with something not needed for that purpose. (Do we need all those close ups?)

Intimacy, we have seen, arises from the fact that the camera and microphone can convey to the viewer greater detail about something than the eye normally can. This extends intensity. Not only are we forced to look at X rather than Y and cannot change at will, but we have to see X with the given degree of detail. Any detail we see that is not to some important point is redundant.

There is a sense, we have seen, in which the camera doesn't lie. This is its photographic 'neutrality'. Of course, photography and cinema can and have been used for all kinds of obviously far from neutral purposes, but – in a straight untampered with case – what was before the camera is what you get in the final image. This forcedness, again, suggests that nothing should be in the image that does not serve a meaningful purpose. (Even if the meaningful purpose at play can itself be questioned.) Why should a viewer be forced to see something utterly irrelevant? A good question to ask when considering any film is: 'Was every shot in it necessary?' If the story could have been just as effective without it, then it should not have been there. (This consideration applies to length of shots, too, so all this touches upon editing as well.)

Filming on location presents some obvious problems here – there is a great deal in a natural or man-made environment, such as a city street, that is incidental. It's just *there*, like it or not. To some degree, that is acceptable. If one wants to show a character walking down a city street or across this or that natural environment, one expects to see lots of stuff that is irrelevant to the story. Somewhat paradoxically, perhaps, this *makes* it relevant – but only minimally so. All we need to know is that the character is walking through a given environment feeling a particular way. Beyond that, though, unnecessary detail should be kept at a minimum.

Memory can be a good criterion here for what is of value. Ask yourself what you can remember about a film. Some of the most memorable cinematic images come from an earlier time of cinema history when either all (or pretty well all) shots, including assumed exteriors, were shot inside a studio. Why? The artificiality *reinforces* the artificial nature of cinema, the strangeness of seeing through the cinematic image that we have already discussed. In short, it works *with* cinema not against it.

Secondly, everything inside the studio as it is under the camera lens is there by design. Every bush, every bit of street furniture, is there and been given the place it has because it serves the purposes of the story. The environment and even the assumed weather and the way it is designed, coloured and lit is under total control. Ask yourself whether the iconic scene in *Singin' in the Rain* (Stanley Donen, US, 1952) in which Gene Kelly dances through the street and swings from the lamp post, would have looked anywhere near as good and served the psychology of the character nearly as well had it been shot in a real street with ambient lighting while there happened to be a slight drizzle. The degree to which that scene would have expressed the necessary intensity of romanticism would have been reduced from 10 out of 10 to 1 out of 10. I considered the *Singin' in the Rain*-like scene in the recent *La La Land* (Damien Chazelle, US, 2016) to be an affront to Kelly but at least its makers had sufficient grace to film it in a studio (or make it look as though it was. In fact, the way that latter film *looked* was its one saving grace.)

Go on location, though, and danger lurks – simply because control is loosened. This is acknowledged in the fact that in many modern fantasy films the external shots are made to look artificial by digital manipulation – very often the sole cinematic feature they have. In the past artificial exterior backgrounds were supplied by paintings on glass screens. Wyler's film *Ben-Hur* (US, 1959) was shot at Cinecitta Studios in Rome. The famous chariot race was filmed in the studio lot but only the lower half of the picture was actually a set. One could apparently see modern day Rome in the background, so this was hidden by painting. Today, a 'green-screen' and digital imagery would be used but the purpose is the same – to regain control of one's film from what would otherwise be there. Even when exteriors were used wholly for many scenes, as say in the westerns of John Ford, the choice (famously Monument Valley) was careful. It was wild and craggy, and Ford seemed even to have the rising dust under his control. Many of the scenes in *Mamma Mia!* (Phyllida Lloyd, US, 2008) are clearly natural settings, yet attention is paid to the quality of lighting. The romantic quality of the Mediterranean look is emphasised.

Use just what is there, though, together with ambient lighting, as seems to happen with so many lower-budget (and hence so much 'serious' cinema) and one is handing over control of the cinematic image to that which is *not* art. The result is a flatter, blander, duller, less expressive image. This, in turn, places much greater weight in telling the story on elements that are not intrinsically or exclusively cinematic – performance, and script (though editing remains, as can music – if it is used). Brilliant! 'This film has all but given up being cinema,' I often want to shout. (I have more to say about this elsewhere). Even filmmakers of the French 'New Wave' of the early sixties (especially, I think, François Truffaut) who specialised in exteriors, gave their shots poetry – and their social and political messages were more powerfully expressed because of it. On the whole, the original forms of what was called '*cinéma vérité*' (French: "truth cinema"), originating in France were like this. Although such films certainly displayed a kind of new rawness and an edgy, nervous, naturalist motion unknown to more studio-bound product, they were never simply careless. They never looked *merely* bland and naturalistic.

As ever, though, one can choose one's own saints and sinners here. To some extent the present book is about the nature of the cinematic image and the aesthetic rules that follow from this nature. It is also about what questions one may usefully ask. That, I hope, is what makes it principled rather than just a personalised rant, but what does or does not fit the bill is up to you. I would say though that one would have little difficulty finding sinners with respect to the present area of concern – especially among filmmakers of serious, socially, politically, issue motivated cinema who are focused so much with their issue that they sometimes seem to forget that they are making a film.

The sin of lack of luminosity

As we saw in Chapter One, any image can have luminosity – take one of Turner's sea pictures, for example. However a cinematic image shines down on us from a screen (hopefully a larger than life one) – standardly in a darkened environment. The nature of the beast is that watching a film is not like observing goings on with our own eyes. Thus, the work to be done by the cinematic image is not simply, in a superficial or naïve way, merely to visually *resemble* reality. Film theorists Ralph Stephenson and J. R. Debrix point out that when watching a film, what matters instead is how readily the cinematic image can be accepted *in its own right.* The impact it has is not perceptual so much as psychological, emotional, and aesthetic. They write:

> "To move us a work of art must possess both authenticity and credibility but the authenticity and credibility which we demand of a work of art are not those which we require of natural objects. In our eyes the two worlds are different and we do not adopt the same physical reactions or attitude of mind towards them. The real world appeals to our senses more than our imagination, while the world of art is designed to work the other way round."[75]

They say of art that it,

> "is a process in which the artist makes use of his experience, intuition, or inspiration, selecting and arranging it to create beautiful and true artistic objects which to a greater or lesser extent imitate reality and that through these objects he communicates his experience to an audience."[76]

This, of course, requires that the filmmaker always use their imaginations. Certainly, bland, photo-copying naturalism is marked by loss of cinematic luminosity.

The role of imagination

Imagination is crucial in understanding the work of cinematic image. On the imagination, the philosopher Anthony Kenny writes,

> "The imagination is clearly not a means of acquiring information about the world outside us in the way that the senses are. One cannot discover the way the world is simply by imagining. None the less there is a sense in which we can increase our knowledge of things by using our imagination. It is similar to the way in which we can learn to see things better by drawing them or modelling them. Using our imagination can increase our sensitivity to other

> people and thus our ability to inform ourselves about what they feel and are likely to do. Works of the imagination may teach us about human beings, great works of fiction are the means by which the human race extends its self-awareness."[77] (p.121).

I entirely accept all this but it *does* seem to imply that the image should never be overly naturalistic in terms of visual resemblance. The cinematic image must feed our imaginations. We need to know how the image uniquely expresses reality and how it produces its effects in us. If the image does not glow in our hearts as much as in our eyes, it is failing as a cinematic expression of the story being told and the characters being revealed – and an overly naturalistic image is too bland to glow. Nature needs help when it comes to us on a screen.

We can see things imaginatively in ordinary perception, of course. The philosopher Mary Warnock says,

> "There is, then, a strong philosophical tradition which gives to imagination the task of allowing us access not only to the natural, external world as a whole, but also to the minds and thoughts and feelings of other people. . . . We are separate, certainly, each with his own point of view, but we are not irrevocably shut up in our own bodies, peering out into the world (including the world of other people) whose real existence remains problematic. That we are not so boxed in is shown by the existence and the efficacy of language. . . . Human beings are capable of grasping and understanding the world of which they form a part. They are observers, but not observers made of wholly different stuff. Their existence is in space and time, alongside all material objects, and alongside other humans."[78]

That we are not boxed in – even inside a cinema – I would say is also shown by the efficacy and dream-likeness of the cinematic image. The question for our evaluation of films, then, would be how efficacious its imagery is, and I would say that it is only efficacious if it feeds our imaginations. As the American silent-film director D. W. Griffith once said, "The task I am trying to achieve is to *make you see*." He was not stating the obvious. We do not just see the world, we see it *imaginatively*. Likewise, we don't just see *extra* things through the cinematic image, we see the things that are there anyway more *imaginatively* – and the image is there to help, or *should* be. "Imagination is more important than knowledge. Knowledge is limited. Imagination encircles the world." That's a quote from Albert Einstein. In similar vein, Mark Twain wrote, "You can't depend on your eyes when your imagination is out of focus." Cinema, like all art, is at its best when it focuses our imaginations. I don't want a film merely to inform, no matter what its message, I want it to expand my imaginative insight into the pain and joy of the world. Don't misunderstand my position – the good and evil in the world is still what ultimately matters – it's simply that we arrive at a deeper understanding of them through art, including cinema, when the art enables and stimulates our imaginations. And art can only do that if it is itself imaginatively made.

The sins of camera angle

Standard eye-line or just below eye-line angles are commonly deployed – and these are right by default. Crowds filmed from a higher angle can commonly be found and very recently drone shots have come into (perhaps far too much) use as a substitute for more imaginative visual thinking. Few filmmakers seem to deviate from the defaults, though, perhaps in fear of making a mess. My response is simple: if one lives in fear of making a visual mess, one should choose some other line of work not force the medium into one's own straight-jacket. One should overuse nothing, of course, but the unreal nature of seeing the world through the cinematic image calls out for a far more imaginative use of camera angles – as the masters Orson Welles and John Frankenheimer knew. If you stick to a common default, as did Ozu (just below eyeline) it should be to satisfy (as it did in Ozu) the psychology of the narrative rather than ease one's fear of over doing things.

The sins of design

Mostly design (of set, makeup and hair) seem right I have to say – just not all that imaginative. On the whole, a filmmaker has succeeded in this department if these things do not make themselves too visible. That said, there seems little attempt to use these things more imaginatively. The main exception has to be the use of special make up to simulate injury in popcorn-level action and horror films. And, of course, again, the general sins of naturalism come into play.

The sins of animation: The threat from Digital Life Forms

Few things sadden me more at the moment (aren't I lucky?) than the fact that everyone talks about taking their kids to see any latest cliché-ridden and completely uninventive *Trash Animation* (Dogsbody Pixel, US, Anytime) and practically no one beyond enthusiasts sees *The Secret of Kells* (Tomm Moore & Nora Twomey, Ireland, 2009) or *Song of the Sea* (Tomm Moore, Ireland, 2014) or *Loving Vincent* (Dorota Kobiela & Hugh Welchman, Poland, 2017) or *The Breadwinner* (Nora Twomey, Ireland, 2017) – some of the finest animations in all cinema. While *Song of The Sea* lacks the extra dimension of mediaeval strangeness to be found in Moore's earlier *Secret of Kells*, it certainly possesses every bit the same degree of magic and charm.

These films remind one that animation, at its finest, is the most wondrous of modern art forms. True, it has been over sentimentalised by post-'Uncle Walt' Disney, over-mechanised by the ravenous, unthinking, half-awake demands of breakfast TV for the otherwise screaming children, and cleansed of visual depth by the life-sucking programming code of Pixar's soul-less computers, but it comes back to life in the films I mention above. The colours have a thickness and unreality reminiscent of three-strip Technicolor and cast their enchantment upon us. The spell glows down irresistibly from the screen. The animation has the bursting playfulness of a long-loved toy you just can't put down. The characterisation reaches straight to the heart without the worry of trying to work out just precisely what it is that is reaching it, and the story somehow sinks in without the need for too much hard reflection. Good animation has at one and the same time both a delicious superficiality and primordial depth. Most of all it is simply and endlessly just watchable without having to trouble oneself with intellectualising the content. (Tell me a greater compliment that can be paid to a piece of cinema.)

Why aren't the best of animations more successful? (Though *Loving Vincent*, a film about the events surrounding the death of Van Gogh, did reach a wider audience.) One major factor is the persistent delusion that cartoons are 'just for kids'. This means that many folk have never noticed the (quite deliberate) intimations of German Expressionism in Disney's *Pinocchio* (US, 1940) or the simple yet delightful drawing of contemporary small-town America in his *Lady and the Tramp* (US, 1955). The dream-like flow of Japan's finest hand-painted productions leave the cinematically blind unmoved, as do the charms of Sylvain Chomet's *Belleville Rendezvous* (France, 2003) and the fascinations and deep humanity of his *The Illusionist* (France, 2010) and the partially animated *The Congress* (Ari Folman, Israel, 2013). Alas, I feel that the clunky interpretive lens of 'Just for the kids' has made decent animation almost extinct in more popular cinema.

Puppet – stop motion – animation must not be forgotten, either. It is almost a kind of cinema all its own, given that it employs photographic imagery. I recall the magic of the puppet version of *Hansel & Gretel* (John Paul, US, 1954) set to Humperdinck's lush operatic music, even if it looked over clunky at times. More recently we have *Anomalisa* (Duke Johnson & Charlie Kaufman, US, 2015). This isn't just *The Woodentops* for grown-ups. The 'stop-motion' puppets at play here are about as unsettling as any you'll ever see. A man in the business of psycho-motivation becomes himself unhinged in Cincinnati. (Just the place for it, I suppose.) He is going through an anomalous phase in which his ordinary world seems alien. He meets Lisa, also something of an anomaly. The film conveys an oddly fascinating and utterly absorbing sense of unreality. The stop motion is as convincing a visual representation of a fractured mind as you can get. One is drawn into its world of strange movement. First-rate cinema.

There have been a number of other heights of excellence: the rather primitive but nonetheless enchanting *Felix the Cat* (black and white animation - now there's a thing), the *Steam Boat Willy* stuff from early Disney (casting his future super-star,

Mickey Mouse), some of the animation in Disney's 1940's *Fantasia* - especially the bit accompanying Stravinsky's 'The Rite of Spring'. Then there's some of the rather ignored Max Fleischer stuff from over a half-century ago (check him out on YouTube). It was he who devised the 'Rotoscope', a means of animating movement by tracing over frames of live action film. Finally, we have a whole raft of abstract shorts - pretty well a genre all its own.

I suppose there maybe something to be said for the content of *Inside Out* (Pete Docter, Ronnie del Carmen, US, 2015) it's just that I'm incensed by Pixar's generally flat, tedious, bland animation. It has all the magic of a wall painted in mild sheen Dulux. *Up* (Pete Docter & Bob Peterson, 2009) is better in its appearance but not by much. That our children should be fed on a diet of such utter disenchantment, frankly, angers me. It simply looks dull and uninspired against even the least of the greater achievements of animation. Not only does that make it thoroughly bad cinema but it will entirely flatten out children's visual imagination. (Now I'm really spitting blood.) *Song of the Sea*, in contrast, will challenge and develop their sense of visual beauty. Teachers everywhere should be planning to get hold of it.

The sins (and virtues) of the digital age & digital FX

The digital age has, in a sense, saved cinema. Old, deteriorated films stocks that went through a camera a century ago that have pretty well any picture left on them at all can now be scanned. Information missing from one frame may be found on a neighbouring frame and the whole thing retrieved and restored. It is now possible to get half-way decent images on a smart phone and imaginative, professional films such as *Taxi Tehran* (Jafar Panahi, Iran, 2015) made surreptitiously to avoid censorship and intended for cinema release, have been made that way.

One problem is that when cheaper equipment is used, the image looks less cinematic and more like video. I am aware that I walk a tightrope here in an already well-worn debate, but it's still important. Images may be crisp and clear but have little texture or feel. The aesthetic distance is therefore much reduced. One sees the world in a rather bland, less visually rich way. I should ram home this point as hard as I can. The texture and feel of an image give it bite and extra strangeness. A cinematic image is empowered if it has a slight oddity to it and if it induces a slight sense of unease. In this way, it adds to the mystery of the cinematic image and straight away at least leans towards *proper* cinema. It helps to keep the viewer psychologically involved. Any film in which the imagery has no visual *feel* to it at all I am inclined not even to *call* 'cinema'. I rather think that this lies behind my tendency to watch almost any film at all, however bad it may be in other respects, and look upon it as at least failed cinema, and look upon the bland, textureless imagery of too many of today's films and regard them as belonging to another medium.

Traditionally, texture was created by film grain but as film stocks became 'better' this was reduced, though even in a high definition digital transfer one still has a sense of it. I think it is also created by the tradition of soft focus. Lighting is key, too. Texture can be created by allowing light to skip across a surface, though this is a bit of a cheat since strictly speaking this technique exaggerates the texture of seen surfaces rather than the image itself. Nonetheless, it adds to the strangeness of the experience so it will do. Even ultra-high levels of definition will do the job since it can provide a level of resolution that seems different to ordinary perception. Defining 'feel', though, is difficult. We can *sense* it and that's about it. The best I can do is to say that feel is determined by how far the form of an image can be (in some sense) separated off from the things, places and people one sees *in* it. It is what gives the viewer the impression of seeing things *through* the image rather than seeing those things directly.

This defect in lack of feel can be put right by using high-end equipment such as the Arri Alexa range of cameras but the coming of the digital age is not helping film aesthetics. There is a crucial sense in which it is not even helping film preservation, either. Unless a film is committed to 35mm and kept in suitable conditions it could well just disappear in a few years. Film stock deteriorates slowly (and today's Kodak stock can last a very long time) but we all know what can happen to a computer file.

The greatest cinematic sin in connection with digital technology though must be that too many popular films nowadays are simply effects driven. Whereas in the deeper past one could go to a cinema belonging to a big chain and often catch some of the greatest films ever made, such places have been reduced almost to games parlours. Too much popular cinema has returned to its roots – the fairground. Stories are dull and unimaginatively told (despite the desperate and merely trendy vocabulary - usually containing the word 'dark' - that is often employed to justify them) and the whole experience is reduced to a theme park ride – 'FX-driven drivel rules – OK!' Cinema has always used special effects, of course, but they used to be employed in the service of storytelling. Nowadays what is still called a 'story' is made to serve the effects. There may be a place for this, of course but to call it cinema just because it employs the same medium is already to embrace something dumbed down. O dear! Good films do still get made, of course, but some months I feel my only choice at the cinema is between seeing some dull, visually retarded tale of grim life (at the 'art-house') or some effects-obese trash that hardly rises to the level of puerile spectacle (at the multiplex).

The sin of the zoooooooom:

One might expect, given that we do not have zoom eyes and my thesis that the cinematic image offers us a strange way of seeing the world, *and* that this strangeness should be aesthetically exploited, that I should approve the use of the zoom lens in cinema – but I do not – or at least not entirely.

Zooming in flattens the apparent perspective. Strictly, a zoom lens, which is a lens with a constantly changeable focal length, does not alter perspective. Perspective can only be changed by physically moving towards or away from a subject. What the zoom lens does, as its focal length increases, is magnify an inner portion of the image. Nonetheless, it has a flattening effect. To zoom in looks less convincing than physically moving in (moving the camera physically towards a subject). It is, of course, easier to achieve and can occasionally be effective but too often it is done for reasons of economy without due thought given to the needs of the image.

One classic trick is to dolly in while zooming out, or the reverse. (A dolly keeps camera movements smooth, though these days there are other mean of doing this.) Done with sufficient precision this keeps everything in the image in (more or less) the same place throughout the move but changes respective sizes of things. It can have a very disorientating effect. Hitchcock famously used it to great effect in *Vertigo* (US, 1958).[79] However, the effect of getting closer to a subject seems heavily reduced if a zoom in is used. The subject is simply taking up more screen space. A rapid zoom in can convey a sense of panic or paranoia but psychological intimacy is not enhanced, only an increasing physical closeness can do the latter. Similarly, though zooming out can be useful for slowly revealing the context in which a subject is placed (a telling thing to do) it is not the best device for distancing the viewer from the subject. Only physically distancing the camera can do this effectively. Thus, zooming in and out must never be used as a cheap alternative to moving the camera. One's choice must be led by the psychological demands of the story. Apparent perspective is a very important phenomenological factor in a film and the drama and psychology of a shot depend upon it. Zooming and camera movements in and out have different emotional profiles. The zoom lens has its own phenomenology and too often it is used indiscriminately.

The sin of abandoning 24 frames

This sin is something of a loan rider in that it is hardly ever committed, at least not in the making of feature films. One tends to find it only in contexts where it is no sin in any case – such as video gaming and special theme-park cinemas. I once saw such a film photographed and projected in a process called 70mm 'Showscan' at 60 frames per second. Its images looked more solid than 3D. The film began with a man (seemingly natural size) standing behind the screen and poking it outward. That is exactly what the audience thought was happening. In fact, it was a projected image. It is, though, worth mentioning, for high frame rates have crept into mainstream cinema – just. Peter Jackson used the technique (at 48 fps).

Since the very early days of cinema, when it was realized that industry standards were required so that films could be shown universally, certain standards arose. 35mm became the standard gauge of film and filming and projecting at 24 frames per second became the standard frame rate for sound film. It gives the film enough physical speed to have a reasonable quality soundtrack. It also reduces visible screen flicker. Different frame rates have different kinds of visible effect and 24 fps became the *look* of cinema. It gives the image a certain kind of texture. Go higher, which may be useful and desirable in all sorts of contexts, and one simply leaves behind what has been identified as cinema.[80] There were even reports that very high frame rates were inducing headaches.

The young may say that keeping to 24 fps as a standard is nowadays just old fashioned and that the only reason we don't like higher frame rates is that we oldies are just not "used to it". The trouble with this creaking *ad hominem* argument is that it cuts both ways. I could just as well say to the youth, "Well you don't so much like 24 fps because it isn't new" (or some such thing). Who cares? I have set out a case here not just a set of personal preferences.

The sins of 3D

The very *fact* of 3D I am inclined to call a sin. At best it is a mere curiosity – until it starts merely to annoy. Again, I am inclined to think that it changes the look of the image so much that is no longer a 'cinematic' image, even if one genuinely enjoys and values the experience in other contexts. So, what is wrong?

It may be thought that 3D brings *extra* reality to seeing a film. After all, we do *see* the world with our two eyes in 3D. However, viewing a film in 3D seems less convincingly real, not more. As I view the world around me, I see the world as 3 dimensional, of course, but I can also refocus my eyes on different things and move around in relation to them. One cannot do that when watching a film. What 3D effect gives in one sense, it takes away, or at least restricts, in another. The 3D image compromises matters. It looks more visceral in one way and less visceral in another. It seems entirely uncomfortable to see something in 3D and not be able to feel it or change one's orientation to it at will. It introduces a kind of hollowness to things. This is important because all these other factors are not extras with which we can dispense. Our ordinary stereoscopic perception is, in part, built around them.[81] 3D sails under a false flag. It promises greater visual reality (and is that what we should chase anyway?) yet fails to deliver. Viscerality itself is the wrong thing to chase in a cinematic image, anyway. Whatever its merits in other contexts (gaming, perhaps, though I am no expert in that) the cinematic image works psychologically not physiologically. Psychological distance, as we have seen, is key. 3D seems not to be helpful here. An edge of unreality is one thing, the bucket-load offered by 3D is altogether more problematic, I would say.

Chapter 3: The Sins of Motion

"People will say, 'There are a million ways to shoot a scene', but I don't think so. I think there're two, maybe, and the other one is wrong."

David Fincher

The dynamics of the Cinematic Image

There are parallels between motion on the screen and motion in the world – between, we might say, the cinematics of cinema and the kinematics of the real world. This includes the kinds of motions that we human beings make as we move around. The close similarity between these two words is not coincidental. It flows from the photographic nature of the cinematic image, which records real-world moving things.

First, though a question, keeping in mind that cinema is primarily a medium of motion: Does the cinematic image itself move? Yes, I contend, and quite literally. This follows from our very definition of a cinematic image as an experience of the world beyond the screen, and the fact that *that* world contains motion. But aren't we often told that nothing literally moves on the screen? (See almost any standard textbook on the fundamentals of cinema.) The ground for this strange assertion is that none of the little pictures on a strip of film (or the digital equivalents) actually moves, except of course, *en-masse* through the projector mechanisms. The motion we take ourselves to see, we are told, is just *illusion*. The brain, we are told, 'interprets' the rushed sequence of still pictures *as if* motion was occurring.

O dear! This is one of those many times in life when phenomenology – the *what it is like* to experience something - trumps science and mechanics as the source of the criteria for what is or is not to be counted as real. In the first place, cinematic images (as defined) *change* as a film progresses. We may here follow the ancient Greek philosopher Aristotle and equate motion with change. What he argued, in fact, was that motion is *the actualising of a potential.* For example, a cold poker resting among the burning coals is actually cold but is potentially hot. After a while, it is actually hot and potentially cold. Motion is the change from the one state to the other. The poker has undergone motion even though it remains in the same position. Motion in the sense of gradual change of position is merely a special case of motion more generally: initially I am actually here but potentially there, later on I am actually there and potentially here. Thus, even if I wanted to say (which I do not) that the images on the screen do not move in the sense that they change position on the screen, we can still maintain that they undergo motion.

But why should we not fall in with the common view that the cinematic image does not involve motion in the sense of changing position on the screen? Because motion, in precisely this sense, is what we experience and the experience, at the fundamental level, is what counts in deciding the realities of a cinematic image. Besides, the only grounds that we have for supposing such motion to be illusory are the physical facts about the individual pictures as they are projected on the screen. They certainly do not move (in the required sense) but they are also not the same thing as the cinematic image as we have defined it. In short, what *does* move isn't the same thing as what *doesn't* move. What *does* move (in the sense of changing position on the screen) are the elements within the cinematic image. What *doesn't* move (in this same sense) are the pictures on the strip of film itself. The physical mechanics is simply irrelevant to what *counts* as motion in this case. They are simply part of the *cause* of the experience of motion. Look at it this way: the motion of the cinematic image is perfectly real, it's just that the immediate physical cause of this real motion doesn't move *in the very same sense.* To deny illusion in this sense, though, is not to deny that a cinematic image may involve illusion in quite other ways, as hinted earlier – such as, in some sense, convincing us that entirely fictional action is somehow real. It is precisely because motion lies at the heart of what cinema *is* in these ways, that it must be handled thoughtfully, both in the sense of the movement of the camera and movement *within* the frame, even as the camera itself remains static. But how may we decide what to think?

One thing suggested by all this is that motion on the screen must reflect the intended change to come. We may be watching the wick on a stick of dynamite incessantly burning away. We then wonder if someone will be killed. Someone may be walking down a street. We wonder where they are going, or we may know that and wonder about their purpose, or we may know all or some of this already and wonder about whether they will succeed, or ... You get the point: something is *going to happen* (change *will* take place, what is now potential will become actual) and the motion, whatever it may be must anticipate that coming change in accordance with the needs of the story. (That thought is at the bottom of Hitchcock's famous remark that it is not the bang that is really frightening but the anticipation of it.) The motion we see must have a *narrative* purpose. Any motion, any change at all that we see in the cinematic image, that is irrelevant to the story is *bad* or at least unwanted motion, for such motion will not add up to a coherent dynamic. It will be a motion that is beside the narrative point.

Also suggested is that the motion we see, call it 'phenomenological motion' must be determined by and correlate with either a character's present psychological condition or the film's intention to convey a sense of something, even if it is just a certain mood. In short, motion must have also a *psychological* purpose. For instance, fast motion may convey a sense of getting on with a job without any ifs, buts or maybes, of not being waylaid. It might convey panic, fret, worry about imminent threat, confrontation of various kinds, or just physically fast action itself. Accelerated phenomenological motion goes well with mounting danger or fear or anticipation. (It can be overdone – see almost any visual effects-driven piece of action-man drivel. It's all far easier than proper storytelling.) Slower motion (I do not mean 'slow-motion' in the technical sense – see below) may convey the very opposite of these things: ease and steadiness, constancy, life's (alas temporary) solidities, maybe ordinariness or even boredom. I need not carry on with such examples. Firstly, they are too numerous to capture; secondly, you can imagine them for yourself. My point is that any phenomenological motion must either anticipate or reflect some psychological motion in a character, some intended mood or emotion or some (relevant) physical motion in the things we see. There must be no disparity between the motion you see and what the story is telling you about what is going on.

Motion in cinema must (standardly) reflect or correlate with some motion in the world. If you want yet another slogan: the dynamics of cinema must reflect the dynamics of the world. This is because, in some sense, the world, remember, is precisely what you see. If the motion within the cinematic image must correlate in some proper way with psychological motion, there must be also an *appropriate* correlation with physical motion. The rate of change in one must correlate with the rate of change in the other. To the extent that the correlation fails (perhaps through wrongful editing or the tedious use of slow motion or some irrelevant camera movement) the phenomenal motion will be inappropriate and may well just *feel* all wrong. Given that the world is literally what one sees, *its* motions must be respected by one's experience in the cinema. This is why filmmakers should be cautious in their use of slow motion, zoom lenses and camera movement. Indeed, the consequences can quickly get monumental. Insert one inappropriate motion into a single cinematic image and that image can be compromised. Allow too many to infect a group of cinematic images and there can be serious psychological diminishment. If inappropriate motion goes on to affect too many scenes, the psychological and aesthetic structure of the entire film is brought down. But let's be optimistic, if the director knows what they are about, suitable and even brilliantly telling motions can transform even an otherwise unremarkable film into a smart piece of cinema.

I am aware that all this may seem abstract. That is simply a very common consequence of trying to express in written language something that is essentially experiential. Inside one's experience of a film, though, it is all very real, as can be brought out by looking at a few examples of a range of moods and atmospheres invoked by various forms of motion. I find old westerns a rich source in this context. The cattle movement in *Red River* (Howard Hawks, US, 1948) takes one to the struggles of life in the great west. We feel the big country's harsh resistance to human need. In a later Hawks western *Rio Bravo* (US, 1959) the first scene, set in a bar as a drunk (played by Dean Martin) is without dialogue. The characters' motions are almost balletic as gunman and drunk give and receive humiliation. Rising dust can be important in westerns and John Ford could seemingly make it rise at his command. In *The Searchers* (US, 1956) the dark character Ethan Edwards finds his long-lost niece. We do not yet know whether he is going to kill the girl, for she has been made Indian at her kidnapping by a tribe many years before the recovery - and Ethan hates Indians. But he doesn't kill. He holds the girl aloft in his arms and the dust rises in almost Biblical formation as he utters the words, "Let's go home, Debbie". In the completely different context of Hitchcock's *Vertigo* (US, 1958) camera movement reflects (private eye) Scotty's growing obsession as he follows the strange woman he has been hired to investigate. All these examples show how motion helps tell a story, and it moves our souls in the process. Whenever one sees a film, notice the motion or lack of it and ask the questions: What is it contributing to what one experiences? How is it making that contribution and making it significant?

Stillness as motion

Using Aristotle's wider and deeper concept of motion we can also incorporate stillness under the category of motion. Being still doesn't just mean remaining physically in one spot (which is always relative to a frame of reference, anyway, given that the earth on which we stand is both rotating and orbiting the sun). We can think about stillness as a kind of lack of perturbance in mind, body, or spirit. The mind is never actually completely still, of course. Thoughts and feelings come and go, drift in and out, but they can at least do so non-violently. Insofar as cinema both stimulates and conveys the thought and feelings of its characters and the spirit of the represented situations, it too can do so with a certain stillness and non-violence. Take *Tokyo Story* (Yasujirô Ozu, Japan, 1953). Ozu's camera moves hardly at all. But there is more than physical change in position involved in its motion. Family life is conveyed in cinema's own poetic motion, invoking parallel motion in the viewer's soul. Far eastern cinema does this better than most. In *Poetry* (Chang-dong Lee, South Korea, 2010) an ageing lady's response to crime in her family and the onset of her own dementia, is to find peace in writing poetry. Many a scene moves (in the sense of changing position) so slowly, yet the imagery richly conveys the growing peace in her own soul. *Departures* (Yôjirô Takita, Japan, 2008) gives us what seems at times to be what we normally think of as 'slow-motion' but it is not. An undertaker is simply preparing a body for burial. There is nothing here that is gruesome. There is only deep respect for what the corpse once was. Through death, the character is dealing with life, indeed, with fundamental reality itself. The motions within the film both reflect and respect all this. I think the Japanese director Hirokazu Koreeda knows about this kind of motion, too, most notably in his *After the Storm* (Japan, 2016) and *Shoplifters* (Japan, 2018). One may note also the deep dream-likeness in all these films.

In all these films the viewer is induced into a mode of consciousness to which western audiences are simply not typically attuned – meditation. I say 'meditation' rather than 'contemplation' deliberately. In religious traditions meditation is a kind or mode of largely non-verbal prayer. However, in an extended sense, it can be understood as seeing things in terms of their relationship to ultimate reality (whatever you take that to be). It's a kind of deepened perception. I would say that this constitutes a spiritual dimension of art. It is the very opposite of today's over celebrated, often quite crass, immediacy, for it prevents our being overwhelmed by what is happening and enables us to see matters *sub specie aeternitatis* (under the aspect of the eternal). It gives us an understanding of things far deeper than any other aspect of film (or art) making. I would judge that all the films I cited above (from east and west) do this. This is the experience had while watching the film. Contemplation comes afterwards, when with a soul that has seen and understood, one reflects upon what it all means. (Something that I am doing as I write this.)[82]

We must not confuse all this visual gentleness, though, entirely with stillness in the spirit of the characters. Ozu's film, for instance, powerfully conveys the struggles within the life of the family and the tensions between the generations. It just does it from a spiritual distance, that strange, phenomenal quality of the cinematic image that rides in tandem with aesthetic distance and aids the much-needed meditation. It is in the film and its viewer that the stillness essentially lies, and in the characters, just sometimes. Michelangelo Antonioni achieves a similar telling combination of stillness of imagery with the growing anxiety and disturbing puzzlement of the film's key character in his *Blow Up* (UK, 1966). In my books, this film is an undoubted masterpiece of 20th century cinematic art, though one, paradoxically, about the power of the motionless image and what it conveys. Certainly, the film's own strange, often semi-surreal motions, its odd, almost absurd, tensions (as in the antique shop) and evermore eye-grabbing detail (as the photographer forever enlarges a teasingly revealing photograph of an assumed murder), even the tree branches waving in transient response to the wind, haunt one's mind. Motion that can meet that sort of end is worth every frame it takes up. I may suggest here, in connection with our thesis that cinema is essentially dreamlike in its nature, and desirably dreamlike in its aesthetics, that the reader sees this film, or indeed pretty well any Antonioni film. You will see cinema that illustrates this point far more powerfully than anybody's words can possibly do.

The sins of camera movement & '*Wobbly Camera Syndrome*'

We come now to inappropriate motion of the camera – motion *of* rather than *within* the frame. Motion picture (I'm sorry but I dislike the word 'movie') cameras make all kinds of legitimate movements: panning and tilting are common, as the camera follows the horizontal and vertical movement of the subject. Cameras can also 'dolly' in and out or 'track' action or scenery. Some of these moves are good, others bad. I offer and analyse a couple of examples.

Good moves

In my books, one of the most impressive and moving stretches of camera movement in the entire history of cinema starts by showing a young woman entering a very makeshift, open air, army field hospital during the American civil war. Gradually the camera pulls backwards and upwards. Slowly it reveals a massive raft of dead and dying soldiers and it comes to an end as a sad but still proud, high-flying confederate flag half fills the screen. Yes! The camera itself moved. There were no zoom lenses then, thank goodness. It was what is called a 'crane shot'. The camera sits aloft a mighty crane and onwards and upwards go both camera and intrepid crew. When this shot was filmed it was not so easy physically to move a 35mm motion picture camera. They were very heavy-duty, industrial-strength pieces of kit. The three-strip Technicolor camera used on this particular film was built like a Sherman tank. Moving it was a major undertaking and it couldn't be done thoughtlessly.

Why was this shot right? Because, ever so slowly, we share the previously rather sheltered young woman's expanding perspective on the horror of the spectacle. More privately, we then see that still proud but now almost mocking flag. Wow! In one aesthetically simple (but logistically expensive and carefully executed) shot we get a whole wealth of revealed psychology and meaning, and this could only be conveyed through picture and sound unified in time and motion – in other words, through the cinematic image. It is why it should rate as highly cinematic, *aesthetically* speaking. Moreover, it was important that the change in its perspective be slow and gradual. Realisation had to emerge as a kind of welling up. Sudden jump cuts between separate shots of character entering the scene, close shot of a particular dying figure, wide shot of the whole field and then finally of the flag would, I submit, have given one an inferior experience. The film, as you've probably guessed, is *Gone With The Wind* (Victor Fleming, US, 1939) - one of the greatest of all the monuments of Hollywood romantic realism. (So called because, though the style and approach is shot through with romanticism, it remains real as opposed to, say, abstract or symbolic.)

Camera motion is at its best when in aid the dream-likeness of cinema. In *Last Year in Marienbad* (Alain Resnais, France, 1961) a slow drifting camera follows the key character through the nightmare-like corridors of an ornate hotel that speaks of a very different past. What better a way could there have been of conveying the character's plight of not remembering. (This film could feature as a saintly example in many of our chapters: its use of black and white, of the 'scope ratio', of editing, of production design, and sound. They all work together with the camera movement in brilliant correlation with the necessary psychological and physical dynamics.) Almost every motion in *A Taste of Honey* (Tony Richardson, UK, 1961) conveys the sense of a disturbed dream. In *Lawrence of Arabia* (David Lean, UK, 1962) we see a distant camel in enduring motion across a screen filled with desert. This seems right. The way is long and dry and hot, the landscape vast, the journey lonely (though at times Lawrence has a companion). At most, the camera drifts, as does the subject. The motion here also allows us to take in the breath-taking scenery and its monumental features. Had Lean gone in for shots in. which the camera just washed across the landscape like some mad, alien flying beast, that whole wealth of meaning would have been lost. In motion, then, dreamlike-ness can be freed to express a deep reality. Yet I can think of few contemporary serious films that display any sense of all this.

In Hitchcock's *Young and Innocent* (US, 1937) we have a good example of going the other way in a crane shot. In this scene two characters are searching for a man who has a twitch in his eye. He is somewhere in the hotel we see but the place is crowded and they do not know where to start looking. The shot in question starts with a ceiling high overview and cranes slowly down to the band playing to the dancing, jazz-happy gathering. Eventually it stops at an extreme close up of a coloured "drummer man". He is the one with the twitch and, far from being happy, looks very afraid of something. A cut from the couple to, say the band and then another to the drummer man would never have done the proper job here. The audience has to wander a little, as if psychologically being with the couple in their search. Identification should come not in a near instant but should sink in slowly and mysteriously. Hitchcock achieved this effect marvellously. A further example, and one for enthusiasts of plenty of hand-held vibrance is the 'silent' film *Man With A Movie Camera* (Dziga Vertov, USSR, 1929). A particularly overwhelming sequence comes in the middle of the film. This, however, has distinctive psychological point – as if the business of making the film and reflecting on what a motion picture camera can convey is itself overwhelming. Kenneth Branagh is a more recent filmmaker who uses rapid, almost overpowering, camera movement - as in his *The Magic Flute* (UK, 2006) and *Belfast* (UK, 2021) - but it is always purposeful and well controlled.

In all the above examples the motion can be seen as the realisation of psychologically significant potential. Moreover, they are all *about* something important (to the story, at least) and all have a clear psychological unity. What *cinematic* images these films have.

Bad moves

In the various Ring & Hobbit jobs of Peter Jackson we see cinematic loss. These films are lauded by many but all I can really recall of them are endless camera moves that, while technically clever, often seem far too diverting. In one or two instances, the unrelenting swishing motion of the camera as it passes over the monumental landscape of New Zealand's wild and vast places, ended up making me feel as though I had been rushed along in some theme-park's tasteless simulation of a helicopter ride when the rotors had just failed. Jackson should have seen *Lawrence of Arabia* and taken note of how to direct a film properly, for Jackson's camera was precisely that mad, alien flying beast that Lean properly shunned.

I can think of few more recent tragic examples of bad moves, though, than in the film *Son of Saul* (László Nemes, Hungary, 2015) It is tragic because the film is otherwise worthy. (Who cares if an all-round bad film fails in one major respect particularly.) Set in a Nazi concentration camp, it tells the story of a prisoner who is obliged to burn the corpses of his own people. The film is heavy with claustrophobic power. In parts, it is unendurably chilling and the central part is played with flawless conviction. It is also refreshing to see the power of suggestion used so effectively. (One directly sees very little of the surrounding horrors.) Instead, one shares the characters perceptions. So far so very good, then. Alas, it is also unbearable in another sense – cinematically - consisting mostly of wobbly, hand-held close-ups and endless back following. Back following may or may not reveal significant potential and be about something important, as it often is in this film, but it is terribly inefficient as storytelling because it is too drawn out and damnably uninteresting to watch. There is one dramatic recent exception – a scene from *Bohemian Rhapsody* (Bryan Singer, UK, 2018). A (very steadily controlled) camera – a 'Steadicam', perhaps, back follows Freddie Mercury up some stairs to a large open-air arena. Here we need to follow him, not merely watch him coming out, because we need to share his experience of fame and 'get' the adoration he is afforded as he reaches the top of the stairs.

Because of its almost clinical implications, in its capacity to induce nausea, I call the bad kinds of motion described above as 'Wobbly Camera Syndrome'. If this puts pressure on the leading actor, who is almost always in shot, it puts even more on the poor viewer. At best it conveys consummately Saul's strategy of coping with hell. But used as unrelentingly as it is in that film, it becomes the very negation of cinema, and after two hours of this eye-straining stuff, I almost gave up the will to live. This is a crying shame for in other respects it deserves our attention and admiration.

Not that all use of unsteady handheld camera is a symptom that constitutes the syndrome. Take *The Hurt Locker* (Kathryn Bigelow, US, 2008) about a bomb squad during the US invasion of Iraq. There appears to be plenty of hand-held camera on display here – but it all seems entirely appropriate. The technique can clearly be used to convey an atmosphere of edginess. Where mines can be found all over the shop, I'm sure there's plenty of that. Another good example: in *Gladiator* (Ridley Scott, US, 2000), at the beginning of a battle, the camera begins to shake, quite deliberately and even severely, until the screen is filled with an abstract of dashing, darting patches of colour. This violent abstraction coveys beautifully the chaos of battle.

The problem is that once a reason can be found for a problematic technique, too many film directors jump on the bandwagon. "I want it to look edgy". Who cares what a filmmaker *wants*, it's what is appropriate that counts – and, too often, it just isn't appropriate? Frankly, one is often left with the impression that handheld cameras are used for financial reasons. It's not just that it saves money on not having to hire a tripod but that one can get through more filming per day if one has a cinematographer following an actor's back with a camera on his shoulders than one can if one has to construct different set ups. It must save on editing time, too, but it certainly saves on the need for cinematic imagination.

But why is it problematic in the first place? There are two reasons. One is the sheer nausea that it can induce in the viewer, especially if overused. The second reflects the photographic realism of the cinematic image. (Recall Chapter 1.) This suggest that, without otherwise very good reason, the camera should behave as our conscious perception does for any given shot. What enters our eyes as we move our faces and walk around is a bit of a darting mess but our actual perception is quite selective. We *see* a solid, stable world. Very well, the cinematic image should respect this reality. This point raises itself in many places. The crucial question any director should ask themselves is: does human perception normally behave like this? If it does not – and in the bad examples I cite, we see the infringement – then do not use the technique without overriding psychological necessity. I call this the 'Occam's Razor of Cinema'[83], a principle that can, and should, be applied to any cinematic technique. Of course, sometimes things do seem necessary. At times of extreme nervousness, for example, the world around us can visually seem less stable (as in *Hurt Locker*). Humanly impossible moves (and I count as possible the use of real or imagined transport as possible) should be used with suspicion, too. It is obviously possible to be transported in a way that produces the moves I cite above from in *Gone With The Wind* and *Young and Innocent*, since the camera crew went up and down with the crane. In this respect, Jackson's wild swingings above the New Zealand landscape are a lot less plausible.

This raises the issue of other means of producing motion: aircraft, helicopters, drones, and the like. Clearly, where such shots replicate possible human perception there is no problem. Here are two good examples. First of all, we have *Human Flow* (Ai Weiwei, Germany, 2017), a documentary about mass migration across the globe. This uses drones to emphasise the scale and, quite literal, flow of people. Though I think the film overlong (half-way through one feels one's got the point) this kind of camera movement at least seems appropriate. Even given that there are times (perhaps) of infringements of what would be possible in daily human perception, this is clearly justified psychologically - perhaps even philosophically, given that we need a raising of awareness of the sheer scale of the problem. Weiwei's imagery certainly has huge scale.

Remember also that it is not my thesis that rules should *never* be broken, only that we should treat them *as* rules (or, in keeping with modern weasel words, 'guidelines for good practice') to begin with. A second example is the noir-ish, Spanish detective story *Marshland* (Alberto Rodríguez, Spain, 2014). This begins with drone shots showing a slow, twisted, almost unreal landscape from directly above as if it were an abstract puzzle. This is great given the general nature of the story and the puzzle to be solved. It conveys also a sense of eerie desolation. Too often, though, drones are used seemingly because they are a new 'boys' toy' and one simply wants to whisper in the director's ear, "Do grow up", as if addressing a merely tiresome child.

Sometimes, however, camera movement just seems to get out of aesthetic control altogether. Take *Beasts of the Southern Wild* (Benh Zeitlin, US, 2012) This is a rare, possibly unique gem of magical realism utterly and gratuitously ruined by such excessive wobbly hand-held camera moves that it renders the whole thing is at times unwatchable. On a far more accomplished note, we may end this section by citing *Casablanca* (Michael Curtiz, US, 1942). Watch it, take note of the ways in which the camera movement (limited anyway) blends in with character movement and editing to push the story dynamics along, then sit back and admire *real* filmmaking. Indeed, any really accomplished film from Hollywood's great days would do.

The sins of slow motion

'Cheap', 'cheesy' and even 'cringe-inducing' seem to be appropriate words for describing what slow motion is most of the time. It has its place both aesthetically and in special effects (explosions may be slowed down a bit because they happen very quickly) but when it is used merely as a bit of poetic-looking light relief in a film that is otherwise as lyrical as a ride on a 1940's double-decker bus, it leaves one wanting to scream. It was used effectively, and almost invisibly, by Arthur Penn at the end of *Bonnie and Clyde* (US, 1967). One really needed to see that pair come to a horrible end and it would have seemed less horrible and too mercifully fast had there been no slow motion. Similarly, the repeated slow motion sequence in *Zabriskie Point* (Michelangelo Antonioni, US, 1969) gives extra dimension to the feeling of the film.

McGinn says of slow motion that, 'it frees the screen figure from the constraints of normal motion, rendering it weightless and exempt from physical law . . . the human body takes on some of the privileges of the immaterial realm . . . no longer shackled to its own bulk and density".[84] He adds that we yearn sometimes for such freedom, the "annulment of the flesh". This is a powerful observation and it captures much of the strange dream-likeness of the cinematic image generally. But . . . but, we do need a focused psychological point. In any case, we must remember that while dreams can be powerful they do not standardly happen in slow motion, despite the curious conception that slow motion is dream-like. Good uses of slow motion, though, are rare. Thus, if a filmmaker lacks sufficient visual imagination to create a certain kind of atmosphere for their product or focus our attention on some emotional detail in *real* time, I am inclined to think they should seek employment in some other line of work. Antonioni was a rare exception.

Chapter 4: The Sins of Colour

Strictly, like the sins of motion, the sins of colour fall under the heading of the sins of appearance. However, colour is also such an important particular here that I think it deserves a chapter all to itself.

The sin of using colour at all

The British film director Bryan Forbes once said that black and white are the true colours of cinema. In similar vein, McGinn cites Peter Ustinov as saying that he filmed *Billy Budd* (UK, 1962) in black and white "because it is more realistic". This paradox, I firmly uphold. Too often we make the mistake of thinking that colour *adds* to a film when, in fact it subtracts. (I thank my brother Andrew for this observation.) But what exactly is subtracted? And why does it matter?

In a fairly obvious, perfectly dull and tediously literal sense, colour enables us to see what was before the camera in the full visible spectrum. Given that we standardly see things in colour and that the cinematic image is photographically realistic, we may think that colour *should* be the obvious default. After all, don't things look *more* real in colour, given that they are coloured in real life? If not, why not?

We need to keep in mind, though, *all* the features of the cinematic image, including the features of form, not just any one of them, such as photographic realism. All of cinema's features should work together. But then one must ask whether they are *all* of equal importance *all* the time, and I would say that they are not. Yes, they are all important but one of them may have, in any given film, a kind of leadership role. It may be the focus of the image, its psychological *intentionality* (or what-its-aboutness), its intensity – any one of all the features we have discussed. This is what determines the purpose of the image. If having a full colour spectrum doesn't contribute to this end and especially if black and white does it better, then colour is clearly redundant.

Remember, though, in sticking to black and white, one is not abandoning the essential photographic realism of the cinematic image, nor even reducing it in any psychologically significant (as opposed to merely pedestrian and literal) way. One is simply manipulating it in some special and pertinent way. But is it legitimate to play about with reality? It had better be: it's what drama does, and it does so inevitably. Firstly, it has to *select* from the real. Drama is not and cannot ever be *fully* real, it just has to be real in the sense (for cinema) that it both satisfies photographic realism and respects the reality of the subject in the required way. Black and white, because of its sparse, stripped down nature, can give us, by default at any rate, better psychological focus on what really matters. If the colour of the things shown is not of first importance, then why should it be captured photographically? Too often, colour simply dilutes what really matters, makes things too superficial. This is the sense in which colour standardly subtracts.

There is something else also that makes the ubiquitous use of colour a sin against the cinematic image. The psychological weight of the cinematic image lies in its conferring sufficient aesthetic and psychological distance between viewer and what is seen. By default, colour reduces that distance precisely because it is more naturalistic – it's just is the way we standardly perceive. If we value distance, it should be used sparingly, only when it actually does add something important to the experience of watching a film. In contrast, black and white, through its ethereal translucency, helps us maintain our distance in a fairly obvious way – it is just not the way we see. Though dreams are not in black and white, the extra distance of the medium also aids what we have seen to be the powerful dream-likeness of cinema.

So, we can conclude that black and white's way of being *un*real is of great importance all round. Looking up at a screen with gorgeous black and white cinematography gleaming down on one instantly sets us up in a strange place with respect to what we see. We relate to it in a more special way. Things are there before us realistically but in a way unfamiliar enough to enable us to be moved by *how* people, places and things appear to us. It says clearly, this is the *character's* world, and it is being revealed to you on the screen. It offers, as Ustinov was hinting, a much starker realism. Colour, by contrast, psychologically places what we see in *our* standard perceptual world. It subtracts psychological distance – by default, at least. Colour, especially today's colour, can so easily offer no more than bland naturalism, though black and white can, when used thoughtlessly can also lean towards blandness.

At its best, though, to watch a black and white film is almost to see something ghostly or mysterious. One is aware of the specialness of the seeing. It has a soul different to that of colour. Colour and black and white convey mood and atmosphere and track the reality of what we see in very different ways. Precisely because black and white is less naturalistic, it conveys the essence of the characters and situations in a special, sharper way. In this sense we can say that black and white is perfectly *realistic*, it is just less *naturalistic*. That's what gives it its special aesthetic powers. One's eyes penetrate a black and white image where they frequently just gaze at colour, or worse, just superficially look at the image. Black and white, in being less naturalistic, may give an image more depth than full colour HD 3D.

I am not suggesting that all black and white films are, by default, superior to any colour film. That would be a clearly ridiculous conclusion. Nor am I saying that all black and white films imaginatively exploit the powers of their monochrome station. This is not surprising, for cinema was born black and white. Colour photography started much earlier than is commonly supposed but it was not there quite at kick-off. The technology and chemistry was just too difficult at first. We should be thankful for this, for inferior minds may well have chosen colour by default, and black and white photography may never have got started. It took time, though, for its aesthetic development. What I *am* saying is that black and white has special aesthetic and psychological power, and this is particularly pertinent to the nature and dramatic narrative and psychological potential of cinema.

Nowhere in cinema is the strange relationship and different powers of black and white and colour made clearer than in *A Matter of Life and Death* (Michael Powell & Emeric Pressburger, UK, 1946). Action takes place both on earth and in heaven (or at least heaven's antechambers) as the life of a wartime RAF flyer hangs in the balance. Colour (old Technicolor 3-strip) and black and white were used to distinguish these places. The more obvious option would have been to use colour for heaven and black and white for earth. Heaven is supposed to be the brighter and more hopeful of the two places, after all. Surprisingly, the filmmakers reversed this. It worked. Earth is the more familiar place, so it was filmed 'in colour', just how we see it. Heaven is not known to us as yet, so it cries out to seem less familiar – at least in the sense of being less naturalistic. Brilliant!

When should colour be used?

I said above that if we value aesthetic and psychological distance, colour should be used sparingly, only when it actually does add something important to the experience of watching a film. We come now to consider when this may happen.

I must be frank. If someone answered "Never", I could just about live with that. There isn't that much that colour can do that black and white cannot. Think of all the (metaphorically) colourful, swashbuckling adventure yarns in the 1930s. They don't seem much reduced by their (literal) black and whiteness. Great landscapes, desert, exotic places, glamour and fantasy hardly ever seemed restricted. We can go back earlier still. Perhaps Abel Gance would have photographed his *Napoleon* (France, 1927) in colour had it been possible (it was in fact tinted in places) but its monochrome cannot be said to hold it back as a great epic. Indeed, it is one of the most powerful of historical adventures ever filmed. It works the other way, too, of course. David Lean's *Lawrence of Arabia* (UK, 1962) was indeed better in colour but it would have only been 5% restricted had it been filmed in suitable black and white.

Nonetheless, colour has been used too many times, to brilliant effect, to deny it a proper – indeed, truly noble – place in cinema. Let us look at some examples. We have already mentioned *A Matter of Life and Death*. In *Gone With The Wind* (Victor Fleming, US, 1939) and *The Red Shoes* (Powell and Pressburger, UK, 1948) a rich colour array, conveys both glee and romanticism. In the former film this is shown as decadent and on the way out.

Of *Red Desert* (Michelangelo Antonio, Italy, 1964) Jon Beasley writes:

> "Antonioni once said of a Mark Rothko painting, "It's painted anxiety." . . . This Technicolor masterwork was Antonioni's first colour feature, and presents us with one of the most emotionally illustrative and evocative uses of pallet in cinema history. Every inch of the frame was considered. Even entire streets and groves of trees were painted black to emphasize the sooty surroundings of a factory, or fruits (and the vendor selling them) were painted grey to heighten the impact of a purple jacket against auburn hair.[85]

This blackness of the industrial landscape is hugely expressive of the fact that the film's character Giuliana (Monica Vitti) is killing herself from within.

In his *Vertigo* (US, 1958) Alfred Hitchcock uses colour possibly with more subtlety than one will find anywhere else in cinema. Novelist and screenwriter H. Perry Horton observes an instance of this richness:

> "Jimmy Stewart's character, Scottie Ferguson, is represented by red - his clothing, the furniture that surrounds him, the door to his apartment - while Madeline, the object of his obsession, is represented by the hue directly opposite red on the colour wheel, green - her dress the first time we see her, her car, the sea she plunges into causing Scottie to rescue her and initiate their relationship. As these two characters come together and grow closer, so too do their colours co-mingle. After Madeline's suicide attempt, Scottie takes her to his apartment, where amidst all his cherrywood furniture he dons a green sweater, taking her colour as she has taken his heart. When she awakens, he hands her a red robe to put on, thus taking possession of her, metaphorically, by dressing her in his colour. And this is really just the tip of the iceberg."[86]

In these films colour is used specifically to enhance the symbolic dream-likeness of their imagery. One of the main roles of colour is described by David Bordwell in his *Poetics of Cinema.* He is also making reference to *Red Desert* (Michelangelo Antonioni, Italy, 1964)

> "...we can read any scene's color scheme in two registers simultaneously: as psychological verisimilitude (Giuliana sees her life as a desert) or as authorial commentary (Antonioni-as-narrator says that this industrial landscape is a desert)".[87]

I think the same applies to *Vertigo.*

Colours are well known to be associated with different moods and many films exploit this well. This is all well and good so far as it goes but notice from the above descriptions that something special is going on with respect to the above films. In neither of them is it merely some generalised psychological response to colour that is being called forth. Nor is colour used simply because it depicts landscape, glamour, or exotic circumstance (even though some films do this beautifully as well). In these cases, more precise and subtle effects are intensified. This is using colour cinematically.

Some filmmakers today, especially in the more popular market may have a good general sense of colour psychology but in too many more serious films, the colour looks bland and conveys nothing. Colour is so ubiquitous nowadays that, beyond some sensitivity to the right colour pallet for the psychological reaction and mood intended (with more rather than less meaningfulness) little attention seems to be paid to the opportunities it offers. My motto: if you don't use it, you lose it.

The sins of blandness

These are the twin sins of much modern cinema. Colour is used by default, regardless of need and it is either bland or too full of un-nourishing visual calories. More serious and intelligent lower budget films often seem to suffer from the former, perhaps because they do not have the money to spend too much time on suitable cinematography. The resulting imagery is flat and contributes near zero to the psychology of the film. So long as the cinematographer gets a useful image on the film, all is regarded as acceptable – or at any rate, so it seems to the viewer. High budget, popcorn-level action films are full of colour but the nearest they seem to get to intelligent visual expression is a bit of carefully lit darkness every now and again. It's all very psychologically superficial – and this is aided and abetted by bangs and blasts in the surround sound effects.

A Brief History of Colour

Colour origination these days (whether on film or digital) tends to lend itself to unthinking naturalism. This has not always been the case, though. Colour has been around in cinema in various forms since quite early times, starting with tinting and hand-painting individual frames of film. Though colour cinematography soon followed, it never gained real popularity until a company called 'Technicolor' developed its various systems, culminating in their famed 'three-strip' process.

Colour film works by separately recording the three primary colours of a scene – red, green and blue. When projected with white light, these colours then make up the full colour spectrum. Each colour is recorded on its own dedicated layer on the colour negative film. Appropriate dyes are incorporated into each layer and actual colour emerges when the film is chemically processed. (It's more complicated than that but this simple version it will serve our purpose.)

Technicolor's three strip process differed from more modern colour film in that the three layers were on three separate reels of film. The cameras were massive, built almost like tanks. Where a 'blimp' was required (these were heavy-duty surrounds for motion-picture cameras that dampened the sound of the mechanism so that it would not be recorded on the soundtrack) the resultant piece of kit was so large that some cinematographers called it 'the enchanted cottage'. The cameras ran three separate reels of black and white films. Light from the lens was filtered in such a way that each strip recorded only its own primary colour. There was no dye carried in the film itself. The resulting images were black and white. Each strip recorded (in black and white) only its own primary colour. These strips were then dyed with the appropriate colour afterwards. On printing copies for cinema release, each layer with its own dye was transferred onto a single strip of film. (Again, it's more complicated than this but the complications are unimportant here.) Voila! The result was a full-spectrum colour film.[88] This three strip process, which led to the expression 'glorious Technicolor', lasted until the early 1950's, when the Eastman Kodak company's 'Eastmancolor' – a more modern combined-strip process (called a 'monopack') replaced it. (Here, the three layers constitute a single strip of film.) The latter was simpler, could be used in ordinary cameras and suited better the newer wide screen processes that were emerging in that decade. Technicolor survived as a company – it is still there but 'Technicolor' on the film credits came to mean only that the company processed the newer kinds of negative films. [89]

Aesthetically, though, I do not believe that Eastmancolor and its clones did cinema any favours. Look at any film photographed in the old Technicolor, and one notices how painterly they were. Technically this is because the dyes were applied *after* the photography. This gave the process a certain magic and the process almost forced filmmakers to be expressive. It gave the filmmakers a great deal to think about in this respect. In contrast, more modern colour film stock (and nowadays digitally originated colour) forces plain accuracy of colour and (if one is not very careful) blandness – the very opposite of how a cinematic image should look.

The sin of *dis*colouration

As with teeth, so with cinema: discolouration is unattractive. I cannot leave this chapter without discussing the once very threatening sin of the 'colourisation' of black and white films. This sin brings us full circle to a point I made earlier: adding colour where there was none in a film is not to add anything worthwhile but to subtract something worthwhile. Watch Frank Capra's *It's A Wonderful Life* (US, 1946) in both its original (though carefully restored) and colourised versions. If you prefer the latter, I can communicate with you no further.

Chapter 5: The Sins of Sound, Music & Emotion

Recall my acid test for good cinema. What one hears in a film is just as important as what one sees. Indeed, what one hears (even if one is not paying it much direct attention) affects what one sees to such a high degree that the soundtrack should be considered pretty well a part of what we will call the 'cinematic image'. The meaning of that image changes not with just what one sees but also with what one hears, even if the sound has gone silent. Indeed, in some deep sense, what one sees changes in tandem with what one hears. If two cinematic images are visually identical but are accompanied by different sounds, or if one has no sound at all, then what one *sees* are two fundamentally different images. To take perhaps a rather unsubtle example, instead of seeing a happy face, for instance, one sees a sad one. Music makes a difference to how we see something, too.

The sins of music – or its absence

Nonetheless, it may seem odd that we should have music in film at all, unless it is part of the action in the story. That brings us to the big distinction in all sound in film – between the 'diegetic' and 'non-diegetic'. Diegetic sound (including music) is sound that is a part of the action. It includes the voices of the characters, sounds made by things within the world of the story, noise emitting objects in the story and music coming from sources within the story world, even if they are sometimes 'off screen'. Non-Diegetic sound is any that is *not* part of the world of the story. It can include theme music, narration, and music used to evoke an emotional response. Not that matters do not get complicated. Many sounds are difficult to record while shooting, others (traffic noises, odd snatches of irrelevant conversation, aeroplanes overhead, and so on) may be impossible to exclude. The problems are worse, of course, when location shooting. The sound can be messy and indistinct, so sometimes outdoor shots are made silently and sound, including some dialogue, is added later in a studio. The 'Foley artists' (named after the man who developed the technique) are adept at reproducing sounds like footsteps, swishing clothes, banging doors, breaking glass, and using sounds actually made by things that are not the things we see on the screen yet whose sounds they are supposed to be.

Sometimes the distinction between the diegetic and non-diegetic is played with, as music that is non-diegetic becomes diegetic in the course of the story. In *South Pacific* (Joshua Logan, US, 1958) the nurse sings the song, *I'm gonna wash that man right out of my hair* in non-diegetic fashion but it becomes clear that we are supposed to take it as diegetic at the point when we see her lover overhearing her. David Lean uses the lush Rachmaninov *Piano Concerto No 2* in his romantic drama *Brief*

Encounter (UK, 1945) as non-diegetic theme music but it becomes diegetic when the Celia Johnson character plays it on her gramophone.

In musicals, the songs are often non-diegetic, and we must keep in mind that it isn't really the *characters* who sing in their story life. Rather, it's the performer who sings and does so to express the emotions of the character. I make this point to address a criticism I once heard from someone who couldn't stand musicals on the ground that real people don't (usually) sing their way through their daily lives. This is true but simply misses the point. (Curiously, this person loved opera.) The point at play here can be generalised. Performers may not only *sing* in order to express the emotion of their character but *dance* or even *act* in a particular way for the same reason, even though it is not always what the character is doing in the story world. Sometimes an actor may be able to portray all the (relevant) emotions of the character in the context of the story being told, but – precisely because the cinematic image is at a distance from reality – this is not always possible – matters need extra help, from music or whatever it may be.

Often it has been the case that the singer one hears is a different performer to the one sees on the screen, also. An opera singer called Marni Nixon sang (uncredited) for many female stars whose own singing was not up to scratch: for Audrey Hepburn in *My Fair Lady* (George Cukor, US, 1964), for Deborah Kerr in *The King and I* (Walter Lang, US 1956) and for Natalie Wood in *West Side Story* (Robert Wise, US, 1961).

Whether diegetic or not, though, and however it may be originated, music needs to be appropriate. I'd say it often is but too often it is not – this is where the sins come into play and inappropriateness can occur in a number of ways: it can be present when it should not be or be badly timed or it can also be absent when it should be present.

The first question a filmmaker must ask about music is not what music to use but whether music is necessary at all. It is, perhaps, not obvious why non-diegetic music should be necessary. After all, we do not live our lives (and nor do the characters in a film live theirs) with music emanating from the clouds. (The equivalent of diegetic music abounds, of course - perhaps too much - in places like supermarkets) But this just misses the point. What we see in a standard fiction feature film is *never* life, however realistic its depiction, but a *representation* of life. We are *shown* life in a special kind of way. But because of the distance involved in seeing through a cinematic image, we cannot share the feelings of a character in a particular situation quite as directly as we might do in 'real life'. That leaves a gap that often needs filling, and because music is a medium of emotion, it is clearly made for the job.

The world of cinema has known this since pretty well its inception. So, how does music fill the gap? Wordsworth understood poetry as emotion recollected in tranquillity. Perhaps this covers only *some* poetry, but it invites an analogy. A film is life seen from the distance of the viewer – what I've called 'the gap'. Music can, in some sense, fill that gap and help make cinema a kind of poetry. This is because both poetry and music involve the arts of rhythmical and melodic composition. It can do this in a number of things: in establishing a mood or just in providing a sense of something important concerning what a film is about. It can help paint a picture of what the characters are feeling, and assist our empathic reaction. In short, it conveys and has emotional significance. It can help narrative progress as characters move around in stretches without dialogue. In fact, philosopher of music Jerrold Levison understands the role of film music as having a narrational role. It can itself be a storyteller.[90]

The place of music in film, though, is as yet far from exhausted. It can create an atmosphere, help us to expect something, but musical motifs can help us also remember aspects of character and situation. It can unify a cinematic image stretching over several shots. It can act in unison with the image or in counterpoint. It augments and completes our perception of what a film is about. Philosopher of aesthetics and film Noel Carroll has called film music "modifying music".[91] He suggests that (at any rate in the classical Hollywood tradition) it functions in a way analogous to adverbs in language. I think this captures something of what I am saying. It can do all this boldly and consciously or it can work less obtrusively in the background, but its emotional power cannot be denied.[92] Cinema is akin more to poetry than to prose – it is caused by the unique kind of aesthetic and psychological distance created by the cinematic image. However, whereas spoken poetry is, so to speak, its own music, a collection of film shots is not. An utterly music-less film can be too silent, like a mute dream. We long to react but we are left unaided, with an idea short of a full interpretation. Music can be the thing that sutures the subconscious mind of the viewer to the film.[93] Moreover, though dreams do not come (standardly) equipped with non-diegetic music, its presence in a film helps to intensify the dream-like capacities and powers of the imagery. Thus, music can increase the narrative and psychological yield of a film.

Think of a couple of Hitchcock films. How would *Vertigo* (US, 1958) or *Psycho* (US, 1960) stand without their Bernard Herrmann scores? The shrill, shrieking music of the shower scene in *Psycho* unifies the multiple shots into one extra-frightening cinematic image. The longing, winding, drifting, entwining music in *Vertigo* emphasises Scottie's growing obsession with the woman he is following – and again welds the separate shots into one gloriously flowing, dream-like cinematic image. Indeed, this scene is a masterclass in how music may seamlessly integrate the elements that contribute to the emotional ebb and flow of a film. How far could we really share the feelings of flight and fright, of mystery and longing and emptiness of Laura Jesson (Celia Johnson) in David Lean's *Brief Encounter* (UK, 1945) without Rachmaninov's Second Piano Concerto? As she runs through the dark, wet streets, the music enables us to be much closer to the character.

Think also of genre in particular – traditional westerns, epics, 'rom-coms', thrillers and noirs. The kinds of musical score each employs helps make a film *belong* to a genre. It does so by suggestion as much as anything. Think of the many moods and moments of the grand symphonic score by Miklos Rosza in *Ben-Hur* (William Wyler, US, 1959). Music like that did not exist in ancient times (though Rosza researched music and instruments that did and incorporated ideas he had picked up) but, aside from other things, it suggests the grand power of ancient Rome. Music can make films *big*. Mostly the music that does all these jobs is, of course, non-diegetic. That said, diegetic music can suffice. Diegetic music in various contexts can set mood, for example, just as well as can non-diegetic music. (Sometimes music switches from one to the other – as in *Brief Encounter*.) It matters not, also whether the music has been written for the film or already exists – it is how well it does its job that matters.

At its deepest level of functioning, music, just like cinema, deals with the contours of time. Philosopher and theologian, Andrew Davison says that a serious side of music,

> "comes in its relation to time, development and change. It is in this way that music concerns itself with those temporal matters that are so interwoven with value in human life: with sameness, repetition and difference; change and stability; interweaving and support; tension and resolution. These make up the texture of music, just as they make up the texture of a human life."[94]

He goes on,

> "It is through these mainly structural elements that music presses upon matters closest to the human heart: upon fullness and emptiness, sadness and joy, determinacy and indeterminacy. It deals with them in ways familiar to us: in terms of change and evolution, of departure and return, of sameness and difference, of expectation, fulfilment and the unexpected".[95]

Davison is writing about the connection between music and theology but one can see an instant summary of its connection with the fiction feature film.

Given all I have said, one may suppose that the absence, or even just plain shortage, of music in film would be one of cinema's most cardinal sins. It has to be absent sometimes in a film, of course, if it is to be effective, and the filmmaker has to know when it should stop and start. That said, much of the time I think it is far too absent in today's more serious cinema. Why? One reason may be cost. Many lower budget (or more modestly budgeted) films simply cannot afford too much music. (Think of how many times when music has been for a single instrument, frequently the piano.) This is no excuse because if one can only afford to make inferior product then one should simply not bother. But reasons for musical silence can run deeper.

Sometimes the absence of music is experimental, as in *Festen* (*The Celebration*, Denmark, 1998) where director Thomas Vinterberg follows the rules (in cult-like fashion, called 'vows of chastity') of 'Dogma 95', a movement devised by Vinterberg and fellow director Lars von Trier. For your enlightenment here they are:

1. Shooting must be done on location. Props and sets must not be brought in (if a particular prop is necessary for the story, a location must be chosen where this prop is to be found).
2. The sound must never be produced apart from the images or vice versa. (Music must not be used unless it occurs where the scene is being shot.)
3. The camera must be hand-held. Any movement or immobility attainable in the hand is permitted.
4. The film must be in colour. Special lighting is not acceptable. (If there is too little light for exposure the scene must be cut or a single lamp be attached to the camera.)
5. Optical work and filters are forbidden.
6. The film must not contain superficial action. (Murders, weapons, etc. must not occur.)
7. Temporal and geographical alienation are forbidden. (That is to say that the film takes place here and now.)
8. Genre movies are not acceptable.
9. The film format must be Academy 35 mm.
10. The director must not be credited.[96]

The reader will not by this stage be surprised to learn that I would replace the word 'chastity' here with 'infertility' or 'impotence'. Home movie makers, at any rate those who know nothing of cinema, comply with much of this by default, but this fact serves only further to blind me as to why doing so should be regarded as a virtue. So far as I can see, this post-modern chaos is fit only for jaded not-too-sophisticates, not some interesting venture. His lack of non-diegetic music, hence, I regard as unprincipled nonsense, and his general approach as something which has all the depth of a roadside puddle. The rules are but rules on how to look trendy. Thus, I move on to deeper reasons.

In fact, one has very much the impression that at some of the deeper reasons I have given for supporting the presence of music in film are understood by some filmmakers as reasons for its absence. (Note, I here refer to the absence of non-diegetic music. Diegetic music is fine, given its appropriateness in context, though even this too is often absent.)

Precisely because music has a heavily emotional role in a film there lurks always a risk of sentimentality – and in some eyes, even putting oneself in a place of such risk is sinful. Writing in *Time*, Richard Schickel says, 'Sentimentality is a kind of fascism, robbing us of judgment and moral acuity, and it needs to be resisted." The music in the classic film *Gone With The Wind* (Victor Fleming, US, 1939) may be thought (superficially) to reduce the film in this way (and, incidentally, to support considerable rebuke, and pressure it received in the summer of 2020 for its apparent racism. It had been removed from at least one streaming service, though has now been thankfully replaced).

I think the charge against it is baseless, though. When I watch *Gone With The Wind*, I see a piece of grand Hollywood romanticism of a long-gone cinematic age. Do I see racism at play? Yes, it's quite clearly there. I don't think though that the film can or should be seen in the same horrific light as, say, Leni Riefenstahl's pre-war film, *The Triumph of the Will* (Germany, 1935). *That* film is repulsive not because it is simply *about* Nazism, or contains examples of Nazism going about its terrible business. Rather, it *celebrates* Nazism. In some way it does indeed sentimentalise Nazism. Indeed, it renders Nazism as an admirable sensibility. Does *Gone With The Wind* do the same for racism? I don't think so. It shows up, of course, but depiction of racism is not racist all by itself. Certain intentions and attitudes behind it might have had racist elements, of course, and many of the kinds of events and characters it depicts are racist. The music in *Gone With the Wind* is hardly irrelevant to the kind of film it is but, again, it does not celebrate racism. Rather, I would say, the music simply emphasises what is historically happening in the various phases of its story.

What, though, of the more general charge of the association of too much music giving rise to sentimentalism? Firstly, I want to say that in my books there is nothing wrong with sentimentality in any case – at any rate so long as it is in its proper place. *The Wizard of Oz* (Victor Fleming, US, 1939) has it in spades and it remains a favourite. In any case, sentimentality has a proper role. In the first place, nothing can be sinfully sentimental if it could (in the context of the narrative and situation) plausibly happen. There really are happy endings in life, or at least phases of life. There are decent people who tend to do the right thing. Self-sacrifice and redemption do exist, as do empathy and goodwill. To scoff at such things would be a far worse sin than any indulgence in sentimentality.

Secondly, we should judge all art which depicts these things very carefully and tease out our own motives for judging it sentimental if we are inclined so to do. Sometimes we will find that what superficially seems like sentimentality is not really so. I would not, for example, see *It's A Wonderful Life* (Frank Capra, US, 1946) as being sentimental in the least. It's simply decent. When we can no longer tell the difference, we are lost. What brings hope into a darkened world is never merely sentimental. We should perhaps, keep in mind what being sentimental actually *is* – to be exaggerated or over-indulgent with emotion that itself is superficial. But we have to be able to argue that this is what is *actually* going on, not just assume it because emotional music is at play. Moreover, as with many other sins (camera movement for example) we can only gauge the degree of sin in the first place by seeing it in context. Taking this point seriously, perhaps we could say that even *The Wizard of Oz* is not sentimental at all because the context is right for its style. All that said, an overly schmaltzy treatment of happenings in certain grim tales would be quite wrong. Music can certainly risk this – but it would be music of the wrong kind or music badly used that would be offensive, not its mere presence.

Of course, there is always a risk of being overly emotionally manipulated by the presence of music but again, we have to be careful. For an artist to say, "This is what *I* feel" and I want you to feel it, too, does not seem intrinsically wrong. It can be an invitation rather than a manipulation. In the war film *The Victors* (Carl Foreman, UK/US, 1963) it is Christmas and we see a soldier (if memory serves, found guilty of desertion) being executed by firing squad. It is accompanied by the song 'Have yourself a merry little Christmas'. Here the music served the purpose of irony and, perhaps, the longing everyone had for returning home, something that the victim would never experience. This cinematic image is vastly more powerful than it would have been had it been bereft of music. The audience just had to feel what its makers wanted it to feel. It was, after all, what the audience *ought* to feel. Music can help emphasise the grimness and even horror of certain scenes precisely by this method of contrast. I therefore entirely reject the view that music somehow automatically puts in harm's way of sentimental manipulation.

Some directors, though, eschew music for (on the face of it, at least) better thought out reasons. Here are excerpts from four eminent present-day directors justifying the absence of non-diegetic music in their films. (Though there's not much by way of diegetic music either.)

Nuri Bilge Ceylan, the great contemporary Turkish director of *Uzak* (Turkey, 2002) and *Once Upon A Time in Anatolia* (Turkey, 2011), says,

> "I don't like music in cinema, it seems to me like a crutch; if you cannot express something in cinematic ways, then you call the help of the music to

underline it. I'm not against it, but if possible I try not to use it. In the editing, I try many pieces of music, but eventually I decide not to use any. And also, the sound of the atmosphere is the nicest sound for me in the cinema, so I prefer to use atmospheric sound instead of music. Because music kills things."

(From an interview at the BFI Southbank in London, reproduced by *The Guardian*, 6 February, 2009)

Ceylan does, it must be noted, used the second movement of Schubert's Piano sonata No. 20 in A Major to some beautiful effect in his film *Winter Sleep* (2014). Apparently, this is a tilt to a much earlier French director Robert Bresson, whom Ceylan admires, who used it in his film *Au Hasard Balthazar* (France, 1966).

Can music in films "kill" things? It's like any other technique, I would say – its *inappropriate* use can kill things. All this amounts to, though, is the observation that techniques are intrinsically dangerous things. One has to know how to handle them - in art as in nuclear power. (I might rather teasingly suggest to Ceylan that he comes close to killing things, too, in coming close to an inordinate length in many of his films.) Is music, though, necessarily a crutch? Yes, I would suggest, if it is enabling something mediocre and shallow to pretend it has more depth than it really has, but this hardly seems the right way of talking about *all* its cinematic roles, most especially the ones I have mentioned above. In any case, Ceylan *contrasts* the use of music with being cinematic and this is a profound error. As we have understood matters, the soundtrack - including any music – is a part of what it *means* to be cinematic. It is an aspect of the cinematic image. He correctly stresses the importance of "the sound of the atmosphere" but this, of course, is perfectly consistent with the presence of music, just so long as it is not ubiquitous. Ceylan gets away with the absence of music because of the depth in his imagery in other ways and his penetrating Chekov-like scripts, but I would suggest that at best, it is making matters more difficult for oneself in terms of conveying feeling, and at worst, dicing with death – especially if, like Ceylan, one makes films many hours long.

Luc Dardennes, one of the famous two filmmaking brothers from Belgium has said,

"We have a difficult relationship with music. We don't use music in our films. We love music in its own right, but not so much as part of a film. The rhythm of our storytelling is through the filming and through our care with relation to how characters are being watched and followed. We feel there isn't much room for music in that rhythm. We feel music is extraneous, and we feel it breaks the natural rhythms of the characters and their actions and emotions."

(*Daily Review* online, November 12, 2014 - https://dailyreview.com.au/the-dardenne-bros-on-two-days-one-night-and-why-they-dont-like-music-in-their-movies/)

I have some other serious issues concerning what I call the sins of raw naturalism of Dardenne's film *Two Days, One Night* (Belgium, 2014) but it is telling to see here the connection with music. To maintain that music has no place where rhythm is concerned seems plain perverse. One wants to gulp, "Eh?". In any case, just following the characters around is itself a sin. It becomes dulled and does so precisely because, as we have seen, the cinematic mage is not life itself but a *depiction* of life, seen from all kinds of distance. This means that one should use the various resources available to depiction. Luc Dardenne seems to be denying all this. Music could aid the efficiency of their story telling at the kinds of points he mentions. Did the presence of some music in all the grim tales told in cinema's past have no place?

Cristian Mungiu, a celebrated Romanian director with a few music-less Romanian films under his belt: *4 Months, 3 Weeks and 2 Days* (2007) *Beyond the Hills* (2012), *Graduation* (2016) has said,

> "We don't use music. But I want to have a very rich soundscape. I really believe that this is a very important layer, which gives spectators the feeling that this is reality, if the sound carries all the elements that are in everyday life. You won't notice them, but I need to have them there. Some people work with very clean sound. I don't work like this. I try to have the dialogue recorded as clean as I can, but then I add a million extra layers. I think it's important to have all the elements which the frame allows you to have because they contribute a lot to the atmosphere. The sound is also important for the rhythm of the shot. We do the same take with the actors, just without the camera, to get the sound very clean. . .. for example, we have a million layers of sound. The sound has the same role that music does in other films. The soundscape keeps up the rhythms. But it's natural sounds. It's the TV sound - maybe, it's a bit louder than you'd listen to it. It's this guy on the second floor who is repairing something in his apartment. He's drilling. Then, there's this telephone that rings that nobody has the time to answer. This helps a lot with the tension in the film."
>
> (Interview on-line, https://seventh-row.com/2017/06/01/cristian-mungiu-sound-graduation/)

Here, then, we have yet another odd case of embracing rhythm and eschewing music – "Curiouser and curiouser", as Alice commented when she fell down the rabbit hole. However, Mungiu wants to have a very rich soundscape. Good! But one may legitimately ask why and how music is supposed to subtract from that richness. Notice that he says, "The sound has the same role that music does in other films". As we have seen, though, this is simply problematic. In any case, we have also seen that music can enhance rather than subtract from realism. At least it *can* providing we do not equate realism will dull naturalistic carbon-copying authenticity. At bottom, I suspect these directors make that mistake. Mungui seems to think that his naturalistic soundscape *keeps up* the rhythms but I would question this. Their very clunking naturalism is precisely what lacks rhythm.

Again, the director makes the mistake of linking too closely film with life itself. It ignores the distance. These directors are right in wanting to maintain rhythm but wrong in ignoring the blunt yet fairly obvious fact that our natural daily movements and presences in life are somewhat apt to *lack* rhythm. Life itself is too full and messy for that. I would say to them all that to desire rhythm, which they *ought*, is already to desire a degree of artificiality, to want the inevitable gap between life and film filled. This being the case, why exclude music, a medium made in heaven to help out at this very point? Of them all, I think that Ceylan is the only one who appreciates the distance and is somehow able usefully to fill it with picture, dialogue and diegetic sound alone. However, music can help transform film into a kind of poetry and poetry acknowledges, respects and crosses the gap. Thus, it is always *more* penetratingly and powerfully realistic.

Our fourth contender for the throne of trendy perversity is Asghar Farhadi. In talking about his music-less film *A Separation* (Iran, 2011) he acknowledges that music can fill a gap and explains how he fills it *instead.*

> "I have to compensate for this gap by using the sound design. For example, just the ambient sounds, the rain, we have the trains - I'm using this to fill the gap that the music is not filling."
>
> (Interview in: https://news.wjct.org/post/asghar-farhadi-more-questions-answers)

Here I have nothing to add save that the difference between Farhadi and Ceylan is that the latter succeeds – to a degree. However, I do not deny that some of the films on the table here have *nothing* of interest to say or have little by way of penetrating insight. Far from it. I say simply that they fail to understand fully enough the role of music and mistakenly see it as the enemy of their true cinematic ambitions.

Sometimes non-diegetic music may be held to reduce the sense of immediacy required by the director. One wonders if this is not at the bottom of some of the objections here. My response is that immediacy itself needs careful handling. If it pretends that there is no gap between life and film, then delusion already rules. Still, the absence of music at any given point may be needed in order to give a special kind of feeling to that gap. In *The Gospel According to Matthew* (Pier Paolo Pasolini Italy, 1964) the Italian director, does just this in expressive periods of silence. But it is not without music and some appropriate Mozart ennobles certain scenes beyond measure.

Sometimes other sounds must dominate and indeed are more powerful without music. In *The Trial of Joan of Arc* (Robert Bresson, France, 1962) a fire crackles away. In Hitchcock's *Torn Curtain* (US, 1966) there is a murder scene in the kitchen of a remote farmhouse in which one can hear only the hiss of gas escaping from the oven as a man's head is being dragged toward it. This works in exactly the opposite direction to the use of the shrill notes in his *Psycho*, but it works. Note, though, that these are not broad, naturalistic soundscapes but single exaggerated sounds designed for the purposes of a making a particular point – just *like* music.

The idea of films without music is not recent, either. In 1931, Fritz Lang made *M* (Germany). He'd never been a great user of music and the film has a strange, eerie feel without it. (Or *nearly* without it - there is the sound of a whistle playing Grieg.) Hitchcock's *Rope* (US, 1948) uses none (though a character does briefly play a piano). These films compensate, though, by using other sound (from streets and so on) *expressively* rather than *naturalistically*. It is the latter sort of soundscape that can make films feel so emotionally barren. To use various sounds expressively, though, is to use them *as if* they were music, not entirely to use them *instead* of music. I think that the general conclusion, then, to be drawn from this is that while music, especially non-diegetic music, may not always be necessary to complete the expressiveness of a film, *something* must, and if there is little expressiveness at play and we are left with mere reliance on naturalism, the film will seem barren.

Music and Emotional Manipulation

Many may still think that music is too emotionally manipulative, so we must look into the whole issue of emotion at a deeper level. While one may legitimately complain about deliberate emotional manipulation in films or being led by the nose towards trite feel-good nonsense, I think that much confusion is caused by of a poor general understanding of what emotions are and their use in art. In the first place, emotionalism is too easily confused with sentimentalism – a kind of trite manipulation of emotion. More problematically though is the mistaken idea that the life of emotions is quite distinct from the proper, cooler, logical, rational side of life. Emotions are supposed to 'get in the way' of clean reasoning. Thus, there are deeper issues at play: one has to ask what emotions are being addressed, what values are being explored, what insight is being conveyed. In exploring all this we will come to see that the modern sin in much serious cinema is not so much emotionalism but lack of proper emotional expression in the films themselves, particularly the sin of supposing that because we have to avoid sentimentalism, we have to avoid an emotional approach altogether. Precisely *that* is the nonsense.

What is emotion?

First, though, another stretch of philosophical thinking is required, for we must ask just what an emotion is. Firstly, I argue that the most viable view is this: passions (or, to use the more modern psychological word, 'affects') are, indeed, involved in the core emotions but only as a component. I will do this by showing that the 'emotions as pure passions thesis' fails to describe fully the phenomenon of emotion. Further, I will show how it is more productive to take emotions (typically) to be complex states involving affect (passion), cognition (judgement) and desire (including motivation). I will show how emotions are an essential *part* of our lives as rational creatures. This more complex view of emotion is much discussed in the current philosophical literature of emotion.

I will take the emotions as pure passion thesis to involve the following combination of claims. Firstly, they are pure affect (raw feelings and no more). Secondly, they 'come over' you. In other words, you are their passive recipient and can no more decide what to feel than you can decide what to see given that your eyes are open and you face a particular scene. Thirdly, they *contrast* with episodes of rational thought (which are cool, logical and, perhaps, better for us). Finally (and relatedly), they contrast with the normal functioning of rationality, occasionally overwhelming us. According to this scenario, we have a rational side and an emotional side; head and heart; logic and feeling. If we swallow this whole, without question – as I believe too many serious filmmakers have - we can soon believe that our minds occupy two distinct universes. Just *that* is, I will show, the delusion.

This picture of the emotions is perhaps supported by the view that many emotions are associated with (and, perhaps, trigger) certain involuntary bodily changes (quickening of heart rate, palpitations, dryness in the throat, and tightness around the stomach, for example). It is also bolstered by the (seeming) fact that, while we may have some rational control over what we think, we have no such mastery of how we feel. Such a view seems also to offer a ready explanation of the motivational force of emotion: our feeling of red-hot anger explains why we 'hit out'. Emotions can, indeed, sometimes be impassioned. Perhaps there is sufficient truth in this picture to capture popular thought about emotion. Carolyn Price sums it up nicely: emotion is passive, bodily, an externally triggered force, standing in need of control, and can lead to impetuous behaviour. In contrast, reason is active, belongs to our true self, is of the mind, is the controlling influence, and leads to considered behaviour. This popular dichotomy is what is quite inadequate.[97]

What is wrong with this popular picture of matters? Five issues stand out. Firstly, it assumes that emotions are all just *one* kind of thing. It will quite naturally emerge from what follows that I take this blunt assumption to be false to the phenomenology (the 'what it is likeness') of emotion. Secondly, in reality, emotional episodes seem sometimes to leave conscious feeling quite behind.

Thirdly, emotions seem to possess intentionality – they point to or make essential reference *to* something, whereas pure affect does not. Fourthly, emotions as motivations seems to suggest desire as a necessary component. Finally, emotions seem a perfectly normal part of a rational life.

The view I wish to put forward is this. Emotions are typically complexes of affect, cognition (judgement) and desire. This is an ancient view found in Aristotle, Aquinas and Spinoza.[98] Crucially, however, this view allows that not all three need be present at any given time. This 'emotions as complexes' view promises to address the above issues. That feelings (pure affect) are involved in emotion hardly seems questionable. Affect can often be the most phenomenologically pronounced part of an emotion, giving it, so to speak, its distinctive flavour. It seems inconceivable that a subject could ever be angry or hopeful, fearful or jealous, infatuated, hostile or anxious, without sheer affect being involved at any stage whatsoever. I will, therefore, assume that affect is typically implicated in emotion.

Affect, however, need not always *actually* be present. I may, for example, feel angry with you about a sufficiently important missed appointment. At first, I am conscious of a distinctive kind of negative feeling towards you. However, in the course of time that feeling dies down. However, I may from then on continue to act towards you in a rather cold manner, perhaps without recognising that I am doing so. I may, quite sincerely, profess that my anger is left behind, yet continue to judge you in negative terms, avoid informal contact with you, and fail to involve you in my life in the positive way I used to. Others may judge, without saying so to me, that I 'still hold a grudge against you'. All this may happen quite without conscious feeling on my part. Indeed, my lingering anger may be clearer to others, especially if there is a sharp enough contrast between my earlier and later behaviour towards you.

An objector may here say that the affect is still there but that I am simply no longer conscious of it. The force of this objection will depend on whether one thinks there can be unconscious feeling. In any case, such an example still tells against the popular view that emotions are pure passions, for that view seems strongly to suggest that the affect be raised quite high in consciousness. So, whether truly extinguished or merely pushed underground, that affect may not always be accessible to or (sincerely) acknowledged by the conscious mind. Either way, this seems to present difficulty for the 'emotions as pure passions' thesis, for during the later (apparently passionless) stages one may still truly be said to be angry. The 'emotions as complexes' thesis offers a solution. We remain angry because the other components are still present – I judge you in a certain way and desire that our contact should be constrained in certain typical ways, despite the absence of the felt passion.

Emotions seem also to possess intentionality. They are, as we may put it, world-directed, they point to or somehow involve extra-cranial items. I am never merely angry, I am angry with *you*, I never merely fear, I fear *something* - a vicious looking dog, and so on. (My anger and fear may indeed be generalised over many objects or it may have no clearly specifiable object at all, but even in the latter case it is still intentional in that it directed on that unrecognised and unspecifiable object or state of affairs.) Anger may also involve *normative* judgements. My anger at you, for instance, seems at least in part, to be my judgement that you have sufficiently wronged me. Note: it is not just that my coming to such a judgement *causes* my anger. That would be consistent with my anger itself being pure affect. Rather, the judgement seems built-in to the emotion itself, a part of what my anger just *is*. It is hard to see how a pure affect thesis of emotion can explain this feature.

This intentionality has inspired a variety of more thought-based (or judgement-based) conceptions of emotions, for thoughts and judgements are pre-eminently intentional affairs. (One always thinks about or judges *something*, again whether vague or not.) It has been argued, though, that this move simply ignores the fact that affects in themselves can have intentionality. John Deigh asks us to distinguish between being aware of a difference and having the *concept* of the things involved. He gives an example of sharps and flats in music. One is somehow aware of the difference without having the appropriate concepts. Now consider emotions. In what he calls 'primitive contexts', he maintains that we can distinguish (have) the emotions of fear, horror and disgust without invoking any concepts. The differentia here (whatever is being differentiated) are simply given in immediate experience. What is happening here is that our fear or horror are being directed at the world (and thus have a kind of intentionality) independently of any thought or conceptually articulated judgement.[99]

I think there is something to this. Deigh gives the example that scariness can, at least sometimes, be just a 'direct property of the way a thing looks or sounds'. Indeed, and it has to be admitted that this possibility has scarcely been explored. (Though it has been exploited in film.) However, it seems harder to account for anger in these 'primitive' terms and perhaps the same can be said for many other mature emotions. If this is so, then we seem to require the admission of judgement in the make-up of (typical or mature) emotions in order to account for their intentional content. That would be the cognitive ingredient of the emotion.

Desire (or at least the disposition to desire) also seems constitutive of certain emotional states. Could I really be angry (even given the presence of some appropriate affect and judgement) if I had no built-in desire to retaliate? I need not always *actually* strike out but say I claimed anger while failing to show *any* of the symptoms usually associated with anger towards someone? Say instead that I continued responding to that person in a warm, affectionate and generally positive manner. Would it be appropriate to say that I am really angry? Another brief example: can I be jealous of you without any disposition at all to desire what you have (even if it is not consciously recognised)?

Further, emotions seem to have a role in nourishing our long-term plans. Given this, it is hard to see how if there is no associated desire. Desire motivates. As Richard Baxter has written, 'As man is not so prone to live according to the truth he knows unless it deeply affects him, so neither does his soul enjoy its sweetness unless speculation passes into affection'.[100] Emotion may, thus, keep alive practical rationality and planning - but not just by judgement (or even compassion) alone. We seem also (typically) to need the motivational force of desire. Most importantly, human sensitivity would be set at zero without emotion. That would leave little of importance with which rationality could then get to work on. Understanding reality is emotion dependent.

So far, then, we have seen just how complex a state an emotion may be. They involve affect, normative judgement, intentionality and ways of looking at things or states of affairs (in the literature what is called 'concerned construals'). Moreover, they can be rational. I fear what a Trump may do, or a Putin, for they are dangerous, ruthless and powerful but such an emotion is surely perfectly rational. The mistake we make about emotion comes when we focus on any *one* thing and take *it* to be key. The mistake then initiates inadequate theories of emotion – theories that fail to recognise and keep track of all that is involved in the having of an emotion.

Our conclusion? Emotions are not standardly pure affect, for affect alone cannot seem to cope adequately with all the features of our emotions. The emotions as complexes thesis seems to be on all fours with the phenomenology of our emotional lives, as I think our examples show. Moreover, I would contend that any decent theory of the emotions just should be true to this phenomenology. Alas, the popular identification of emotion with raw affect is kept alive in popular culture, sometimes quite overtly. Think of two characters from different phases of the popular *Star Trek* series – Mr. Spock and Commander Data. They are supposed (when on their best and most efficient form at least) to be without emotion, a characteristic that supposedly allows them to focus on what is purely logical.

I think we have revealed enough about emotion to show that, despite superficial appearances, such creatures are not really conceivable. Fictitious characters can sometimes *seem* conceivable only because of our standard willingness to bracket out some crucially relevant consideration. The fact is that emotion is an essential *part* of our lives as rational creatures, not something opposed to it. Only a diminished conception of what it is to be rational (a historically modernist abomination in the history of thought) can lead us to suppose otherwise. To the extent that we could relieve ourselves of emotion we would render humanity considerably diminished.

Spock and Data, I submit are failed, and even dangerous, copies of rational humanity to the extent that they are supposed to lack emotion. They are not exemplars. Of course, emotions can be turbulent, bothersome and even dangerous themselves at times - what can be right can always go wrong if we are in the least careless. But emotions are necessary if we are to be led to better things. If they can occasionally 'cloud our judgement' they can be moved, even commanded, by virtue. As embodied creatures, emotion is part of what we need to be led to the good. They are an embodied response to life itself. In the 13th century the philosopher-theologian St Thomas Aquinas recognised all this. He also recognise that emotions (he called them 'passions' but he meant more than we seem to mean by mere 'affect') often arise in the 'sense appetite' – in what we desire. As such emotions need to be governed by virtue, above all, love. Love just is the recognition that something is fitted for the kind of creature we humans are, and it desires it for the other. This is a built in part of being a rational creature. We just need to hold to the ancient idea that we humans need to be trained in governing our emotions by the commands of virtue.

Being rational is thus far more than being purely logical. Logic is part of the story not the whole of it. Being rational involves a whole raft of capacities: being logical, arriving at sound arguments, being able to arrive at abstract and generalised judgements, being able to distance ourselves from the here and now, being able to entertain possible scenarios far from the ones that obtain at a given time – and being able to accommodate appropriate emotion. Perhaps it even involves training ourselves into appropriate emotional response and giving up the psychological myth that they must inevitably lie beyond all rational control. I commend this more ancient view of the whole issue.

What has all this to do with cinema? There is nothing merely superficial or necessarily puerile or sloppy or sentimental about emotional life, even if it can sometimes be that way. It is a deep and essential part of our rational humanity. There can no reason to think that cinema (or any art) is diminished by using it to provoke or suggest emotion, and much reason to suppose that it is ignoring it that is diminishing. What is important is the quality and depth of the emotions that are being invoked, what human values are being explored, and what extra insight is being conveyed. In short, what matters is how virtuously a film may be governing our emotions.

Moreover, cinema is particularly good at emotion, conveying and using it are two of its great strengths. This is true of music, too, and why music is so important to a film. A medium that can yield such riches should not have its riches demoted on philosophically inadequate grounds. A filmmaker who avoids exploiting emotion on the grounds of fear of falling into sentimentalism or emotional manipulation (as opposed simply to displaying it in the characters) needs simply to be a better, more imaginative and more intelligent filmmaker.

But just why is cinema so good at emotion and how can it be involved in a productive way? Dream theory, I think answers the first of these questions. Dreams are "emotions dressed in sensory clothing", remember – and the very nature of the cinematic image reflects this at its core. Films also relate strongly to the emotional aspect of our memory – individual and collective. This is evident in the slew of post-war 'war' films and the post-'Wild West' westerns. A film must immerse us in an appropriate emotional context if it is to do an effective job, even if we come to reject some of their messages, for not to do this is a failure to address ourselves as rational creatures, though films must do this job in an emotionally coherent, holistic and justifiable way. It is important that films imaginatively engage our 'emotional intelligence' and not merely appeal to what I like to call our 'emotional gormlessness'.

In general, to fail to address us at the emotional level in this way is a double failure: firstly, it is to ignore what cinema essentially is, and secondly it ignores what we human beings essentially are – failure that is to address us as fully functioning human beings, rational creatures in which emotion is built into our rationality. I am not, of course, saying that a good film should constantly promote (or try to) a level of high-pitched emotional intensity. I simply maintain that emotionalism in a film is a legitimate and essential component of the psychological space of good cinema. The power of cinema lies essentially in its emotional life and offerings (where emotion is construed as I have argued it should). Film is as forceful a medium as any for showing us how emotion, judgement, thought and action are interdependent, especially if we think about a film afterwards and, perhaps discuss it. Indeed, I think this is the quality of cinema that most justifies its place in our education system – at all levels. And, remember, in this section I am not talking primarily about the emotions shown by the characters and expressed by the actors (though that is important, too) but how the film as a whole is dealing with emotion – the quality of its emotionalism.

Further, a film may use its emotional force (not just the emotions of the characters) to provoke its viewer in justifiable ways – to snap the viewer out of ignorance or lack of care. Films that deal with wider social and political issues do this – at their best – but they risk failure if they try to do this without using emotion. They really do have to prod one into caring for their characters. This sort of provocation should not be seen as mere manipulation because it provides some insight or leads one to a sufficiently imaginative involvement. It is in this, I think, that we can find the sinful in so much of modern serious cinema – one is not emotionally engaged deeply or soon enough with the characters. Why then should the viewer persist with such a film?

Not that this sin is altogether new. A movement in cinema called 'New Objectivity' enjoyed some prominence in Germany in the 1920s, though that was more specifically a move against the then popular expressionism in films. The films of Georg Wilhelm Pabst are of importance here. While the terms 'objective' and 'subjective' are too philosophically slippery to generate anything much beyond confusion, to the extent that the former is meant as a way of avoiding emotionalism in film, I consider it a deep error. But, once again, I suspect that much of the culture behind serious cinema has lost touch with a proper and fuller emotionalism in film (save for the blunt portrayal of the fact that a character may be emotional). This is something which, thank goodness never afflicted the serious movements in the past – such as Italian post war 'neo-realism' and the various 'new waves of the sixties', otherwise we would not now remember them

Thus, frankly and bluntly, emotion (properly and richly construed) is what cinema does best. It need never be reductively melodramatic or superficial, even though it sometimes is. By its very nature, coming to us as a kind of ghostly apparition dressed in sensory clothing, somehow detached from and yet still somehow *about* and connected to reality, the cinematic image calls out primarily for an emotional response rather than (primarily) an intellectual one. Emotion is precisely what is shaped to fill the enigmatic gap between image and reality. Though intellectual consideration may have an eminent place on later refection, it is more than just a bit of a pity to spoil the journey itself by too much focus on the intellectually imbued destination while one is still on the way. 'Just sit back and let it wash over you' is the proper advice to give oneself as one takes one's place in the cinema seat. (If the film allows it, of course.) Emotionalism no more gets in the way of a proper appreciation of effective cinema than water gets in way of an invigorating swim. Water and emotion are necessary ingredients in their respective activities. I think that this is at the bottom of why it is so difficult (something of which I am acutely aware of as I write this book) to write about cinema, for doing so is precisely an intellectual activity – more than ever when one is providing a philosophical analysis. It is also what makes reviewing good films far more difficult than reviewing bad ones: one is trying to put into words something that finally transcends language. One can but reach for the more poetic metaphor. Clunky literalistic lenses just do not bring any relevant focus to the job.

In fact, emotionalism is part of what has been called the 'poetics of cinema'. It is no coincidence that poetry is another medium which has a strong dream-like aspect. Indeed, poetry (much of it at least) could be called dreaming in *literary* clothing, though perhaps, as has been observed, in tranquillity *after* the action, as opposed to film, in which the poetry is very much simultaneous with the action. I feel this when watching the very finest of westerns and in the aforementioned Italian neo-realist films. Cinema's language is very much the vocabulary of emotional signal and symbol. To ignore all this, is perhaps the most grievous sin with which a film may damn itself.

Music, I contend, can be a useful way in which film can intelligently appeal to and move and govern our emotional lives, even if in some films it often slides into being part of emotional banality. The music may lead us into a way of judging a character. It may lead us into expectation. It can also be in counterpoint at times. The possibilities are almost endless, so let not our cinema ignore it.

More sins of sound

The first thing to note is that good sound in a film should hardly draw too much overt attention to itself. In fact, no one aspect of a film should – sound (music or otherwise) editing, performance, cinematography, design, and so on). What should attract one's attention is the *whole* image. That principle simply falls out of the fact that *all* aspects of a film contribute to the overall effect of what I have been calling the 'cinematic image'. They are all *in* consciousness, perhaps (or sometimes just about) but never the *focus* of consciousness.[101] That must always be the role of the cinematic image. I am thinking here, of course, about one's primal enjoyment of a film. On later analysis one may be intensely interested in the way some aspect of a film has contributed to the overall effect – as I am here.) But sins there are in sound generally: poorly recorded dialogue in low budget films, deafening Dolby noise in a popcorn comic-book job, the sudden use of music because a director sees the need for a short lyrical stretch in an otherwise dull naturalistic film. This is not just a sin of sound either, it can creep into vision also (as in a shot of a merely post-card beautiful countryside). This sin particularly annoys me for it seems to be admission that the rest of the film will not do as it is. It *should* do.

Part of the problem I think with film sound these days is the fact that it is now clever enough, almost, to do anything. This leads to two sins. Firstly, sound in films is overstretched. It is pushed too far beyond reasonable limits and gets far too complicated and messy. Without the best of reproduction equipment in the cinema it can be impossible to hear distinctly everything that is intended. In low budget films the same fault occurs at the opposite end of the spectrum – it's not that the sound is too complicated but that it's not recorded as clearly as it should – especially dialogue – or so it seems to a viewer (and hearer) of the film. Secondly, it means that filmmakers give themselves too much to play with, a capacity that frequently exceeds their actual imaginations. In the days when certain things just couldn't be done, no one could do them wrong, but it also meant that imagination had to be used. Mostly sound was kept simple.

I am sometimes encouraged to suppose that, getting on in years, my own hearing is failing a bit. Well, so it is, and a friendly audiologist at that estimable organisation 'Specsavers' concurs. I especially think this after I've seen a film in a cinema with pretty well all the faults I've mentioned and understood little of what I've heard. Then I go home, play an old film and – *viola* – the sound has been crisp and clear. This hardly seems too much to ask of an imaginative filmmaking mind. I appreciate that makers of certain films have to appeal to a certain kind of audience – the kind that seem to like a fairly constant stream of miscellaneous loud noise. I may worry about their future mental (and auditory) health, and it may act as relief for the kind of pressures that these days tragically typify work environments, but be that as it may, it seems to make film a different kind of medium to cinema. Cinema emerged from the level of the fairground but it can hardly return to it and remain the art it became.

The motion picture journal *Variety* recently ran an article on sound complaining that sound was generally less well understood as a medium of expression than the visual aspects of the image, saying that, "movie critics rarely single out the work of sound people; adding insult to injury, if they do mention sound, they often credit it to Dolby, i.e., the equipment rather than the artisans". It goes on:

> "The 1926 'Don Juan' and 1927 'The Jazz Singer' pioneered sync sound in movies. Hollywood's uneasy adjustment to talkies was spoofed in the 1952 classic 'Singin' in the Rain', which depicted a movie's sound coming from one microphone on the set. That image over the years has turned into a compliment (filmmakers want audiences to think they're listening to the actual noises) but it's also a slight. It discounts the complexity involved in creating sound for any scene. It also leads to an ongoing sore point: In the early days, sound people were technicians, trying to wrangle new machinery; but to call current behind-the-camera folks 'technicians' or to call these 'tech categories' is to overlook their enormous creativity."[102]

This may isolate an important point, and I certainly do think that many film critics seem to have a poor understanding of how a cinematic image is constructed. Many film reviewers seem hardly even to mention the impact (or lack thereof) of important aesthetic elements in films, and this failure may be because of the tendency to see them as 'mere technicalities'. If some aspect of a film – and recall that sound is a vital part of the cinematic image – is regarded in this poverty-stricken way rather than as art, then the problem isolated in the article quoted will remain – as will the inadequacies of reviews. But the problem is not just that some alleged "enormous creativity" of the filmmakers will be "overlooked" by mere critics. Forget the critics, the more fundamental problem remaining will be that matters will scarcely develop beyond mere technical cleverness, in the first place, and there will be little chance of film's further development as art unless filmmakers take *themselves* to be artists, rather than managers of technicality. They, after all, not the reviewers, are the ones that actually make the product.

Chapter 6: The Sins of Performance

The sins of acting styles

Acting styles have changed a good deal over the history of cinema. Look at silent films, especially very early ones, and one notices a style that went with stage melodrama. Nowadays, all-round authenticity and naturalism are standardly the things, especially in more serious cinema – but not always to good effect, I will argue.

This was brought home to me a few years ago when our local film club celebrated its 10th anniversary with a showing of *Lawrence of Arabia* (David Lean, UK, 1962). It was very well received by all members – but one. This one complained that it was spoiled by over-acting on the part of Peter O'Toole. He, of course, played the title part of Lawrence. I utterly disagreed with this judgement but I could see what was behind it. O'Toole, I argued was not *over* acting but simply acting in a style that has nowadays all but disappeared. What was that style? What was it trying to do? And, why is it a sin that it has all but disappeared?

O'Toole was, I believe, acting out aspects of Lawrence's character and making these aspects stand out. I will call this '*aspect* performance'. This is entirely justified by the fact that what matters in the events covered by the film is not what the character was like *all-round* but what particularly motivated him at the times concerned. Foreground, or not far off, is far more important than having the entire background slowly revealed – throughout the film. Nor does it, or *should* it, matter that the man himself would not have entirely resembled O'Toole's screen performance at any given time. The man himself was just *that* – the whole man, whatever that may have been, but in the film certain aspects alone are what matter. These aspects needed to be made clear and are made clear – by O'Toole's pointed performance, by the almost poetic power of his speech and dialogue, and by the way in which he is presented to us in the film. Giving us something merely more authentically plausible would have diluted the key aspects of Lawrence that the film sought to bring out.

Once again, I issue the reminder that cinema is not exactly the same thing as life. Cinema is seeing but it is selected seeing, focussing on this or that. The cinematic image has, as we have seen, *particularity* but it can also particularise all the way down. Each emotion can be focused on – and *needs* to be focused on. Knowing too much of the character or being made able to see too much of the character disables this focused particularisation. In the case of TE Lawrence, it would also have demystified the enigma that surrounded his life and thus ruined the very purpose of the film. If you want a balanced biography of the man, then read one, would be my advice. Do not blame a film and performance that are more about the legend. A cinematic image is a very particular, peculiar and distinctive way of being acquainted with a character, and this brings its own distinctive potentials and demands.

I believe that until recently nearly all film performance was aspect performance, more or less along the lines I have described. Actors were never much required to make the mistake of trying to cram into their performances too much generalised authenticity. By 'authenticity' here, I simply mean acting in such a manner as would perfectly reflect what might plausibly be revealed by that character if they were actual people in an actual situation or mere carbon-copies or photocopies of such. By 'generalised' I mean acting in a way that tries to give too much of the character at each moment, or even over an entire film. That is life, not good cinema.

I am not saying that the resulting exaggeration should be too great, only that some exaggeration, or rather, *focus*, is needed if a film is to work. This reflects a crucial difference between *acting* a character and just *being* that character. No matter what we face in life, we respond in a way that reflects our whole selves. We are often (quite unthinkingly) exhorted to 'be ourselves' yet there is a strong sense in which we cannot be anything else. If we behave more deferentially towards some people than others, or are nervous or shy in certain situations, then being these ways just *is* a part of our whole character. We just *are* being ourselves. A performance, though, is *by its very nature*, something more focused and selective. This needs to be exploited not ignored or played down. To *perform* a life is not – quite literally – to *live* it or *be* it. To perform (or be required to perform) under the delusion that it should be other than this is a profound error.

Aspect performing may not earn our respect for revealing the all-round character but it does hold our attention in a way that fits the nature of the cinematic image – its intensity, its focused down particularity, its luminosity, its power to move. Popular cinema still has some of this. I was struck, as were many, by Gary Oldman's playing of Sir Winston Churchill in *The Darkest Hour* (Joe Wright, UK, 2017). This covers the time in which he was first made prime minister during the early days of the Second World War. There was no attempt to give us the whole man. It was Churchill the Hero that we saw, not Churchill the X, Y or Z, at least to any real extent. Focus was entirely on his inner and outer response to events at the time being covered. More than this would have entirely ruined the thing. It was about how Churchill was transformed into that national hero – full stop. Any more about the man would have been simply beside the point. We need to follow the story being told; we need to know the character only insofar as this serves the story. If you want a history lesson, study for an OU degree, watching a feature film serves quite different, though not necessarily less penetrating, purposes. This isn't, of course, to assert that films must not, never are, nor ever *can* be concerned with fundamental truths, only that such truths as they can reasonably be expected to convey are, in some sense, narrower. Certainly they will be narrower than an exhaustive and completely balanced biography or history of the times can be – even given the highly questionable assumption that such could exist in the first place.

An actor may be interested in their character on a wider front – of course – but, if so, this has more to do with what motivates and shapes the performance than with justifying what it gets across. It is certainly the case that film acting (or parts of it) went through something of a revolution in the 1950s with the coming of the school of 'method' acting. Marlon Brando is the textbook case here and *On The Waterfront* (Elia Kazan, US, 1954) perhaps the textbook film. Here it may well be observed that the focus was on a more realistic style of acting. But 'realistic' in this context seems to mean more focus on the lives of ordinary Joes rather than on more exotic or glamorous characters. I do not think that Brando's performance is anything less than aspect performing. I think that the same can be said of other 'realistic' performing – those in the post war Italian 'neo-realist' corpus, say, or the various 'new waves'. In both these cases, the actors are performing their parts as though their characters were in a kind of dream. It is the dream-version of life that we see. This, remember, is what cinema is best at. Dreaming about someone, I think, focusses on aspects of characters we know. This is because those aspects are somehow psychologically important to us, if only subconsciously. Very well, if the cinematic image is dream-like, as I have argued, then the characters appear in a kind of dream and they should be performed in a dream-like manner.

Let's now look at some of the sins. This is difficult because the sins should not necessarily be attributed to the performer. I am not writing here about *bad* acting. (As a matter of fact, I feel that most actors are pretty good – and far better than most directors.) I am concerned with what acting, specifically in film, should actually *be* – good or bad. No matter how well *executed* a part may be, and no matter to what degree that execution can be attributed to actor, screenwriter or director, it fails if its very conception is faulty. What I am arguing is that too much focus on pure authenticity, especially at the expense of focus on particular aspects, is a faulty conception of what acting actually *is* (or at least what it is supposed to be or what it is best at doing). Nor here am I remotely suggesting that an actor should not try, in some sense, to "become" the character they are playing. Let's get it straight, I am not writing here about acting *at all* in any direct way, still less about how actors prepare. Frankly, I am not, either by experience or knowledge, remotely qualified so to do.

Strictly speaking in the extreme, I am not even writing about performance. My focus is what and how something about a performance comes across in the cinematic image. I am subjecting some of those 'whats' and 'hows' to philosophical analysis in the light of what I have argued a cinematic image actually is. Recall our finding concerning the nature of the cinematic image, especially that it is a strange combination of photographic realism and all sorts of ensuing characteristics (intensity, luminosity, distance, particularity in the extreme, selection, and so on) that, frankly, are very *un*realistic – something called 'form'. These are characteristics that direct, unmediated experiences of raw waking life either do not have at all or do have only in a completely different sense. Remember, the cinematic image is reality revealed *un*realistically. This, recall, is the fundamental paradox, of the cinematic image. However, recalling Chapter 1, in this context I use the word 'unrealistic' in a special sense – that of the cinematic image not being exact carbon-copy of real life. This is not remotely to deny that they might be perfectly realistic in a deeper sense – that of conveying something importantly real.

One consequence of this paradox is that there is something curiously but quite literally superficial about cinema. Photographic realism doesn't even go skin deep. Materially it conveys only the surface – of things, places and people. If it is to convey any depth it must therefore do so by artifice, that is, as we have suggested before, by intensifying and enlarging that surface. In that sense, cinema is more a magnifying glass than a mirror. Old-fashioned acting with its exaggerated gestures did just that. (Though perhaps it could commit its own sin of exaggerating too much.) Generalised authenticity, mere carbon-copying' of what one would see in real life, just plain 'playing down' in too subtle a manner, fairly obviously, goes against this nature. Generalised authenticity is what you get from life itself, inevitably: life just *is* reality coming across realistically (no matter how bizarre or seemingly surreal some situations may be). Cinema, in contrast, is life coming across by artifice. If a performance looks – on the surface – too much like the real, ordinary thing, it will get across less of the in-depth reality that can, and *ought*, to be conveyed by cinema. Note, I am not denying that moments of intensification, in drama, excitement, fear, love, hate, and so on, cannot come across in real life situations. Of course, they can, but they come across in different ways because we are physically immersed in the situation. In cinema we are not – detachment rules, remember. Nor am I denying that cinematic performances can be subtle. They can, but the subtlety has to be more selective and focused and intensified. Without this we have a denial of the powers of cinema.

Despite all I have said here about authenticity, in the sense of carbon-copying, as a sin, there is one sense of the word 'authentic' in which a good actor just *has* to be authentic. I do not mean here (as is so often said) that the actor has to convince the viewer that they *are* the character they are playing, for this is literally impossible. We (the audience) *know* they are not. We *may*, recall, be said to 'celieve' that we see an actual living character. Celief needs more exploration than I can give it herein but one consequence is that it has different implications from its parent concept 'belief'.

These differences, I feel, include the ways in which characters come across. The audience is, strictly speaking, engaged in a special act of make-believe. The actor (alongside everyone and everything else, visible and invisible) are strictly *aids* to this act. Being a good aid to this make belief (celief) could pretty much serve as a definition of good film acting. The sin of over-authenticity, of mere carbon-copying, arises when performances are not focused enough solely on what matters at the time or that the emotional aspects that are in the performance are subdued rather than reinforced by the way the performance is presented in the image, and this is precisely what's happening if the performance or its surroundings are just too naturalistic. I suspect that the sin of over-authenticity is primarily one of storytelling (as we shall come to see later) rather than performance more narrowly. It is that the whole approach feeds into and affects performance. Under its delusional incapacity to distinguish between looking *artificial* and exploiting the necessary *artifice* of cinema, carbon-copying what one may see in life prevents actors (and directors) focusing what matters to the cinematic image. There is one kind of over-authenticity in performance, though, that seems so common now that I deal with it separately.

Mumbling

Real people, in real life, do not always speak clearly, and even when they do various accents can be a problem for someone who is not familiar with the local brogue. In some contexts people will mumble. Sometimes there is a need for such people and occasions to be represented on film. What should the actor do? It should be clear to any filmmaker not held in totally unthinking thrall to the practice of carbon-copying authenticity, in speech as elsewhere, that if an actor is playing the part of a mumbler, the last thing they should do is *actually* mumble. The reason for this is also simple – the audience will not pick up what is being said, or at least struggle so to do. If the intention is that we should remain in the dark then all well and good but as often as not this is not the case.

While watching the film *Macbeth* (Justin Kurzel, UK, 2015) I became almost incensed. Is this Shakespeare I hardly hear before me? I wondered. Michael Fassbender (an otherwise excellent actor) could have been mumbling through a patch of Scotch mist, Marion Cotillard, as his delightful wife, could have been whispering sweet sonnets in his ears, and the rest could have been a convincing background noise in a charming highland pub for all the sense it helped make of the drama. It is simply dramatically and narratively irrelevant that any real Macbeth might have 'spoken like that'. Such an atrocious approach wouldn't even make

Shakespeare relevant to a broken-bottle-wielding, hard-drinking motor mouth in a Glaswegian bar. To complain in this way is not being an elitist snob. It is simply to insist that one should be allowed to know what is going on. If such speech is held to be necessary, then subtitles should be provided.

Directors are as much if not *more* to blame than the actors here. The director is the boss. It would be poor excuse for them to think that, because they already know the script well enough, the audience will be with them. I think that the more sophisticated recording apparatus and techniques misleads filmmakers, too. More can be captured than ever before and made at least audible. Googling this topic reveals that some will find the excuse of blaming inferior cinema equipment. This is nonsense. Dolby 'Atmos' is not the answer here, escape from muddled-headedness is. Filmmakers must cease thinking that telling the truth about a character or realistically portraying a situation or emotion requires an unthinking worship-like attitude to bland naturalistic carbon-copying. We need sound to be audible, of course, but audibility is not the same as clarity, and unless what should be made clear to an audience is actually made clear, a sin has been committed. If a mumbling character is being portrayed, then that character should *sound* as though they are mumbling but the actor should get this character aspect across without *actually* mumbling. It's called 'acting'. After all, if a suffering character is being portrayed, it should not be necessary for the actor to suffer – not in the same sense, at least. I am reminded here of Laurence Olivier's advice (or so the story goes) to Dustin Hoffman during the making of *The Marathon Man* (John Schlesinger, US, 1976). The story is that Hoffman had deprived himself of sleep in order to get across better the feeling of the character he was playing. Olivier's response was terse: "Why don't you just try acting?'. We should remember that advice nowadays.[103]

It is one thing to innovate and experiment with new technologies but entirely another to be wilfully, or even accidentally, obtuse. Besides, technology should always aid the storytelling. It has absolutely no other use whatsoever. All this matters very little for a bad or mediocre film, of course, but it spoils some otherwise good ones. The aforementioned *Macbeth* is one of them. *Brokeback Mountain* (Ang Lee, US, 2005) is another, as Heath Ledger drones through certain lines. This, though, is a topic in which one can engage in hours of fun, isolating one's own favourite collection of sinners. I find American 'indies' one of the worse classes of film hereabouts. The accent doesn't help, of course, but watch almost any old piece of Hollywood – from the bad, through the mediocre to the great. One encounters all sorts of characters including the scarcely articulate, yet one can tell what each is saying – all before Dolby even existed.

Film stars, and the sin of their absence.

I do not make any reference here to the human sins of this or that film star. Numerous and fascinating as they may be to the more tabloid and celebrity minded of film-goers, I am more concerned in the present book with any sins there may be in their use (or rather their absence altogether) in films. But first some of their virtues – characteristics that pretty much make an actor a star rather than just an actor.

Firstly, the great film stars of past years were good at *aspect* performing. They brought out particularly strongly, an important aspect of their character's lives and emotions and did not worry (indeed, they were not required to worry) about being plausible in a more authentic, purely naturalistic, carbon-copy sense. One was presented with a concentrated profile of characteristics made individual through the screen persona of the star. One knew what to expect. Yes, that meant that they were mainly stereotyped. In turn, this meant that a film didn't have to spend so much time and effort on character development that one got lost in during the first thirty or so minutes of running time.

Relatedly, the stars of old were not referred to as 'gods' and 'goddesses' without good reason. It has often been remarked that, in appearance and role, they resembled the divinities of classical paganism – *super*-entities that have playful control over our psyches. One knew what to expect or even when one's expectations may be thwarted. Their faces shone down from the screen like celestial objects, as divinities were seen to shine down from the sky in our pagan past.[104] They could mean something special to us, express an ideal. They could give focus to an issue in the way that bland, all-round, more naturalistic acting cannot do. To be sure, such lofty perception helped maintain a background of vice and sinfulness all its own, but that is a further matter. I recall here a remark from film star Lauren Bacall: "The industry is shit, it's the medium that's great". It is the latter we are addressing in this book. It is the latter which owes much of its greatness to the film star.

Sometimes, again like the pagan divinities, they would surprise, even delight, as Humphrey Bogart did in *African Queen* (John Huston, US, 1951) and as Captain Queeg in *The Caine Mutiny* (Edward Dmytryk, US, 1954) but you still expected, and received, a no-nonsense character. Having stereotyped characters is alright, too. After all, most of we ordinary humans act in stereotypical fashion about 99% of our waking time – it's normal. If we didn't behave in this way, others would have no idea of what to make of us or how to deal with us. People most familiar to us and our dearest loved ones would have little idea of how to approach us. Life would be terrible if we were not, in some degree, stereotypes. Of course, we may want a film's characters to have some depth, but that can and did happen in the case of many of the great stars. Did James Stewart's Scottie in *Vertigo* (Alfred

Hitchcock, US, 1958) or his George Bailey in *It's A Wonderful Life* (Frank Capra, US, 1946) not reveal any depth just because Stewart exhibited in them his usual stereotyped characteristic of dependability?

The distinction between stage and film acting comes into play at this point. Philosopher of film Stanley Cavell has observed that, "For the stage, an actor works himself into a role; for the screen, a performer takes the role onto himself".[105] Philosopher Noel Carroll expands on this by citing Erwin Panofsky who points out that "stage actors *interpret* their roles, whereas film actors . . . because of the intimacy of the lens vis-à-vis the actor, *incarnate* theirs".[106] (My emphasis.) Philosopher Arthur C. Danto says, "the movie star is a metaphysically complex personality, retaining a personality so strong as to swamp the role he or she plays to the point that we speak of Elliot Gould rather than Philip Marlowe as doing this or that, as though roles were like lives through which a Hindu soul migrates".[107] For Cavell, Carroll says, "movie stars merge their own being with the characters they portray. In a sense, the character *is* John Wayne or Marilyn Monroe".[108] (My emphasis.) Stanley Cavell again:

> "[On the stage] the actor's role is his subject of study . . . [b]ut the screen performer is essentially not an actor at all: he is the subject of study . . .. (That is what the content of a photograph is – its subject.) On the screen the study is projected; on the stage the actor is the projector. An exemplary stage performance is one which, *for* a time, most fully creates a character. . .. An exemplary screen performance is one in which, *at* a time, a star is born. After *The Maltese Falcon* we know a new star, only distantly a person. 'Bogart' *means* 'the character created in a given set of films'. . . . if those films did not exist, Bogart would not exist. The name "Bogart" would not mean what it does"[109] (My emphasis.)

There's a lot in all this to get one's head around and it is part of what Danto seems to mean by talking of a "metaphysical complex", but with due nuancing here and there I think it all sounds credible. The nuancing should include acknowledgment of the fact that it may take a great deal of performance skill on the part of the star to pull all this off convincingly. We see on the screen only the result, not the inner process involved in getting there. From the screen shines Danto's unified 'metaphysical complex' – agreed – but getting there might be a more varied matter. Remember, that whereas stage actors have to project their characters, film actors just *are* a projection of their characters – no projection on top of the one that cinema provides by its very nature is required. The true star is just a more impressive and glowing projection.

Are stars in some sense, though, "acting themselves"? Yes. A stage actor *does* (performs) while a star just *is*. However, despite the large degree of merging of performer and character, they are still in some sense *acting* the part, not simply *being* it without any further ado. They have to *do* their part in creating the character, after all. Perhaps a star is somehow a hybrid entity – both be-er and do-er. Moreover, if one thinks that 'acting oneself' requires little talent, one should try it – and be prepared for embarrassing failure. We should remember also that a star may convincingly merge with some very different kinds of characters – John Wayne certainly did that, as did Bogart. Many of the 'greats' did. Robert Mitchum once said that one of the greatest stars was Rin Tin Tin . . . a dog . . . so there couldn't be too much to it. I think there is, it's just that Mitchum was a 'natural'.

The close up, not something available on the stage, accentuates some of these points. We know the character more intimately. In a much stronger way we no longer intuitively think of a performer *and* a role, just the human presence on the screen. The implications are colossal. It is in the very nature of the cinematic image to try to make a star out of the performer, even if only a minor one in an overall constellation. The cinematic image, as we have seen, is a strangely distanced way of seeing the world. This means that the thing upon which it is focused becomes more vivid as it glows down from the screen. This strange way of seeing makes what is seen itself strange, somewhat distanced, as if from another reality. Yet the distance of the cinematic image is a paradoxical thing, indeed, for it is not a measurable distance, and it allows what crosses it and reaches the viewer to be closer to us than almost anything else can be.

Traditionally, stars have fitted this model of cinema. They have been strange beings seen large and dominating our souls. Film stars convey reality in a way ideally shaped for the medium of film. They could accommodate what matters in the strange, detached focus that so marks out the nature of the cinematic image. Think of Charlton Heston as *El Cid* (Anthony Mann, US, 1961). He was a fine actor but here as elsewhere (as Moses and Ben-Hur) it was his status as a film star, with all its inherent qualities, that made the lion-sized contribution to his portrayal of true nobility and honour. Think also of Anthony Quinn as *Zorba the Greek* (Michael Cacoyannis, Greece, 1964). It was Quinn the star as much as Quinn the actor who put the zest in that strange, hypnotic part.

Today, film stars in this sense hardly exist. Famous names exist of course, as does celebrity status, but these days everyone wants to be a 'proper' actor instead. Just this is the sin, for if there is anything in what we have just seen, it grinds against the nature of the cinematic image and no matter how beautiful a film is in other respects, its beauty will always be constrained by the fact that we are greeted with essentially stage performances merely adapted, toned down a bit in gesture and so on, for the camera. No longer are true stars born. Gone with them are the true genres (as we shall see later) which are a star's proper dwelling place in the galaxy of cinema. Alas, much of what has traditionally been identified as cinema has gone with them.

I must add here, a proviso. I am not saying that acting in a non-film-star way or context necessarily produces non-cinema. That would be too exaggerated a thesis. If one wants a contrast, I would say that much good acting can convey the substance of the ordinary, but only stars (like divinities) can convey the essence of the *extra*ordinary. I am simply, though importantly, saying that the idea of the film star in the traditional sense was a huge cinematic element in films and that it flowed from the nature of the cinematic image as a breeze flows from the sea. I am also saying that we should rue its passing.

Chapter 7: The Sins of Space and Time

The sins of using – and misusing – cinematic space

We have noted that what and who are 'in the frame' is clearly important. A conversation may be filmed in standard form. First there is a shot containing the two conversing characters so that the viewer knows that a conversation has begun and who the participants are. This followed by alternate closer shots of each character as they speak and react. This approach feels different to a conversation in which both characters are visible all the time. In other contexts, too, scale should also be on the director's mind as shot is being planned. Is Atlanta on fire or is an individual character tearful?

One of the most brilliant psychological and dramatic effects of creative use of scale can be seen in a famous shot from Orson Welles' *Citizen Kane* (US, 1941). Kane is still a boy and is playing freely and joyfully in the snow outside. The shot shows Kane alone, enjoying life, but then pulls back inside the house. Kane becomes boxed in by the window frame. The shot pulls out further and we see him now boxed in by both the window frame and a group of adults discussing his future. What a brilliant match there is between the psychology of the story and the cinematic image by means of which it is being told.

One can only dream of such brilliant cinema nowadays, I fear, but a remarkable example from recent times comes from the film *The Favourite* (Yorgos Lanthimos, Ireland, 2018). Lanthimos' camera is kitted out with pretty well 'fish-eye' (extreme wide angle) lenses as Queen Anne strides through the palace. The picture has warped verticals that seem to bow to her as she passes by. What a wonderful visual fit that is for the queen's psychological disintegration. What a wonderful contemporary example it is, too, of using space to convey a dream-like impression, even though dreams do not (I suppose) typically come with distorted wide angles).

The needs of general image composition and scale, though, are not always observed, and I follow up with a few sins of getting wrong the visual, and thus psychological, scale of an image.

The sins of scale - the close up

A particular kind of use of scale is the close up. It is held that the close up was invented by the American silent film director DW Griffiths about a century ago. Filmmakers came to recognise its power but also knew that it should be used sparingly. Of course, grandeur and large scale are not always needed. Times of intimacy are also required in building up a relationship with a character. McGinn quotes film theorist Bela Balazs on this:

> "Good close-ups radiate a tender human attitude in the contemplation of hidden things, a delicate solicitude, a gentle bending over of intimacies of life-in-the-miniature, a warm sensibility . . . [they are] in the heart, not the eye . . . the face loses all reference . . . we see not a figure of flesh and bone but an expression . . . emotions, moods intentions and thoughts, things which though our eyes can see them, are not in space . . . we can see the bottom of the soul."[110]

This is true and powerful, and again reminds us of the dream-likeness of the cinematic image. I am reminded of the telling close-ups of Celia Johnson in David Lean's *Brief Encounter* (UK, 1945) and *In Which We Serve* (UK, 1942) though some of these things are conveyed in other kinds of shots as well. It's all a part of what McGinn calls "the pleasure of looking". We can, in a film, look in ways hived off from us in daily life, gazing rather than seeing.

In lower budget 'serious' cinema today, however, the temptation seems to be to use as many close ups as possible. For one thing, like the handheld camera, it can save enormous time and expense. One needs to pay less attention to background, which will likely be out of focus anyway, and the actors, usually pretty good, can shine. Unfortunately, it also reduces a film's visual impact. See a film almost made of close ups and each one lacks impact and suffers from reduced meaning; see a film with just a few close ups and there's at least a chance of both. Close-ups give us (obviously) more intricate and facial detail. If that is what is needed at a particular point, then fine, but one also often needs to 'feel' the context and the environment – the missing 'space' which Balazs mentions. Emotional intimacy is reduced, not increased, by the over-use of the close up. The stance of a character's whole body can be telling, too - if we can see it. All this seems obvious I have to say and not in the least controversial.

Perhaps less obvious but still, I think, true is the human specialness of the close up. I recall reading somewhere that it has a kind of sacredness. I think this captures the matter perfectly. One is graciously permitted to get especially close to a character. In the cinematic image the optical closeness comes across as emotional and personal closeness. This should be a respected perspective, quite aside from the fact that we often need to see the emotion in its context. Close ups need not come all at once, either. A slow 'dolly' in from a wider context-building perspective to a bigger close up as a character speaks or responds can be psychologically useful. On the whole if you see a close up and are not feeling the 'wow factor' then the visual tactic is not working. Close-ups should be used when they have a dream-like impact.

The sins of aspect ratio. The inexcusable sin of cinematic obesity.

This is yet another aspect of scale. Though epic films, great musical extravaganzas, colourful and exotic yarns and general large-scale spectacles have been made in black and white in the academy ratio – and very successfully – it can hardly be denied that they call for colour and wide screen ratios. Both *Ben-Hur* (William Wyler, US, 1959) and *Lawrence of Arabia* (David Lean, US, 1962) needed colour and width.

The scope ratio (approximately 2.35:1) though, was not welcomed by some – on cinematic grounds. The old joke about its being suited only to pictures of snakes and funerals did its rounds. More elegantly and humorously, Orson Welles, who never used the process, said that "Man is made in God's image. To enlarge that image is not to glorify but to deform it. It's a sort of joke, and one doesn't joke with God. . .. It can happen to us to dream in colour and sometimes in black and white, but never in CinemaScope". There were worries that this wider ratio would make films look too theatrical. Steven Roberts writes:

> "It was supposed that fewer cuts would be necessary to maintain continuity as the camera could capture actors moving dynamically within an expanded area from a fixed perspective, as a theatregoer typically views the stage. The close-up, it was predicted, would become less common as the human face now appeared larger in scale and would be plainly visible. Shot scales would therefore be recalibrated, using more distant shots for dialogue in widescreen tableau."[111]

I could say 'Amen' to that in many respects and Welles' comment about not dreaming in 'scope' resonates about what I have to say about cinema resembling dreams. But resemblance is not exact identity. Such films as I mention above gain by filling the visual field of the viewer, especially horizontally. I would respond to Welles by pointing out that the dream aspect of the cinematic mage can be enlarged when the story and subject demand. The physical size and scale of the image fits the magnificence of the spectacle under construction. I am inclined to think that anyone who has seen the two films mentioned on a television only (or even at a cinema not equipped to show them in their original photographic processes – or close to) has not seen these films at all. One has done no more, as my brother likes to put it, "monitored their progress".

Filmmakers had to learn how to use 'scope' properly, to be sure – and did. There was a time when the 'widescreen' techniques, especially those in the so-called 'scope ratio' were reserved for the bigger, lusher spectacles. Now, however, this ratio is used all over the place. We can see too much of value in the ratio to pay heed to the above worries. Wide ratio films can be just as cinematic as those of narrower ratio. Nonetheless, different kinds of subject call for different ratios and the wider ratio's essentially different visual dynamic has nowadays become too much abused or ignored. What is visually suited to desert, ocean and battle is now frequently used – and just to rub salt in the wounds, replete with close-ups – in the most intimate of dramas. Too often even the demands of picture composition remain unobserved but even when they are (even carefully) considered, using the scope screen should not be used by default. Its unique psychological, even physiological, features and opportunities are just too special. Using them in an inappropriate context, even when one has composed the picture carefully, is an affront to cinematic space and how *that* space is supposed to match the psychological demands of the story. Different ratios demand different dynamics. It no good using the 'scope' ratio in a documentary style or with just too much handheld camera movement. Extra width demands greater steadiness at the tiller. The visual needs of the story should never be ignored, nor the visual dynamics of ratio violated.

It is not that the scope ratio should be exclusively reserved for the grand but there should be a narrative need. Here are two examples. In the days of the British 'new wave' in the early 1960s, mostly about working-class domestic stories, one notable film nonetheless came in scope: *Billy Liar* (John Schlesinger, UK, 1963). This was set not in the desert of Jordan or in ancient Rome but in a northern town. It starred (among others) Wilfred Pickles not Charlton Heston. Nonetheless, the story called out for scope, for it was also set in Billy's imaginary world, something too big for his boots and his character, if not his fancy. Scope captured his fantasy world of 'Ambrosia' perfectly. Standard narrower ratios typified most of the rest of this group of films. (Though, by this time, the narrower still 'academy ratio' had disappeared.) One can never stiffen too much any rule of cinema for such an attitude would blindly rule out too much inventiveness and thus too many good films, but I do think that the demands of the story to be told should be observed. All other things flow out of these. A motto: "Story first, shape second." To think in reverse here is to invite narrative distortion and cinematic obesity. Even the now common modest widescreen ratio of 1.85:1 (midway between the old academy ratio and 'scope') is still too wide for many story purposes, I believe. It makes it more awkward to frame a face, for starters and compositionally it is neither tight enough (as is the academy ratio) for some purposes, nor, unlike scope, expansive enough for others. It is far too easy to forget composition and leave image elements all over the place. I would say that is lamentably common, though the greater directors, such as Hitchcock, once used the mid-range ratio of 'VistaVision' very effectively – as in his *North by Northwest* (US, 1959). I welcome the more recent comeback of the 'academy' and other narrower ratios, though filmmakers almost need to re-learn how to use them appropriately.

The sin of merely photocopying physical space

I have already said quite a bit in this book about space and will have more to say about the sin of what I call the 'photocopying' reality approach to filmmaking later on. Here I want to explore more the sin of photocopying real, physical space – just as it supposedly *is*. Real physical space together with its tightly defined geometrical perspective is certainly what is in front of the film camera, but we acknowledged earlier that it also has a psychological force. Because of what I have described as the 'strangeness' of the space in a cinematic image (see Chapter 1) the latter has the potential for its own special kind of psychological impact. The bland photo-reproduction of the physical space in front of the camera misses out on all this. (In fact, missing out the special potential of the cinematic image, a potential born of its very nature, in the blind copying of ordinary perception is at the bottom of many of the sins revealed in this book. Art is never just reality, nor ought it aspire to be a mere copy of it. It's a special kind of perspective on reality and should convey its own unique insights.)

I think the world of art once knew this better than it does now. In fact the danger, if not yet quite the rot, set in as far back as the 15th century in Florence, when architect Filippo Brunelleschi famously showed the world his "demonstrations" of linear perspective. Before artists came to master (or perhaps be mastered *by*) the geometry of optical perspective, they were freer to represent the objects and characters in their art in more psychologically flexible ways. The significance of what we saw was not constrained by optical perspective. To the extent that a film is photographic one can argue that it is necessarily so constrained. But then there is that awkward 'strangeness' of the resulting image, and its resulting power to reveal more than ordinary perception ever can. The cinematic image is never delivering reality in the ways of ordinary worldly perception. Rather, it is revealing dimensions of that reality by employing the powers of its own built-in imagination, though under (hopefully) the vision of the filmmaker. This imagination transforms how we see the objects in the image – or at least, it ought to if it is to do what art can do best.

Fortunately for art, the restrictions didn't last forever. In painting, Picasso showed us how space could be used imaginatively, and in cinema, Alfred Hitchcock comes readily to mind. Take his famous shower scene in *Psycho* (US, 1960). If the viewer of this shocking event were a fly on the wall merely witnessing what was taking place, they would almost surely feel shocked by the brutality and the sheer horror of it all (taking it to be real). But the filmgoer sees more. The cinematic image makes visible what is invisible to the witness of the real event because it requires reflective imagination to do the trick. Blood and water swirl in frightful eddies. The knife is seen splitting through the space. The pulled down curtain is the undoing, through imaginative visual space, of the victim that somehow completes the sad course of her own earlier crime. All these things fill our specially stimulated imaginative awareness of space. Both witnessing the real thing and watching the film are nightmares, but the added dimensions of the cinematic image give point and insight to the nightmare one experiences that just wouldn't be there for the real witness. Both witness and filmgoer are shocked but the latter offers no mere shock, it is shock held in a kind of reflection, and this gives the filmgoer value-added insight into what has happened. The filmgoer has a *gaze* upon the horror; the witness merely sees it happen. The special gaze experienced by the viewer of the film is aided by the film's imaginative use of space. Hitchcock does this in many places – in the dark spaces of Uncle Charlie's face in his *Shadow of a Doubt* (US, 1943), and the spaces in his *Vertigo* are filled in Scottie's obsession. I consciously came upon this special kind of use of space in 1961 when I saw William Wyler's *Ben-Hur* (US, 1959). As Christ is crucified the wide screen space is filled with a river of water washing away the blood that humanity has spilled. There, space somehow fills and serves our strongest spiritual sensibilities. In general, the space in the best of films serves the psychology and the insight; in ordinary worldly perception space merely contains what happens. Seeking to photocopy the latter is a considerable sin in visually blander, supposedly more authentic films. It becomes an authenticity that conveys less of reality not more. The bland photocopying reality has been a visual turn in the history of cinema that has done no favour for deeper levels of realism, for cinema is no *mere* window or mirror, and no more is it a mere branch or kind of virtual reality. Cinema should transform our perception of space not merely repeat it.

The sins of time & length

How long is *too* long?

How long should a film be? It seems simply arbitrary to propose a limit. A typical feature films these days may be around two hours long. In earlier days they used typically to be shorter. It's a question of what customers feel is value for money. In olden days a visit to the cinema would include a 'B' feature (around an hour long) a cartoon, perhaps, and a newsreel as well as the usual ads, trailers and, of course, the 'main' feature. The length of each part of this 'programme' usually had to be limited to fit into an evening's cinema-going. There have always been exceptions, though. In the 'silent' era we have Abel Gance's *Napoleon* (France, 1927). In 1939, came *Gone With the Wind* (Victor Fleming, US) and in 1959 William Wyler's *Ben-*

Hur (US), all weighing in at several hours. Indeed, some of the most popular films ever made in the 1950s and 60s, were the 'big epics' and sumptuous musicals – pretty well all long films.

The answer to my opening question must be, presumably, that the story be allowed to dictate the length of the film – an epic story dictating an epic length. Put at its simplest – the longer the story, the longer the film. But perhaps this is just a bit *too* simple. The demands of the story cannot, all by themselves, justify the length of the finished product. The story itself still has to be told *well* and with decent degree of narrative efficiency. If one is justifiably bored by a film it simply doesn't matter how long it is, one will either leave the cinema or wish its time to be over. (As I grow older, and feel I have less time left, I tend to opt for the former.) In general, I would conclude that whether a film is too long (or even too short) depends on the demands *and* the quality of the story being told and how well it avoids the whole vast raft of other sins covered in this book. There are, however, other more specific areas to be considered and I now move on to these.

Torture on the rack or times of calm reflection: the sins of '*s l o w* cinema'

I have described a certain kind of camera motion (such as endless hand-held back-following) as 'cinematic laziness' and as indicating a certain lack of visual imagination (though it makes a film less expensive to make as well) but the same could be said of a certain kind of stillness. The camera will be firmly mounted and motionless for minutes on end, not untypically at medium range during a conversation, or worse still, shots will be stretched out - spaghettified - as though having fallen through the cinematic equivalent of a black hole, focused on a room say or some other location. The virtues of varying shots and in cutting between them seem frequently to be missing. The result: the serous loss of cinematic dynamic.. As we have seen, stillness *can* be good (as in Ozu) but one has to know what one is doing with it. It still needs a touch of magic to work well, otherwise it is like being stuck in concrete. The film *Ava* (Sadaf Foroughi, Iran, 2020) a politically important film seems to me a textbook example of this specific failure. In short, too many of its shots are (visually) almost endlessly tedious. It is the cinematic equivalent of listening to a good story being told by someone with a monotonous voice. This is the cinema of politics to be sure but the cinema of politics is still supposed to be *cinema*. Why this is not recognised more than it is by reviewers shows only, I want to say, just how far we have gone along with sheer laziness and even incompetence in film making. Peter Bradshaw writing in *The Guardian*, for example, judges, "Ava is made with superb technique and real style." Sometimes it does work here, to be sure – it's almost inevitable that some still half-alive remains will float – but not to the extent that Bradshaw suggests.

Torture on the rack is becoming all too common in serious cinema, these days. It seems to stem from a phenomenon called 'slow cinema'. 'Slow cinema' has in recent times become something of a darling of the art-house crowds but it is surprisingly difficult to pin it down in a handy definition. Given that one's perception of just how 'slow' a film may be varies a good deal, this is hardly surprising. There do seem to be some general characteristics at play, though. It has been said that slow cinema "revels in stillness and quietude", that "characters are developed through movement and actions more than dialogue", that it makes heavy use of static, long duration shots, and slow pans which have a "narrative focus on the more mundane aspects of life". "Situations are frequently shown in long shot, allowing the audience to rove around the frame, not necessarily focusing on the protagonists".[112]

All this seems to constitute an accurate enough description of slow cinema and may elicit some approval, but of course, mere description does not, all by itself, provide a justification. Are the mundane aspects of life, for instance, always relevant, and even if they are, how much focussing on do they need? We need to *see* the mundane nature of events, not personally *endure* them. Many films have these characteristics occasionally and to some extent but seem also to be aware of reasonable limits. Black-hole type spaghettification seems to me to be beyond such limits – in cinema as in space travel. There are, of course, entirely one-take films (or *fake* one-take films) but which are not slow in any extreme sense: *Rope* (Alfred Hitchcock, US, 1948) *Russian Ark*, (Aleksandr Sokurov, Russia, 2002) and *1917* (Sam Mendes, US, 2019). But vagueness is, perhaps, inevitable given that the epithet 'slow' will depend on how an entire film holds together rather than its satisfying some arbitrary limit on time and speed.

Directors such as the Hungarian Bela Tarr and Nuri Bilge Ceylan from Turkey come readily to mind as primarily makers of slow cinema but others partake, either by diving headlong into it in particular films, as did Alfonso Cuaron in his *Roma* or by dipping into the idea to some extent, as arguably does Claire Denis in her *High Life* (France, 2018). I will illustrate my concerns with slow cinema by considering two acclaimed cases: *Roma* (Alfonso Cuaron, US & Mexico, 2018) and *Uncle Boonmee Who Can Recall His Past Lives* (Apichatpong Weerasethakul, Thailand, 2010).

While *Roma* is made up of parts which are too long, and *is* thus too long, at least it is, mercifully, not overly long as a feature film. *Roma*, though, is a case of 'slow cinema'. I must be blunt. This film is probably the longest stretch of yawning, self-indulgent tedium to which I have ever borne witness. Although it is not overly long in clock-time, weighing in at around 2 hours 15 minutes, this film makes coronavirus lockdown seem short. Every shot, just about, is racked out until long after it has made its point. Yes, there are evocative moments of tenderness and it gets across the kinds of injustices that are faced. (So did *Chambermaid*, another recent similarly themed Mexican film (Lila Avilés, 2018) and much more efficiently.) It is about a year in the life of a middle-class family's maid in Mexico City in the early 1970s. Cuaron has said it is '90 per cent from my own memories'. All the same, notice the stunningly obvious: the Emperor Cuaron simply has no clothes here. Perhaps it is supposed to be the cinematic equivalent of Proust, but apart from my suspicion that no such thing is possible, it fails here altogether and dies luxuriantly while still in what it takes to be the prime of its life. It consists purely of a series of still photographs that just about manage to move around – like over thick custard. It's a cinematic sin against time and motion, a gorgeously photographed, wide format, B&W bore. In response to the whole movement of slow cinema I utter a simple reminder – a film should be 'well-tempered' (nicely timed) just like good music and good instruments. This allows for considerable variety in both shot length and running time, but once the timing is out, wherever that point may be found, the film is lost.

But why no Proust? I take this simply to reflect the difference in function between sentences and pictures: both can evoke, suggest, haunt or just plain bore, but while sentences *describe*, pictures *show*. Moreover, no matter what depth of description our sentences may convey, they will always be limited. More description is always possible. We can always take almost endless stretches of well enough written, pertinent description. Showing, in contrast, presents us with equivalent amounts of information *all at once* or at least over much shorter periods of time. Of course, a picture may limit showing as well: a black and white image, for example, is silent as to the real colour of things. Nonetheless, a few seconds of even black and white imagery in a film can show more than even a whole page of written description. It's just the nature of the medium. This suggests that playing the cinematic Proust is an impossibility and it further suggests that trying it on is ill-advised. One has to understand how differently words and pictures resonate in our minds and how much mental and emotional space they respectively take up. Slow cinema treats showing too much like written description in this respect and hence, in some sense, fails to be cinema at all.

Uncle Boonmee is the story of a man who lays in his death-bed having mystical experiences and visions of bizarre visitations from the dead. Yes, it is infused with a certain magic but we are left too much to contemplate our own navels in its telling. Both of these films were favourites of the 'art-house' specialists and reviewers whose priority seems too often just to seem 'cool' and 'with it', but I suspect that they admire the *wrong* qualities. Good photography, even when almost transcendent, as it is in both films, is not itself great cinema, and inward-looking navel-gazing is not motion as cinema knows it.

None of this means that cinema cannot successfully convey memory, longing, nostalgia and the like in a dwelling, evocative manner. Ceylan films, in large part, do that. Cinema can also convey almost mystical states, too, as it did in *Poetry* (Chang-dong Lee, South Korea 2010) – a film about an ageing woman who takes to writing poetry during oncoming dementia, and *Departures* (Yôjirô Takita, Japan, 2008) about a redundant cellist who takes a job with an undertaker preparing the bodies of recently deceased. The best of far eastern films often reflect slow, quietly respectful ways to life's issues, encouraged by the religious and cultural traditions of the region. If Ozu was still directing, his films would be declared 'slow cinema' in this sense. Ingmar Bergman's films are often in some sense slow, as well, but they also do a great deal of psychological work.

Contemporary slow cinema is occasionally defended, rather sneakily, by appeal to these kinds of directors. Such defence, though, often seems based on the failure to observe the essential distinction between the psychological demands of the story being told and sheer slowness just for the mere sake of dwelling on things. We all know how pathological the latter can easily become. One simply cannot justify either torture on the rack or sheer self-indulgent emptiness and tedium by appealing to films that, while maybe being in *some* way slow, are nonetheless masterpieces of fullness and deeper motion. *Mirror* (Andrei Tarkovsky, Russia, 1975) invokes childhood memories, like Cuaron's film, and it is full of slow, haunting, dreamlike interiority and motion. Like Cuaron's film it is also loosely autobiographical, but while Tarkovsky pushes at cinema's extremes (here and elsewhere) he never seems to do so with such self-indulgent excess as Cuaron. *Mirror*, is a saint; *Roma* a sinner. Give us *too* long with a single cinematic image (not necessarily just one shot, remember) and we begin to get restless. There can be a perfectly proper cinema *of* slowness without the sort of thing that gets called 'slow cinema'.

This may seem paradoxical because we can happily stand (never mind even the comfort of being seated) in front of a great painting and contemplate *it* for much longer. This, however, simply reflects the different demands of the two media. The painting much more calls on its viewer to provide the context surrounding what we see. The cinematic image, because it has motion (even if only in the wider sense of that term) provides more of its own context. The latter involves us in a different kind of way also precisely because of its photographic realism. Though we are not quite there, in the action of the picture, we are looking at the action in a way closer to ordinary perception than is the case with painting and its ilk. Cinematic seeing is (in a way again difficult to pin down) imaginary seeing, as is a painting but it is a very different kind of imaginary seeing. Because the job of the cinematic image is to show (visually reveal) things that we then see imaginatively, my conclusion is that, while a cinematic image can take its time, a director can dice with death if it is overdone. Moreover, we must not lose sight of the rather simple and obvious fact that while we can always choose for ourselves how long to look at a painting, the film-viewer alas is not the one who can shout, "Cut!". Another difference is this: contemplation in reading and looking at a painting (or even a photograph) can be enjoyed *during* the acts of reading and looking, but contemplation of a cinematic image seems more suited for afters. This seems precisely because cinema involves motion in the way that reading and seeing a still picture do not. But if cinema essentially involves motion then motion (in some sense) there had better be. If it is insufficient, in *any* sense, as it often is in slow cinema, then something is going badly wrong.

Slow cinema has also been justified by claiming it to be some sort of antidote to an otherwise constant focus on frenetic, brain fragmenting motion, as Russell recommends:

> "People are searching for ways to escape the fast pace of the modern world and our constant connectivity. Why not find it by relishing the moments of stillness, the static shots of landscapes, the experience of ordinary people living ordinary lives, found in slow cinema."[113]

This appeal for adequate rest periods during a busy working-life, though, seems just feeble. As we have seen, plenty of films that move more readily than the congealed gravy of slow cinema do that. Take *Waltz With Bashir* (Ari Folman, Israel, 2008). It involves haunting memory even *as* it simultaneously keeps up the action. It tells the story of a soldier as he copes with nightmares, memories and unresolved feelings brought on by his teenage experiences in the 1982 Lebanon War. We must never embrace the simplistic equation: haunting, lingering memory and / or static landscapes = slow telling.

Slow cinema, especially when combined with a heavy-duty running time does, though, raise a question not thought about too much. That is, how legitimate is watching a film in episodes. Long films have often (historically) come with built-in intermissions (though this seems regrettably to be ignored these days in theatrical showings - a sin, we might say, of film exhibitors). When I recently saw the restoration of Gance's Napoleon, though, it came with *three* intermissions one of which was long enough for a meal in the establishment's own café (it was a special showing). When I recently saw *Gone With The Wind* at home I did so over two evenings. So, why not take slow cinema in chunks? I'm not convinced that this is the answer, though. It may help both to take it less painfully and appreciate more of its approach but it would still fail to address its central sin – that of going against the nature of the cinematic image. Besides, they still take up "great swathes of our precious time", as Nick James (being critical of slow cinema) said in *Sight & Sound* (February 2010). Moreover, the problem with much slow cinema is not total runtime in any case.

Another lurking sin is that slow cinema seems as contagious as the coronavirus. I do not think that I exaggerate more than a tad in judging that pretty well almost every other film I see these days (in the art-house context at least) has, to some degree, caught the infection – the symptoms are just too obvious, though sometimes I am left with the impression that the directors just don't know whether or not to go the whole hog. Looking on the brighter side, at least Bela Tarr's imagery looks beautiful. Indeed, the imagery in his *The Turin Horse* (Hungary, 2011) is nothing short of transcendent. It would have made a great short but alas weighed in at over two and a half hours. Its imagery, including its use of time and space, is beautifully dream-like even though one wants to wake up far sooner than the film allows. However, so many directors of 'art-house' pulp these days seem to have caught on to the notion of slow cinema even though their imagery, and cinema in general, is simply tedious. The techniques of slow cinema are used, quite unthinkingly, as though they constituted a suitable default position. This seems sinful whatever one's wider judgment may be on more full-blown slow cinema.

Cinematic participation and the sins of navel-gazing

I have discussed critically the tendency of slow cinema to focus on the mundane aspects of life. Associated with this are episodes of what is often called 'navel-gazing'. These are often somewhat morose and perhaps rather unhelpful episodes of over-focus on the grimmer features of our lives and, at worst, times when we can see 'no way out'. We humans may indulge in navel-gazing every now and again, of course, and sometimes characters in films must legitimately reflect this. But we may ask how a properly cinematic depiction of such episodes should go. What does the viewer need to take in?

The answer: firstly, and most obviously, the fact *that* a character is navel-gazing. But, of course, we also need to participate cinematically in their feelings and lives – and fully so. But cinematic participation ought not to be an endurance test. We do not need to *share* in the navel-gazing but rather (and again) be *shown* it. Should we even get the 'full monty'? Sure! In some sense we need to get inside the character, but we do not need to go full-time with them. Exactly what cinematic participation and its many modes is, in a broad sense, is what this book can be taken to be all about. Briefly, it concerns the ways in which we engage with reality *through* the cinematic image. On our present matter, though, we may note that edited highlights (perhaps in this case 'lowlights' may be better) is one aspect of such participation. These give us *all* we need to capture and feel the weight of a character's episode of navel-gazing. We need to empathise in response to the character's mournful contemplation and hopelessness, not altogether join in. I rather think that traditional *noir* did this best. In the lesser known noir film *Detour* (Edgar G. Ulmer, US, 1945) we have a case of almost an entire film (though of 'B' picture length) devoted to a study in the navel-gazing of its main character. We sympathise, we empathise, we 'get inside', and we understand – as fully as we ever can without our own lives suffering similar misfortune. Yet, we still have a cutting edge. We still have cinematic motion – not all that fast, but detectable all the same – and that motion takes us places. Cinema is a special kind of depiction of life, one which gives us 'cinematic participation', not (remember) a mere and tedious photocopy of it. The latter simply tends to make it look as though the filmmaker, like the character, just has no idea where to go or what to do next, so just serves up more mogadon.

The sins of heavy weather and wasting cinematic time

Associated with torture on the rack are the sins of making heavy weather of things. Too much serious cinema in our age suffers from this. The filmmaker wants to make a film about a serious subject. Fine, so they should. The characters live difficult and deprived lives full of problems, victimisation and even despair, tedium at the least, violence at the worst. Their lives lack any hint of love and care (or they have lives where these things go wrong). Their lives are heavy-duty, industrial-strength stretches of sheer toxic misery. Well, we all know that things can be just that way for many. What is less clear is why life should be that way for a viewer of the films. Is it that the viewer should *share* the misery through the medium? What does that achieve? It might 'raise our consciousness' of some issue, I suppose but it will have had little impact if we leave the cinema bored stiff.

In any case, a representation should never be confused with what is represented by it. Life has been 'nasty, brutish and short' for too many throughout all history. For centuries art has properly represented that aspect of life, but the art itself has been exciting, adventurous, vibrant, or at the very least visually interesting. It has also been sensitive to its subject matter, conveying what needs to be conveyed. Too many of today's filmic explorations of misery fail to convey the misery with soul-engaging vibrancy because they too tediously immerse themselves in the misery they represent rather than take the trouble of standing at a suitable aesthetic distance from it, even though, recall, cinema, by its very nature, calls out for this space to be exploited. Sympathy and engagement simply give way to boredom. In that way, such films fail even to invoke sufficient sympathy.

Some contemporary films do offer some kind of interesting visual engagement. The Russian films *Leviathan* (2014) and *Loveless* (2017) by director Andrey Zvyagintsev express wonderfully the massive corruption of business in Russia and the unloved life of a child who goes missing. It isn't that life's heavy-duty-ness in these cases is given a light touch or is merely sentimentalised, but that it comes with a certain visual beauty. The Japanese director Hirokazu Koreeda also can weave a lovely cinematic story of sad human issues. At one time beautiful films about serious subjects used to be far more common (if not exactly weekly). They include many of the films from the British and French 'new waves' made in the late 50s and early 60's. Post war Hollywood had *On The Waterfront* (Elia Kazan, US, 1954) and other Kazan films. All had a vibrancy and life of their own. Now too many serious films seem like merely dull, lifeless photocopies of the difficult lives of their characters. The shots do nothing, or too little, and seem to last too long. Their cinematic time is wasted.

Barry Salt has said of editing that it should aim at, "what a spectator before the scene would see, standing there and casting his glance from this point to that point within it."[114] This, I think, may be a good rule of thumb, it can often make things acceptable visually. Alas, I fear that it can also make for easier, less imaginative film making. We should never merely accommodate some dull, hard replica of a dull, hard life. That is, in the end, a kind of *dis*respect. The cinematic image is made to enable us to witness harshness and brutality with passionate engagement and help us gain a longing for a world in which the suffering will no longer be. Failure in this endeavour is not just aesthetic, it is moral. Instead of developing the right emotions and thoughts, we simply want the film to end. Ugliness needs beauty in its depiction, so that the ugliness can be seen, clearly and uncompromisingly, as the absence of beauty.

The sins of editing: *Cutting sights*

Editing is important. Orson Welles was moved to say, with his customary heavy-duty emphasis, "The notion of directing a film is the invention of critics - the whole eloquence of cinema is achieved in the editing room." Director Francis Ford Coppola says, "The essence of cinema is editing. It's the combination of what can be extraordinary images of people during emotional moments, or images in a general sense, put together in a kind of alchemy."[115] This real mystery of film editing, as famed editor Walter Murch observes, is that it works at all. He says of film editing that, "it represents a total and instantaneous displacement of one field of vision with another, a displacement that sometimes also entails a jump forward or backward in time as well as space".[116] This reminds us of just what an *unnatural* thing cinema really is and is yet another strong reason to think that an over degree of naturalism goes against its nature.

Yet, it does work and the way in which a film is cut or edited is crucial. It can make obvious differences to pace and storytelling. Good editing may save a film even, if only just, from being bad so that it ends up being merely mediocre, but it can also give a good film some extra life and charge. Decisions are legion when it comes to deciding just what is to make it into the final film. What about a simple conversation? Does a scene concentrate on the character who is talking or the one who is reacting – or both (as is fairly standard)? If the latter, when do you cut? If a character is revealing with their face what they see, how much of what the character is seeing needs to be shared with the audience? Keeping things hidden can also be very effective. (See the Lean example below.) An editor must know when to hang on (given the footage) as well as when to cut. It has been observed that the final cut of a film is also, in some sense, the final rewrite. Of course, the film editor needs sufficient filmed material to work on. A big part of the director's job is to make sure that this is the case. But editing can also have some more subtle effects – especially on the emotion conveyed by a performance.

There is a well-known phenomenon called the 'Kuleshov Effect' which illustrates this. Lev Kuleshov (1899-1970) was a Russian filmmaker and theorist of cinema. He became fascinated by the effects conveyed by the way in which shots are juxtaposed. In 1921, Kuleshov set up a cinematic demonstration which gave the phenomenon its name. In this demonstration, the film showed the face of a well-known actor. It cuts to a plate of food. This is followed by a shot of the same face followed by a girl in a coffin. Finally, we see again the actor's face followed by a shot of an attractive young woman. Audiences thought that the actor conveyed, most subtly, hunger, sorrow and lust. What a remarkable performance. And so it was but it was not acting talent that did it. It was simply the arrangement of shots. The shot of the man's face was the same each time round. Here, the editor is, in some sense, the actor.

That was a simple experiment and, of course, it would be a non-sequitur to assume that the actor has nothing to do with such effects in films generally. Kuleshov's own footage is lost, though the experiment has been repeated. The expression on the actor's face, arguably, must also not be too expressive, in order to leave maximum potential for the editing to do the job. Nevertheless, that editing affects one's perception of a performance can hardly be denied. One hardly knows what is possible until one gets in the cutting room. I recall David Lean once commenting that he received some complaints that he should never have shown the hanging in his *Great Expectations* (UK, 1946). In fact, he didn't. Here we have pretty well the opposite of the Kuleshov effect. The camera remains on John Mills' face all through. The audience merely felt that they had witnessed the hanging courtesy of Mills's acting. Lean pulled off a similar trick in his *Doctor Zhivago* (Italy/UK/US, 1965). Armed cavalry charge a defenceless mob. One sees a few items being dropped but one witnesses most of the massacre through the face of actor Omar Sharif.

What constitutes good editing has been the subject of some impressive treatises. Walter Murch proposed a 'rule of six', saying of a good cut that it must: (1) be true to the emotion of the moment, (2) advance the story, (3) occur at a moment that is rhythmically interesting and right, (4) acknowledge what you might call "eye-trace"

-the concern with the location and movement of the viewer's focus of interest within the frame, (5) respect "planarity" - the grammar of three dimensions transposed by photography to two (the questions of stage-line, etc.) and (6) respect the three-dimensional continuity of the actual space (where people are in the room and in relation to one another)."[117] Things can get confusing if these things go wrong. Emotion Murch places at the top of the list. The integrity of emotion in the story must be maintained at all costs. Again we see the necessity of the needs of the story ruling the roost.

More classically, the Hollywood director Edward Dmytryk outlined some rules of editing:

Rule 1: NEVER make a cut without a positive reason."

Rule 2: When undecided about the exact frame to cut on, cut long rather than short." [stay on the previous shot longer].

Rule 3: Whenever possible cut 'in movement'. [It makes the cut seem less obtrusive].

Rule 4: The 'fresh' is preferable to the 'stale'.

Rule 5: All scenes should begin and end with continuing action.

Rule 6: Cut for proper values rather than proper 'matches'.

Rule 7: Substance first—then form.[118]

One can have a bit of intellectual fun matching this list with Murch's. For Dmytryk it made editing less obtrusive and pretty well invisible – it still had its effects but it worked quietly in the background serving the story and not drawing attention to itself. In general, it is instructive for the interested filmgoer to understand the ways in which films are assembled and have a good grip on how this can profoundly affect the psychology of a film. Viewers may also benefit also from an understanding of the varied approaches to film editing across the world and throughout the history of cinema. It is good to be acquainted with a knowledge of montage, 'invisible' editing (as Dmytryk's Hollywood editing style is called) and editing for symbolism, to understand how editing a scene can give the audience a sense of the 'geography' of a scene and the psychology of the situation and characters, to develop an awareness of the suggestive powers of editing and the relationship between editing and the progression of time within the narrative.

A director, too, needs to understand the needs of editing, where and when to use 'continuity editing' (where shots are assembled in a transparent, temporally linear flow of uninterrupted action) and not make itself too visible to the viewer, when to cross-cut or use an establishing shot (to show location) or a cutaway. The latter can be used to collapse the flow of time as tension builds or to establish context. The Japanese director Ozu famously uses so-called 'pillow shots' for this latter purpose. In the middle of a family drama he will show, say, the street outside, composed in serene beauty. This establishes the environment of the characters and reveals their wider living space. However, this sub-section of this present chapter cannot function as a general treatise on film editing. No doubt editing can be good, bad or indifferent in accordance with many of the criteria I have outlined. Here, though, my job is to reveal a range of defects (sins) that can be found in modern cinema.

Sins of *lack* of editing

A recent bad habit in too many films, as I made plain earlier, is to have a camera simply back-following a character around. This cuts down the sheer amount of cutting to be done and time spent on the imaginative effort of considering its effects. Alas, it also cuts down on the impact of the shot, often guaranteeing its absence altogether. It is all too often an example of what may be called 'ill-temperedness'.

It is a part of the capacity and the power of the cinematic image to move more freely around time and space. While there is a place for extensive camera movement and even entire one-shot films, as we have seen, to use it simply as a cheaper alternative to editing reduces the level of cinema involved. It also makes storytelling less efficient. Endless back-following shots force us to take in all kinds of detail and context that is irrelevant, or only partially relevant. We have already examined a sample or two of where it works and where it is simply tedious under 'The Sins of Movement'. Long takes, as we have seen, can also be cinematically valuable. In Ozu one has long but very measured shots which are replete with the motions of emotion. Editing can be open and free, as (along with the camerawork) as it is in much of Jean-Luc Godard. (His *Breathless* (France, 1960) – is a classic here.) It can be sharper and more biting and still measured and careful, as it is in, say, *Brighton Rock* (John Boulting, UK, 1948). It is a sin against the power and magic of cinema, though, to show a wilful disregard or plain ignorance of all that good editing can offer and it usually betokens an utter lack of visual imagination in storytelling. All it really achieves is a kind of egalitarian opening into filmmaking for those who should never be allowed behind a motion picture camera.

Sins of inappropriateness and lack of range

Transitions between shots used to be many and various: cuts, dissolves, wipes, fade-ins and outs and montage (under one of its meanings). All of these, apart from (traditionally and standardly, the cut) convey passage of time between two shots but they do so with different effects.

Cuts

Standardly these just shift our points of view. They can also convey what a character is looking at. Without any further ado, if the viewer sees, say, a shot of a character turning to face something and there is a cut to another person or object, one takes it that this is what the character sees. It can, however, be used more sharply and distinctively to convey the passage of time, even up to eons. The famous cut in *2001* (Stanley Kubrick, UK/US, 1968) does this as we witness the transition between a bone, having been thrown into the air by an excited ape-creature, to a spacecraft in orbit around the Earth. It pointedly poses the question of whether human-kind ever really changes in its need to explore (either peacefully or aggressively). Equally famously, in David Lean's *Lawrence of Arabia* (UK, 1962) we have the cut from Lawrence blowing out a match (which echoes some meaning about his character from an earlier part of the film) to the opening scene in the desert.

> "We marked a dissolve, but when we watched the footage in the theater, we saw it as a direct cut," [Editor Anne V. Coates told Justin Chang in *FilmCraft: Editing*]. "David and I both thought, 'Wow, that's really interesting.' So we decided to nibble at it, taking a few frames off here and there." Ultimately, Coates only had to remove two frames to satisfy the perfectionist director.[119]

Such cuts are called 'match cuts' because the two shots cut together are matched by some action or subject matter. In the example from *Lawrence of Arabia* Lawrence's lighted match, which he famously blows out, is instantly replaced by the rising sun, soon to burn, in the desert. Match cuts have been used elsewhere. Michael Powell and Emeric Pressburger use one similar to that in *2001* in their *A Canterbury Tale* (UK, 1944) A shot of a fourteenth-century falcon cuts to an aeroplane during the Second World War. It makes, of course, a similar point. In Satyajit Ray's film, *The World of Apu* (India, 1959) we have a cut between a cinema screen, which two characters are watching, to the window of the carriage in which they are going home. A particularly suggestive match cut can be seen at the end of Alfred Hitchcock's *North by Northwest* (US, 1959). Cary Grant pulls Eva Marie Saint up from a cliff edge at Mount Rushmore and there is a cut to him pulling her up to his bunk on the train. One can have match-dissolves, too. Watch the opening of Orson Welles' *Citizen Kane* (US, 1949). A small lighted window in Kane's palace is kept in the same position on screen through a series of dissolves spanning various parts of his now decaying estate, showing that what once shone powerfully is coming to an inevitable end. This is cinema that calls for speechless, even weeping admiration, as is the entire tale that follows in this film.[120]

The match cut, though it conveys a kind of jump, should not be confused with the common or garden 'jump cut'. The former conveys (often a kind of symbolic) continuity; the latter conveys *dis*continuity. Jump cuts seem ubiquitous nowadays. One is enjoying a shot (perhaps of a decision for future action) then there is a jump to a later time to a shot *of* that future action, sometimes with the sound in the second shot coming a second or so before the picture. We have seen that editing, according to Edward Dmytryk, should be pretty well pretty well invisible to the audience. It should still have its effects but it should work quietly in the background serving the story and not drawing attention to itself. There is merit in this for the simple reason that it is the story being told that really matters. Technique matters only insofar as it serves the story. The jump cut, in contrast, draws much attention to itself. I think it would be a hopeless exaggeration to conclude from all this that that jump cuts are *necessarily* bad. (Pretty well no technique is. The criterion is how well and appropriately they are used.) The jump cut has been around since cinema's early days. The early French director Georges Méliès uses the jump cut in some 'trick' shots. Though Dmytryk's continuity and invisibility thesis came to rule classical Hollywood (the style that ruled most popular cinema) the jump cut was used in the French 'new wave' in the early sixties, most notably by Godard in his film *Breathless*, mentioned above.

The technique can be fruitful if only because it keeps the pace going and serves storytelling efficiency. It can also amplify the tension in a series of shots and build up narrative momentum. Mike Bedard, illustrates some examples of these and other good uses of jump cuts in these ways.[121] He mentions Guy Ritchie's crime thriller *Snatch* (UK, 2000) in which he uses jump cuts as a hyper-efficient way of introducing us to new characters. Compare this with two other famous crime films from different ages of cinema in which a number of participants have to be introduced. In *The Italian Job* (Peter Collinson, UK, 1969) each character is introduced in a comedic yet still reasonably sharp way, and in *The League of Gentlemen* (Basil Dearden, UK, 1960) this process is more measured yet still sharp. The sheer ubiquity of the jump cut, though, illustrates how films have become generally more frenetic and perhaps explains in part the proliferation of the exaggeratedly slower forms of cinema that we discussed earlier. When there was no toxin, one required no antidote.

However, the jump cut can so readily become a bad idea when it simply confuses a viewer, especially when used to link two shots whose narrative connection is far from obvious. These days, one can feel as though one is being merely dazzled by the technique – and being left confused rather than having proceedings kept clear. The jump cut seems obviously to be a bad idea unless there is a very good narrative or psychological reason for it. The sin, then? What is good for some specific purposes is no good at all for others. Almost certainly, if it used too much as standard practice for far too many transitions, the chances are that it will be used inappropriately. Why should it be pretty well standard practice nowadays? Surely, the earlier methods better suit various subjects. The question of how characters are introduced is key in storytelling, and the virtues and sins of various methods belong to a discussion of storytelling as much as to editing specifically, but jump cuts have become far too commonplace it seems to me.

Dissolves

Dissolves are made by overlapping one shot with another. They can convey the passage of time or, in the case of *Citizen Kane*, above, the surveying of things within a single space. Dissolves do not appear to be used much nowadays. Partly this may be due to their giving rise to momentary colour clashes on the screen. They were more popular in the classic days of black and white where this was not a problem. Mainly, though, the change seems stylistically driven. Cuts can be used instead, and while they may involve a rather jarring jump, they are simply sharper. Often one feels that this is what the filmmaker wants, so it may seem justified enough.

This is a pity, though. Dissolves can jolly a film along in a gentler manner. They are less 'in-yer-face'. They almost say, "Just sit back and enjoy it, we are moving along as fast as is required". If gentler films are not what is wanted, then precisely *that* would be the sin. One shouldn't always *want* sharp-edged suddenness. Isn't there a part of life worth filming that just *is* gentler? Should not this be as encouraged as much as rawness? The lack of dissolves may seem to be a minor issue but I think it reflects a more serious fault line in modern culture, one that values no-nonsense grabbing and less consideration.

Wipes

Here the following shot replaces a previous shot in a swiping movement across the screen. The typical wipe will move from side to side, or maybe at an angle. There are variations. Wipes can come in various forms. In past cinematic ages they were common enough. A filmmaker could have fun with them, and the audience in taking them in. They could induce a slight, but not unpleasant, disorientation. They gave the impression of rush without a cutting edge, of youthful enthusiasm that is not simply induced by drugs. All this, of course, implies that their almost complete absence in today's films says something about what, these days, we think of as fun.

Fades

In fades, the present cinematic image slowly disappears into complete darkness and the following image slowly and gradually appears out of that darkness. There can, I believe, be a certain magic about that. Remember, a cinematic image is a rather magical entity. This is due, recall, to the fact to see the world through a photographically realistic motion picture is a strange and flexible business. To open and close this strangeness in the more easy-going manner of fades seems more to respect it, to say of it that it has a value to which we should doff our caps and approach (and leave) willingly but without undue haste.

Fades can vary in time. A good move would be to fade out slowly and respectfully at, say, the sadder end of one shot and fade in more quickly to the next, especially if it is supposed to bring in fresh hope – all without slicing through one's eyes with a cut. Really you filmmakers of today! The psychological possibilities of all the combinations are endless. Do use them! Some contemporary filmmakers can still use fades with proper effect. Quentin Tarantino does so in his *Pulp Fiction* (US, 1994). He fades out right after a car smash. This smash is not just part of a mad, cinematic rush, it has an effect on the lives of two of the film's characters. The fade gives the audience the time needed properly to digest such moments; the cut tells us that there is no time to think, that we must get on with the job. The ubiquitous use of the cut says something very different: "Don't bother thinking at all, my film couldn't withstand such scrutiny". Good filmmaking is rarely rocket science, but it very much depends upon having the visual imagination to perceive and convey psychological and narrative opportunities.

Classically, a whole film has faded in and faded out. Again, this is a gentler technique. It says, "Our story has ended, We hope you have enjoyed it. Thanks for coming but for now, goodbye – and remember, you are most welcome to our next film". Ending a film with a cut almost says, "We're done with you now, so you can just go away and think about it. I've been in your face and now you can get out of mine. I've got my next film to think about". O yes! Even something as simple as this has its psychological implications. It has its narrative implications, too. If one needs to end a story with the implication that the misery is to continue unabated, then by all means let us have the cruel cut. A cut rather than a fade in may also be appropriate to start a particular story. It can function as a sharp insertion into its world – as if one has just been ignominiously and violently dropped into it. It can say, "Take notice! You at the back of the cinema, pay attention!". This can, I suppose, be appropriate in limited contexts. In other contexts, though, let us have a more welcoming visual tone, and if the film ends on a more resolved note, let it say 'goodbye' nicely. Then I, for one, may indeed come and see your next film. Even using the closing caption announcing 'The End', now not standardly used (perhaps because there is still an hour or so of 'end credits' to come) can let us exit the story world more comfortably.

One has to be careful with fades, though, and here we come to what could too easily be a sin with older cinema. Used too frequently, the fade can slow things down just too much. They can make a film seem too episodic in contexts where this is hardly meritorious. In the over three and a half hours of running time of William Wyler's *Ben-Hur* (US, 1959) I do not think there is a single fade-in/fade-out (apart from the beginnings and endings of each of the two halves flanking the intermission). Wyler knew he had to keep up the momentum. Fades reduce momentum by their very cinematic nature. They should only be used when this is precisely what is needed by the narrative.

Montage

'Montage' means different things in different contexts. Here I mean it simply in the sense of being a sequence of shortish shots, often linked with quick dissolves and intended to condense time yet provide relevant information that links two major scenes. Classically, it was often used to convey a journey. In a musical of the 1930s, a theatrical troupe may be moving between American cities. The shots within the montage might well show the wheels of a steam train speeding down the track, the excitement in the 'cars', newspaper headlines announcing the arrival of the gang in the next city, and so on. These days the gang would be in New York in one shot and on stage in Chicago in the next - in one sudden cut. This is *not* (or not necessarily) efficiency in storytelling, it leaves out something we may need to know: the eagerness of the players, their tiredness after a long journey, and the expectation involved. Of course, we do not need to know any of the details of the journey (though sometimes, as in Billy Wilder's *Some Like It Hot* (US, 1959) we do) but we may well need to know the sort of thing I have just outlined. It's all a part of the overall story. Besides, it is important in setting a mood and tone, and inducing a sense of rhythm. Come on filmmakers, aren't these all highly cinematic matters? The montage sequence is one of the most versatile emotional tools in the editing suite – only dullards, or those so immovably serious, will leave it out. Yet left out it too often is. Another kind of montage has replaced it – the fast *cut* sequence of shots that come at the viewer like bullets from a cinematic machine gun. Again, this can have its place and be genuinely exciting but it has little else and certainly little charm.

The prevalence of the cut over these other transitions, as I have hinted, says as much about the kinds of films we are given and supposed to *want* as it does about style. Or, better, one should note that style itself reflects prevailing moods and attitudes in our culture. A constant preference for the cutting edge betokens, I want to suggest, something ugly at play in the human psyche – a kind of 'gimme it now, or else I'll cut you up' - and this spiritual ugliness is played out as much in the way films are put together as it is in other cinematic (and wider) ways. The general cinematic sin, though, is that filmmakers too much ignore the subtler powers of the wider range of transitions. No wonder that slow cinema is beginning to prevail in places. At least it can stop the world long enough for us to get off.

The almost total domination of the cut says something else, too – or is, at least a part of a bigger and more worrying thing about today's film world. I write of the polarisation of cinema into the popular, pop-corn fed, casual, BBQ'd trash of the multiplex and the constant drip feed of the heavy-duty, industrial-strength, 'grim tales of the grim' that grace what are called 'art-houses'. The latter very often really do call for more of the cruel cut, though perhaps not quite as constantly as we get it. The former calls for the cut only because it is dominated by the 'Marvel' culture and the latest in the 'Fast and Furious' franchise (or whatever the latest variants on these species may be). Pretty well gone are the days in which popular cinema – even from Hollywood – gave us some of the very finest cinema that was ever made: intelligent, witty, thoughtful, artful, rich, telling, perceptive, yet (often at least) still thoroughly entertaining and popular material. I mentioned one such above from Billy Wilder. Writers and directors who are that inventive, intelligent, wise and clever and yet endlessly entertaining – I think – scarcely even exist anymore – and the present-day economics of filmmaking, which seems to demand either rapid success or obscurity, doesn't help to nurture any. Certainly, though, that past films from directors of such cinematic genius can these days only, or at least mostly, be found in 'art houses', well away from the grasp of the appreciative but perhaps less knowledgeable film-goer, is discomforting and worrying. It is also deeply depressing for a lover of cinema. However, just now and again, I will then catch a little masterpiece, they can still be found, and I am encouraged.

Chapter 8: The Sins of Storytelling

The cinematic image, or at any rate a suitably related series of them, makes what we call a 'film'. A film is an ideal medium for telling a story. Storytelling is not an essential characteristic of a film because one could have a cinematic image, or continuous series of them without their having to tell a story. Nevertheless, unless one is creating something purely abstract, it is hard to think how any series of cinematic images can be related save through their telling a story, at least of sorts – fiction or non-fiction. Even abstract films can often be thought of as telling a story, even if it's no more than the story of a line walking across the screen in an interesting way. Even a single cinematic image, of a horse galloping, for example, presents us with a very simple story – the story of the galloping of that horse at that time. Storytelling, then, comes naturally to cinema.

Cinema, however, clearly opens up further obvious golden opportunities of storytelling. Even the very early exercise in cinematography by the Lumière brothers tells a story of sorts, though its viewers were probably far more fascinated by the sheer phenomenon of cinema than they were the very simple story the Lumière's were telling. Be that as it may, more interesting stories were not too far behind. Audiences like stories, and films, like books, that do *not* tell them are doomed to occupancy of a lower floor in the human heart. We are immersed in an engrossing story as in a dream (and maybe daydream). I have spoken of 'aesthetic distance' but it is precisely *that* distance, as if we see things through a kind of vacuum, that draws one closer to the characters and their stories. Good films must surely follow this. However, to do this well the filmmaker needs to be blessed with a good helping of visual intelligence. A film will inevitably be marred for the lack of it.

Alas, this present book wins no awards here. Not only does it not tell a story, it is a work of pure analysis. Worse even than that, it is a work of (largely) *philosophical* analysis. I couldn't possibly have chosen a genre less likely to hit the best seller list or be taken up by Hollywood. That sad but inevitable prospect doesn't matter, though, because my book is not in the business of telling a story. Narrative flaws in books and films that *do* tell stories are much more serious. Matters of storytelling, though, quickly become rich and complicated. Two questions are key when you have a story to tell in film: What do you tell – or show? and How do you tell it – or show it? That is where the sins (and virtues) come in.

The sin of not telling much of a story at all

The first and most grievous sin lies in not telling a story at all, or at any rate, not much of one. In popular cinema the spectacle of special effects seems to rate much higher, but why should it be found in more serious cinema? There is a sense in which ordinary life is not a story – not really. Stories *tell* of life; life just is itself – a series of more or less and variously related events of differing importance.[122] Memory may be selective but life is not – everything is there. Too many serious filmmakers seem these days to fail to recognise this important distinction, so in wanting their films to 'be like life', they avoid too much story – as though this itself is a weakness. No matter that humankind has thrived on stories since its earliest thinking days or how much we have learned about life from stories, no matter how much these noble aims have for millennia been a major part of the very purpose of stories, we now have a *new* insight: the story is to be rejected, or at least not constructed so as to look much like one. This is because story is artifice and therefore not real – not the cool thing to do according to the 'in-crowd'. As a result, their films can so often reduce to mere photographic reproductions of life's events. Mere photographic reproduction reigns. No matter that we have, too often, to wait for ages for 'something to happen', no matter if we cannot make much sense of anything for the first 30 minutes or so of run time, these things are not what is important to such filmmakers. Anything that smells of story must be shunned. No matter that there seems to be little discernible or intelligible structure, all we need is that succession of chaotic, unrelated or only partially or problematically related events – just like real life. Gosh! What a darned easy way to write a screenplay. If a character is taking a pee in one edifying image then staring out of a window in the next – all without any obvious connection – well, that's life mate. Indeed it is but I am pleased to be in, so to speak, the 'out crowd' with regard to this approach. (I will not grace it with the word 'philosophy'.)

Dreamlike films with narrative shortcomings

There are serious films that come from a different direction. The Hungarian film *Body and Soul* (Ildikó Enyedi, Hungary, 2017) comes to mind. A love story set in a slaughterhouse, this rather strange and attractively fanciful though unfortunately boneless job won the 'Golden Bear' award at a Berlin Film Festival - and there are indeed things to like about it. Parts of it are very beautiful, and it is an extremely beautiful dream-like film. Certainly merely naturalistic photographic reproduction does not rule. There is a real sense of oddity and unfulfilled longing. The psychologies of both dream and daily life are well conveyed. The problem, I feel, lies in its structure. There is no real tension to it. (This is one of the most difficult things for a filmmaker to achieve.) There is too much vacant staring. (Always an easy get out when a director runs short of ideas.) Some good ideas (such as a remark that one should feel sorry for the doomed cows if one is to survive a slaughterhouse job, and the imagery of cattle being slaughtered) are left dangling and unexplored. For all its genuine qualities, then, it never seems to raise its overall shape and purpose above the level of a line of occasionally rather fascinating washing pegged out to dry. It's got the right looking flesh but needs the skeleton. Visual intelligence may abound while narrative intelligence is sadly lacking.

Body and Soul is not on its own among recent (at the time of writing) films in having some good dream-like stretches but is challenged in the way it tells its story. Craig Robert's *Eternal Beauty* (UK, 2019) goes much the same way. This film acts well enough as a vehicle for Sally Hawkins playing a schizophrenic with considerable conviction but as a piece of cinema it is very mixed. There is an interesting, rather charmingly old-fashioned use of music and increasing stretches of dreamlike (or nightmare-like) cinematic promise, especially in her visions, and it is as sympathetic an exploration of schizophrenia as I know, but then (apart from the final stretch) it idles down into plodding pedestrianism. One cannot do cinema just most of the time and rely on the actor to carry it for the rest.

Then we have the Chinese *So Long, My Son* (Xiaoshuai Wang, 2019) at over three hours. This is a saga tracing the lost and found fortunes and lives of two families over three decades of cultural and political revolution and its attendant human upheaval. No initial pressure, then. Yes, it's deep, dense and nicely dream-like but three hours of doubt, depression, disappointment, dissolution, disagreeableness, death and Chinese dumplings is hard work to get through. Besides, it breaks my first rule of cinema: never make a film over three hours long without either including a chariot race or some other mark of distinction. This has neither and offers instead only a confusing narrative structure.

Yet if one is really concerned about life and its issues, and we want to tell the world about it and its sadness, wickedness, prejudices and social injustices, then our film must have a skeleton – and its bone structure must lie in its telling a story, preferably a good, well-constructed one, with strongly related events that spell out some kind of solid meaning. It will otherwise be, at best, just a drifting and occasionally attractive jelly-like entity, and amount to nothing much at all. At the very least its impact will be much reduced, or stay with one less meaningfully. It is precisely by the artifice of strong storytelling that points are put across and, by lack of it, that point-making is reduced in its power or influence. This is why many serious filmmakers were once also very often popular filmmakers also. Think here of Frank Capra, William Wyler, David Lean, Billy Wilder. Yes, they were spinners of good yarns, magical yarns to a point, yet something like Wilder's *The Apartment* (US, 1960) relates more powerfully, and with wit and intelligence, the injustices and exploitations of the workplace (of its age and place, of course) than many a piece of 'serious' cinema about such themes can even hope to do nowadays – and all because it has become cool to shun proper storytelling. Too much so-called serious cinema is, as a result, all too easy not to take seriously. It fails to be intelligent filmmaking at all. Please give us a good, well-constructed story that grabs us from Scene 1, just as good 'social issue' films of the past did. Of course, this takes real talent. I should not exaggerate. The more common sin is simply to downplay on story and up-play certain events. This, however, is already bad enough. Let us look at some specific sins in this area.

The sins of story structure

The sins of ubiquity

Something is ubiquitous if it can be found pretty well anywhere at more or less the same time. As individuals we occupy one place in the world at any given time. If we want to occupy somewhere else we have to move, and the journey may involve anything from moving to the kitchen to fix a drink or going on a flight to the other side of the world. There is no escape from the travel if one wishes to be somewhere else. A single image, given its standard total occupancy of the screen, is hardly ubiquitous – they come one at a time - but tightly bound collections of them often are. We can be in one place and one time now and a different place and time after a single, instant cut. Remember also that a single cinematic image may consist of more than one shot, for it is often a collection of associated shots. In that sense – having parts, at least, in many different places at the same time or existing as a whole over at least a short stretch of time, cinematic images can have something pretty well like ubiquity. This ubiquity, however, can be a two-edged sword. All too often a film can be just *too* ubiquitous.

Multiple story lines are a good example where care needs to be exercised. They can be used effectively. This is sometimes called 'hyperlink' cinema. Alejandro González Iñárritu's films *Amores Perros* (Mexico, 2000), *21 Grams* (US, 2003) and *Babel* (France, 2006) have been cited as good examples, and I am happy to go along with this judgement. Steven Soderbergh's *Traffic* (US, 2000) is another effective use of the technique, as it examines the illegal drug business from a number of angles: a victim, a lawman, a politician and a trafficker. At the level of more popular cinema, *Love Actually* (Richard Curtis, UK, 2003) is a clear example as it tells in simple parallel the stories of several different couples negotiating their love lives.

This technique can easily go wrong, though, and let tedium reign. This may, of course, be because the storylines themselves are told in just too dull a way, in which case we are simply left wondering how much more we can take, but there can also be frustration and confusion as we wonder what 'x' has got to do with 'y' and begin not even to care. *Cloud Atlas* (Tom Tykwer, US, 2012), though sometimes lauded, gets my vote here. It is a kind of global atlas of how our lives can affect each other – from past, present and future. Adapted from David Mitchell's 2004 novel of the same name, it tells six different stories across very different time periods and places. Each story is told from the point of view of the main character in the next. But connections seem just too loose and hard to take in. (It may have worked better in the book but I was hardly inspired to experiment.) This left me feeling that while it might be fitting stuff for lovers of far-out mysticism, it seemed more than faintly ridiculous and even just plain daft to a cinemagoer. I simply got lost in its uncontained kaleidoscope. Despite its clear pretentions, this dizzying effort is not remotely of the standard of DW Griffith's silent classic *Intolerance* (US, 1916) a collection of four tales exploring intolerance, separated by centuries and linked by shots representing Eternal Motherhood.

There are many kinds of narrative structure and this is not a textbook on the alternatives. In connection with multiple story lines, the guiding principle would be that a film should have a certain kind of unity. There may be several different stories but it should still be just the *one* film. Moreover, one should have a clear understanding – while one is watching the thing – of what binds the stories into one. The unity should not remain obtuse. As ever, we will each have our own examples of the saints and sinners. The filmmaker Terrence Malick, I am inclined to think, has skipped between these extremes with ease. However, I would say to filmmakers that if they cannot ensure clarity with complexity, I am inclined to think it a good idea to keep the story structure as simple as possible.

I am not suggesting that one should be required to check in one's brains at the box office – that would exclude *2001: A Space Odyssey*, alongside other great treasures. The call for clarity is not the same as the call for naivety. Almost all of the world's finest, deepest and most subtle pieces of cinema have consisted of single story lines (perhaps with pretty well and clearly connected sub-plots). We should never forget that blunt fact. There should be no sense of clutter on the screen and one should certainly never be left feeling as though matters are just all over the shop, floundering and wondering quite what is supposed to be going on in the fog. Simple (not naïve) should be the default position of the filmmaker's switch. Any deviation can cause even the intelligent viewer simply to lose track, and with it, interest. Ideas for multiple, and even over complex storytelling should certainly come with a severe risk of failure warning.

I suspect that there is a fundamental difference here between literature and film. In literature we can take complex and multiple storylines much more in our stride because we can pause every now and again, and take stock of the position, think about it a bit for a while, become as best we can, clear about just where we are. We can even, so to speak, rewind and refresh our memories. A film, in contrast, is relentless. Even if we see it at home and can pause and rewind, that is not how a film is supposed to be seen. (It can be *studied* that way, of course, but that is a different matter.) It is even something of an affront to the very nature, and particularly and especially the motion, of a cinematic image to be pausing and re-winding. In any case, what is one supposed to do in a cinema? There is a sense, then, that (by default) the cinematic story calls for simplicity in narrative structure by its very nature that doesn't apply to the written story.

The sin of having to wait

There are many ways in which a story can legitimately have us wait. A fairly obvious if rather banal instance would be a 'whodunnit', in which we are made to wait before the guilty party is revealed. In any case, we have to wait for whatever the resolution of the story may be. Likewise, there are many legitimate ways in which a film can be a slow-burner, in which problems and conflicts develop slowly. Besides, we often, at least in more serious films, need to give some time for character development and for our understanding of character relationships to be enriched. One thing, all good storytellers need to remember though is that the wait and slow-burning stretches should never be merely boring. We should never be left suffocating in sheer, unoxygenated tedium while the characters and relationships are being developed. We may need to wait for almost anything at all but we need to find the story compelling or intriguing right from the off.

The sin of the yawing credits

Stories should never be lazy, nor should character and relationship development. They should draw us in as the opening credits close – and even these can bore us easily these days as we have to wind through up to a dozen or so logos of companies who have had a financial hand in getting the film made, often followed by simple white credits against a black, music-less background. (Compare such openings with films of old in which even the opening credits announced the drama, conflict or comedy that is to follow.) These days I often feel a mouth-stretching yawn coming on before the film proper even gets under way, especially in more low-budget, supposedly serious cinema.

The sin of not being given a reason to care tuppence

When the yawning credits are followed by a half-hour or more of even more yawning development, during which time little is done to promote much by way of sympathy or engagement, the boredom becomes unbearable. We need to be given reason to care, right from the off. Characters may be good sorts, bad sorts or complex sorts. They may be fine and happy or torn and in distress. The characters may be depressed, down-hearted, despondent, desolate, discouraged, desperate or just plain bored, but the viewer should *never* be. Life is simply not long enough to waste any of one's time struggling with a film, waiting to care. Remember, cinema is not life, it should *tell* us a story of life.

Take two, now old British films: *Saturday Night and Sunday Morning* (Karel Reisz, UK, 1960) and *Lawrence of Arabia* (David Lean, UK, 1962). The first tells the story of the tangled relationships of a bored, young factory worker called Arthur Seaton (Albert Finney); the second, a bored young army officer, T.E. Lawrence (Peter O'Toole) who seeks adventure and test and not minding if the pain hurts. Neither film wastes a single moment in developing its leading characters. We see the rebelliousness in Seaton's eyes and hear it in his mouth in the very first crisp shot. We see Lawrence's self-destructive drive for excitement in the motorcycle ride that kills him, again right from the off. In neither case is everything about the protagonist revealed before its proper time, but we are given straight away motivations that lead us to care in some way about them or at least to tickle our intrigue. We are led to take up at least some sort of attitude towards them. We want it to go on. We want to find out more. We are not bored. We are not left like Rhett Butler, not giving a damn. Forcing upon us some immediate indication of character in such ways from the very start of the film is not emotional manipulation. Nor does it rule out possibilities for further character deelopment. On the contrary, it invites our interest and care, and if a filmmaker cannot be bothered to issue a proper invitation to their story then I become Rhett Butler – and with complete justification. In both these films we wait for, and eventually get, further developments, further complexities and subtleties. I am not, of course, saying that there was once a golden age of cinema in which there were no bad or boring films. But if they kept their audiences waiting in tedium it was at least *counted* as a flaw, a fundamental failure in storytelling. In contrast, it seems to be developing into something more like standard practice more recently. Let's look at some far more recent films for which the waiting is just too dull. I deliberately cite here films that have received high critical ratings and that do indeed have some otherwise decent cinematic qualities.

Take the South Korean film *Burning* (Chang-dong Lee, 2018). This is a slow burning mystery. Jong-soo meets Hae-mi, a girl who once lived in his neighbourhood. She asks him to look after her cat while she's away. When she returns, she introduces him to Ben, a man she met on her trip. But just who is Ben? And what of his strange hobby? Unfortunately, it is also a question of who really cares, at least for a long while. This is an example of wasted talent, for the second half of the film is nothing short of orientalist Hitchcock. We are drawn into a fascinating, deepening and darkening mystery with considerable style. The first half, though, is a mix of dull film-making (complete with hand-held, back-following camerawork) and sheer tedium. One comes too close to giving up before the action comes together, and since it weighs in at two and a half hours, initial attention should not be a lot to ask for. Frankly, one half of the first half could be simply snipped away. The result would increase its story-telling efficiency by a good 100%.

Sometimes a film breathes poetry but is starved on story. Oliver Laxe's *Fire Will Come* (Spain, 2020) seems an excellent example here. A curious fellow from the Galician wilds is released after imprisonment for setting fire to a forest. He seems to have it in for the greedy eucalyptus. After his return to his home village to live with his elderly mother, he helps around the farmstead, looks after sick cows, and is indifferent towards the neighbours. You may think that this is a good idea for a story but you'd be wrong. It *is* the story – or the bigger part of it. The whole thing looks gorgeous and Laxe's 16mm camera captures beautifully the countryside that famously looks like Cornwall on steroids. And it isn't just pretty postcards either, there is a properly cinematic poetry to it right from the start as we see, still in the dark hours, a mysterious light and drifting smoke haunting a burnt-out forest. In fact mystery haunts the whole job. The characters are equally largely unknowns, and remain that way. All this is, of course, good news but despite these clear merits the initial development was far too laboured and far too long. It made me wait a cool forty-five minutes before I even cared a jot. Even though the whole film is of modest length, weighing in at under one and a half hours, this seems, to me at any rate, still too long a time for what this film has to say. The problem is the story – or lack of it. Nothing is developed, it has no structure. One may argue that this accurately reflects this phase of the character's life, but an audience needs more getting-on-with-the job-ness - or I do! Frankly and simply, I spent too much time being just old-fashioned bored.

On the whole, though I felt quenched somewhat by the visual poetry, I was left hungry for something to happen. There's a lesson here, a principle if you like, and one of which too many of today's bright young filmmakers seem to be completely unaware: film should be poetic but not *solely* poetry, especially not just mystical poetry. Even poetry has its own kinds of structure, of course (on the whole) but this job doesn't have much of even that. Many directors, who nonetheless still like chancing their arms, may simply not have the talent for creating structure of course but I thought Laxe *had* grasped this. His previous film, *Mimosas* (Spain, 2016) had that same mystical air, mysterious gaze and free, poetic flow, but one sensed also that it was taking one through the different phases of a single, unifying journey. In short, it was telling a story. There was at least a sense of search. Basically, it had narrative structure. Without that, one can feel just too lost for comfort – as a viewer abandoned in a wasteland.

Next up is *Force Majeure* (Ruben Östlund, Sweden, 2014). A family travels to the French Alps for a skiing holiday but a threatened avalanche spoils the enjoyment. The worst – physically – does not happen but the family's life has been shattered as doubts remain over the father's actions. There is some skill here in relating true cinema to character psychology but the weaknesses are multiple. The characters are left too unsympathetic and for the first half an hour they do nothing except dwell on being disagreeable with each other, brushing their teeth and peeing. (What is it with so many present day film makers who imagine that social realism is enhanced by having a strong focus on toilet practice? I can only suppose it's easier than plot development and character exploration and story-telling. Hitchcock once humorously observed that "Drama is life with the dull bits cut out." He'd have to have another think these days.)

I, Olga (Petr Kazda & Tomás Weinreb, Czech Republic, 2016) tells the story of 22-year-old mass murderer Olga Hepnarová. In 1973, she drove a truck into a group of people in Prague. It is based on a true story. The film presents itself as a smart but cool-headed anatomy of a disturbed young woman who turns herself into a murderer. In some respects it is reminiscent of Polanski's 1960's *Repulsion* (UK). The superior black and white cinematography helps with that, though the young woman looks less mistily gorgeous than Catherine Deneuve. But I digress, the sad fact is that it would be a poor tribute to the earlier film. It only really begins to smarten itself up in its final reel. For the most part it is a combination of shapeless navel-gazing (or, rather empty room-gazing), repetitive shots that look like nothing more revealing than a series of vaguely suggestive and disorientating stills and lots of ultra-explicit sex that quite gratuitously exceeds any demands of characterisation. For too long it quite simply lacks pace, tension, structure and even pretty well any meaning. That, of course, may well have been the life of Olga but it should not have been made the life of the viewer.

Drifting, structureless preamble is also evident in *Lean on Pete* (Andrew Haigh, US, 2017). This tells of a teenager who gets a summer job with a horse trainer and befriends the fading racehorse, 'Lean on Pete'. It, too, has its merits. When did you last see a film with a genuinely hopeful, feel-good ending which wasn't simultaneously a meaningless stretch of flummery, candy floss and miscellaneous emotional sticky stuff? Here is one. It's about disappointment and only partial recovery. Charley, the teen, has lost his mum and then loses his dad. He becomes involved in work with a laconic, blunt, low-level race-horse entrepreneur, engagingly played by Steve Buscemi. When the racehorse is condemned, Charley takes the horse and embarks on an epic journey of rescue. This is the point at which the film comes to cinematic life. Charley's experiences in the big, wide, beautiful yet cruelly indifferent country are poetically captured, aided by a winding musical score which underlines Charley's twisting journey looming with danger. There's no sentimentality here, just harshness and humanity - a beautifully exhibited mixture. It's a different matter, though, for the first twenty or so minutes. One feels the point is being laboured (or even forgotten). It would have helped had the first key moment come sooner. A delayed hook in a film always causes me frustration. What makes this flaw all the more a pity is that it is otherwise a mature and fine film with a wonderfully unforced, attractive central performance from the boy. One is genuinely moved in places.

Sweet Country (Warwick Thornton, Australia, 2018) is an instructive case of both saint and sinner. Set in the outback of the Northern Territory in the early 20th century and concerned with the violence and prejudices of the whites against coloured folk, *Sweet Country* is, in many ways, as fine a piece of cinema I have seen emerge from Australia. It has far greater cinematic qualities than the director's earlier *Samson and Delilah.* (Not the 1950s Biblical epic!) Its tensions and perceptions become vividly portrayed on the screen. Indeed, there are some wide format visuals at play here of which David Lean would have been proud. They aren't just pretty pictures punctuating psychological inertia either – as is too often the case. They have real dramatic significance. We are involved. A suitable scorpion-like musical track would have perfected it, I think.

Alas and alack, there is another much more serious flaw. For the first twenty-five minutes or so – up to a crucial incident – the film, though still looking good, seemed to me rather static. The narrative structure has a weak start. We are introduced to the characters, and we know who we don't like, but there is little forward thrust. This flaw seems all too common. Slow action should never seem unexciting, unmotivating or lack direction. In this film it does seem this way, at least for that first lazy stretch. Frankly, it all seems far *too* slow. It makes its points still but in a rather plodding if not exactly lecturing manner, as if set in a narrative vacuum. I wanted desperately to say, "I've got the point, now *please* can we get on with it?"

Sharp, precise story telling is vital if one is to hook the hearts of the viewer because this is what sets up the necessary profile of emotional dynamics. Here, it's a bit like getting on a creaky, unoiled push-bike that only begins to find its wheels after one has struggled up the first hill. Again this is a pity because when the film does find its way, its cinematic power gives life to every shot and every line of dialogue. There is interest too. For one thing, in our terribly anti-establishment days, it is refreshing to see a local Christian landowner and a judge as the whites who have the greater understanding and more charitable attitudes (even accepting that the Australian establishment and church have a great deal to answer for at this time).

Finally, I present *House by the Sea* (Robert Guédiguian, France, 2017). Close to a harbour near Marseille in the depths of winter, the family of a now ageing and paralysed father return to their once shared home to care for the old man and air their regrets (and non-regrets - a far worse tendency) in front of each other's eyes and ears. Hardly a promising start one might think and, indeed, Guédiguian's film dices with nothing short of death for two thirds of its running time. It is the revealing depth of its dialogue (at first at any rate) that comes to be its only real saving grace, and this, at least, impresses from the start. Unfortunately, it is also the only thing that moves much at all for the first hour or so - and occasional, mandatory shots of rugged nature and splashing waves do not help. Guédiguian's earlier *The Snows of Kilimanjaro* (France, 2012) suffered in a similar way, I seem to recall, though not to the extent on display here. Its shots and scenes are nearly as clogged up as the veins and arteries of the old man.

I realise my own eccentricity, of course, but I like my cinema to move about a bit. (It is called 'cinema' - 'motion pictures', is it not?) Alas, this thing moves around as heavily as a dying, flat, lumpish, bottom-feeding fish. Despite its good intentions and engagingly philosophic reflections (and Jean-Pierre Darroussin's impressive selection of coloured jackets) the film echoes rather too effectively the paralysis of the old man. I half expected both to drop dead, too, half-way through. But, very slowly, the more perceptive moments, if as yet still too few and ephemeral, become increasingly evident, and interest slowly starts to grow. Then - the nearest thing I've ever seen to a miracle on screen saves the day, for both family (who are becoming ever more jaded) and film (which has secured so far no more than mere machine-dependent survival). Some of the family discover three young Arabic children ('illegal' refugees) in the hills, hiding from the authorities (armed soldiers who expect to find nothing but dangerous terrorists). A slightly older girl is silently feeding two much younger brothers. A fourth has already died. Heaven meets earth at such moments as these. Christ is seen, bringing light into our self-imposed darkness, and through those who have scarcely yet learned to think.

From that moment the film is lifted out of its self-generated swamp. It could so easily have become soppy but one knows it isn't going to. Instead, as the family takes in the children, whose reactions reduce one to tears, the film becomes almost translucent and filled with quiet but determined life. Even the old man's head is finally turned in symbolic acknowledgement. Every single moment of this final act - the fear, the hope, the misery and mystery of life, is revealed by the quiet, unassuming detail at play. Few things on screen have been more genuinely wonderful to watch. Few stretches of cinema have been so clearly and distinctly transformed in front of one's very eyes. It becomes pretty well the cinema of the transcendent. Not bad progress for a piece that starts out as the cinema of near-death.

This also illustrates a core take-home message of the present book. The space and time of the cinematic image are never mere replications of the physical space and time in which events are depicted, they have their own potential and reality. Thus, the cinematic image, when its potential is realised fully, is an instrument of transformation of events, place, time and space, never a mere recorder of these things. The same can be said of the chiaroscuro of the cinematic image, the way in which its areas of light and darkness can have a potential for fictional world-building and meaning. To understand this one general point is to understand most fully the nature of the cinematic image.

Back to the films that disappoint, I choose here recent examples that simply stick in my own craw. Do characters need to be developed? Should there be slower burning stretches? Do matters need proper exploration? Of course, especially in any cinema that is beyond the simplistic and naïve, but the slower stretches still need structure and storytelling clout. They should not be there standing inert and lazy, or just looking pretty, or even just giving a bit of background. They should be doing important work in preparing us for later developments. There should be something imperative, rather than merely relevant, about the slow burn, otherwise it's just a time-filling waste of dramatic space.

In all these cases, as in many of the films by Asghar Farhadi, the renown Iranian director of *Everybody Knows* (Spain, 2018) *The Salesman* (Iran, 2016) *About Elly* (Iran, 2009) *The Past* (France, 2013) and *A Separation* (Iran, 2011) – otherwise accomplished dramas, one after another - we have to wait for a crucial moment before their story-lives really get underway. Just *that* is the sin. What a film should do is *build up* to a crucial moment – in mounting tension, growing excitement or just increasing expectation. None of these things need lead to naivety or over simplicity. Let me ram this home. There is nothing wrong with films being slow burning in principle but it should be substance, not mere preamble, that burns. Then the crucial moment can come very late. Such films have been made over the decades, from *Black Swan* (Darren Aronofsky, US) in 2010 back to *Rosemary's Baby* (Roman Polanski, US) in 1968 back to *Rear Window* (Alfred Hitchcock, US) in 1954. But in all these and many others what we have is slow burn, not a slow lukewarm pre-death. My recommendation? If you can't tell a story keep away from a motion picture camera save for making family holiday videos, no matter how clever you may be in other cinematic respects.

The sins of (lack of) particularity

As we saw in Chapter One, while the word 'man' can apply to men general – a photographic image of a man is always of a particular man. The focus is always on the individual, though not necessarily, of course, on the very same individual throughout the film. It can be on groups or even crowds, course, but even then it is always on *this* or that *particular* group or crowd. No one *sees* man, we see either *a* man or *a* group of men. We do not see man's cruelty to men, we see *this* man's (or this group of particular men's) cruelty to *a* man, or group of men. This has implications for the ways in which films get across their points. Stories must emphasise what is happening to individuals, they can never be a general treatise. One should always ask of a film if insight is forthcoming with respect to a particular individual or group. A film cannot be solely a political or social campaign. Films that are centred on the latter have to be particularly clever in other ways to rise to the level of cinematic art. Sergei Eisenstein's *Battleship Potemkin* (USSR, 1925) is certainly that clever in many ways, but at what cost? Yes we still, inevitably, see particular groups (of sailors and civilians) and what happens to them but the film is so busy dealing with issues that I have to say that I find it rather cold and uninvolving. This, then, is a pretty *old* sin. It does not seem to be a general worry nowadays, though. That said, there are plenty of instances nowadays of films in which one feels that an issue outweighs other aspects of cinema. I return below to this important point.

The sin of chasing and overvaluing originality

Any new film is original to some trivial extent, of course. Even remakes that use originals as templates – such as the flat, dull remake of *Brief Encounter* (Alan Bridges, UK, 1974) or Gus Van Sant's futile gesture of *Psycho* (US, 1998). Both remakes were at least in colour, while the originals were in black and white (though this fact certainly didn't make them better). Remakes frequently (though not always) flounder if only because what makes the original seem worth remaking in the first place is their superior nature. One can always legitimately make another, fresher film of the same novel, of course, though even then one is dicing with death if the first adaptation was any good. One instance where I am inclined to think the remake better is *The Talented Mr Ripley* (Anthony Minghella, US, 1999). The original was *Plein Soleil* (aka, *Purple Noon*, René Clément, France, 1960). However, I am not here interested in the issue of remakes if only because to the extent that it may be a sin, it is hardly an exclusively modern one. In any case, when a film is described as original, what seems to be implied is that its originality is more than merely trivial. My question here, though, is whether it is altogether worth chasing originality *at all* – even when it is more than trivially originality that one is after. After all, what is usually meant by 'original' is '*importantly* original' or '*interestingly* original'.

If a new film really is importantly or interestingly original, my question may be thought to answer itself. Of course it's worth doing. A sin, though, lurks in confusing originality with quality. This seems more recent, too. Sound films replaced the so-called silent films, colour replaced black and white as the default choice, and some kind of widescreen replaced the old academy ratio. These changes were largely motivated by economic rather than aesthetic demands and many thought that they ruined the art of cinema – and, for a time, I rather suspect they did. It took a while for filmmakers to learn how to adapt and get the best out of such innovations. Frankly, though, I am not all that interested in whether or not a film is properly original. I would sooner it was just *good*. Look at the history of other arts. Was every piece by Bach truly and importantly original, or every novel of Jane Austen, or every painting of Rembrandt? Of course not. Their overall styles and ways may have been but, having established that much, they went in for quality and development. Constantly chasing newness and entertaining the urge to 'say something new' at every touch and turn is at best futile and at worse stupid.

To be fair to filmmakers, the word 'original' often comes from reviewers (who should know better) and marketing departments. The latter, of course, use 'original' as an 'attractor' word rather in the way that a manufacturer of shampoo may use the word 'natural' as an adjective to go with 'ingredients', quite regardless of whether the product so described does a better job on one's hair. My favourite recent candidate to have received the accolade 'original' is *Victoria* (Sebastian Schipper, Germany, 2015) a film taken in one shot. We have earlier seen that there are much earlier films made this way.

Some original films – and here comes my caveat – are original in some significant enough way but are still either poor or at least annoying in other ways. In other words, they are original in a *bad* way. Again the film *Victoria* comes as a ready example. Its shots seem continually shaky as the cinematographer endlessly chases the protagonist down the streets of Berlin. This kind of originality, though, comes at too high a price – that of triggering my vertigo. Sticking with Germany, another candidate was *Toni Erdmann* (Maren Ade, 2016). This is certainly not original in its deadpan comedy (which works rather cleverly, I must make clear) but *is* original (so far as I know) in the sense that it dices with death in stretching it all out at close to three hours. I have heard some films being described as original when they are pretty well sickeningly just more of the same. My intuition is that this applies most notably to 'the grim cinema *of* the grim'. On the whole, I suspect that chasing originality, or thinking that one has achieved it, is tremendously overrated. Good ideas are what we really want, followed by good filmmaking, whether the results are particularly original or not. Apart from that, my message here is simple. If one sees a film because one has been attracted by the epithet 'original', ask yourself two questions: Is it *really* original? And, if it is, is its particular originality worthwhile?

Human Realism: 'Authenticity', 'Carbon Copying'

I have already said things about the sin of over-authenticity. I think that the source of much sin in performance lies pretty much in the sins of storytelling, especially where over-authenticity rules, so I now move on to this.

The sinful turn in truth telling: dreamless, disenchanted carbon-copying of life.

A kind of bare-faced authenticity occurs when a filmmaker refuses properly to exploit cinema's own deep audio-visual artifice or form and a film is made to look more like a mere photocopy of life, as if the viewer were simply present to the events as they would be if they were just bluntly *there* - when, in other words, the film looks just *too* naturalistic. This is what I call 'carbon-copying' (or 'photocopying') reality. I argue that this actually *prevents* a film from conveying more forcefully the deeper aspects of the reality it represents. In short my thesis is that over-naturalism works against a deeper degree of realism. The fundamental mistake is failure in making the distinction between naturalism and realism. We have already seen how this affects appearance. Here we examine its affects upon storytelling. A blunt example: Elia Kazan's *On The Waterfront* (US, 1954) is full of stylish cinematic artifice, yet it conveys the deep reality of life in its setting far more forcibly than almost any more naturalistic film does nowadays. I distinguish here what I take to be several priorities of the authentic, carbon-copying, naturalistic film:

N1. The medium of cinema becomes less visible. There's a focus on the 'fly on the wall' approach. Films often look like TV documentaries with the camera following the characters around as the action proceeds, often with a hand-held camera. There is increased licence given to something often identified as 'immediacy'.

N2. Picture composition is less important. One is shown what has to be revealed but the aesthetics of *how* a thing is shown is not key.

N3. The performance is down almost to the actor and script alone. (The director spends much of their time exclusively on performances, or *seems* to have done.) Aside from distinctions between close up and longer shots, the aesthetics of cinema plays a minimal part in contributing to the psychology of the story.

N4. The lighting is usually less key. It can often look quite flat. All that is necessary is that you see what the director intends you to see. 'Fancy cinematography' is seen as a distraction from the business in hand.

N5. Editing is not seen aesthetically. Often characters are just followed around and things will be seen on the screen that are unimportant. (Though a certain suitable pace and geographical logic must be maintained.)

N6. Music is often less important. Most of the emotion comes from actors and script.

N7. In general style is far less visible or even hardly present at all. One might say that the only allowable style is that there should appear to be none, except to give a more or less 'documentary feel' to the film. In fact, it's better if there's no real style at all because it gets in the way of the naturalism. A film should contain no more style than life itself.

N8. The narrative must avoid the symbolic and things must be presented quite literally. In fact, there should be as little story or plot as one can get away with. The attitude often seems to be that too much story gets in the way of the authenticity and the issue. Stories, after all, have to have a structure and life does not (in the same sense at any rate).

N9. Strict authenticity in the sense of carbon-copying should be observed at all times. The fictional space of the story (if that is what we can call it) simply mirrors what would be the actual space of the action as if the latter were real.

N10. ATHENTICITY OF VOICE RULES, OK? *In extremis*, actors are frequently allowed to mumble their way through an entire film (because that's what the 'real' character would do). Never mind that the poor audience cannot discern a single thing said. (For a prime example of this see *NEDs* (Peter Mullan, UK, 2010). 'NEDs' stands for 'Non Educated Delinquents' and the film is about violent street gangs in Scotland. This needed subtitles as much as any non-English language film.)

N11. Telling a gripping story is out, or not much to be bothered with. We have already seen off that one.

At the bottom of all this, either consciously or simply through unthinking influence, lies the 'Realist' thesis we discussed in Chapter 1. It can *seem* all too clear that photocopy-like authenticity goes well with both Photographic Realism and Appearance Realism (Naturalism) both of which we have discussed earlier. Cinema's photographic realism, however, as we have already made clear, is a *way* of seeing the world that was before the camera – and, by imaginative extension, the events, characters and so on in the story told – but it is a way of seeing that works best *non*-naturalistically. The cinematic image is, by its essence, a *non-natural*, purely imaginative way of seeing. There need be no prohibition, therefore, on imaginatively exploiting its potential powers. Indeed, the nature of the cinematic image as a way of seeing seems to call out for imaginative seeing in ways that cannot apply (certainly in the same sense) to our daily perceptions of life. We can understand more clearly a situation or a character in a film than we can in the normal run of daily life because we can attend to what matters about them in a deeper and more focused way. The almost complete rejection of these 'formal' powers amounts, I would say, to an almost complete rejection of cinema. Naturalism, then, is not, as too many filmmakers seem to think, the *key* to deeper authenticity and realism, but rather a bar to it.

The sins of grim cinema of grim life

A kind of cinema that seems particularly susceptible to naturalistic treatment is what I have called 'the grim cinema of the grim'. There is absolutely nothing wrong, of course, with having a large diet of films that intelligently and insightfully portray life in all its variations, including those which explore the issues of all that makes life grim. (Though it would be nice to have some equally intelligent and insightful cinema of life's joys, too - something that the typical modern formulaic 'feel-good' films signally fail to provide.) Sticking with the grim cinema of the grim, though, the mistake ('sin') is to think that because the films are *about* the grimness of life, the film itself must be grim, in the sense that it must offer the viewer a grim experience in the watching of it. As is typical of such cinema, there is an over-concentration on the issues and the drama and only a dulled concentration on the mode of their presentation, even though the latter is what half of cinema actually is. We need to realise that there is no 'zero-sum' game at play between the styles of artifice available to cinema and the needs of realism such that the more one gives space and time to one, the less there is to give to the other. There is no competition here for the life-affirming resources of a film, for it is precisely through duly elaborated style that realism is given its due force. Realism is always far more than the conveyance of momentary event, far more than the surface. It is inevitably life-affirming because it involves depth and larger vision in which we can see, understand and feel deep down the rightness or wrongness of something. Realism in art never merely shows us the visible surface, it educates our emotions and understanding. I think that all the best and most penetrating, in short the *most* realistic, artistic expressions of life's tragedy, wickedness and sadness, as well as its joys and happiness, happen in a kind of mysterious territory beyond the more prosaic, trimmed down, carbon-copying forms of representation. All we are really given by that is an invitation to visionless platitude, a hard-nosed momentary concern with all the depth sucked out.

Writing in similar vein, though not about cinema, the philosopher and theologian David Bentley Hart compares other approaches as being, "rather like attempting to understand the flight of a swallow by attaching anchors to its wings".[123] Truth can never be simply identical with naturalism. To think so may be alright for journalism, and even then I am not sure, but it is the most egregious error in all of cinema. The cinematic image was born as an enchanted world. Its range of spells and audio-visual potions are all discussed in this book. Not to use them is certainly a crime against the art, a kind of dumbing down of cinema's power, but it is also a crime against reality, for it fails to convey its deepest truths. These deeper truths, as they can be given in the form of cinema, call out to be expressed in the contours of that form, in its special varieties of appearance, sound, space and time, not in the dull-minded, pedestrian audio-visual literalism that denies the powers of cinematic art by regarding cinema as a mere *mechanism* of conveyance of reality. Even the camera, despite its engineering and looks, is more than a mechanism. Rather, it is an instrument in the larger process of transforming our vision of reality – all the way down.

Films with dreamlike enchantments and force

Think of some of the greatest films of grim life: the post war Italian neo-realist films, including *Bicycle Thieves* (Vittorio De Sica, Italy, 1948); the films of the French and British 'new wave' movement; the new cinema from America in the fifties, including Elia Kazan's *On The Waterfront* (US, 1954) and his other films. (See his *East of Eden*, (US, 1955) for a really cinematically imaginative and powerful film about the frustrations of youth.) All of these are instances of the 'cinema of the grim', yet all are also masterpieces of cinematic form, with crisp, arresting, yet at times also reflective, poetic cinematic styles - and they all convey the grimness through well-constructed stories that vary in pace according to the needs of the narrative moments. Indeed, Martin Scorsese said of the Italian neo-realist film *Rome, Open City* (Roberto Rossellini, Italy, 1945) that it was "the most precious moment in film history". That remark may, I feel be extended to the whole movement.

The finest of cinema of the grim leaves one with an invigorated sense of anger that life can be such a way. One simply *feels* more involvement with the characters and more sympathetic with their plights. This is because one is able to be more imaginatively engaged with them through the special powers of cinematic form. Grim life must never merely be shown with dull, merely carbon-copying authenticity, as if one mere merely watching it take place as one is walking down the street with its unfortunate protagonists. It must be *revealed* through the poetry of cinema, experienced dream-like as in a nightmare, not merely shown. *Then* it has staying power. This, of course, requires huge visual imagination on the part of the director. Present grim life in a uniformly grim, tedious and un-invigorated way and the viewer is simply bored - or at least I am.

Today's filmmakers would respond, I am sure by pointing out that what matters is the *issue*, the social or political reality, and that getting out *that* message should not be diluted by some assumed aesthetics of cinema. WRONG YET AGAIN. Cinematic aesthetics is never merely icing on the cake, something that hides the substance (the issue) or covers it with the goo of sentiment. Nor does it dilute the issue; it reinforces it, gives it extra weight and power. It is cinema's own unique and glorious means of conveying and expressing the issue - which can be as grim as death - with the force, meaning and memorable beauty that it deserves and needs.

One of the most frightening yet accomplished pieces of cinema of the grim I have seen in recent years is *Margin Call* (J.C. Chandor, US, 2011) - though, less usually, this film tells the story is about an episode of (potential) grimness of the *rich*. It follows the key people and events at an investment bank, over a day, in the early stages of the financial crisis of 2008. At one stage in walks the big boss (played with the mischievous, even devilish, deliverance of a petulant public school headmaster by Jeremy Irons). He has come to make the big decision. At the crucial moment he stands against a window and explains that he is there to guess what the 'music' (financial gains and losses) may be in a year's time. He confesses that he can no longer hear the music, after just having learned that the bank is on the road to ruin in very short order unless they sell the items on their books rapidly. He is framed so that he is at the extreme left edge of the image looking through a window into the darkness of the city below. The cinema expresses the emptiness now that the music has stopped. A large area of financial darkness is all that he faces. The image expresses also just how little perception such people had of their being the direct cause of the impending disaster. (Though, of course, the economic behaviour of we millions of ordinary Joes hardly leaves us with entirely clean hands.) I do not think I have ever seen a more vivid, hellish or sobering cinematic representation of nihilism anywhere else in films. A blander more naturalistic representation, chasing nothing more than strict carbon-copying and endless close-ups would have denied the film all that power.

Just how full of hate does the world have to be before we recognise the one vital, life-blood necessity of cinema: that it must shine in the darkness and throw light on things, in accordance with its psychological, and even its very physical nature, and not merely indulge itself or even partake in the darkness under the pretence of higher authenticity? Just what tortures does the world have to endure before we realise that it must also be able to reveal the difference between right and wrong, with no conveniently compromising over-complexity behind which we can all hide – i.e., without the 'moral maze' which tends to leave us just . . . lost?

This places *Belfast* (UK, 2022) Branagh's tale of boyhood experiences in trouble-torn Belfast in the late 1960s firmly on the side of the angels. This makes it not "manipulative, and sentimental", as The Spectator rather snootily observes[124], but truer. The dialogue and performances are spot on and Branagh shows his firm hand on tiller. Even what I normally complain about, the nervous, almost giddying, camera movements (especially in the early shots when the violence first comes to play) seem to have purpose and are carefully controlled, and the largely black and white cinematography beautifully conveys a combination of recollection, nightmare and tension. If there is a flaw at all it is that the imagery looks too smoothly video-ish at the times when it should have been at its grittiest. OK, Italian post-war neo-realism and British 'new wave' it is not (the only British filmmaker capable of those truest hights of visual poetry is Terence Davies) but it's still lovely stuff – and it shows due inventiveness, especially in its morally urgent use of clips from *High Noon* (Fred Zinnemann, US, 1952)and *The Man Who Shot Liberty Valance* (John Ford, US, 1962). The key point is, though, that Branagh does not present things blandly but instead uses a wide gamut of cinematic form to put across his points. And, note well, all this blurs nothing of moral importance but, rather, casts upon it that much needed light.

Though dreamlike imagery used to abound in cinema at all levels and has nowadays taken a very severe dive, it does still exist in contemporary serious cinema - just. *Capernaum* (Nadine Labaki, Lebanon, 2018) is a good example. Charting children on the edge of society amidst chaos, pain, loss and casual violence, this film possesses enormous audio-visual dreamlike power. One follows a boy, aged around 12 as he struggles to survive and finds both the cruel and kind. The impact of all the grim horror is unrelenting without mistake but one is swept along with the cinema and the soundtrack. At one point, the boy rides on a big fairground wheel and sees the world's beauty from above, only to descend, as if doomed, to the chaos and darkness below. The yearning, aching music adds a necessary counterpoint to the endless suffering, as if to convey the fact that it all matters. But this film is not parochial. It shows us just what our fallen world can do to the poor and dispossessed. It makes us all ache with shame.

Then we have *Happy as Lazzaro* (Alice Rohrwacher, Italy, 2018). In a remote Italian village, peasant workers are held in feudal captivity by an exploiting aristocrat. Among them is Lazzaro, a simple minded but saintly young man who is in turn exploited by his fellows. He dies but they all meet again many years later. This is a rather weird but charming and gentle fantasy come allegory illustrating the fascinating fact that we always tend towards obscuring light in the world, and thus always enslave ourselves. Filmed in 16mm, it is often deliberately photographed to give a sense of a dream of a past age, especially in the first half of the story. Only Lazzaro, saint or angel, happy and innocent to the last, does not taste age. There's a simple, absorbing, inventive beauty at play here - things are often seen in long shot, as if we are reflectively detached from the action - and parts of it move the deeper regions of the soul.

Next we have *The Guardians* (Xavier Beauvois, France, 2018). World War 1 ravages, kills and damages in the background but the women work on the land as their men-folk are at war. Watching this film is rather like sipping a late summer wine whose flavour contains a rich bitterness, all in telling counterpoint to Michel Legrand's haunting score and some well-honed cinematography. It focusses all its efforts on the people surviving in an outwardly idyllic but utterly uncompromising environment. Life without their men is hard. But where Beauvois really shows consummate perception, as in his *Of Gods and Men* (France, 2010) is on life's spiritual troubles in times of conflict and sacrifice, when, as one line puts it, the living are buried underground and the dead lie on top. Both camera and performances reveal with full dreamlike force the beauty of the human soul enduring pain and loss. And one cries.

Waiting for the Barbarians (Ciro Guerra, Italy, 2019) is worth looking at, too. From the director of the impressive *Embrace the Serpent* (Colombia, 2015) and *Birds of Passage* (Cristina Gallego & Ciro Guerra, Colombia, 2018), two further films with dreamlike force, comes the tale of a local administrator (Mark Rylance in top form) of an isolated desert outpost of an unknown empire from an unknown time in the past. 'Barbarians' is the term used by the empire for the local tribes. Although all live in peace, forces within the empire, represented by Colonel Joll (a threatening Jonny Depp) want to stir up trouble. It isn't and could not possibly *be* one, but this film has some of the look and feel of an old-fashioned epic. Unlike the latter genre, the music is minimalist but effective. Some may think the dialogue contrived but this would be to misidentify its place. It isn't meant to be naturalistic, it is a poetic, dreamlike expression of a moral war. The administrator ('magistrate') is a good, peace-loving man who helps a young barbarian woman after the colonel has been on a rampage of torture. The film's theme is simple but elemental, but only a hard-nosed cynic could call it 'simplistic'. It is a powerful portrayal of empire and evil, of how imperial fear and efficiency gives rise to evil men, and how a good man will inevitably suffer tortures just by being good. It all makes a welcome change from the usual crop of mere dull recording of what goes on in our darkened world. There's something almost operatic about this film. Ciro Guerra is the sort of cinematic director we need to cultivate.

Another recent film of dreamlike force is *The Invisible Life of Euridice Gusmao* (Karim Aïnouz, Brazil, 2020). The sheer colour, energy and passion of every image here would put almost Gaugin and Van Gough in the shade. This is pure cinema of loss, longing and gift, as Christ looks down almost invisibly on Rio. This film washes through one's very blood stream and lives in the aching soul. There could be no better reminder than this film that the cinematic image should never be a mere visual adjunct to the meaning of a film. The image *shapes* the meaning, in its very essence and moving form. It is a pretty well flawlessly magical mix of cinematography, design, performance, pace and music.

Finally, as a cinematic treat amidst the outbreak of Covid, we had the latest film of *Pinocchio* (Matteo Garrone, Italy, 2019). Pinocchio is, of course, one of the world's greatest stories, a kind of 'coming of age' with an old-fashioned moral: be kind, accept rational authority and sage advice when growing up, and do not lie, even though it's all just so hard to do. This is a message we badly need in today's world in which the brainless and heartless 'follow-your-own-dream-and-do-your-own-thing-at-all-costs', egalitarian, libertine clap-trap philosophy dominates from top down. Garrone does not fight shy of one single thread of this, and I feel refreshed by it. Another refreshing feature is that the effects, which are quite wonderful, serve the story rather than substitute for it. The dialogue sparks and the performances are a splendid mix of the bizarre and the authentic. Alas, it isn't quite flawless: the music tends towards drippiness and thus fails to enhance the otherwise excellent combination of weirdness, magic and shocking believability. Many scenes genuinely touch and I particularly appreciated the nativity-like setting, among straw and sheep, when Pinocchio emerges as a 'real' boy – at the dung end of the world. That's at the close, of course. For the most part, Pinocchio is portrayed as wood come to life in curious semi-human form. There's an alien strangeness, even a nightmarish oddity at play here – one wonders just what kind of creature Pinocchio is, yet there is also sheer adorableness in the character and one roots for Pinocchio's potential becoming reality. Other puppets (but with strings attached) also lend a kind of strange, sub-real existence. Much as I take Disney's now very old film to be one of the greatest masterpieces of animated storytelling, I like Garrone's conception. It's the one that hits our age as it needs hitting.

Despite these gorgeous exceptions, though, blander more naturalistic material seem too much to rule. I rather conflate naturalism with authenticity here, of course, because that's what the films do, but another way of putting the issue would be to say that more naturalistic looking films deny themselves a fuller and deeper authenticity by denying themselves the capacity to express more fully what is all too frighteningly real. Next time you watch a film about grim life – at any level – ask yourself how much deep work their cinematic images are doing.

The sins of S&V

As McGinn points out, the film viewer is almost a voyeur by definition. This is because the cinematic image has such features as close-up and psychological foreground. It positively invites the viewer to *look into* things. The screen draws one into "the posture of the voyeur". He goes on, "the unreciprocated gaze into the private world of the other is amply catered to by the by the cinematic medium".[125] Does this rule in sex scenes without further ado?

The sins of in-yer-face sex

"Sex is the sphere in which the animal and the personal meet", observes philosopher Roger Scruton. He rues that "modern discussions [of sex] have been conducted in a 'scientized' idiom which, by its very nature, removes sex from the sphere of interpersonal relations and remodels it as a relation between objects."[126] We are simply to be understood as biological entities, where 'biological' is to be understood scientifically. (This follows Freud and other supposedly scientific writers on the subject.)

Whatever one makes of the Scruton's wider judgement here, and I am inclined to accept it, I take it as a profound truth that the arena of sex is unique in that it cannot, in humans, be understood purely as a biological urge (even though I am willing to acknowledge that it evolves from such). Being human (having a rational soul as the ancient philosopher Aristotle has it) transforms the urge into something else even if it retains some its urge-like qualities. It cannot be modelled on hunger or thirst without hopeless distortion.

This 'something else' is always a relation involving a kind of desire between two individuals. I would want to say that it has (acknowledged or not) a spiritual dimension. It is a unique and ultimate joining of flesh into one, where flesh cannot be conceived simply as bodily where the word 'body' is understood exclusively in terms of physical science. Indeed, it is hardly obvious that the body as a whole can be conceived in this way, though since the time of the 17th century philosopher René Descartes, who placed the soul in an entirely non-material arena, it has been so conceived.

One does not, though, have to follow Descartes in separating body and soul entirely in order to appreciate that body cannot be understood in purely material terms which can then be scientised. One simply has to reflect upon bodily experiences and then engage in a modicum of philosophical reasoning based on that reflection. Consider one's pains and one's joys or one's vision and hearing, our capacity for memory and reasoning – the stuff of our rational and conscious lives generally. It seems neither too quaint nor too exaggerated to label these as activities of the soul, even though they involve bodily organs. Body and soul simply cannot be ultimately separated as Descartes thought.

However, this does not mean that we can conceive our bodily natures purely in scientised material terms.[127] As Scruton puts it, "The concepts and categories that we use to describe the embodied person are far removed from the science of the human body. What place in such a science for smiles instead of grimaces, for blushes as opposed to flushes, for glances as opposed to looks"[128] The concepts we use to describe ourselves as embodied persons take us as conscious, intentional, self-aware agents not as things. They situate us in a world of meanings not just of interactions, the latter being the preserve of science. Sex, as it is known to humans at least, is a denizen of the world of meaning and significance. It is not merely a pleasurable physical interaction because it is more than a physical interaction to begin with – or, at least, more than an interaction understood purely in physical terms.

So far, so good, maybe, but also 'So what?', one may respond. What's all that got to do with its being a sin, if it is one, to show sex in a film? These important preliminaries should alert us, though, to the fact that sex is a very particular department of the intimacy of soul and body – to what transforms a *thing* into a *person*. Why, though? After all, we humans can join together in a number of ways, many of which are special in one way or another – conversation, engaging in a joint project, and eating together seem also to be clear examples.[129] Sex, like these other examples, has a further feature – it is always *intentional*. Note well, though, I mean 'intentional' as a philosophical term of art which pertains to activities that point to or reach out to something further. Consider thinking, hoping, or desiring. These are intentional because they always require something, as it were, to *point* at, to represent, or to be about. Intentionality is, in short, mental directedness. One always thinks *about* something, hopes *for* something or desires something. This wider concept is what is meant when a philosopher says that something is intentional.[130]

However special various private activities are, though, and however hidden they are from more objectively measurable traits, sex is more special still. Sex, as we observed above, is a joining together of flesh in a special and unique way but the desire involved in this joining is always intentional, in the wider sense, in that it is always desire for a unique other. But it is also desire for a unique kind of joining, one that transforms both parties to the act – the transforming of two into one – a spiritual, not just physical, joining. It is, necessarily, a transfiguration of persons. This is what makes rape so terrible, worse in a special way than other forms of physical assault. It is a spiritual affront in an act that should be a spiritual joining. However physically satisfied the rapist may be, they have desecrated what sex actually *is*, rather than simply having illicitly engaged in it. It contaminates the very act it involves. It is also why one cannot put on the human sex act any measurable physical value. It is placed, by its very nature, beyond the remit of science.

One doesn't have to go so far as rape, though, to desecrate or contaminate this joining. One only has to *look*. The sex act should not be kept hidden simply in the way that, say, a private or confidential conversation should be hidden, or even a kiss. It should be hidden because it involves a joining that excludes others from any kind of participation *at all* – including looking. Private conversation can never be violated in quite the same way. Sex (properly understood) is between two *intrinsically* – by its very nature. An additional unwanted ear to a private conversation may be bad in all sorts of ways and require apology but it is not in the same territory as sex. An eye on a sex act can never be an unfortunate, merely unwanted intrusion, it is (by the very nature of the sex act) turned into a participation where participation is desecration, even a denial of its being the kind of joining it involves. Given also the qualities of the cinematic image that we call intensity and intimacy, this would make the present sin a worse intrusion still.

Merely avoiding voyeurism (if one includes in that getting sexual pleasure from watching sex) can never be sufficient defence, either. Even voyeurism is never merely a psychological perversion. More seriously, it – alongside just looking - is a metaphysical denial of what sex is. This is what makes it a perversion in the first place – a corruption of something sacredly excluding of others. Accusations of mere prudishness or old-fashioned-ness or unwillingness to explore reality hold no water here. Not watching sex is the virtue of giving sex what it calls upon *us* to give – the proper recognition of its nature; watching it is the vice of refusing this recognition, of spitting on a gift belonging to its proper participants. In acquiring the habit of thought that one is merely avoiding the vice of prudery one is contaminating one's own person. Matters get even more serious. Virtue can never be understood as a mere means for obtaining a good life. It is already to live a good life. Similarly, vice is never a mere hindrance to good living, one that can perhaps be compensated for elsewhere. It is excluding oneself from good living, and denying oneself good living can never be a rational and entirely free choice of what we call 'lifestyle'. Vice is the very denial of one's own humanity, the refusal to accept the gift that makes personal, rational choice possible in the first place. (Instead of just going with some fashionable flow.)

Where does this leave sex on the screen, though? After all, that is play acting, make believe sex, not *real* sex. (Although there are exceptions – so I am given to understand.) There is some nuancing here, though, on the word 'real'. The actors may not be having real sex but the characters in the story world of the fiction certainly are. In short, it is real sex in the world of the story, and in some sense we are to take this world as real, even though we see it through the image. The desecration, so to speak, seeps through.

That, then, is what makes a sin out of in-yer-face sex in film (or any other photographic representation). Looking is precluded in both life *and* cinema in this case. This does not, of course, preclude its other sins, the most usual of which is the sheer tedium involved in watching it all. The reason for the tedium, though is not just a matter of personal taste. It is caused by the fact that, as often as not, it puts a hold on the story. It is a narrative flaw, though one that allows a filmmaker who is challenged in terms of cinematic imagination to continue making feature length films out of stories that should be much shorter. These other sins could obtain, of course, even if one rejects my case against the main sin or if one has swallowed the modernist myth of sex as a form of mere physical appetite, urge or even recreation. If one accepts this reductivist (I would even say 'eliminativist') picture, there would, of course, be no more principled a reason for excluding from films in-yer-face sex than there would be for excluding in-yer-face eating. (Though don't forget the other associated sins.)

Nor can we make useful (and maybe just convenient) distinctions here between what is pornographic and what is not, or what is intended as (or taken to be) voyeuristic and what is not, or what is supposedly done with taste and what is not. *Any* film that explicitly displays a sex act is committing the main (and serious) sin. That is why I have not needed in this section to cite any films as particular sinners is this regard.

To finish off we must also never fall for the excuse that showing the sex is a dramatic or narrative *necessity*. First of all, even if it were such a necessity, the price would be too high. Fear not, though, for it is never necessary. That would be to deny the power of suggestion – as often as not a power that exceeds that of direct depiction - something too many modern filmmakers have forgotten in many contexts. Of course, the art of suggestion is terribly inconvenient to the cinematically challenged filmmaker, for it requires at least an artisan level of cinematic skill and imagination.

After writing this section my attention was drawn to a different kind of sex scene, one more nuanced and, in a sense, less in-yer-face. The example given was from the film *Don't Look Now* (Nicolas Roeg, UK, 1973). As the couple make love, two things become apparent. First of all, the flesh on flesh shots are intercut with later shots of their dressing for dinner. This cleverly places the scene in a wider, and important, context, as if saying that the sex is part of a wider life. Secondly, even the flesh shots themselves were not quite so in-yer-face. It was clear that the couple were involved in comforting each other in grief over the recent death of their daughter. This both worked and seemed justified but this is because it wasn't *simply and solely* a sex scene, let alone an entirely in-yer-face job. Its explicitness was in the very least highly nuanced. Still, one can legitimately ask if more suggestion could have been used.

The sins of 'in-yer-face' violence.

There are many questions that could be asked about violence in films: Where is it necessary or justified to show it? Does watching violence in films encourage violence in behaviour? If violent behaviour is encouraged, does it affect some groups more than others? Is cartoon violence (or any violence sufficiently removed from reality) perfectly safe? Is there too much extreme violence in modern films?

What counts as violence in addition to the more obvious higher measure of physical harm done to a person or persons?

Each of these questions requires (and has no doubt received) many thesis length studies but they do not concern me here. The question I want to deal with is: given that a stretch of violence in a given film is proper and justified in order to keep the narrative realistic, *how* should the violence be portrayed. I will restrict myself to physical violence, such things as knifing, shooting, torturing and fighting. Human beings sometimes do violence to one another. For some, such acts are rare or non-existent, for others it is a part of daily existence. If one is making a film about characters who are either the victims or perpetrators of violence it would simply be disingenuous not to show it. I also take it as a given that it would be inexcusable for any film that purports to be a serious exploration of violent characters and films to gloss over the effects of violence – on all concerned. Gratuitous violence I take to be violence shown for pure effect and which is *not* dictated by any purer cinematic, psychological or narrative need. I take it that such filmic violence exists. I also take it that such portrayals of violence is its own sin, but it is not this is not my quarry either. I simply point out that gratuitous violence is a sin, not because it is violence but because it is gratuitous. Nothing in a film should be gratuitous, not even love, peace and gentle goodnight smiles. Nonetheless, I restrict my concern to violence that is *not* gratuitous. My question is how this non-gratuitous violence is to be shown to maximum effect.

Many filmmakers seem to think that the only honest way of being true to the violence and its effects is to get up close and personal and reveal the damage done as close-up as a lens can get. It is unpleasant but, "get a life", we will be told, one shouldn't seek to cloak it or sanitise it to protect merely sensitive souls. They can always switch off, exit the cinema or just close their eyes. (Gosh! If I closed my eyes to every sin, I would scarcely see a modern film at all.) However, we will be told, what we should face up to needs to be *in* our face? My response to this is a "Yes, but". What exactly *is* the most effective and powerful way to see the violence represented, honestly and with no holding back – just as it should be?

As elsewhere in the book, I seek a principled answer by drawing upon the very nature of the cinematic image. Remember that a cinematic image has two contrasting aspects. Insofar as it is photographic it is realistic: seeing an X in a film is, in a strong way, seeing X itself or seeing X being portrayed, just as if one were directly perceptually present to X. On the other hand, a cinematic image also has *form* in the way that ordinary perception does not. (Recall Chapter 1). The form of the image gives it additional potential and powers and it distances the viewer from the events seen. This distance allows for, even *calls* for, some very different responses. One does not, must not, and simply cannot react to a violent act on film as one may in real life. One cannot come to the aid of the victim or phone for an ambulance or make a witness statement to the police. That's left to other characters in the story, given that they exist or want to in the relevant part of the story world. But distance from the story world also allows and calls for a different (if overlapping) range of emotional or other psychological responses. In particular one may (and should be if the image is a good one) have some moments in which one can absorb further insight. In contrast, reflection and insight in a real-life situation have to wait until appropriate, maybe lifesaving, action has been seen to.

This special distance is not always best respected by the in-yer-face approach. I draw again upon the fight scene in the western epic *The Big Country* (William Wyler, US, 1958). Two key characters are brawling and most of the fight is seen in extreme long shot. This gives the viewer appropriate and important context. Here are two characters thumping each other and the sheer pointlessness of the violence is markedly represented by seeing them, and the fight, as puny in comparison with the 'big' open country. The point is made visually that the country's demands and challenges are far more important. Seeing the blood squirt out, Sam Peckinpah style, would have ruined the thing. Similarly, and again, in the war film *The Victors* (Carl Forman, UK/US, 1963) we have a military shooting squad execution scene filmed largely in very long shot, there being only a few medium shots and a clutch of close ups of soldiers witnessing and reacting to the scene. What we largely see is a snow covered landscape, and what we hear is Frank Sinatra singing 'Have Yourself a Merry Little Christmas'. Cold, strict indifference is conveyed here, alongside shame. This is an aspect of violence, too, and it is missing far too prominently in the in-yer-face approach.

Physical violence is cold, even when committed in what we tend to call the 'heat of the moment'. The coldness of violence is often far more effectively captured in reaction shots of other characters. Perhaps the most famous and best loved example is to be found in the scene in *Bambi* (Walt Disney, US, 1942) when 'mother' gets shot. Two further celebrated examples, already discussed under editing, come from David Lean's hanging scene in *Great Expectations* (David Lean, UK, 1946) and the massacre scene in *Doctor Zhivago* (Italy/UK/US, 1965). Seeing such stuff *through the soul* of a character is frequently far more telling than witnessing it for oneself. This fits the special and indirect way in which the cinematic image actually works.

I have just used a curious expression in the context of violence on the screen – 'best loved'. How can something horrible be 'loved'? One is not loving the violence, of course, one is loving the beauty of its portrayal and the truth and insight that its indirect showing reveals. At the very least it is a powerful reminder of what we stand in constant need of being reminded – the wider context and deeper implications. The indirect approach is almost always finer, better, more effective and more revealing in this respect. We have lost too much of this in the course of our crude, let's-be-explicit age. Almost always the indirect approach is best but not absolutely always. Sometimes having the violence in-yer-*own*-face can make a more powerful point than seeing it through or in the face of another character, as it did I believe in the boxing scene in *Raging Bull* (Martin Scorsese, US, 1980) mentioned earlier. That scene, though, captures the dance-like aspect such fighting can have. Most of the time though, it seems a sin against the power and narrative and psychological potential of the cinematic image to thrust the actual acts of violence too far in the viewer's face. That approach is almost always restrictive and unrevealing, it's just easier, less imaginative and lazier, filmmaking.

The sins of (lack of) symbolism in film story-telling

In briefly discussing Sergei Eisenstein's *Battleship Potemkin* (USSR, 1925) I said that a "film cannot be just a political or social campaign" and that its focus on this left me rather cold. No one, though, can deny the cinematic power of its symbolism. Symbolism can make for powerful cinema and, of course, it fits in with the thesis that the cinematic image is dream-like. Cinema's primary appeal is to the senses and emotions more rather than to a stricter, unadorned, abstract intellect. This is the territory where symbolism can have a home despite its purpose in Potemkin being more ideological and abstract. Symbols are also pictorial, we can take them in at a glance, no words need be involved, high degrees of meaning, significance and connection can be conveyed in a single shot, and they can be part of the sheer playfulness of the way cinema can make connections. Symbolism can enrich our experience of what cinema can do and illuminate a point in a uniquely powerful way, as it does in Potemkin – even if, for other reasons, it does so rather coldly in that film. Concepts cannot be represented in pictures directly because pictures are pictorial not linguistic, but connections of a conceptual, social or political nature can be conveyed very powerfully by symbols, and insights can be established. It became an established part of early Soviet film art.

Why then the lack of it nowadays? Save for limited amounts of cinema it has been standardly ignored, of course. At least *non*-diegetic symbolism has. (Symbolism that is not within the narrative world of the film.) Audiences in most places and times have become deeply unfamiliar with its use and do not seem to take to it easily. (The image of the baby in the monolith at the end of *2001: A Space Odyssey* is a grand exception, of course, though I know it put off many film-goers.) That said, every technique has once been new and unfamiliar. Serious filmmakers may also think symbolism too much of an adornment, but I think this reveals simple ignorance. The only recent (at the time of writing) serious film to contain much overt and obvious symbolism of the kind I am lauding here is *Bait* (Mark Jenkin, UK, 2019) a story of a fisherman who needs a boat. This is a curious but powerful little number, filmed in standard 16mm black and white in academy ratio on an old clockwork Bolex camera with genuine gritty film grain and what look like digitally added scratches and other imperfections.

What might be called diegetic symbolism has been perfectly familiar, though. Compare Potemkin with a rather engaging much later naval yarn of ye-olde-worlde injustice at sea, *HMS Defiant* (aka *Damn the Defiant*, Lewis Gilbert, UK, 1962). Here, too, sailors are treated badly, and there is a shot of maggoty food which symbolises the injustice. Most audiences seem to have preferred its symbolism to come in such diegetic clothing - through character, place and objects *within* the story world. Waves crashing on the beach (*On the Beach*, US, Stanley Kramer, 1959) and trains entering tunnels (*North by Northwest*, Alfred Hitchcock, US, 1959) come to mind as indicators of sex, for example. (And can function as efficient narrative placeholders for the act itself.) Certain film stars counted as symbols in themselves: we had the sex symbol, the symbols of the various genres. In westerns, for example, these would have been the gunslinger, the marshal, the drunken 'doc', the 'tart-with-a-heart', the honest homesteader, and so on. In fact, a genre could be half-way defined in terms of its symbol set, but I come on to that issue later.

Even studio logos used to be symbols of high achievement and magnificence and strong independent living: MGM's roaring lion, Fox's searchlights, Paramount's mountain, Universal's rotating globe, RKO's towering transmitter, Columbia's torch bearer and Republic Pictures' no-nonsense eagle. Some of these still exist, though they don't mean what they used to mean. (I vaguely recall seeing a first MGM film with a mere unanimated, logo-ised lion that didn't roar and thinking that the all that damned thing symbolised was the downfall of the once mighty empire that produced *Ben-Hur*.) Nowadays we get a slew of pathetic, merely trendy animated, unimposing, and often silent, logos that also, alas, reveal the scale, magnificence and importance of what we are about to see. We do have a company called 'Dogwoof' – I kid you not – a distributor of documentary films whose way of announcing their arrival is a barking dog. What I say, with due respect to Dogwoof, is that barking dogs are to roaring lions what today's cinema is to past cinema. (In fairness, I should add that they have presented to us many a good documentary.)

Discussing symbolism is difficult if only because almost anything can – at a sufficient stretch – be regarded as symbolic of something. An entire scene, for instance, through *mise-en-scène*, colour and performance may signify, love, say. A whole area of the study of signs and symbols – semiotics – has and continues to enjoy a big place in film theory but I will not divert myself here with such inflation. [131] My own thesis here is much simpler: the sin of the lack of more overt and obvious symbolism in overly naturalistic modern cinema counts as a sin because it denies the medium some of its most primordial power.

The sins of being *anti*-auteur

What is an *auteur*?

"A director must be a policeman, a midwife, a psychoanalyst, a sycophant and a bastard."

Billy Wilder

"I think, at the end of the day, filmmaking is a team, but eventually there's got to be a captain."

Ridley Scott

"I'm not averse to the Stalinist approach to filmmaking, just as long as I'm Stalin."

Alan Parker

Take the following three films: *Lawrence of Arabia* (David Lean, UK, 1962), *The Searchers* (John Ford, US, 1956) and *Citizen Kane* (Orson Welles, US, 1942). Each film has a very different and distinctive style. So much so that each has been said to have an 'auteur' (French for 'author'). A film auteur is the (putative) 'author' of a film, much in the sense in which a novelist is the author of a novel. Usually, but not always, it is the director who puts his or her particular stamp on a film. We must not, though, link the notion of auteur with the idea of a particular style. The director William Wyler comes to mind here. He is well known for never having had a recognisable 'Wyler' style. In fact he deliberately avoided having such, always maintaining that it is the story, not the director, that should dictate the style. I think this applies to many an auteur. In any case, however, a film can still have a unique auteur, even if one with a flexible attitude towards style.

The French term 'auteur' is used for historical reasons. The concept came about among a group of young French film theorists in the 1950s. (*Cahiers du Cinema* was a key publication.) Francois Truffaut, of French 'New Wave' fame, coined the phrase "la politique des auteurs". 'Politique' here simply means 'policy' or 'programme'. Indeed, the whole 'new-wave phenomenon in the history of the cinema in the early sixties in France and the UK was pretty well built on the notion of the *auteur* – with some impressive results. It has an impact on the way in which a film is to look and how it is to be valued. It involves very much a personal style or a unique way of looking at matters in a wider sense. When auteurs become established one should quite readily discern their films.

Criticisms of auteur theory – and some responses

Film making is artistically collaborative

During the 1960s, though, auteur theory came under suspicion. This is because it focused too much on the supposed authorial role of the director. It ignores (or *seems* to) one crucial fact about film-making: it is very much a *collaborative* affair. It's not like writing a novel or painting a picture or even composing music (where performers and conductors can make a difference). It involves a great variety of skills, many of which have been discussed in this book. Some of the people with these skills – the cinematographer, production designer, editor, musical composer are no mere technicians, either. They are key *creative* contributors to a film. Their contributions matter to the look, sound and feel of a film.

The auteur theory has also come in for some grief of a more philosophical nature. This emanated originally from the 'New Criticism', a school of literary criticism. The key argument here is that auteur theory commits what is called the "intentional fallacy". This comes into play when we interpret works of art by thinking about what the author *meant* (intended) by doing things a certain way. All that is less important, so it was argued, than the experience of the viewer (or reader).

I'm not sure how moved we should be by all this criticism of the notion of an auteur. I do not doubt for one moment that films involve any number of key skills, nor that such skills are so specialised that no one person can be a master of them all, at least not technically. Nonetheless, I fear that today's popular auteur-denial is just one more unmerited tilt to a merely fashionable egalitarianism. Thus, we may wonder whether the real bearer of the sins hereabouts is not so much *Auteur* Theory as *No-Auteur* Theory.

We can firm up some thoughts here firstly by considering the role of the (as yet putative) auteur of the films mentioned above. Secondly, we can ask whether one person can still be a Master of All Arts. Thirdly, we may question whether the essential collaboration involved in making films refutes Auteur Theory? Finally, we can question whether the intentional fallacy is even relevant.

Each of the films mentioned at the outset of this section is arguably the work of an auteur. That auteur tightly controls everything: the script, the look, the performances, the cutting and so on. David Lean, for instance, has been known (in making his film *Great Expectations*) to sack a cinematographer in mid-stream because, upon seeing the rushes the morning after a shoot, he did not like the look of them. Some auteurs have a style that is so distinctive and well-known that their name has taken on adjectival form, allowing us to describe crisply a film from another director made in a similar style. (eg: 'Hitchcockian').

The auteur doesn't have to be the director. It can be the producer – Disney, for example. No one who sees *Pinocchio* (US, 1940) says "I've seen a Norman Ferguson (et.al) film". He was one of the film's directors but who's heard of him? No! One calls it a 'Disney' film – and rightly so. Disney was the one with the final artistic stamp. Others simply had to use their considerable skills, and creative powers, to follow suit. *Gone With The Wind* (US, 1939) is arguably a David O'Selznick film *not* (simply) a Victor Fleming film. (Both an earlier director (George Cukor) and cinematographer - Lee Garmes - did not continue because of Selznick's authorial demands.) In other cases, the fact that a film had a certain producer with a powerful liking for a certain style is at least as important as the fact that it had a particular director. Arthur Freed comes to mind – the real auteur of many later MGM musicals, or at least of their style. Always, however, *the* auteur is the one who supplies the creative vision for the film – director or otherwise. Most of the time, though, if there is a discernible auteur at all, it is the director. *The Searchers* (US, 1956) is very much a John Ford film. *The Big Sleep* (US, 1946) owes its due to Howard Hawks. One could go on.

One person cannot be a Master of All Arts

But can one person still be a Master of *all* Arts, at least in the sense that the putative auteurs of the above films are supposed to be? Not technically, perhaps, though Lean knew his photography and had been a professional editor of feature films. Hitchcock had also been an editor. We have already seen how Lean took control. Hitchcock provides us with an even more dramatic example. He and his then provider of music, Bernard Hermann, could justifiably have been counted as joint-auteurs of some of the world finest pieces of cinema, including *Vertigo* (US, 1958). Despite this, he and Hermann parted company for music written for his later film *Torn Curtain* (US, 1966) (As I understand it, something more trendily 60s was needed than Hermann could, or was willing to, provide.) This shows that some directors at least have been in the position to make themselves the auteur by sheer force. Good!

There is, however, a further suggestion: an individual person can be a Master of All Arts in the sense of just knowing what they want and knowing what is best. Hitchcock, Lean – any of the brightest and best directors fit that bill. Even Orson Welles who, as he made *Citizen Kane* admitted he knew nothing about cinematography and the technicalities of filmmaking (and was delighted when celebrated cinematographer Gregg Toland walked into his life and said he'd like to be part of the show). However, Welles knew well enough how to tell a story and how it should look. Welles was the auteur of that film and was, in the relevant sense, the Master of All Arts. The fact that one may need others to help one realise one's visions is a further issue. The auteur does not need all the skills, they simply need all the appropriate sensibilities. Even the fact that the chief others are no mere technicians but creative artists in their own right, as are all good editors, sound mixers, screenwriters, cinematographers, production and costume designers, make-up and hair specialists, and who are deservedly celebrated for their contributing achievements, does not prevent there being a 'Master of *All* Arts' in some still strong sense. The vision can be *one*, and belong to one, despite the necessary artistic contribution of the *many*. It is a simple conceptual error to confuse vision with contribution, or even collaboration. What matters is not the fact of collaboration, or even the necessity for it, but to what (and who's) vision all the contributions and collaborations are in service.[132] I conclude that the fact that filmmaking is necessarily a collaborative endeavour does not refute auteur theory.

It is precisely because the cinematic image is, by its very nature, a single, psychologically and aesthetically unified thing (as is a painting) that its creation should be similarly unified. Who precisely does the unifying is an interesting further question but if it's done by committee, divided up in accordance with the principles of democracy and guided by a very misguided notion of egalitarianism, one can expect the result to be a dog's dinner. Dictatorships are far better in art, I feel. In art they achieve unity of vision and purpose – just what is needed. Of course, the dictator needs to know what they're about and many fail to have a sufficiently well-defined, distinctively meaningful and decisive vision. They would be classified as auteurs only in the extended sense of being the authors of rubbish. Where such unfortunate directors are let loose, artistic chaos can be expected to fill the inevitable aesthetic and storytelling vacuum. If *one* 'policy' is not specified and turned into standing orders, everyone will have their own, and only an occasional and purely accidental compatibilism could ever be expected to emerge. Armies can fall apart if that happens and that includes the army required for the making a film. It's all a matter of degree, of course, but if one wants the best of films, one needs the highest degree of 'cooperation' in the service of *one* vision, followed by recognition and compliance. The essential principle – one single vision – applies, of course to *all* arts. It applies to theatre and even to music where an interpreter is needed at the point of performance. And one auteur there is. There is something unified about all (recognisable) performances of Elgar's *Enigma Variations*, no matter how much some 'young pup' of a conductor thinks they've got something new to add.[133] A single auteur is required, I am inclined to say by the very nature of art, it's just that, in many arts – novels, poetry, painting - the one creator is all the creative army there is.

The intentional fallacy

Or is it? Let's look further into the 'Intentional Fallacy', which has been seen to be a problem hereabouts. The term originated in literary criticism but can apply elsewhere as well – wherever there is an alleged author. It is called a "fallacy" (which is, strictly, an error of reasoning) because it is supposed to reveal the mistake of thinking that one can assess a work of art by appeal to the purpose (the 'intention') of the creating artist.[134] It was a reaction against the common belief that the correct interpretation of a work of art is given by what the creator intended. *That* was what you really had to know, though it may often be held to be obvious from an inspection of the work itself.

But why is *that* a mistake? For one thing, once a work has been published, many other interpretations can (and often do) come to life, so there is no reason why the author's interpretation should take pride of top place. I am not entirely sold on the second part of that but it matters not in any case, because a work's having many interpretations does not mean it has many creators. It simply means that there are many understandings of what has been created – and it is still what the author has given us that is being variously interpreted. Even though there is no such thing (I think this is true) as an *uninterpreted* way of seeing an artwork (even seeing it *as* an artwork is already at least the beginnings of interpretation) what is being variously interpreted is still the *one* thing. An interpretation is a way of organising one's understanding and experience of something, not to create alternative versions of it – except metaphorically.

Film makers do not work in a vacuum

Another issue lurking here is that the putative auteur did not create their work in a vacuum. Many forces and assumptions of a philosophical, cultural, historical, ideological and political kind influenced the work, even discounting any human "collaborators" there may have been. Many films have been made in the context of an industrial pipeline. Doesn't this refute the notion of the auteur? Not at all. A sensible version of auteur theory does not *have* to insist that the author is free from influence, it needs only to accept, as do we all, that the author's *way* of understanding (or even sub-conscious use of these influences) plays into what the author creates. Criticism of an *artwork* may legitimately be based on these factors but not criticism of auteur theory. To the extent that the exponents of auteur theory are led ignore other clearly important matters, then *they* can indeed be legitimately criticised but all this simple confusion leaves auteur theory itself completely intact purely as a descriptive theory of artwork creation.

More importantly, it also leaves intact the thought that an artwork *needs* an auteur if it is to be among the best of its type. I am prepared to think that the very best films have been what one may call 'auteur' films, even in the days of the Hollywood dream machine industry. Indeed, some of the very best auteurs worked in that context. Even at worst, all this would mean is that the real auteur is the factory (studio) boss rather than the individual director – Sam Goldwyn, Louis B. Mayer, and so on, come to mind. I am sure that many of today's CEOs in the world of film financing cannot tell films from brands of toothpaste, and care about the difference even less – but then, *they* tend to manufacture franchised trash. They are auteurs (if I can use the term still) of the cinematic equivalent of the Big Mac.

In any case, the industrial context of the production doesn't by itself exclude the notion of an auteur. After all, many past artists had to give the patronage system upon which they depended (the Church or the king, and so on) the sort of product they wanted but nobody can sensibly conclude from this that Mozart was not the composer (auteur) of his own music. Studios, of course, simply do not exist these days in anything like the old sense, even though some of the old names and logos still do: MGM, 20th Century Fox, Paramount, and so on. In days now well gone, these studios employed people in a more standard way. People learned their trades within their walls. But the best of them also learned how to become auteurs. Nowadays the young depend on 'film-schools'. I think learning was in a better position in the past. Mistakes were not necessarily lethal. There was no need for rush in acquiring and developing skills and artistry on one's way. It all seems a bit more solid and reliable that going to school then being plunged into life or death. On the whole, good cinema needs its properly brought up auteurs. My general conclusion, then, is that auteur theory is more sinned against than sinning.

Such thoughts as these may go well beyond the intentions of the original auteur theorists but so what? Nothing I have discussed refutes auteur theory *per se*. Nor does the fact that many a time the auteur's intention may be neither knowable nor clearly discernible. That the receiver cannot recover all the meanings the giver intended to give certainly means that the receiver has to fall back on his own interpretation, but it tells us nothing about whether those intentions were pivotal in the creation of the gift. It's merely the misfortune of inevitable ignorance. Another point: author intention is hardly irrelevant to the *moral* evaluation of an artwork and, therefore, to its aesthetic evaluation, as I will argue later. Who, for example, can say with confidence that Riefenstahl's awful, Nazi, Hitler-fawning attitude is not relevant to the evaluation of *Triumph of the Will*? My conclusion: auteur theory can stand as a simple descriptive theory of how many films have been made and the notion of an auteur can stand as a necessary condition for the making of a good film.

I am not saying in this section that all films have a discernible auteur or that they cannot be at least passable films with some decent characteristics if they *in fact* have an author only in a very extended sense of the term. In the old Hollywood studio system, each major contributor to a film tended, in true assembly-line fashion, to get on with their work on a film in the expected way then, on the following Monday morning, find themselves assigned to the next project. Even the director would quickly move on. Only in the more prestigious films made by box-office successful directors can we see much individual artistic clout at play. Yet for all that, each operator of each cog in the whole machine worked (consciously or not) in accordance with a single vision. Auteur theory still stands.

What really matters, then, is that a film be the result of a singular, unified, imaginative *vision*. Maybe that vision could be regarded as the real auteur. So long as everyone on the film shared that vision, the outcome would be a truly authored work. It's just far more likely that such a vision would be formed, and adhered to, with strong, pretty well dictatorial power from – well, someone.

The supposed sins of cliché – and 'tropes'

These two features of storytelling (tropes and cliché) get mixed up. Perhaps this is inevitable given that (a) both are used repeatedly, (b) there is no clear-cut distinction between the two and (c) the trope can easily become cliché. Tropes can be understood as storytelling devices or images that convey something more than is literally shown. Usually they get across the sort of thing (the genre, for example) one is looking at. Thus, one might classify as tropes the use of artificial life forms and aliens (which suggest science fiction) or the gunfight showdown (a western). It may be an object that keeps the story moving on – a bomb that has yet to explode, a valuable jewel as it makes its rounds or remains hidden, stolen money, something special that maybe two or more characters are keen to get their hands on. One of my favourite examples of this comes from the film *Charade* (Stanley Donen, US, 1963). A young widow, several crooks and an American government agent all want to get hold of a dead man's wealth. Each has what they take to be a legitimate reason for claiming it, but they don't know where it is or even what it is, though it stares them in the face pretty much throughout the entire film. The film is driven by this device and only when a special context makes the penny drop does the climax come. In *The Maltese Falcon* (John Huston, US 1941) the falcon statue itself is the trope. Hitchcock popularised the word 'MacGuffin' for these types of tropes, though there seems to be no exact definition.

The lack of precision is also inevitable, though this doesn't matter too much for our present purposes. A key difference between a trope and a cliché is that the former is not a term of evaluation but of description. There is nothing obviously wrong with employing tropes in films. In fact, to the degree that they help tell stories with efficiency and promote a sense of excitement (given that this is the aim of the film) they are entirely a good idea. Where things go wrong (supposedly, at any rate) is when they turn into clichés. They do that when they become overused, poorly used or unthinkingly used as an easy substitute for storytelling intelligence. Naturally, determining that point is a judgement call. I can only suggest asking oneself whether or not their use in a particular film *seems* dull or overdone. Since certain kinds of trope are indicators of genre, one's estimation of them might well depend also on how much one values genre.

The sins of cliché may seem too obvious to spend much time on – so I will not. Such sin is also, of course, far from uniquely modern. Cliché can, as always, make a film tedious. One knows too many times what is going to happen next and it all seems too much an easy substitute for a more thoughtful approach, whether they are clichés of storytelling, character, music – whatever. So, are clichés things we should 'avoid like the plague'? Fun aside, while such avoidance is normally a good thing and subversion of cliché can be an interesting and humorous policy, I wonder if we can sometimes get too pompous about cliché – to the point where *avoiding* it becomes the sin. Let us see what some of the virtues of cliché may be. After all, I like keeping my feet on the ground.

Clichés, we should keep in mind, can be useful storytelling devices, especially if one is telling of adventure or mystery or romance (together with many other categories) and one wants to keep the plot moving along – as one should. In my view, it takes a hard-nosed purist, one who values far less than they ought, to think this unimportant. Clichés can sum things up nicely – characters and situations - in a handy, crisp manner. They will always be inadequate for deeper purposes of character and situation analysis, of course, and philosophically they will *never* do. Never say to me, "Beauty lies in the eye of the beholder" unless you enjoy watching someone choke to death in front of you. It is my favourite example from the department of completely unthinking aesthetics. But cliché can give one a quick fuller character when needed in a context in which one has no time to waste – and such contexts may not be without value. Even though cliched characters may hardly be convincingly real as individuals, the best of them mark out general profiles of human characteristics that can be morally useful in storytelling, especially when it comes to celebrating the good profiles and abhorring the worst.

Next, we can sometimes encounter what some may regard as cliché but others think are profoundly true. I really *do* think that adopting the policy of an eye for an eye and a tooth for tooth leaves the world blind and toothless, whether to say it is cliché or not. The Bible and Shakespeare, of course, are the two favoured sources here. We can too easily confuse idiom for cliché, too. It seems obvious that I am entitled to report that I have butterflies in my stomach when I propose certain films for our local film club. The sin then, if there is one, is to be found more in *how* certain devices are used that the mere fact that they have a continuing use. My case here is that they *can* have a use in all kinds of storytelling that are perfectly legitimate. Sometimes, cliché and cinema can go together happily, just like – well (what else?) – rhubarb and custard.

Take the film *1917* (US/UK, Sam Mendes, 2019). Two young British soldiers on a WW1 Mission Impossible (should they wish to accept, which of course they do) have to take a message behind enemy lines to prevent the massacre of 1600 men who are heading straight for a trap. One can, on this much information, readily understand my expectation of the worse from this. It didn't seem much of a story, for a start. I also wondered if it would take the attitude that a story is a bit beside the point anyway when you're on a stomach-churning theme park ride. I also do not like mere visceral impact parading itself as cinema. My worries, however, were soon dispelled, and pretty well totally.

I can readily see why some should not regard it as without serious flaw. It gives us no new insight into the horrors of war – though, as I have already made clear, originality is an overrated virtue, and the word is usually attached to what is distinctly unoriginal in any case. But why worry? How original a film may be is far less important than how well it does its job, I think. More to the point here, though, one may suppose that it might rely a little too much on the usual clichés of war cinema: a British soldier being killed by a German officer after the former had, with typical Anglo-Saxon decency, rescued the man from a burning plane; the discovery of a frightened, ragged, young, half-starved but nevertheless pretty little maiden, complete with baby child, hiding in the shadows - and so on - though presumably these things *did* happen. Perhaps these are more trope than cliché, in any case. One might also complain that some of the bit characters come across as a bit *too* stereotyped - though there surely were such characters. I think that we complain too knowingly about such matters sometimes. I think we would certainly be doing so in respect of the present film. Besides, we're *all* clichés to a point. We'd be damnably unpredictable and difficult to deal with if we were not.

Mendes, though, steers round (almost literally with his ultra-mobile camera) these weaker aspects (if that's what they are) and keeps well focused on his true dramatic and visual intentions. Firstly, we feel constantly very close to the main characters, both sympathetically played: how they feel, their frights, their concerns, their humanity. Psychologically, as well as visually, we never leave their side. Secondly, and mainly, the film conveys better than any other I know the danger, the fear, the close death and constant decay, the never-ending muck, rats and remains and ever-present stench that must have characterised trench warfare, and Mendes does it with eye-popping visual aplomb. Forget what you may have read about its being all done in one take. It wasn't (though the takes were very long). It was made deliberately to *look* that way. That's not a cheat – looks are important to cinema, are they not? Standardly, I do not much like the technique, I have to say (fake or otherwise). I always wonder what is supposed to be inferior about cutting – but here, at least, it works. The visual seamlessness captures well what must have been the sheer unrelenting, unrelieved experience of the real nightmare. Moreover, the essence of the nightmare itself is captured with a horror that almost seems almost unreal at times, as though it is an evil magic conjured up by a vengeful wizard. (That's Roger Deakins' superb cinematography.) In contrast, its moments of unsteady peace seem equally unreal. (That's Newman's almost wistful Elgar-like score at play.) In general, the soundtrack is well mixed, and further emphasises the hard to take in horror of our witness to the passing show. There's certainly nothing merely in-yer-Dolby-deafened-ear about it. (Though I'm glad I didn't see this in its Imax version.) It is one of those times when the look, sound and air of magical unreality reflects, I think, what the participants themselves must have experienced in their own very real nightmares and more hard-to-believe relieved moments. Never does Mendes allow mere viscerality to rule the roost, it's all pure cinema, take your eye away for a single moment if you can. In short, it is an astonishing achievement and a beautifully told story – even with some measure that is arguably cliché. My general conclusion? Avoid getting too snooty about cliché.

The sins of *The Age of the Algorithm*

Cliché is one thing, but algorithm quite another. Cliché may (legitimately) help storytelling become more efficient; algorithm indicates that one is watching only a commodity. Expensive films these days have to satisfy the algorithms of those who provide the finance. Nothing much matters than getting into one's film A, B and C because doing so increases the chances of financial success and avoiding X, Y and Z because these are known to spell financial failure, or at least lean that way. One of the things such films have to do is satisfy to an acceptable degree the cultural demands of the many parts of the world in which the film has to succeed if it is to make money at all. One will, of course, be told that it's just giving the pundits what they want, and to some considerable extent that is right. Alas, it also guarantees films that are almost completely mindless, gormless FX-driven drivel of industrial-strength, heavy-duty grade. It pretty well rules out intelligent, imaginative, challenging, thoughtful, properly emotionally engaging product. Hollywood, and other places may just as well be manufacturers of Coca-Cola. If this died one day because people got fed up with it, it would not so much mark the death of popular cinema as evidence that its death happened some time ago. I can sometimes smell the corpse of cinema before even the hotdogs every time I walk past a multiplex.

One sin a film can never commit: films from books.

It seems frequently observed, and genuinely felt, that when a good book is adapted for the screen, it is simply impossible to rid one's evaluation of the film of one's evaluation of the book, often to the detriment of one's evaluation of the film. I think it a profound error to think that way. I can easily see how it arises. One loves the book, so the resulting film must not offend. I can see that but ask, offend against *what*, exactly? It can hardly be that the film reflects the book only problematically or partly – can it? That is inevitable given the core fact that film and book are two fundamentally different kinds of media. Books *describe* and films *depict*; books employ *language*, films use *images*; books *tell*, films *show*. This much is clear, of course, and frequently acknowledged, but I think we then often go on to miss the depths of its implications.

These are? While a book may well have deep value, and the film from which it somehow 'comes', little or none, the value (or its lack) in each case must nevertheless arise from some profoundly different set of characteristics, each set being peculiar and essential to its own medium. One must therefore see the film entirely as its own entity – another kind of thing altogether, not a thing merely distortedly begotten of the same kind. One must love both media, but that love must be cashed out as love of some very different intrinsic types of expression if it is to amount to anything.

I find it a helpful aid to thought hereabouts to cease thinking of a film as an *adaptation* of a book right from the off. (Even though, in a trivial sense, it remains one.) The very word 'adaptation' is problematic: it points to the book as primary (though it only really comes *before* in time) thus rendering the film somehow secondary. In turn, this tempts us to assume (if perhaps subconsciously) that, being an adaptation, it must almost inexorably be not quite as good, or perhaps pure, as the 'original', no matter how good it may be according to its own nature. This would be a serious failure of evaluation.

Correlatively, one must cease also to understand the book as the 'original' (as opposed to being the work that simply came along earlier) even though it is the item that provided some core ideas and characters. In a crucial respect, the film is just as much an original (of its particular type) as the book is (of its particular type). I'm talking aesthetics here, of course (that beauty comes from different elements in each case) and even hinting at metaphysics (that each medium has its own quite different fundamental nature). The book simply provides some 'raw material' and perhaps also some inspiration. It cannot, though, impress its intrinsic characteristics, beauty and structures on to the film, for film simply cannot accept its forms. Film is no mere lump of wax upon which a book can force its all-encompassing impressions. The film must be allowed to develop its own very different form, if it is to live at all, and given license to express itself according to that form. The only alternative is cinematic death.

Thus a film, if a failure, is a failed piece of cinema not a failure relative, in some sense, to the book's literary success. So, 'don't let a favourite book become the film's fate' would be my own go-to slogan here.

Chapter 9: The Issue of Morality and Goodness in Cinema

A critique of Aesthetic Autonomism

Can a film, or any work of art, retain any of its aesthetic qualities regardless of any of its other qualities, including that of taking a repulsive moral stance? The view that this *is* the case is called 'aesthetic autonomism'. According to this view, a film can be aesthetically beautiful despite its moral repulsiveness or dubiousness. An artwork can be evaluated aesthetically without drawing upon any matter outside the aesthetic realm. Aesthetics is, so to speak, its own master. If this is true, films such as *The Act of Killing* (Jerry Oppenheimer, Denmark, 2013) – discussed below, or Riefenstahl's *The Triumph of the Will* (Germany, 1935) could be regarded as beautiful pieces of cinema, because of their cinematic qualities, despite the fact that the first gives a platform for evil people to act out (pictorially) their own evil, and the second celebrates Nazism. Being an aesthetic autonomist doesn't mean that one approves of the evil, only that one can still admire wonderful cinema without having to worry about the ethics. Autonomism may sound reasonable enough and it has enjoyed considerable high-ground in modern thinking. After all, the connection between morality and beauty isn't obvious. Cannot a morally evil person be beautiful?

I wholly reject aesthetic autonomism and defend its opposite thesis 'ethicism', which maintains that an artwork's aesthetic qualities are closely related to, and even dependent upon its moral properties. However, we need to refine the question. Firstly, by 'repulsive moral stance' I mean encouraging or celebrating that which is evil, or even giving illegitimate airing to something evil. This is something beyond the mere *showing* of evil. A film may well be *about* something evil or feature evil characters and doings if it is to be true of various aspects of the human behaviour. 'Good cinema' needs more precision here, too. I refer here to the aesthetic values of what I've been calling the 'cinematic image'. So the question is whether the positive aesthetic qualities of a film can survive a film's repulsive moral stance (as just defined) without themselves becoming either devalued or eliminated altogether. (I simply take it as a fact that films are open to moral evaluation.)

My answer to this more precise philosophical question will be a firm, 'No!' My position is this: a film that serves ugly, immoral purposes has whatever aesthetics qualities it may otherwise have had rendered null and void. Put it this way, the moral ugliness empties out whatever aesthetic value it may otherwise have enjoyed. I will not begin my argument too abstractly though. Rather, I will start by giving an example of a film I take to be morally repulsive and an example of one I take to be morally virtuous. I look at their various effects and then return to my argument. I then offer a series of philosophical arguments to defend my position and follow this with a treatment of a modern philosopher (Kant) who has offered a strong defence of autonomism. A reader may then skip these more formal and difficult philosophical arguments and go on to the next major section. (I hope you won't, for justification is key.)

The sins of repulsive moral stance in a story

I open my case with my review of the film I mentioned above - *The Act of Killing* (Jerry Oppenheimer, Denmark, 2013).

> "The only challenge in listing the moral flaws in this misbegotten, gut-wrenching, utterly unedifying, pokey little exploration of Indonesian cultural life is knowing just where to start. I could mention the director's complicity in allowing two young children to watch the most sickening scene ever photographed for a film. That said, I suppose he didn't wish to risk being throttled with a wire in the home of his own leading man. What did we see? A thinned out little nobody being given the resources to seek relief from the memory of torture and murder by pretending to have his methods inflicted upon himself. Just what made the director think that this would make worthwhile watching? And just how are we supposed to react? With a clap of admiration for sheer physical and mental endurance, perhaps?
>
> All this, however, dwindles into insignificance compared with the fundamental flaw - that of giving these still threatening, morally shrivelled up nobodies a platform to play on and the instruments to play with. Just where is the point of enlightenment supposed to be found here? I don't accuse the filmmakers of deliberately presenting these men as film stars, or even of actually doing so by sheer careless oversight. Rather, the deep moral error lies in giving them the opportunity of further deluding themselves by believing even yet in the possibility that they might come across as glittering 'freemen' saving their vulnerable country from a destructive communist conspiracy – as saviours of all that shines. It is one thing openly and unabashedly to show evil for what it just is - empty, life-denying banality. That is a *good* thing to do. It is quite another to give that evil a technicoloured stage from which it can sing its own unmelodic song, as though it deserves a place to be heard alongside all comers. This makes for shallow even-handedness perhaps - but that's the least of its miserable effects."

Oppenheimer is capable of reason, though, so what has the director himself got to say by way of justification? On the film's own website he says, "The filmmaking method we use . . . is best seen as an investigative technique, refined to help us understand not only what we see, but also how we see, and how we imagine. (The resulting film may best be described as a documentary of the imagination.) These are questions of critical importance to understanding the imaginative procedures by which human beings persecute each other . . ."[135]

"A documentary of the imagination"? "Investigative technique"? Give me a break. Quite frankly this is gobbledygook. His film goes nowhere at all in helping us to understand anything at all. Oppenheimer's words ring with thin intellectual loftiness. Worse still, I have seen it added that Anwar is the bravest and most honest character in the film. This is breathtakingly offensive. Anwar is not brave at all, he is merely self-advertising, and even what honesty he does show is limited largely to the simple 'I did it' variety – and in circumstances in which he faces little threat. How much real honesty does he show about the poisonous little character he made of himself?

The self-delusion of the director is further displayed by the following curious fact – nowhere in his statement is the word 'evil' used – even once – at least as far as I have seen. Perhaps he thinks himself too much a modern minded and sophisticated intellect to use so antiquated, and religious sounding, a word. I have to say that I find its absence to be part of the filmmaker's preposterous pretence that we are dealing with something more complex and interesting than evil can ever claim to be. That is a modern-minded self-delusion indeed, and one shared, by too many influential people these days. I am pleased to distance myself from them.

For these reasons I was all set to confer upon this poisonous nonsense what would have been the so far singular award of 0 out of 10 - but for its ending. Here at least we see its glittering main star made physically sick by the faint glimmer of realisation that there is something about himself that simply won't do. Here at last was a picture of a thin, puking ghost of a soul just about recognising his own self-prescribed descent into hell - and not liking what he saw. This is the film's sole insight. So (a sadly non-unique) 1/10 I had, reluctantly, to confer upon it. Or am I being too kind?

On the whole I found no moral authority or insight at all in this film. The occasional stretches of quasi-poetic cinema involving a big metallic fish and girls in pink, dancing against the misty green-grey skies above the jungle (I am not making this up) do nothing to relieve matters. Its moral flaws simply become aesthetic flaws as well. Moral repulsiveness may be shown in a way that is beautiful but a morally repulsive *way* of showing it never can. It suffices only to show just how avant-garde Oppenheimer clearly wishes to think himself.

I am shocked that this film seems to have got away with even so much as existing. A newspaper film reviewer, felt the same, adding:

> I'd feel the same if film-makers had gone to rural Argentina in the 1950s, rounding up a bunch of ageing Nazis and getting them to make a film entitled

"We Love Killing Jews". Think of other half-covered-up atrocities – in Bosnia, Rwanda, South Africa, Israel, any place you like with secrets – and imagine similar films had been made. Consider your response – and now consider whether such goings-on in Indonesia are not acceptable merely because the place is so far away, and so little known or talked about that the cruelty of such an act can pass uncriticised.

Nick Fraser, *The Guardian*, 23 February, 2014

A moral, and very beautiful, cinematic saint

If Oppenheimer gives us one of the most morally repulsive films ever made, I submit David Lean as having given us one of the most morally virtuous – *Brief Encounter* (UK, 1945)

The film tells the story of Laura Jesson, wife of Fred Jesson, someone who seems, at first, to be the most boring man in Britain. She is also the mother of a couple of very precocious children – the sort who get fun out of going to the circus and pantomime. One can easily imagine young Bobby as mastering his Meccano. (This is the most British of films ever made.) The family is comfortable and middle class. On one of her frequent shopping expeditions to the nearby town of Milford, always taken by train, she gets a piece of soot in her eyes from a passing steam express. (Can you remember all that romantic soot and smoke and steam? This is a Britain now very long gone.) A handsome man, one Dr. Alec Harvey (played by Trevor Howard) appears by her side. "Please let me have a look, I happen to be a doctor", he says to her, as he removes the annoying speck with a nicely laundered middle-class handkerchief.

This encounter is not only very brief it is also quite casual. The film, though, wastes no time in conveying the Britain of the time. The rushing steam train is a telling and rather obvious metaphor for the oncoming speed of the affair to follow. The story begins near its end as Laura and the doctor sit in the station café saying goodbye – the decision to part by now having been made.

I could go on about the efficiency with which David Lean gets on with things and quickly establishes the psychology of it all. This is story telling of the first order, but what I want to concentrate on is a very important contrast. Laura may have led some sort of romantic dream life with the good doctor and here she is, very much in real life, submerged (I don't think that's too strong a word) in a reality that seems tediously domestic yet founded at least on rock and trust. That's going to be important.

The dream, however, is explored. There is a sense of danger, to be sure, but it is quickly supressed. Laura's emotions are now being led into an ocean swell. She returns home to a domestic crisis. Young Bobby has been knocked down by a car.

He's not badly hurt but it brings Laura back to reality in a guilty crack: while she was gadding about with a doctor, her son was in an accident. Time rolls on, though, and Laura is shopping in downtown Milford again. But the dream is too well bedded down not to spring to life again. The doctor arrives. He's in a bit of a rush but they promise to meet again. At this point there is one of Celia Johnson's finest ever pieces of eye-acting. Her eyes are dancing with nervous excitement and quite suddenly she registers a glimpse of real danger – but it doesn't make any difference. They have now fallen in love. At times, Laura tries desperately to see sense, halfway realising the depths of deception into which she has descended. "It's awfully easy to lie when you know you are trusted implicitly", she says at one point, "so very easy and so very degrading". Indeed, but once you're there, you're there. And what is she losing? She's losing purpose and becoming blind to what she knows and loves.

Throughout the film Rachmaninov's Piano Concerto No.2 draws us into Laura's love-dream – sometimes as background music and sometimes being listened to at home on the gramophone. If one is going to use established music, especially classical music, in a film, one had better make it a character itself, and Lean, I think, pretty much does this. The 'Rach 2' is one of the most highly romantic of all piano concerti but, like all the best of such stuff, it's also full of longing, loss and despair. (Bryan Forbes does the same thing with the Brahms No.1 Piano Concerto in his *The L-Shaped Room* (UK, 1962) though this time the male lover is working class.) In much of today's cinema despair, purposelessness and hopelessness would reign supreme. (I know. I see most of it.) In this film, however, we see hope. Laura *does* re-awaken, not altogether but fully enough to realise what she must now do - make the break and return to purpose and the more solid reality in which she can truly be at peace. A dream may sometimes linger but with little solidity.

Brief Encounter is a film which, from today's perspective, can easily come in for a bit of stick. It's too sentimental. It's too stilted. It's too politically irrelevant. It's too polite. "Wrong! Wrong! Wrong! and Wrong!", I want to say. It has the manners of its age, to be sure, films almost always do, but it is not sentimental in the least. It poses a serious question about where we can find reality. And far from being stilted, the story flows like a river, and we follow its twists, turns, eddies and flurries without effort. Most of all, if it is politically irrelevant, this is only because its theme transcends politics.

Let's be blunt, Laura chooses truth over falsehood, reality over illusion, and goodness over temptation. She is offered the world of her dreams and chooses the world she has already been given, the world in which she is really most alive. Celia Johnson takes on the challenge of conveying all that and does so to perfection. *Brief Encounter* is about getting lost and then being found. It is about sinking into unreality and then rising back up to reality. It is about recognising what is solid and what can really bear the weight of life. Most of all, it is about seeing what is good and what is right and sticking to it in full recognition that one's life does indeed depend upon it. It is about moral courage. It is, in short, one of the most realistic of films ever made. The bigger point here, though, is that its rich aesthetic beauty seems strengthened by its being in service to something morally beautiful. The philosopher Iris Murdoch once said, "Art and morals are, with certain provisos, . . . one. Their essence is the same . . . love".[136]

All great films are somehow deeply moral films and a variety of films fit this bill. They laud moral value and make clear the centrality of their core value: forgiveness: *Les Miserables* (Bille August, UK, 1998) and *Invictus* (Clint Eastwood, US, 2009); self-sacrifice: *It's A Wonderful Life'* (Frank Capra, US, 1946) and *A Man For All Seasons* (Fred Zinnemann, UK, 1966); grace: *Babette's Feast* (Gabriel Axel, Denmark, 1987) and salvation: *Ben-Hur* (William Wyler, US, 1959) and, in a sense at least, *Groundhog Day* (Harold Ramis, US, 1993). And many good films deal with the wages of sin: *Brighton Rock* (John Boulting, UK, 1948) and *Citizen Kane* (Orson Welles, US, 1941). There is something elemental about being shown the virtues at work, and the vices for what they are. It can lead us to wisdom and, as St. Thomas Aquinas has said, "Of all human pursuits, the pursuit of wisdom is the most perfect because in so far as a man gives himself up to the pursuit of wisdom, to that extent he enjoys some portion of true happiness."[137]

But while all this can show us that films lauding moral rectitude can leave us with hope (and to value the film as a whole) and films that laud evil can lead us to nihilism, it is not yet entirely clear how these things can affect our aesthetic evaluations. I thus return to this crucial question. Remember: I am not talking of films here that are *about* evil – all kinds of good film can be that - but about films that *laud* it, give it too much place, or even think that it is worthy, or even possible, for it to be considered part of the dialogue of rational discourse. (Which might more fairly characterise *The Act of Killing*.) One can certainly have a rational discourse *about* evil, just as one can have good films *about* it. I am about to embark on such discourse, but why can't evil (or its re-enactment) play some kind of *part* in the good stuff, as Oppenheimer seems to think?

Keep in mind here that I am not just pointing out that a film's corrupt moral values can spoil our appreciation of its aesthetic values. Almost anything, including poor storytelling can do that. Besides, that would leave its aesthetic values themselves essentially untouched. Rather, I am going to argue that a film's moral corruption leads to its aesthetic corruption (if there is anything of potentially aesthetic value at play in the first place). I am saying that moral cinematic corruption either reduces or even eliminates its aesthetic potential altogether, even though a film remains visually untouched. Beauty and morality have that kind of intimate natural connection. We do not say of some moral decency performed beyond the call of mere duty, "What a beautiful thing that was to do", for nothing. However, a little philosophical thinking – of an ancient, and I am inclined to say, more rational, kind - is required in order to establish this monumental claim. I must here give a caution: decent philosophy can never be made easy and the going can get a bit tough for the rest of the discussion of the sin we are presently considering. If the reader has been moved at all by what I have said so far and feels less at home with more logically difficult argument, please skip a rather lengthy patch. I make no apology for its inclusion, though, for it is necessary to the process of raising mere complaint and gut distaste, however well founded, to the level of a carefully reasoned case.

Ethicism: A Defence (Aesthetic and Moral Beauty and Ugliness)

The First Argument: Participation in the good[138]

Under the influence of the Platonic and later Christian traditions of thought on the matter, what mattered, what had to be sought, was *the* Good. Note the capital letter. Yes, we should seek to do good things but in order to do good things one has to be able to recognise *the* Good. In his best known dialogue, the *Republic*, Plato points to an important parallel: light from the sun makes other things visible and knowable. Similarly, *the* Good (and keep in mind that we still associate light with goodness) makes things intelligible, understandable. (In the Christian tradition Plato's 'Good' become God, Love itself, the creator and sustainer of all things in addition to being the source of wisdom and intelligibility.)

In Plato, all that truly exists is said to 'participate' in the Good, and to the extent that this happens, things become more themselves and more intelligible – we can know better what they really *are*. It's a bit like having more light shed upon them. For example, I *know* that the gin that I drink is a good one (as opposed to one that tastes like the product of a child's chemistry set, or just a watery non-entity) just because it *is* a good gin. It's *more* a gin, and therefore more *knowabl*e *as* gin, just because it *is* a good one. *Intelligibility* (knowability) is thus intimately linked with what a thing, most fundamentally, *is*. (In the jargon, epistemology is linked with ontology) and a thing truly *is* the X you know because of its degree of goodness as an X – and its degree of goodness is understood as degree of its participation in *the* Good.

Truth and beauty enter the picture, too. We often talk of a 'true friend'. What we mean is that such a person is *more* of a friend, a really good friend. Again, this will be because this person, *qua* friend, participates in *the* Good. On the whole, what we regard as true, is true, because of this participation. Complete falsehood participates in *the* Good not at all. Now think of something that is beautiful. Again, it is beautiful because it is in some fundamental sense good. Its measure of beauty depends on its degree of (participation in) goodness (*the* Good). These three things remain, we might say, truth beauty and goodness, but the greatest of these is goodness – the Good. This should ring bells in later Christian scripture where St Paul tell us, "These three remain: faith, hope and love. But the greatest of these is love." (*1 Corinthians*, 13) In Platonism *the* Good (in Christianity, Love) has sovereignty. Without this 'Sovereignty of The Good' we would be left with – well, nothing good (or, hence, intelligible at all). Without goodness *at all*, we would be left with literally nothing *at all*. This includes no value at all, including no aesthetic value.

One may, of course, just not accept all this ancient philosophy, and much modern thought has indeed rejected it. In modern thought things don't exist because of anything higher in which they have to participate. Nothing has, so to speak, to earn its lunch in order to exist. They are physically caused and then just bluntly exist. If you go along with modernism here you may well be freed from ethicism on this count, at least, but you will also owe some intelligible alternative account. Good luck!

That's good. What about evil? In the Christian tradition evil is seen as privation. As darkness is seen as absence of light, so evil is seen as absence of good. Absence is the key here. Evil is not some existent entity or force that happens to have some alternative (and rather unpleasant) qualities. (That's *Star Wars* or 'Harry Potter' thinking, not proper philosophy.) One may object by pointing out that evil often *seems* like a force because we have to fight it. It can even be palpable. True, but these are consequences of the absence not positive qualities of a real presence. Darkness, too, has consequences and can seem tangible. In some sense we have to fight *it*, as well. In a room without light, for instance, we have to take care we do not bump into furniture, or fall, and perhaps break a bone. For all that, darkness is still only the absence of light. It does not have its own existence, still less sovereign existence. (When Christianity claims that the devil is on the losing side, it is not making a possibly falsifiable empirical prediction, it is uttering what it takes to be a *metaphysical* necessity. It's a bit like saying that only light can show you the way. This is true no matter how deep and extended the darkness in which you are presently plunged may be.) Being an absence, evil cannot participate in rational discourse – there's nothing to participate. It cannot add anything – and thus cannot add intelligibility – to anything. Good, though, *can* because it is what gives us the light of rationality in the first place.

What *affects* the whole can, if it is poisonous, or even just lacking, *contaminate* the whole, and that includes its aesthetic qualities. Aesthetic qualities that become contaminated become less like aesthetic properties. Why? Remember Plato: beauty can only exist insofar as it is part of something bigger – *the* Good. To the extent that they fail in this participation, beauty ceases even to *be*. Aesthetic qualities then may survive their plunge into darkness in the sense that they may retain their same visual aspects, it's just that these aspects have been aesthetically nullified by a crucial kind of absence. This is what happened to *The Act of Killing*. We tend to understand aesthetic values as depending on some stand-alone range of qualities. We then wonder why these cannot persist when other qualities (such as moral qualities) change. But under the view canvassed here, this would be impossible. Certain audio-visual qualities may be *necessary* to a film's having aesthetic value but they are not *sufficient*. Beauty simply runs deeper than that.

The Second Argument: The Relationship of Purpose and Nature

But what if one rejects this Platonic conception in the first place? There is a second reason why aesthetic value cannot run free of moral value. Films of moral rectitude invite morally improving questions. More! The experiencing of the film itself makes one want to ask further questions about the virtues it explores. Films revelling in evil do not. They simply leave one in the mire, as does *The Act of Killing*. Sure, you can ask such questions *later*, and be led to do so by having seen the offending film, but the experience of the film itself simply makes one sick.

I submit that part of the role of aesthetic values is that they serve to enhance what is good not what is poisonous. I am not talking here simply of guilt by association. It is not that the aesthetic values of a film are reduced or eliminated by keeping bad company, nor even obscured. Rather, it is that it is no part of the very *nature* of such values to be a part of the general stench. The nature and purposes of a thing are closely related. If the one changes, so does the other. If what might otherwise have been aesthetic qualities serve what is evil, they come to have a purpose that is alien to their nature. Thus, to that extent, their nature itself is transformed: the otherwise aesthetic qualities, in short, *cease to be* aesthetic qualities because they have become cancerous. The aesthetics of the cinematic image are inevitably rendered null and void. At bottom, this second argument, I think, is a simple extension of the first. *The Act of Killing* illustrates this principle in almost all its cinematic imagery. That is, I suppose, some sort of an achievement.

The Third Argument: Truth and Aesthetic Evaluation – and the relationship with morality

So far we have focused on goodness as an essential feature of aesthetic value. That is, something bad about a film's aims and purposes negates its aesthetic qualities. But we may also link it to truth. We can ask whether truth itself is an aesthetic virtue of a film.

Firstly, I will clarify the question. I will follow this up with an examination of the issues involved, focussing on the so-called 'No Truth' theory and T.S. Eliot's critique of this.[139] I finish by offering an account which defends ethicism.

What exactly is the 'no-truth' theorist denying? Certainly not that art works can contain truths – of course they can. Both films and novels contain many truths, both incidental and ones that are crucial to the stories they tell. Nor is the 'no-truth' theorist resting on the fact that fiction, because it is fiction, states many falsehoods. There is a real sense in which *Great Expectation*'s Pip did not play at Miss Haversham's because neither he nor Miss Haversham existed. What we really want to know is whether art works must contain, or perhaps encapsulate, truths that are significant to their just being art works. And this question applies to truths of any stripe – trivial or profound, metaphorically or literally expressed. For example when Blake described the tiger as 'burning bright in the forest of the night', we are not asking whether the metaphor expresses a truth and, if so, what truth. Nor are we asking whether, given its truth, it is terribly significant as a truth. The no-truth theorist is not concerned to deny that truth has at least that much connection with literature. Rather, we are asking whether its truth is relevant to our evaluation of the poem which contains it. Essentially we want to know whether considerations of truth are relevant to what makes a work a work of art. Is truth-telling aesthetically important? The 'no-truth' theorist answers, 'No'.

One way of construing the question is to take it take it as involving necessary conditions. Is truth-tellingness a *necessary* condition for something to count as an artwork? Here the 'no-truth' theorist seems already to occupy the high ground. Some poetry, for example, is mere word-play. Some consists in deliberate nonsense cleverly constructed to make its lines sound as though they possess the syntactic structure of ordinary truth-value bearing sentences (e.g. 'Jabberwocky'). Even in cases in which literary material does contain truth-value bearing sentences, there may be no truth (of the relevant kind) revealed at all in the reading of it. This may be so of complete fantasy novels. This seems to be no reason, though, to deny such works the status of literature, nor even the status of *good* literature (i.e., aesthetically valuable literature). After all, we read, and enjoy what we read, not just to have truths revealed to us but also for fun, diversion and entertainment – and some of it at least may be clever, aesthetically pleasing material. Films may be like all this, at least occasionally. Many of the arguments I cite here arose specifically in connection with literature but I think they can be transferred over to film – and other art-works.

TS Eliot does not insist on truth-telling as a necessary condition, but thinks that we could construe the (relevant) question in a different way and ask whether the 'no-truth' theorist is correct in denying that truth-telling is *ever* relevant to an assessment of an art-work. In particular we must ask whether truth-telling is *aesthetically* relevant. Isenberg, a proponent of the 'no-truth' theory, thinks not.[140] He starts off with an innocent enough premise: when something is said to us, we have to understand it before we can give our assent. He then goes on to conclude that, 'that it should be possible to understand without being concerned with truth and falsity'. But can we? And even if we can, to what extent can we? We may be able to understand that a work is a putative artwork without being concerned with its truth and falsity, but can we appreciate or properly evaluate it as such without bringing in issues of truth at all? Not with respect to anything serious, surely.

Consider the well-known Shakespearean line which tells us that, 'Love's not time's fool'. Can we really understand this line independently of our belief that love tends to have a unique way of transcending the passage of time, and independently of our belief that time has an intimate connection with change? Say someone did not think that this was true of love or time, they would surely then be at a loss to understand the metaphor. Its force would be completely dissipated. Belief here underlies evaluation.

What of the evaluation, though? I think that we must here side with Elliot and point out that very often what we most value about an artwork is the fact that it states a truth, often a profound truth, in a way that is powerful, elegant and economical. One might just say a way that is *beautiful*. It may force such truth upon one in ways one cannot easily ignore; it may offer a new insight into the place of such truth in one's life. A film may do this in a primarily audio-visual way but that simple line from Shakespeare fits the bill as well as anything. If we simply did not believe that certain things were true of love and time (and their relationship) it seems plausible to suggest that we just wouldn't value the line as much as we do. Its beauty would be considerably diminished because it would no longer have truth to hang on to. Of artwork which is merely playful and expresses no truth, such as Jabberwocky, I think we should see such work as being parasitic upon the paradigm cases in which truth, even deep truth *is* expressed and *is* key to its evaluation as an artwork. Indeed, any playfulness possessed by such things as nonsense poems seems to depend upon this relationship. It *sounds* meaningful and even true to say that, "The slythy toves did gyre and gymble in the wabe", and if it didn't we wouldn't think it playful in the first place. We are making believe, admittedly in a quite well extended sense, that it expresses a truth. It matters, crucially, to our evaluation of it. This seems to be the whole point of the game.

We can extend this line of thought by observing a connection with the very nature of make-believe. In reading fiction or watching a fiction feature film we are engaging in make-believe. (We 'celieve' what it says, recall.) We take to the make-believe world much of (but not all) the very same mental set we take towards the real world. (What else?) We respond to it in ways which at least reflect the ways we respond to the real world. It is almost, as has been occasionally observed, as if we are running our thoughts and feelings 'off-line'. (That, of course, makes a significant difference.)[141] Our responses are, in this case, directed upon what is actually false (because the work is one of fiction) but which we nonetheless imaginatively take to be true, as if the characters and situations parallel possible real ones. In engaging with fiction we are safely insulated from the real-world consequences of our responses. Yet what we watch or read is still important to us and it elicits to some degree a range of real-world-*like* responses. Why? Again, I think that a plausible answer is that truth just matters to us. We *need* to understand the nature of human situations; we constantly desire (at least in our more reflective and better moments) a better grip on the truth of the human condition. Art has its unique role in all this. Further, we are strongly inclined to think of such a role as being at least a part of a work's aesthetic dimension. This is all we need to refute the 'no-truth' theory. Truth just *is* relevant to aesthetic evaluation in any deep sense of the word 'aesthetic'. With respect to other narrative arts – fiction film and theatre, for example, there seems no reason why one cannot take a parallel line to the one we apply to literature. Such arts can access truth in similar sorts of ways fiction literature can.

I could end on this point and rest content that the essential connection between truth and the aesthetic evaluation of artworks applies only to narrative arts – arts that tell a story about we humans, but this would be to hold short. In cases of non-narrative arts the issue of the relevance of truth-tellingness is complicated by the fact such arts do not seem to consist of the sort of elements that can function as the primary bearers of truth-values. How, for example, can a symphony tell a truth? I think, though, that music can be more or less truth-telling. This is because music ('pure' music, I mean, not just quasi-narrative stuff, or music with words) can be emotionally truthful to something relevant to it. Furthermore, music is used in film in such a way that is often supposed to help reveal the truth about a situation. Here I do not just mean how it may, in some way, *express* a truth about its composer's feelings, even if it does. Rather, I mean that it *reveals* to us truths about the emotional structure of a character's situation, in a very forceful way.[142] One feels one has a better grasp of the nature of these emotions (and, perhaps, of how to fit them in their proper place in life) through listening to the music. I think that pure music is revelatory of important truths. It is precisely because the 'Rach 2' conveys in its own ways the true characteristics of love, longing and loss that makes it suitable for *Brief Encounter* in the first place. Moreover, the very aesthetic distance involved enables us to perceive all this far more clearly than we ever could just by undergoing the emotions themselves.

And what of painting? Even the way in which paintings can be, as we sometimes say, 'true-to-life', this seems not to be the same, exactly, as truth-*telling*, the way novels and films may be. But truth seems still to be involved. Imagine a painting of someone 'warts-and-all'. While such a painting may be more true-to-life in respect of the person's actual appearance, a painting without the warts-and-all may be truer to something else – say the subject's distorted self-conception.

Moreover, the issue is further complicated by questions concerning the ways in which a painting may be considered realistic.[143] Picasso's *Guernica* is, in some respects the most intensely realistic portrayal of war I have ever seen. My point in this (slight) diversion into other arts is simply to issue the reminder that truth telling is a multi-faceted business.

In conclusion, we might make the following observation. The 'no-truth' theory belongs to a long tradition of autonomism in aesthetics – what could be called the 'The Tradition of Grand Independence of Aesthetic Experience'. This doctrine maintains that aesthetic experience exists in lofty isolation from operations involving other kinds and levels of consideration. It has been said to be independent of concepts, other interests, concerns about the real existence of objects and of knowledge – both in the sense that aesthetic experience demands no further knowledge of the item experienced and the sense that it can deliver no knowledge. I hope I have cast serious doubts on that idea. In the ways qualified above, truth can even be seen as an aesthetic virtue all its own. (Though I give autonomism a further and more detailed consideration below.)

But is truth more than just *an* aesthetic virtue, merely one among many? If that were the case, then other aesthetic virtues may rest content with autonomy from the truth. I do not think this is viable, though. Truth telling and truth revealing are key to a quality's being aesthetic *at all.* We make a mistake if we think that what constitutes an aesthetic value are solely elements of decoration (though they may in some contexts – evaluating the aesthetic qualities of a vase, for instance). Aesthetic value may be *embodied* in the interplay of light and shade and other visual aspects of a cinematic image (and in the choice and flow of words in literature) – what else? - but it does not *consist* of these base-line visible features considered alone. It consists in how these features are supposed to be interpreted and understood. There is more to them than mere decoration. *That* is where considerations of truth enter the scene. And it should be crowned king as it enters. If we interpret and understand certain cinematic images (and words) as being necessarily truth revealing, then that would be a key part of their aesthetic worth. If they do not convey truth in any significant sense they lose aesthetic worth, perhaps to the point of their ceasing to be aesthetically valuable at all.

There is still one more step to take. Even given the argument so far, we may still wonder what morality has to do with it. After all, may not a thoroughly immoral film like *An Act of Killing* or *Triumph of the Will* still be truth telling and thus worthy of positive aesthetic evaluation independently of its moral repulsiveness? No! Truth comes at different levels of significance. Neither of these films is involved with truth-telling at any level beyond the meagre: the former merely indicating the evil acts committed by the characters through re-enactment, the latter the historical fact that many folk in Nazi Germany publicly celebrated a certain nasty form of life. The latter is an important truth historically, of course, but there is no higher truth involved in the film. The truth expressed in *1945* (Ferenc Török, Hungary, 2017) on the other hand – a film that looks at some of the consequences of the holocaust that were less widely known – is much higher, for it tells us about how different people reacted to the evil done. It exposes evil even further. I think that the film *The President* (Mohsen Makhmalbaf, Georgia, 2014) can be counted as a saint, too, as the dictator of a fictitious eastern country has to flee his palace and learns some key truths about his actions on his journey across his country. Hence, we have the crucial difference. It is not just *any* level of truth telling that counts towards a more aesthetic evaluation but *profound* truth-tellingness, the sort that reveals our real depths, or at least something sufficiently significant.

Hence, I do not think that the correlation between moral and aesthetic evaluation is coincidental. I think we resist positive aesthetic evaluation even of truth telling films if the truths they tell obscure deeper and more morally relevant ones. *1945* is not aesthetically better than *Triumph of the Will* in terms of some assumed base-line inventiveness of its cinematic images. Its cinematic images are aesthetically better because they express, even *serve*, the right sort and levels of truth – the profoundly moral ones. Aesthetically distancing ourselves from the moral awfulness, in our present context by focussing on some narrowed down conception of aesthetic qualities, is not only to seal off a correct response to moral awfulness but to downplay the importance and the very nature of our aesthetic evaluations.[144]

Kant

This concludes my case for Ethicism and we may well end here, but we may still ask whether Autonomism (the grand independence of aesthetics, remember) can be rationally defended at all. One significant thinker famed for such a defence is the German philosopher Immanuel Kant (1724-1804). He is well-known for the difficulty and denseness of his argument and even the reader who has struggled this far may fairly wish to skip this section, but Kant has a great significance in the development of thinking in this area. Many reflective people these days think along Kantian lines (here as elsewhere) so I include with an account of my own. It has its cinematic implications.

Kant's fundamental question is: 'How are judgements of taste possible?' In asking this question he is opening up his enquiry as to what it is (if anything) that *grounds* our judgement that something is beautiful. Certainly we make such judgements but in doing so are we doing no more than simply signalling an unsupported approval of a thing's appearance[145] or are we judging that the thing before us possesses a certain quality - beauty?

In some respects we seem to be doing the latter, but there is tension here. This tension is generated by the fact that though we may wish to say of the thing before us that it is beautiful, we seem to base the judgement on a certain kind of effect the thing has on us and we are inclined to think that this *effect* is what makes the object beautiful. So, is beauty simply a certain kind of *effect* something may have on us or is it an actual property of the thing itself? This tension has two consequences. First, it distinguishes judgements of taste from judgements of other qualities that things have, especially physical qualities. A thing's mass, for example is not determined by how a thing *seems* to us. True, one may make a (rather rough and ready) estimation of a thing's mass on the basis of a (series of) perceptual seemings. (One may look at it, weigh it in one's hand, and so on.) However, we readily acknowledge that it is not these judgements that *make* the object possess whatever mass it has: such judgements are guides only. On the question of taste, on the other hand, one may be more tempted to think that our perceptual construal of a thing in some way *constitutes* its beauty: it is beautiful *because* of its effects upon me.[146] Yet, for all this, we still wish to say of the thing itself that it is beautiful.

This should strike us as a puzzling state of affairs. Relatedly, we may ask the question of whether judgements of taste are objective or subjective. They *sound* objective: 'x *is* beautiful', we say, is simply predicating a real property (beauty) of x. We think we can be either right or wrong. Yet if things are beautiful simply *because* of their effect on us, then they begin to seem subjective. Certainly, Kant bases judgements of beauty on their effects upon us. So, how can we have any true objectivity? How objectivity *is* possible is revealed in Kant's analysis of the structure of our experience of beauty. In all this, subjectivity seems best construed as *inter*-subjectivity – a kind of subjectivity which leads to judgements common to us all. Beauty is not something merely 'in the eye of the beholder' in the more modern individualistic sense. He proceeds by means of laying clear four aspects ('moments') of aesthetic experience. (Think about moments as dimensions upon which things of importance turn.) I first offer an account of these 'moments', then then put forward some criticism.

The first aspect ('the moment of quality') is that our judgement that something is beautiful is always accompanied by delight. Here, what we judge as delightful is the way a thing appears to us – the 'representation', as Kant puts it.[147] This is important, for in our aesthetic experience we must, according to Kant, distinguish our interest in the way the thing appears from any interest we may have in the thing's actual existence. Only the former matters.[148] This is Kant's famous notion of the *disinterestedness* of our aesthetic involvement with things, and it distinguishes aesthetic interest from interest of other kinds.[149]

Pertinent to our present discussion is that our moral concern for something, for example, entails a concern about the *existence* of the object (or person) concerned.

Also, our judgement that something is agreeable (a gin and tonic, say) involves the kind of appeal to our senses which necessitates an interest in (indeed possession of) the agreeable thing (and thus its existence).[150] According to Kant, though, our aesthetic appreciation of a thing is in no way related to its mode of existence. Rather, it is a purely *contemplative* matter; we are interested only in the pleasure given to us in reflecting upon the thing as it is represented to us.[151] 'Taste is the faculty of estimating . . . a mode of representation by means of a delight . . . apart from any interest'.[152]

If the first aspect of aesthetic experience is that it is disinterested – in the sense outlined, the second ('the moment of quantity') reveals a further important Kantian notion – that of the *non-conceptual.* Crucial here is the interplay between what Kant calls the 'Imagination' and the 'Understanding'.[153] For Kant, Imagination has an important role even in ordinary perception, playing, in a sense, a gap-filling role. Look at a house, for instance. Our eyes deliver information not from the whole house but just one part of it, yet we still see a *house*; we take it as an object of a kind which has aspects hidden from view. In short, we always see more than the sensory information from our eyes tells us. It is what Kant calls the Imagination that does this gap filling.[154] Construed this way, Imagination is a kind of mental instrument for going beyond perceptually given data. The 'Understanding', in contrast, is the abode of concepts. Again, take the case of ordinary perception. This is *concept dependent*; that is to say, to see a house *as* a house, we see what we see as *falling under* the concept of house. Perception is thus a synthesis, forged by the powers of the Imagination in uniting sense perceptions and the powers of the Understanding in providing the necessary conceptual scheme. It is in this way that we perceive a public, objective and shareable world.

In aesthetic experience, Imagination and Understanding interact in a way not bound by concepts. Concepts are for cognition but in judgements of beauty the Imagination is allowed to act more freely; its deliverances are not be bound by a (set of) concepts. It doesn't have to deliver an object as fit for falling under a concept. Its aim is purely *non-cognitive.* (It doesn't reveal knowledge.) Yet, the Understanding still has a role, only this time it is *regulatory*. It plays a similar role to the one it plays in perception but without imposing a concept. Its role, we might say, has the same general *form* here as in the case of perception but without the definite conceptual content. Put simply, a thing just *looks* beautiful without paying any heed to what sort of thing it is. The regulation is still necessary in order to prevent imagination going wild. It must be allowed some freedom but the freedom must not be allowed to descend into chaos, like the behaviour of a wayward child. We must, after all, have an experience delivered unto us which is fit for the process of aesthetic contemplation.

Kant's example of a rose can help spell out all the abstraction generated by our discussion of the first two aspects of aesthetic experience. If we look at a rose and contemplate and enjoy the experience purely aesthetically we are: firstly, not interested in the existence of the rose and secondly, not interested in it *as* a rose (that is, as being a thing which falls under the concept of rose). Rather, we disinterestedly contemplate its form as revealed to us in its representation.

From what we have said so far we may also now derive a further crucial Kantian aesthetic notion – that of *universality*. Because a judgement of taste is not based on any interest in the real existence of a thing and because it is not concept bound, Kant concludes that it is a judgement that may command universal assent. One may not even know what a thing is, even that it is an object at all in order to judge it beautiful.[155] Conceptual schemes, personal interests, judgements of what we find agreeable, all differ; judgements of taste do not because they *cannot* – there is, so to speak, nothing personal in it from which dispute even can coherently be said to arise. Thus, although judgements of beauty are subjective in the sense that they are based on feeling, they are objective in the sense that such feeling is *common to us all.* This may sound simply perverse. Do we not, after all, frequently *dis*agree? Perhaps, but the disagreements hit matters at the wrong level. Whatever our individual differences, we all have the same kinds of basic mental structures and these occupy such depths that they transcend any possible differences. The mental structures are built into us as human beings and we have them in common.

In the third aspect at play ('the moment of ends') Kant points to the object of one's judgement as having 'the form of finality' This means that the beautiful object has the *form* of purposiveness even though, in fact, it has no *actual* purpose – 'purposiveness without purpose'[156] is the expression he uses. The beauty of a flower, for instance, looks as if it has, in some sense, been planned or is fulfilling some function or has some meaning, though it has not.[157] That one is occasionally inclined to regard the beautiful as ineffable is perhaps connected with this: one would like to be able to articulate a dimly perceived purpose but, when it comes down to it, there is nothing to say. This purposiveness without purpose seems connected to the fact that beauty is generated by the free interactive play between the Imagination and Understanding. We have noted already that this interaction is not chaotic. We are now in a position to add that it is *law-like*, though no specifiable laws can be invoked.

The fourth aspect ('the moment of modality') develops further the notion of universality. Because judgements of beauty are based on deep matters which do not vary with individual circumstance or psychology, they are not just universal but also invite the thought that we all *ought* to find beauty in the same things. 'X is beautiful', if true (and it will be if it satisfies the conditions outlined in the four moments) should find assent from everyone. There are simply no relevant grounds left *upon which* disagreement even *could* be founded?

Though the moments are but four, the conditions covered by them are many. Now we have spelled out the crucial terms, we may summarise Kant's account in the following way. The judgement 'x is beautiful' is a genuine judgement of taste (aesthetic judgement) *if and only if* it is: (a) objective (in the sense outlined above), (b) disinterested, (c) universal, (d) necessary, (e) involving of a contemplative pleasure that everyone *ought* to experience, (f) involving of a free play between Imagination and Understanding, (g) is concept independent, and (h) has the form of finality – the appearance of purpose or having an end. This list is impressive, not just for its length but for the profundity of its members. I will, however, focus on just a two central issues.

To begin with, it may be thought that in concentrating on form and delight, Kant's notion of the beautiful is somewhat light, having a faintly decorative air about it. Cannot our perception of beauty, at any case now and again, go much deeper than this? Can it not evoke emotions that disturb? Can it not involve matters that are far more profound? To some extent this would be unfair, for Kant *did* recognise these deeper and sometimes darker matters, it is just that he did not consider them as belonging merely to the realm of the beautiful. Rather they belong to what he called the *sublime*. The difference lies in the fact that the sublime reaches areas where individual differences do indeed come into play. What disturbs you may not disturb me. Moreover, the difference will be doubtless due to the role played by our individual psychological states. The sublime, therefore, cannot satisfy the universality condition, nor the condition to the effect that all rational minds *ought* to give assent. Further, and in contrast to the beautiful, the sublime has a purposive*less*ness about it. It is far from law-like. Far from being generated by a balanced interplay of the Understanding and Imagination, an encounter with the sublime actually 'does violence to the imagination'.[158] Beauty is neat; the sublime is elemental.

Although, again, Kant is profound here in his many observations, one may wonder whether he is correct in separating the sublime from the beautiful. Might not the correct thing be to drop the universality and purposiveness conditions – at least as necessary conditions. Why not just say that certain forms of the beautiful possess these and others not? Kant was, of course, motivated by a need to find universal conditions of rationality, but this aside, there seems little to recommend the separation. Indeed, there is something in favour of not doing so. Our perceptions of beauty as we ordinarily understand them do seem to fit rather more a spectrum of conditions. At one end, there is indeed, a taking of simple delight at the form of a flower, but at the other there is an aesthetic disturbance to be experienced in seeing a bolt of lightning or the explosion of a star. Further, there is the aesthetic and even spiritual awakening and profundity to be had in our response to certain works of art. The use of the word 'aesthetic' here seems justified by the fact that at least some of the conditions associated with the aesthetic seem satisfied. Firstly, it is subjective, secondly, we still attribute qualities to the objects involved (disturbingness, profundity, and so on) and thirdly there may be something of disinterestedness remaining in such experiences. (An example: awe at a thunderstorm is not the same thing as our being in fear of it. Indeed, to feel the former one must be somewhat distanced from one's individual fear.)

In general, though, there seems to be no sharp cut-off point between responses which should count as belonging to the beautiful and those that belong to the sublime. One's response to a musical phrase, the form (or part thereof) of a painting, a poem, a natural scene and so on may indeed fall within either extreme but may equally come somewhat midway. A second criticism arises from the temptation in Kant's account to think that it can apply equally and solely to our appreciation of art works. This, however, is hardly obvious. Another difficulty is that, on Kant's view - that the pleasure in beauty is non-conceptual - we seem committed to the view that our capacity to make conceptual distinctions has no role in our appreciation of beauty. This seems perverse, especially in the light of what we argued earlier concerning the cinematic image. Worse still, it seems that Kant's account leaves no room for reason-giving, including criticism in aesthetics, since these activities very definitely employ our conceptual capacities. It seems an arbitrary stretch to say that our judgements of beauty do not involve these capacities, especially when, again, we take into account our earlier arguments. One may, I think, say of Kant that his account of beauty, and its entirely non-intuitive separation from the sublime is what it is because it fits his overall conception of reality and morality. A consideration of *that*, however, would take us simply too far from the business of the present book.

Thomas Aquinas

For a better view of beauty than Kant's I think we need to go mediaeval and return to the thirteenth century philosopher/theologian Thomas Aquinas.[159] He was certainly no defender of autonomism. Thomas talked about three essential aspects of beautiful things. First, they need 'integrity' ('*integritas*'). This is wholeness and unity: a beautiful thing must show no deficiency in anything necessary to its being most itself. It has to be itself *fully*. Think of a beautiful thing – a flower maybe - and you think of it as a whole. And that wholeness speaks of perfection, a kind of completedness – as something created to be that way. So, a beautiful flower would be a flower that best exemplified ideal flower-ness, flower-ness as it is supposed to be, flower-ness uncorrupted. That's integrity. Secondly, to be beautiful, a thing must have correct 'proportion' (*'consonantia'*): its properties and the way in which it is ordered should match what it really is, and should show us its proper metaphysical ideal, its end. Finally, says Thomas, it must exhibit 'clarity' (*'claritas'*): "it should clearly radiate intelligibility, the logic of its inner being, and impress this knowledge of itself on the mind of the perceiver".[160] This is why I always wince when someone suggests that a scientific analysis of something – our flower, say – subtracts from its beauty. No! Science qua science certainly *ignores* beauty but nonetheless shows *more* of a thing's beauty because it shows a deeper level of its proper order and unity. It reveals further levels of its radiance. It reflects more of God's glory not less. All this can be readily applied to artworks. A beautiful thing shows clearly what the thing *is*. Thus, if I look upon, say, Michelangelo's 'Pieta', I can clearly and distinctly see that it is a sculpture of an agonizing mother holding her deceased son. A beautiful thing does not cover up or deceive. Ditto, I say, for films. Under this schema better than any other one can see how the beauty of a depiction can express or reveal the most harrowing parts of reality. Indeed, we can see most clearly also why beauty is necessary to such depiction. We can also discern why a depiction that lacks beauty (understood in our now enlarged and deeper breathing sense) lacks also a power proper to conveying such things. Beauty should never be seen as an irrelevant, merely decorative, Kantian delightedness which functions to obscure the harrowing or even downright ugly.

Thomas's account is, thus, very different to Kant's. While beauty involves the contemplation of that which, in some sense, pleases us, it can never be purely sensuous in the (rather specialised and thinned-out) way in which it is in Kant. It runs much deeper. How can we know that we are considering a whole flower, for instance, if we do not know it *as* a flower? How can we know that something has right proportion if we don't know what it is? And how can we see a thing clearly and distinctly as being what it is without the employment of concepts? It seems clear that in judgements of beauty (as elsewhere) we need to be able to identify what it is we are looking at. We can never look at something in an isolated know-not-what, never-mind, who-cares? sort of way, or just look at things with some ideal Kantian detachment and judge it beautiful. That's too limited. We really do need to know and be able to identify the things in question. For example, it is precisely because in looking at Michelangelo's Pieta that we identify it *as* a sculpture of an agonizing mother holding her deceased son, that we can also see that it fits the Thomistic bill with respect to having integrity, clarity and correct proportion - that we can see it is beautiful in the deeper way. I say again, "Ditto for beautiful art, including beautiful films".

It may be thought that my statement above, that "a beautiful thing shows clearly what the thing *is*" is defeated by the fact that some completely abstract image may still be beautiful, and that we can also see beauty in something which remains at best only rather vaguely identified. I do not think these are genuine worries. Even something only vaguely identified (or even not identified at all) and images of pure abstraction come with some kind of implicit interpretation which gives them some kind or level of identity and wholeness (*integritas*). The abstract image (Picasso's *Guernica*, say) stands for something identifiable, and even an arrangement of shape and colour on a canvas may display a holistic meaning of some sort – discomfort or peace, say. As to vaguely identified things or misidentified or unidentified things, these are still understood as things that have their identity and unity, it's just that we remain unsure or just mistaken about precisely what they are. Nonetheless, any beauty that they may retain I would suggest is diminished when compared with the beauty they may be judged to have when they are identified more precisely and known and understood better. A person unfamiliar with and unable to identify chairs (i.e., someone not possessing the concept of chair) may nonetheless (we may suppose) see some sort of beautiful *thing*, but the person who is familiar with just the sort of thing it is, may well see an even more beautiful chair. Beauty can come in grades.

Returning to the cinematic image

All this applies to the cinematic image because such images, by their very nature, are about the world and the things and happenings in it. One may suppose that there could remain a certain pleasing arrangement of colour, light and shade within the cinematic image that could have a level of beauty no matter how morally ugly the film may be of which it is apart. This, however, would be a very thinned out, superficial level of beauty.

Beauty in its fullness is a feature of things, happenings, and so on in the world, not just a decorative and pleasing spatio-temporal array of basic perceptual elements such as colour, light, line and shade. The cinematic image is more than this.[161] We must keep in mind here Merleau-Ponty's 'temporal gestalt' – the meaningful whole. That meaningful whole includes what is happening in what one sees, and this includes, I would say, the spiritual reality of its characters and story.[162] If that is morally ugly in its essence (not just being *about* moral ugliness) the cinematic image will be aesthetically ugly. The morality and the aesthetics are inseparable in our perception because, in the cinematic image, we see not a mere array of its elements in isolation (which can then be discussed as such) but as an always and already interpreted unity. At most, all that one could say is that the bare perceptual elements (and various aspects of form) have some *potential* to make the image beautiful, but for that potential to be fully realised one needs to see the elements in accordance with an interpreted unity, including a moral interpreted unity. Herein lies the essential connection between beauty and goodness in cinema.

The general conclusion to drawn though can be expressed in simpler ways. One cannot aesthetically evaluate a cinematic image, and thus a film, in grand independence of moral evaluation. The two go together, especially in art media that are concerned with truth. The high moral truths of some of the films I cite make their cinematic images more beautiful – not in some metaphorical sense but literally, and significantly. The best art, including the best of cinema is always a deeply moral art, an art that reveals life at its deepest level of reality. It reveals heroism, decency and goodness of character – nobility, even – all absent from films that revel in pointless violence, sexual debauchery and general sleaziness. The latter form of cinema is not simply 'being honest' about reality, it promotes wrongness. It's not just morally abysmal, its cinematic images also lack anything worth calling aesthetic value, however clever they may otherwise be.

The sins of depicting evil. Can evil even *be* depicted?

This kind of consideration seems to be what lurks at the bottom of frequent worries about films depicting the holocaust. On this point, philosopher and theologian Simon Oliver contrasts *Schindler's List* (Steven Spielberg, US, 1993) and *Life is Beautiful* (Roberto Benigni, Italy, 1997). He writes within the tradition that evil is a privation of the good.

> ". . . it is precisely Bengini's refusal to assign any transcendent meaning to the Shoah which renders *Life is Beautiful* an insightful approach to the subject. By contrast, the cinematic spectacle of *Schindler's List*, while doubtless heightening public awareness of the terrors of the Shoah and helping to assuage what Gillian Rose calls 'knowledge-resistance to the Holocaust', nevertheless renders the experience of Jews and Germans in mid-twentieth century Europe too accessible on a pietistic and literal plain, and therefore 'comprehensible'."[163]

He concludes,

> "For the tradition which understands evil to be the privation of the Good which is God, evil dissolves meaning and intelligibility. Yet that dissolution is only made apparent by reference to the more fundamental and 'real' story of transcendent goodness. Because of Schindler's List's self-enclosed and all-encompassing realism, it does little to reveal the incoherence and nihilism of the Shoah beyond the literal portrayal of brutal murder which it renders visible in unproblematic fashion. The problem with such depictions of brutality is that, in their simple literality, audiences become over-familiar with such scenes. At some point, it becomes apparent that one must leave the theatre; one is watching a film. For *Life is Beautiful,* the narrative extends beyond the movie theatre's doors. If spirituality is the faithful search for as yet undisclosed or

unrealised meanings, *Life is Beautiful* is of greater theological import than its realist counterpart *Schindler's List*."[164]

Perhaps some will find some the theological thinking a bit heavy going here but the fundamental point is important in our moral assessment of films. Evil must be transcended; we can only make sense of it *as* evil by contrasting it with the more fundamental existence of goodness. Because of the kinds of distancing it exhibits and enables, the cinematic image is made to convey that transcendence. I agree with Oliver's assessments here. At the very least, *Life is Beautiful* exhibits this grace far more than *Schindler's List*.

Another notable contender is *1945* (Ferenc Török, Hungary, 2017). At the opening of the film we wonder why two orthodox Jews are returning to a village in Hungary after the war bringing with them two mysterious boxes? The villagers believe that it may be to reclaim property that was snatched from their deported families and wrongfully passed on to their present owners, a shameful process in which many of the influential villagers were themselves complicit. Though all is not as it seems with these Jews, and we have, rightly, to await a well-timed revelation of the truth they bring, the film is not essentially a mystery. The film conveys a theological truth: it is about how the very presence of the sinned against stirs up fear, suspicion, overwhelming anxiety and life-sucking guilt in the hearts of the sinful. The false peace and illicit happiness of the villagers, all nicely focused on preparations for a local wedding, are rudely exploded by their own self-induced yet well-earned paranoia. Faces are fearsomely expressive, relationships become strained to breaking point and settled life itself seems threatened, as past wrongs begin to consume the villagers in a fire of anger, terrible alcohol-fuelled realization and hate-ridden defensiveness. These morally unlucky villagers know a shame few of us can imagine. All this Török captures with a truly humanistic, tense, even bursting cinematic heartbeat which punctures the claustrophobia of stench-ridden moral pretence. There's even a sense of nobility to the piece. (How cool is that these days?)

Quite simply, *1945* is one of the very finest pieces of cinema I have yet seen in the 21st century. It's photographed in a black and white that streams down cinematically from the screen with an almost nitrate-like glow. The art direction is exquisitely detailed and evocative. Its story is nicely constructed and the editing never misses a beat. The soundtrack is a brilliantly mixed combination of simple but tension-filled music and sounds heard around the village, revealing the narrative's increasingly despairing song. It all has a windingly unnerving effect and contributes to a tightness and slight, yet almost bizarre, unreality to the feel of the piece. At the end, picture and sound come together to terrifying effect when a storm, fire and a sense of self-destructive doom, all of almost Old Testament proportions, afflicts the village, as the two Jews leave the scene as peacefully as they arrived. It's as if the very wrath of God (however one may understand that) has been unleashed in terrible vengeance and the two Jews must not look back.

For all that, the film is hardly of epic length, sweep or scale, running for a mere 91 minutes, never leaving the village and occupying just the standard screen. Yet, I tell you, Cecil B. DeMille himself could hardly have fathered anything more cinematically magnificent. *1945* may be, in some sense small but it is a large achievement, a consummately beautiful little masterpiece, because of the way it makes its most profound points. Most important at this point, however, is that it does not try to depict evil. Rather, it primarily depicts the consequences of evil and finally goodness. In doing so it reveals evil as a fundamental absence and with that, it reveals more vividly the "incoherence and nihilism of the Shoah". Evil is indeed transcended. We may also note here that because of the moral compass at play in the film, *1945* also intensifies its aesthetic qualities.

So can evil be depicted? Evil happenings certainly can, the sin though lies in the fact that too direct a depiction obscures evil's more fundamental status – that of absence and nihilism. Such depiction leaves evil un-transcended and the viewer merely shocked. I would say that this constitutes the vilest of all sins that can afflict modern cinema.

Chapter 10: The Issues of Genre

What is a genre?

The misuse of the term & a reassessment of genre

There are different ways of classifying stories and with this go some different ways of storytelling. Thus, storytelling codes soon emerged in cinema. This is at the bottom of what we call 'genre'.

The term 'genre' is used too loosely these days. Look at categories of films under almost any streaming service. One will find 'Drama', 'Comedy', even 'Foreign Films'. These may be useful starting points for an evening's viewing but they are hardly genres. How can foreign films be a genre if Hollywood is not? Besides, genres in the classical sense are mutually exclusive. One *can* easily have, say, a comedy-drama. A lot of recent popular films have been such. Take *The Full Monty* (Peter Cattaneo, UK, 1997) for instance. Many of the so-called 'feel good' films of our own day fall under this broad category, but this is not a genre in the classic sense. (Though modern 'feel-goods' come close.) The so-called 'screwball' comedy of 1930s Hollywood does count but that is already to move into a more specific *kind* of comedy. Perhaps the British 'Carry Ons' (or most of them) could constitute a genre too, for the same reason. On the other hand, one cannot have a western-noir, or rather, if one could, then it would be neither of those things in the sense of the original genre. Nor, without further ado, would it be a genre all its own.

What constitutes a genre in the classic sense, however, depends on the *codes* to be found in the film. Codes are systems of signs and ways of doing things in various kinds of film: narrative devices, kinds of music and lighting, and so on. A genre is a particular code set, one that has become established for a particular purpose because it has a particular set of effects. Different code sets will consist of many mutually exclusive elements. One can see a genre also, perhaps a little more loosely, as 'a body of conventions'.[165] They have their own distinctive iconographies. Each influences style and narration its own way. They largely have their own form (in lighting, for example). Of course genres can move from one culture to the next without becoming a different genre, as happened when the Japanese *Seven Samurai* (Akira Kurosawa, Japan, 1954) famously gave rise to Hollywood's *The Magnificent Seven* (John Sturges, US, 1960). Elements of one genre can also find their way into another, as happened in the influence of German expressionism on Disney's *Pinocchio* (US, 1940). Genres themselves, though, are fairly immutable – that's part of their point – and, I would say, their attraction and their unique brand of beauty.

Are their sins in genre?

What I have said seems to raise a conflict between the code and the story. Which is the more important – getting the right code or getting to truth through the story? Put that bluntly, the answer seems obvious – attend to the story, get *that* right, and its characters, never mind mere law-abiding adherence to a code and its dogmas and doctrines. Make the story authentic, make it real, and believable. Codes seem as like as not to work in the opposite direction – or so it may often be thought. But I do *not* think this. Indeed, I sometimes worry about the sheer arrogance and self-assumed superiority in the modern mind. Never mind that for millennia humanity has been moved, fascinated, motivated, morally instructed and had important truths imparted to them by masterpieces of encoded, genre storytelling – from ancient mythologies, through Norse sagas and favourite fairy tales – *we* know better. This arrogance seems to leave some folk craving for bland authenticity and mere pedestrian plausibility, all coming with a dull, leaden literalism. This is simple, and gross, lack of imagination. It is also a lack of insight regarding the fact that truths come in hierarchies: some are simply more important than others. Concentrate too much the mere, dull daily details of life and you will have ignored the bigger picture – and cinema, as we have seen, is ideally suited to the bigger picture. (It is why, for instance, cinema deals in legend and folklore far better than strict historical truth and detail.) We have already dealt with the sins of (this kind of limited) authenticity so I now move on to story-telling codes themselves, especially the big ones – the genres - and give them some re-assessment. In general, the traditional genre has gone. One reason why is that they are understood to be merely formulaic ways of making films - and this is supposed to be a bad thing (as though *new* formulae don't arise in the replacement of old ones in any case – and perhaps ones that are not as good). In any case, code should not be exclusively or naively understood as rigid, truth-repelling formulae.

Codes are the stuff of genre as archetypes are the stuff of dreams – we become absorbed in both, each is what gives its vehicle its gravitas. (Think of the nightmare and the horror film.) As dreams may impart something important to us in a cinematic fashion, the cinematic image can impart something important about us in a dream-like fashion. As McGinn points out, "It's only a dream" goes with "It's only a movie" when reassuring a frightened child.[166] Thus, genre fits well the dream-like nature of the cinematic image.

A reassessment of genre?

Many genre films are among the very greatest films and I think it useful to reassess the greatness of genre from time to time, especially in an age in which traditional genre has all but gone and a fashion has developed in which it is more than likely subverted. I choose three past great genres: the epic, the western and the noir.

Because the chosen few of these are the best of the great, they are the ones most likely, and most interestingly, to survive any re-assessment. Moreover, a considerable amount of time now separates us from them – a half a century or more (from the best). Our culture has changed profoundly in its tastes and attitudes. It thus needs a way to see these films afresh. Fourthly, I am eager to show that genre is not bad just because formulae and codes are involved. Finally, I have some reflections that go beyond considering them purely in terms of genre, on what makes them *great* – suitable for future admiration and endless rounds of technologically necessary restoration.

Examples of genre

The Epic

Just what makes an epic, one worthy of the name at least? Size, sweep, scale, mightiness, cinematic magnificence, a deliberate but not too overdone larger-than-life-ness, high adventure, intelligence but not too much analysis, a certain historicised affectedness in the dialogue but without falling into utter preposterousness. (That takes some doing.) It will tell a tall, heroic, Homer-esque but not by any means silly tale, and convey the sense of historic journeying. Its tale will rest on fate and it will have the feel of Grand Opera, or maybe classical ballet or deep tone poem. It will have the look of a great Renaissance painting, the impressiveness of a statue taken straight from Michelangelo - though animated of course. It will have the majesty and rock-solidness of a great mountain range, yet also the unstoppable flow of a mighty river. It will have monumental settings and magnificent set-piece actions (a chariot race would do, or a desert crossing) but it will also have a sense of the noble - few films of any kind nowadays seem much interested in that. All these elements will all be woven together as a wall-filling tapestry and will be kept going with nothing less than a truly symphonic musical score. Any smaller, more cut-price or entry-level specification could never count. Finally, it needs a stompingly good director who knows how to tell a story without unnecessary complication, delay or tedious psycho-dwelling. And as for handheld shots, even if they could have had access to modern, lighter equipment - and the cameras *actually* used were built like Sherman tanks, often made to run 65mm film - the practice would have been forbidden, on the grounds that it would have ruined the theatre of the epic.

To see one of these things projected on a sports stadium-sized screen in 70mm (the extra 5mm on the release print carried an analogue surround soundtrack) at a well-equipped luxury cinema, seating around 2000 in its single auditorium was an epic experience itself. The 'overture', 'entr'acte' and 'exit' music were part of the show, too. You could buy programme booklets about the film. The admission price was also epic, and in the big cities, the film would run for months (in some cases years) on its first release. This was called 'roadshow' releasing. (General release to ordinary cinemas might be months or even a year or so later.) Going to such a show was never a casual act, there was always a sense of occasion. Usually you had to book tickets in advance, for particular timed performances, like going to the theatre. This was at a time when the normal run of provincial cinemas ran what were called 'continuous performances' in which people could enter and leave the cinema at any time, seeing a film's second half before its first - if they were so inclined and went early enough in the day. (One of the oddest and daftest practices of cinema going in my youth.)

The true epic cannot be made now: (a) it would be too expensive and (b) there's no one around with sufficient gift to direct such a job. Even Ridley Scott's *Gladiator* (US, 2000) - as good as it is cinematically, lacks the necessary size. There are some much later 'near-epics', as I call them, from the East. *Ran* (Akira Kurosawa, Japan, 1985) a tale of mediaeval Japan, is a good example and a close run job, but as impressive as it (and other similar films) may be in various respects, they don't fully meet *all* the criteria I have laid out. The films that do are from a long gone era of cinema: Abel Gance's *Napoleon* (France, 1927), *Gone With The Wind* (Victor Fleming, US, 1939) and from the 50s and 60s - DeMille's *The Ten Commandments* (US, 1956), Wylers's *Ben-Hur* (US, 1959) Mann's *El Cid* (US, 1961), Lean's *Lawrence of Arabia* (UK, 1962) and *Doctor Zhivago* (Italy, US, 1965) Fleischer's *Barabbas* (Italy, US, 1961) George Stevens' *The Greatest Story Ever Told* (US, 1965) and Kubrick's *Spartacus* (US, 1960) and *2001* (UK, US, 1968) – all fitted this monumental specification.

The true epic must be likened to other grand media – music comes readily to mind – ballet, grand opera, the tone poem. *El Cid* is definitely grand opera. When the Cid kills the king's champion in a swordfight not of his own seeking, the champion milks his death scene for all it's worth – just like grand opera. The film's dialogue (as in *Ben-Hur* and *The Ten Commandments*) seems stilted if understood in a naturalistic way, but it just has to have biblical-grade gravitas. When the leader of thirteen opponents helpfully points out that there is only one of him, the Cid answers, "Were you thirteen times thirteen I would not be alone" before he draws his noble sword. *Ben-Hur* (Wyler's version! Bekmambetov's 2016 version – see below – hardly rises to the level of a warbling ballad) is both grand opera and ballet, and has the general stylistics of a grand silent epic, while *The Greatest Story Ever Told* is more like a tone poem. In truth, all epics have something of each, and the cinematic image is ideally suited to such magisterial mimesis. Not that all epics of the genre type and from ages past have been as good as the ones mentioned but uniform excellence is, alas, not a necessary requirement for counting as a member of a genre. Nonetheless, it is the grandness and nobility of the best of the long-gone epics that make them still worth watching and admiring. We have downplayed these qualities far too much in our modern western culture.

Not all recent attempts to recreate such spectacle works. Take another *Ben-Hur* (Timur Bekmambetov, US, 2016). In December 1961, when I was still only 15 years old, I saw Wyler's version, a film that inspired a serious interest in cinema. Had I then seen the later version, not only would this book not exist (which surely would not be a blessing) but my entire subsequent life would have been hugely diminished. Eventually, though, my worst cinematic fears were to be realised. Some popcorn brain in Hollywood decided that it would be really cool to remake the film. The film world is sufficiently inhabited by mediocrities to have made that inevitable, sooner or later. I am fortunate in having lasted over half a century before it actually happened. Fortunately, and unsurprisingly, it shot into obscurity under the shadow of its 1959 predecessor. I have a few reasons that justify that fate:

1. It lacks epic length, epic grandeur, epic scale, epic sweep and epic music - and looks like a postage stamp in comparison with its predecessor.

2. It lacks any hint of nobility, any hint of significance, any real emotional impact and any hint of humour or real humanity.

3. The camera is all over the place, allowing the eye to take in less. (Perhaps a small mercy.)

4. The acting is very weak. (Except Nazanin Boniadi as Esther, who I think is better than Haya Harareet in the Wyler film.)

5. The dialogue is weak, sounding like the script from a Hollywood teenage, high-school movie.

6. The 1959 film was real cinema for about 200 reasons, none of which even could become apparent to director Bekmambetov even if he lived 200 *times* 200 more years.

7. Heston has been replaced by Huston, but the difference in performances by far outstrips even the greatest distance to be found in the alphabet. The former looked like rock and acted a solid part; the latter merely looks like a part and acts like a rock. (Though in more tender moments he ups his game to look more like a pussy cat.)

8. The 1959 film moved the world. This thing doesn't look as though it could move so much as a freshly awakened Roman dormouse.

9. The 1959 version was directed by William Wyler, a master Hollywood craftsman who had already made *The Big Country* (US, 1959) *Roman Holiday* (US, 1953), *The Heiress* (US, 1949) *Wuthering Heights* (US, 1939) and a number of other respected classics. This new film is made by a man whose claim to fame is - wait for it -

Abraham Lincoln: Vampire Hunter (US, 2012). Bekmambetov I judge would be better suited to directing Judah Ben-Hur's little sister in *My Secret Night With Messala.*

10. Wyler's film had a 2-dimensional image and 3-dimensional meaning; this thing has a 3-dimensional image and scarcely a 1-dimensional meaning.

Peter Bradshaw writing in *The Guardian*, added his own comments:

> "Bekmambetov's own narrative drumbeat is set to a relentless heavy thump, and so we reach the famous chariot race scene in pretty short order, via Morgan Freeman having to come on to play a ridiculous, amoral chariot trainer (perhaps inspired directly by Oliver Reed's character in *Gladiator*). The Wyler classic was famous for the terrifying blades that came out of the chariot wheels to carve up your opponents. And what happens this time? How about those knives? Well, it's entirely in line with the film's toothless dullness that this gadget goes missing along with much else. After this, Christ's crucifixion scene simply looks like an anti-climax and the tragedy and miracles concerned with leprosy are more bizarre than anything in Monty Python's Life of Brian. Epic fail."

"Toothless dullness"! Bradshaw, I feel you are being just too kind, though "epic fail" is spot on. It should have been given one award, though – the coveted 'Brass Balls Oscar for Simple Existence'. What we learn from epic successes, though, is significant: how high or low we human beings can go, how good and evil we can be, and how we may respond to the epic requirements of our own lives.

The Western

Even films called 'westerns' these days, a few very good, are not westerns in the traditional genre sense. This is because they do not depend upon the standard codes and characters of that genre. I am willing (if somewhat tentatively) to tender the hypothesis that the true western genre both began and ended with John Ford. (*Stagecoach*, US, 1939 and *The Man Who Shot Liberty Valance* (US, 1962). He who gave also took away. Certainly his film *Cheyenne Autumn*, (US, 1964) was very different, and somewhat yawningly over-stretched and over long. Hints of the true genre certainly lived on, especially in John Wayne films, but only as Sunday's leftovers may be served up as bubble and squeak on Monday. Good as many of the later films are in all sorts of ways, they no more count as true 'genre' westerns than potatoes mashed up with stale cabbage counts as Sunday lunch.

Later 'westerns' could display the toughness and injustices and sudden death in the wilderness but only the genre western keeps proper cinematic track of the elemental and illuminates its depth with a strangely revealing light. Indeed, the genre could be called 'the poetry of the elemental'. Earlier westerns tended to feature robberies and singing cowboys but in genre westerns the community becomes key, and was of a fairly consistent kind. We have the hymn-singing, soil-turning homesteader ('sodbusters' to those who felt themselves in conflict with them) the doctor (not always drunk), the sheriff, the barman and his clientele, and so on. Important also were those outside or on the periphery of the community: the bar-room singer, the ex-gunslinger trying to live a decent life – and, of course, those who were still gunslingers. Then we have the great conflicts: the coming of civilisation and the railroad, the taming of the wilderness, the strength and conflicts of community versus rugged individualism, freedom under sun and stars versus growing civic responsibility, the settlement versus the nomadic, and the relationship between the strong and the weak, between what we may well call the good, the bad and the ugly. Iconic scenery and 'Vistavision'-assisted landscape helps, such as Monument Valley, the great rivers and (mostly) distant mountains. These vast, largely unconquerable features of nature make life dangerous – and danger is something made for conveyance by the cinematic image. The audience participates in this in a way that it simply cannot in ever more carefully qualified and quantified history. My aim here, though, is not to exhaustively describe the genre but just to outline its main features and note that the relevant cinema takes these elements and weaves them into cinematic opera and ballet, something pre-eminently achieved by directors John Ford, Anthony Mann, Howard Hawks and at least once by George Stevens' (*Shane*, US, 1953).

The genre western clearly fits into the 'cinematic image as dreamlike' thesis. The films are not history lessons – not even partial and questionable ones. Cinema can certainly reinforce our ignorance and, often, feed our prejudices if we take them to be revealing historical truth. For these reasons I would be perfectly happy to see many a film being headed up with a cinematic equivalent of a health warning. Instead of the merely misleading 'Based on true events', we could have 'Motivated by legend', or just 'Only vaguely related to the truth', or, *in extremis*, 'You are an ignoramus and likely to remain one if you believe a single shot in the following film'. (Perhaps such warnings could replace some of the crass pronouncements of the BBFC[167] certificate, such as, 'This film contains mild sex'. I like that one.) Note, I am not saying that the genre western was not concerned with truth. It was, it was just not concerned with historical literalism.

History and cinema: westerns and others

Cinema primarily addresses not specific historical details of events but a whole historical sensibility, about the origin and development and myth of a culture, about what has to be done and what has to be faced, about courage and survival, and what these things throw up. (Take *The Alamo*, John Wayne, US, 1960). Such films penetrate reality at a different level or at least in a different way. They say something universal rather than local. At the end of *The Man Who Shot Liberty*

Valance (John Ford, US, 1962) the newspaperman says, "This is the West, sir. When the legend becomes fact, print the legend". Anyone who still thinks that genre follows rigid thinking has simply failed to get all this. Yes, genre has its equivalence of dogma, but here I am inclined to borrow Dorothy M. Sayers' dictum: "the dogma *is* the drama.[168] And the drama is indeed the poetry of the elemental. The western is, as John Wayne himself remarked, "folklore in its purest form".[169] This is why, I feel, that the genre 'Western' should still be watched and, at its best, admired.

I do not think that what cinema does best is teach history. Instead, cinema offers a dream-like vision of reality. However, like many such visions, they are still at some level existentially truth-telling. This, not historical or biographical scholarship, best fits legend and drama as it is presented in cinema. It is not the historical events themselves that much of the best cinema expresses but their dream versions. This involves, essentially, an imaginative level of engagement that justifies playfulness with literal truth but which, at its best at any rate, delivers deeper truth. Cinema is not at its best when it is trying to be prosaic – and historical and biographical details are often exceedingly prosaic. This distinction is brought out in the case of Maria von Trapp and the film *The Sound of Music* (Robert Wise, US, 1966). The fact that this brave soul looked very unlike Julie Andrews is but a part of its imaginative, playful, non-literal approach. On the whole, things were not really like the way in which they were presented in the film, historically or biographically. At the time, the real Maria did not like it for that reason – perhaps understandably. Eventually, I understand, she warmed to it, commenting that it was how it *should* have been. This dream version of reality is, I believe, what cinema does best, and it involves a re-imagining of things. Of course, that which is legend, pretence and dream should be understood as such.

All this is what a genre western does, but legends and folklore are not mere lies, they are part of the dream in which our deepest concerns are anchored. We know that civilisation is built upon foundations of barbarity from which we can never entirely escape. Nevertheless, monumental truth (together with monumental valleys and monumental shootouts) are made to shape the exaggerated stuff of dreams, and the finest of cinema, as we have seen, is made of that stuff. We rightly worry about racial and sexist injustices which are too often left unexplored but when we forget legend we let go of what cinema does best. Moreover, we also ignore a large part of what has formed a culture – something very real.

The days in which the genre western passed away might to some extent have signalled a greater willingness to face the wrongs of the past – that is the good thing – but they also signalled the abandonment of what our best dreams tell us about ourselves – a deep level of truth, remember. They ushered out a poetry we should never forget, and our contemporary fascination with forever more tedious, labyrinthine deconstruction rushes in to fill the vacuum, yielding only acres of screen boredom. If you want a slogan, I favour the following - 'Hang literal, base-line truth in serious cinema, as in all serious art – keep it for the history books'.

One can consider further the depths of truth to which the western can take us through a brief analysis of John Ford's *The Searchers* (US, 1956). I have had the criticism put to me that it was viciously and gratuitously racist. I think, however, that this confuses what the film is *about* with what it celebrates. In fact, throughout the film, Uncle Ethan, the racist bigot, is held by many of the other significant and world-weary characters at best in suspicion and at worst in having a side which is despicable and beneath any decent understanding or affirmation. Even his own brother seems nervous of Ethan's darkness, as he rides into their lives. The general suspicion emerges at several key points: as he constantly dismisses his 'nephew' (Jeffrey Hunter) as a 'half-breed', as he shoots out the eyes of a dead Indian to the disgust of the 'reverend' and lawman (Ward Bond) and as he comes close to shooting Debbie, the girl he had gone in search of, because she had become Indianised. Ethan Edwards hates intensely and he is disliked intensely by many.

True, Edwards is projected as a kind of hero in this film. He is strong – and principled in certain key ways, and he did finally *rescue* Debbie, after all, not shoot her, as we feared. He might have been killed in this endeavour – and that shows courage. However, I rather think we are presented here with a *tragic* hero, a *flawed* hero, even a *doomed* hero, not a genuinely celebrated one. Martin Scorsese (in an American Film Institute interview) calls the character a "poet of hate", one who "hates beyond the grave". Presenting this, I think, is the central point of the film, and is, of course, brought out powerfully by the film's rightly celebrated closing image, showing him leaving the homestead, where he fundamentally knows himself to have no place. The poet of hate has to live his life in isolation from humanity. That final shot is, I believe, one of the finest cinematic images one will ever come across, expressing so poetically – and in full dream-like force - one of the deepest and most epic tragedies of sheer human cussedness. This man cannot help but cut off his nose to spite his own face - all in the cause of some assumed but unnamed and distorted honour. In the end he is on his way out, but this is not presented as being the way things *should* be. We celebrate the power of the cinematic image, not what the image shows us. We are simply shown what, given his character flaw, *is* the case. And we are shown its inevitability. This is what makes it, finally, a great, almost Shakespearian, tragedy. The whole film, in fact, was something of a departure from the tone of the other Ford-Wayne westerns, which usually have to do with honour. It's more radical in that it explores hatred and its implications instead.

Indeed, the film is unsurpassed in the way in which it explores Edward's flaws - his black-heartedness, his turnings away, his deep loneliness. "What makes a man to wander? What makes man to roam?", the film's title song goes. What indeed drives this still large, bullish, tough but otherwise shrivelled up character? The man rejects the respectability (though also of course its inevitable hypocrisies) as well as the safety and even love of the civilised (genre) 'homestead'. In the end he draws back into the wilderness, his only possible home. Tell me that this does not express a deep truth. In fact, this man pretty much rejects humanity. Ford grasps this character abundantly, and respects his toughness. John Wayne (who, in a singularly great performance, plays Edwards) and John Ford draw him with deep perception, but Ford also knows full well that this man has some deep flaws and certainly didn't celebrate them. In fact, I think the film was quite deliberately written, directed and acted to make us feel deeply uncomfortable about this character. Yes, toughness and willingness to struggle against life's challenges are celebrated, as they are in many a fine western, but bigotry and racism are not. This alone makes it a hugely moral enterprise, as all the best westerns were – another reason to watch them again and value them. It might be pointed out here that *The Searchers* transcends as much as exemplifies the genre western, and I am inclined to agree – but it includes what it transcends. Moreover, many other westerns transcend the genre. Take *Shane* (George Stevens, US, 1953) for example, which shines in its telling of a reformed gunslinger, yet still make use of the genres elemental features.

Hence, to say that the genre western tells us no truth worth pondering is no more credible than asserting that Shakespeare tells us no truth on the grounds that his histories do not stand up to more literal research into mediaeval kingship. We are here talking about targeting very different issues and evoking very different responses: the pitilessness of the wilderness, how we respond to almost archetypal character, how difficult building and maintaining honour can be, how (as with the epic) we can face sheer magnitude, and how frail human flesh can respond to the elemental. This is what the great genre western can teach us. Tell me that this little lot is of no importance. Thus, anyone who wants to say that the great genre westerns secure no valuable truth whatsoever needs to visit Specsavers, for they need to replace their clunky literal-seeing lenses for something that will enable them to access a richer and more revealing filmscape. As far as I can see, the only sinfulness of the great genre western, lies in its now being a thing of the past.

Film Noir

Noir, like other genres, also has an intrinsic dreamlike quality that fits the nature of the cinematic image but this time with the aura of the nightmare. This, I believe, reinforces the idea that the natural photographic home of the genre is black and white. Arguably, its visual origins lie in such masterpieces as Fritz Lang's *M*

(Germany, 1931) and John Huston's *The Maltese Falcon* (US, 1941). Its continuing emotional acceptance is sometimes said to lie in post-Second World War cynicism, a cynicism that has not left us. The genre seems also thought never to have left us. Be all that as it may, however, we may ask whether it is really still around or has morphed out of most recognition into merely dark films, mostly in colour, that merely have vaguely noirish settings and themes? I suspect the latter.

There are far too many more lacks, however, for noir not nowadays to be declared dead on arrival. There seems very little around of the crisp intelligence of Raymond Chandler adaptations. There seem to be no regular noir stars, especially of the calibre of Humphrey Bogart and Lauren Bacall – and made to measure for the job. There is still the violence and sudden death, of course. Indeed, there seems to be *too* much of it. The threat level remains high and there is darkness and despair a plenty, but I cannot recall any characters from recent so-called noir film for whom I have much liking, or even sympathy. Sex, which was implied in true noir, will now be more explicit. Aside from the special problems associated with that (which we have already discussed) it is uniquely sinful in a genre that lives at least in large part on the strength of suggestion. (On this front, think of the relationship and dialogue between Fred MacMurray and Barbara Stanwyck in *Double Indemnity* (Billy Wilder, US, 1944).

The more specialised noir notion of the hard boiled has turned into something just hard. Undercurrents can still be found but they seem starkly black rather than more richly dark. Smart cynicism seems to have given way to mere indulgence in the sickening. (Tarantino's 'Hollywood', perhaps!) In fact, about the only things left are the shadows, though these are usually surrounded nowadays by colour, which seems to be imported from a climate where noir doesn't naturally grow. Seeing supposed noir in colour always strikes me as being as out of place as eating a pineapple salad starter on a cold winter's evening when hot, thick pepper soup is called for. It can set me against a film, sometimes unjustly, before I even see it, simply because I wonder what distorted tastes are at play. The studio-based look of true noir is also important, as is the heavy studio rain. (Studio rain I always find one of the more deeply cinematic of phenomena.) The shadows need heavy-duty definition as well, perhaps with as many off-beat diagonal lines as can be mustered. Simply having plenty of them certainly won't do. A heavy-duty musical score, lubricated especially for noir, should be there, too, as should some voice-over narration (an efficient way of getting in more detail, or an element of double cross, without taking the sharp edge off the actual dialogue). To go with the dark, night-time should, of course, dominate – noir is about the night-time of life, after all, and it presents that 'night-time' in a uniquely persuasive, forceful, crisp and tellingly nightmarish way – as it should. That would be my case for watching and valuing true Film Noir. It makes us aware, in its uniquely symbolic way, of the easy seductions and spiral descents to which human flesh is heir. It does not, like too much of its alleged modern equivalent, leave us merely sickened. True genre material, here as in the other examples, has an equally true moral force.

Understand that falling on what I regard as the unnatural side of noir doesn't automatically render a film bad. One would have to take each film as an individual case. It is regarding them as belonging to a recognisable genre legitimately called 'noir' that I find so perverse. The codes that earned the label can still be found hanging in the air but there is often too much complexity in characterisation and less restriction. This perhaps characterises most films these days that are slotted into known genres. Moreover, being restricted in what one can do doesn't seem to sit well in the stomachs of today's more serious filmmakers, despite the fact that the world's best art throughout much of history has thrived under restriction. (A pet thesis of mine is that if one gives an artist of any kind too much rope, they'll hang their art from it and give their audience self-indulgence rather than true inventiveness. Recall the recent plethora of long-running, long-winded films that constitute much of so called 'slow cinema'.)

Too often, also, films called 'noir' seem to have too large a canvas – almost literally – the classic noirs having been filmed in the old 'academy ratio', something that added to the necessary tightness and tension. In general, the instant iconography associated with noir (or *any* traditional genre for that matter) is no longer there, which is perhaps why we have to be *told* a film is an example of 'noir'. When it was obvious, we needed no telling. One may note that we often use words more pointedly when that which they denote either no longer exists or exists only in a deformed or reduced way. 'Community' is my favourite word hereabouts, but I recently saw on a local bus the slogan 'Connecting people to places'. Wow! That's news, I commented. My bother instantly retorted, "Yes! But they only say it because they do less of it these days". The same goes, I contend, for the epithet 'noir'.

Noir was defined and forged by filmmakers such as Howard Hawks (*The Big Sleep*, US, 1946), Raoul Walsh (*White Heat*, US, 1949), Fritz Lang (*The Big Heat*, US 1953), Nicholas Ray (*They Lived By Night*, US, 1948), Jules Dassin (*The Naked City*, US, 1948), John Huston (*The Asphalt Jungle*, US, 1950) and, of course, Billy Wilder in the film mentioned above. In Britain we had Carol Reed (*The Third Man*, UK, 1950). (There are others, of course, I simply cite my own favourites.) The genre didn't entirely die after this period but I think it lost some of its unique charge as it gave way (if not, to be fair, entirely) to the merchants much more of mere shock–directors such as Samuel Fuller and Robert Aldrich.

At best we have something that can be called 'neo-noir', though now even this is getting on a bit. *The Usual Suspects* (Bryan Singer, US, 1995) *L.A. Confidential* (Curtis Hanson, US, 1997) and, perhaps, *Memento* (Christopher Nolan, US, 2000) may count here as really prize examples. But 'neo' can be used too loosely. Often it just means no more than 'influenced by' (which can often mean whatever an author wants it to mean) rather than 'a new brand of' (which it *should* mean). Perhaps true noir cannot exist now – the culture, as hinted earlier, not being suitable for its thriving – but in which case just let's drop the term, and let's not attach 'neo', to it either. I've heard *Blade Runner* (Ridley Scott, US, 1982) described as neo-noir. In some sense (I begrudgingly suppose) that may be the closest, but *Sin City* (Frank Miller, Quentin Tarantino, US, 2005)? Come on! That is good but it is amusing pastiche. None of these films has the special feel of traditional noir – and genres, I believe, are to be defined in terms of *feel* as much as anything. Even the 1973 remake of *The Long Goodbye* (Robert Altman, US, 1973) much as I like it, just has too much of the 70s revolution about it to count that much as noir (in the traditional sense). I will tire neither you nor myself with other putative examples. Often a writer will call a film an example of noir (or neo-noir) just because – at the required stretch – it contains one or two of the original elements, but this is just silly. One needs to harness far more than that if one is to be left with more than a mere shadow of the true genre, otherwise the term becomes so course grained as to be all but meaningless. Another strategy would be simply to define 'neo-noir' in terms that include just a few of the traditional criteria and some new ones to boot. Limits can always be legitimately pushed of course but aside from the arbitrariness of such a manoeuvre, it seems less clear that the new version of the genre is a genre at all. Genre demands strict limits. Going hybrid can hardly count.

Whatever the reason, true noir ('noir' as intended by the French film intellectuals who used the term to classify this unique kind of dark film – thus the French) is, I think, dead, and no number of semantic shenanigans can resurrect it. The really sad truth, the truth that quite properly gives rise to mourning, though, is that a large slice of important cinema is dead. This is a pity in ways that go beyond even cinema, for what true noir teaches us (or reminds us of) is just how easily human life can be made sordid, and just what twisted, darkened and ultimately lethal trenches we can so readily fall into, either through ignorance, through weakness or own deliberate fault, as did Fred MacMurray's doomed insurance salesman in Billy Wilder's magnificent *Double* Indemnity (US, 1944). On the whole, I think we should mourn the passing of all the great, classic genres, for they taught us some truly important, classic and perennial lessons, lessons we seem these days too easily to take ourselves as being far too sophisticated to need. Thus, with the passing of the classic genre goes the passing also of a key strand of human wisdom.

The 'comic book' film: A new genre or just a new sin?

In general, traditional-genre has gone, though there is at least one new one – the Comic Book film. Is the new genre of CGI-driven, comic-book, super-hero films worthwhile?

I recall the film-maker George Lucas saying somewhere of computerised cinema, "We have changed the medium in a way which is profound. It is now no longer a photographic medium. It is a painterly medium". This fact seems innocent enough but it has indeed changed the medium. Part of cinema's glory is founded in the fact that it is photographic (or cinematographic). In that sense, it retains a reality despite its artifice – and despite the fact that cinematography, at its best, is already quite painterly enough, and wonderfully so.

What a magnificent and magical combination cinematographic reality and artifice traditional cinema has proven to be. Change it and we see a horse of a quite different colour. We should, of course, always embrace new and appropriate technology. Good cinema has always done this. Cinema has always been technological, right down to its bones. This is a simple consequence of the need for camera and recording medium, but *is* computerisation an appropriate technology? In some respects, obviously. It has made possible the glorious restoration of many a long past cinematographic masterpiece for starters. But when cinema allows its stories – its very foundations - to be driven solely by its technology, whether this consists of painted backdrops, 'travelling mattes', wide-screen, 'three-strip Technicolor', 3D or, now, its range of digital effects, one is generating not good cinema, but narrative, aesthetic and psychological trash. (In the past only 3D was allowed on any wide scale to do this dirty deed. Nowadays it is common currency.)

Compare our present day 'comic book' adaptations with *2001: A Space Odyssey* (Stanley Kubrick, US, 1968) and one will develop a keen enough sense of the difference I am talking about. That film used the new computer wizardry (though not yet CGI) for art's sake. The computer here enabled a new kind of 'visionary poem', as Martin Scorsese put it. Maybe the new combination of digitisation and visual motion can create a further new kind of great art, an art just as much of the 21st century as cinema has been of the 20th. Great! But one will need a strong narrative, even philosophical vision, to pull it all off (as film-makers such as FW Murnau, D.W. Griffiths and Stanley Kubrick, and companies like Technicolor, had in spades) and all I can say is that, so far, few, if any, have yet come remotely close to realising any similar hope with CGI. And before anyone says otherwise, digital cinema effects now lay well beyond their earliest and clumsiest days. But perhaps hope is still due. We have Scorsese's own *Hugo* (UK, 2011) in our repertoire, after all, and even the comic book *need* not be entirely banal. So, while the current evidence is slim, let us wait and see what lies ahead.

The sins of genre subversion

Today, one hears talk of 'subverting genre'. Subversion is, in my view, the great love of people who have little of value to offer in exchange, but is there *any* value in subverting genre, even remembering that genre itself is not sinful? In my researches I readily discovered a web article titled, '7 films that subverted genre codes (and were all the better for it)' by Charles Baptiste (details in Bibliography). Let us look at some of these, and others and see how, where and even what (if anything) is being subverted and whether the subversion was worth it.

We first deal with *La La Land* (Damien Chazelle, US, 2016), a supposed subversion of the MGM musical genre of the time, in particular *Singin' in the Rain* (Stanley Donen, US 1952). I am inclined to think that this film subverts Gene Kelly more than the bright, cheerful traditional it mimics. I often jokingly maintain that I could dance round a wet lamppost better than Ryan Gosling, but that jest aside how much is there by way of subversion? Only – so it seems, that the key boy and girl (unlike Gene Kelly and Debbie Reynolds in the former film) do not get together. I suppose this is something but, on the whole the later film seems more to celebrate (sort of, at least) rather than subvert the ethos of the former. In any case, why shouldn't we wish to cheer ourselves up now and again? But I would not laud the film. I have seen that film but once and that is likely to be that; *Singin' in the Rain* I have seen umpteen times and I have no intention of depriving myself of what has become an annual yuletide treat.

Next we have *Winter's Bone* (Debra Granik, US, 2010). Man versus the raw forces of nature has long been a feature of certain genres – the western and the adventure yarn, for instance. Though women have been at their side, it has traditionally been the man who fought the wild. *Winter's Bone* subverts this and puts the woman in charge. The film is beautifully played and has plenty of atmosphere which conveys a strong sense of place. The culture and the mixture of motives at play are apparent, even though it lacks a little crispness in its storytelling. My key question here, though, concerns whether what it subverts deserves subversion? And to what extent? Didn't women *equally* fight the wild in the earlier genre jobs – but just *differently*?

The Coen brothers *could* be thought of as great subverters – of sorts. *Burn After Reading* (US, 2008) might be thought to subvert the spy film, *Hail, Caesar!* (US, 2016) the traditional Roman epic and *No Country for Old Men* (US, 2007), the western. But these are special cases. Firstly, they are comedic – they are engaged more in having fun with the tropes of genre than in subversion itself. Secondly, there are simply too many different types and flavours of 'spy' films for them to be lumped together as a genre in any case. *Burn After Reading* is simply of the fun, satirical type. Finally, if *No Country for Old Men* subverts anything (how?) it subverts not the traditional western, set in the 19th century wilderness, but the more modern west with its phones and big cars. As for *Hail, Caesar!*, it doesn't so much subvert the ancient-world epic as make lots of fun of the filmmakers who jumped on that bandwagon at the time. On the whole, I don't think that the Coen brothers are subverters at all but more cinematically clever, witty and intelligent satirists. They are too clever for mere subversion.

The horror genre is sometimes subverted. From more recent times, Baptiste suggests *Scream* (Wes Craven, US 1996). Yes, I suppose this works but much depends on the type of horror one is thinking of. Gone, mostly, are the more story-telling horrors of the past, their having been replaced with the mere easy to produce, merely visceral, shock flicks. Now that's a genre worth subverting for it has no discernible value to begin with. My favourite example of subversion, or at least micky-taking, of the more traditional variety of horror film, though, is *Carry on Screaming* (Gerald Thomas, UK, 1966).[170]

On subverting genre, Baptiste writes:

> "Genre can be a double-edged sword for any filmmaker. On the upside, knowing the genre of your story can help you figure out a character, fix a plot that doesn't hang together or just simply provide you with inspiration. On the downside, you can quickly get stuck in the codes and conventions of that genre, which can lend your film a formulaic, unoriginal feel, however brilliant your idea was."

I find two worrying sentiments here. First comes a plain over emphasis on the assumed default value of originality – something I have already discussed. Secondly, we have the view of codes and conventions leading to formula, as though formula is something iffy. (I have already given reason to reject the charge of iffiness.) Yes genre is formulaic but so is dream. It's a part of how they both work. The *fact* of being formulaic is never as important as the quality of the formula. Cinema is also like food in this respect. It doesn't matter that each apple pie follows a common recipe, only that the recipe followed is a good one and the cook, competent. Inventiveness and playfulness are always to be welcomed but I do not think subversions of genre are better ideas than genre itself. Besides, I rather think that life itself is standardly far more formulaic than we may like to think. That's a good thing, too. We would hardy know where we were otherwise.

Genre is also the very opposite of (human and appearance) naturalism – photo or carbon-copying, which is cinematically dulled out right from the off. There aren't any 'stories-*on-their-own*', there are only 'stories-*as-told*'. The audio/visual *way* in which they are told is paramount. Moreover, to care about the dream aspect of genre (and film in general) is not to cease caring about reality, or descend into some sort of hopeless rose-tinted romanticism. To care about the quality and vividness of the cinematic dream, and what the dream is telling you, is a *way* of caring about reality – a way that cinema does best. Individual preference aside, I urge that filmmakers and film-goers remember all this.

Conclusion

Will the tsunami of sins of modern cinema ever wane? I suppose so. The tide may well turn, it's what tides do, after all, though of course they turn back, too - the cycle continuing. Rebellion is always somewhere in the wind; it is the very engine of change. Isaac Newton got more than physics right when he spoke of 'equal and opposite forces'. Rebellion caused the present tsunami and it will eventually cause its collapse, then return it to prominence again – at least for as long as anything remotely resembling cinema lives on. It is inevitable given what I have called 'the paradox of cinema' – that it possesses both photographic realism *and* form, for there will always be those wanting to give one of them greater prominence.

The various turns towards sin against which I argue in the present book hardly help the survival and thriving of *good* cinema, of course, but there is also a further issue' – whether cinema will continue *in any way at all* that is remotely recognisable – sinful or virtuous. Motion picture imagery of some kind will continue, I am sure, but as its essential technology inexorably moves on so will the forms of its media. Recall George Lucas's observation that digital technology changes the medium. I predict further, even more radical technological innovation that will change the landscape forever, as did the coming of cinema in the first place, and with that change will come a whole *new* raft of sins and virtues. (Though being able to tell a good story, and tell it well and imaginatively, will always be important for as long as humanity survives – or so I very much like to think.) Good art (or good entertainment) simply has to have its appropriate and inappropriate ways if we are to retain any distinction at all between the good and the bad. I will weep a tear, I suppose, if I live long enough to witness the death of cinema as we more or less know it, especially if it comes during one of its higher phases. Too often now, though, it seems already so close to death that I could almost wish that it be seen off altogether and slide into the pages of history. At least there's something untouchable about death, and I do so hate to see the poor medium suffer so much at the hands of its torturers and not-so-cultured despisers.

Bibliography

Andrew, Dudley, *Concepts of Film Theory*, Oxford, OUP, 1984.

Andrew, Dudley / Sklar, Robert / Murphy, Arthur, D / Stephenson, Ralph & Roger Manvell, Roger, "Motion Pictures" in *Encyclopaedia Britannica* March 24, 2020 https://www.britannica.com/art/motion-picture.

Aquinas, St. Thomas, *Summa Theologiae*, 1265-1273

Baptiste, Charles, '7 films that subverted genre codes (and were all the better for it)' Radiance.org, 1 February, 2017, URL: https://www.raindance.org/7-films-subverted-genre-codes-better/.

Barr, Charles, "Cinemascope: Before and After", in Mast, G and Cohen, M., eds. *Film Theory and Crticism,* New York, Oxford University Press, 1985.

Bedard, Mike, 'What is a Jump Cut? 5 Ways to Use Jump Cuts in Film', on the studiobinder.com website, July 5, 2020. Retrieved from: https://www.studiobinder.com/blog/what-is-a-jump-cut/.

Belton, John, *Widescreen Cinema*, Harvard University Press, 1993.

Bordwell, David, *The Poetics of Cinema*, Abingdon, Routledge, 2008.

Carr, Robert, E, & Hayes, R.M., *Wide Screen Movies: A History and Filmography of Wide Gauge Filmmaking,* McFarland, 1988.

Carroll, Noel, "Defining The Moving Image" in *Philosophy Film and Motion Picture*, eds., Carroll, Noel & Choi, Jinhee, Oxford, Blackwell, 2006.

----------------, 'Introduction to Part II' in *Philosophy of Film and Motion Pictures,* eds., Carroll, Noel & Choi, Jinhee, Oxford, Blackwell, 2006.

Cavell, Stanley, 'The World Viewed' in *Philosophy of Film and Motion Pictures,* eds., Carroll, Noel & Choi, Jinhee, Oxford, Blackwell, 2006.

Currie, Gregory *Image & Mind*, Cambridge, C.U.P., 1995.

Danto, Arthur C. 'Moving Pictures' in *Philosophy of Film and Motion Pictures,* eds., Carroll, Noel & Choi, Jinhee, Oxford, Blackwell, 2006.

Davison, Andrew, 'Music and What Matters Most' in Milbank, Alison; Hughes, John; Milbank, Arabella (eds.) *Preaching Radical and Orthodox*, 2017, SCM Press. Kindle Edition.

de Valk, Mark. *The Film Handbook* (Media Practice), Taylor and Francis. 2013. Kindle Edition.

Deveraux, Mary, "Beauty and Evil: The Case of Leni Riefenstahl's *The Triumph of the Will*", in *Philosophy Film and Motion Picture*, eds., Carroll, Noel & Choi, Jinhee, Oxford, Blackwell, 2006.

Dmytryk, Edward, *On Film Editing*, London, Focal Press, 1984.

Eliot, T.S., 'Poetry and truth' in *Theories of Art & Beauty*, ed., Wilkinson, R.Milton Keynes, Open University Press, 1991.

Farley, Edward. *Faith and Beauty* (Routledge Studies in Theology, Imagination and the Arts). Taylor and Francis. Kindle Edition. (2001)

Fiorelli, Lindsey, "What Movies Show: Realism, Perception and Truth in Film", PhD Dissertation, University of Pennsylvania, 2016. Publicly Accessible Penn Dissertations. 1715. URL: http://repository.upenn.edu/edissertations/1715/

Fort, Jeff, 'André Bazin's Eternal Returns: An Ontological Revision', *Film-Philosophy*, (2021) 25:1, 42-61

Galgut, Elisa, "Harnessing the imagination: the asymmetry of belief and make-belief" in *Contemporary Aesthetics*, Vol 12, 2014. https://quod.lib.umich.edu/c/ca/7523862.0012.021/--harnessing-the-imagination-the-asymmetry-of-belief-and-make?rgn=main;view=fulltext. Retrieved: February 2022.

Gaut, Berys, "Cinematic Art and Technology" in *Current Controversies in Philosophy of Film*, Thomson-Jones, Katherine (ed) London, Routledge, 2016, Kindle Edition.

Gray, Tim, 'Sound Is 50% of the Movie, but Hollywood is Often Tone-Deaf, *Variety*, Feb 22, 2018. URL: https://variety.com/2018/film/awards/sound-movie-blade-runner-get-out-phantom-thread-1202705398/.

Hart, David Bentley. *Theological Territories*, University of Notre Dame Press. Kindle Edition, 2020.

Herrmann, Jorg "From Popular to Arthouse: An Analysis of Love and Nature as Religious Motifs in Recent Cinema", in *Mediating Religion: Studies in Media, Religion, and Culture*, eds., Mitchell, Jolyon P. & Marriage, Sophia, London, AC Black, 2003.

Hill, Paul E, *Philosophical Puzzlement*, Self-published on Amazon Kindle & paperback, 2020.

--------------, *Seeing Things*, Self-published on Amazon Kindle & paperback, 2019.

Hopkins, Robert, "Depiction", in *The Routledge Companion to Philosophy and Film*, Oxon, Routledge, 2009, Ch.6.

Hopkins, Robert, "Realism in Film (and Other Representation)" in *Current Controversies in Philosophy of Film*, Thomson-Jones, Katherine (ed) London, Routledge, Ch 4, Oxon, Routledge, 2016, Kindle Edition.

Isaacs, Bruce, *The Orientation of Future Cinema: Technology, Aesthetics, Spectacle*, Bloomsbury Publishing, 2013, Kindle Edition.

Isenberg, A.,in Hursthouse, R., 'Truth & representation' in *Philosophical Aesthetics*, Oxford, Blackwell, 1992.

Kael, Pauline, "Raising Kane", *The New Yorker*, February 20, 1971.

Kalinak, Kathryn. *Film Music: A Very Short Introduction*, Oxford University Press, 2010.

Kania, Andrew, "Realism" in *The Routledge Companion to Philosophy and Film*, Oxon, Routledge, 2009, Kindle Edition. Ch.22.

Kant, Immanuel, *The Critique of Judgement* (1790) in *Critique of the Power of Judgment (The Cambridge Edition of the Works of Immanuel Kant)* eds.: Guyer, Paul & Wood, Allen W, Cambridge, CUP, 2000.

Kenny, Anthony, *The Metaphysics of Mind*, Oxford, Clarendon Press, 1989.

Langer, Suzanne, *Feeling and Form*, New York, Charles Scribner's Sons, 1953.

------------ 'Philosophy in a new key', in *Philosophical Aesthetics*, Oxford, Blackwell, 1992.

Lopes, Dominic McIver, 'The Aesthetics of Photographic Transparency', in

Mind, New Series, Vol. 112, No. 447, Oxford, OUP., Jul., 2003.

------------- *Four Arts of Photography (New Directions in Aesthetics)* Oxford, Wiley, Kindle Edition, 2016.

Marshall, Colin, *Film*, September 3, 2019 (Retrieved from: http://www.openculture.com/2019/09/the-greatest-cut-in-film-history.html).

McGinn, Colin, *The Power of Movies*, New York, Pantheon, 2005.

Monaco, James, *How To Read a Film: Movies, Media, and Beyond*, Harbor Electronic Publishing, Kindle Edition.

Murdoch, Iris, "The sublime and the good", in *Existentialists and Mystics: Writings in Philosophy and Literature by Iris Murdoch*, eds., Conradi, Peter and Steiner, George, London, Penguin, 1998.

Murch, Walter, *In The Blink of an Eye: A Perspective on Film Editing*. 2nd Edition. Silman-James Press, 1992.

Oakley, Justin, *Morality and the Emotions*, London, Routledge, 1992.

Oliver, Simon, 'Representing Evil in Schindler's List and Life is Beautiful', in Jeff Sellars. *Light Shining in a Dark Place: Discovering Theology through Film*. Pickwick Publications, an Imprint of Wipf and Stock Publishers, 2012. Kindle Edition.

Phillips, Dawn M., 'Photography and Causation: Responding to Scruton's Scepticism', in the *British Journal of Aesthetics* (2009) Vol. 49 Issue 4 pp. 327-340.

Price, Carolyn, E*motion*, Milton Keynes, The Open University Press, 2005.

Roberts, Steven, 'High Fidelity Widescreen Cinema: VistaVision Film Production and Style in Britain and the USA', PhD thesis, University of Bristol, 2020.

Russell, Andrew, 'Slow cinema: what it is and why it's on a fast track to the mainstream in a frenetic world', https://theconversation.com/slow-cinema-what-it-is-and-why-its-on-a-fast-track-to-the-mainstream-in-a-frenetic-world-114769.

Salt, Barry, *Film Style and Technology: History and Analysis*, London, Starword, 1983.

Scruton, Roger, *An Intelligent Person's Guide to Philosophy*, London, Duckworth, 1996.

-------------------"Photography and Representation" in *Critical Inquiry*, Vol. 7, No. 3 (Spring, 1981).

-------------------- *Beauty: A Very Short Introduction*, OUP Oxford. Kindle Edition, 2009.

Smith, Jeff, 'Music', in Livingstone, Paisley and Plantinga, Carl (eds.) *The Routledge Companion to Philosophy and Film*, 2009.

Sobchackin, Vivian, "Phenomenology", in *The Routledge Companion to Philosophy and Film*, Oxon, Routledge, 2009.

Sokolowski, Robert, *Introduction to Phenomenology*, Cambridge, CUP, 2000.

Stephenson, Ralph and Debrix, J.R., *The Cinema as Art*, Revised Edition, Harmondsworth, Penguin Books, 1969.

Tersman, Folke, 'Ethics', in Livingstone, Paisley and Plantinga, Carl (eds.) *The Routledge Companion to Philosophy and Film*, Oxon, Routledge, 2009.

Tyler, Parker, *Magic and Myth of the Movies*, London, Secker & Warburg, 1971.

von Balthasar, Hans Urs, *The Glory of the Lord: A Theological Aesthetics*, Edinburgh, T&T Clark, 1989

Walton, Kendal. "Transparent Pictures: On the Nature of Photographic Realism", *Critical Inquiry,* Vol. 11, No. 2, December, 1984.

Warnock, Mary, *Imagination and Time*, Oxford, Blackwell, 1994.

Wimsatt, W.K., Jr., and Beardsley, Monroe C., *The Verbal Icon: Studies in the Meaning of Poetry*, University of Kentucky, 1954.

Wynn, Mark, 'Religion and The Revelation of Value: The Emotions as Sources for Religious Understanding', in *Comparative Theology: Essays for Keith Ward*, edited by T.W. Bartel, London, SPCK, 2003.

Endnotes

---

[1] See: http://alanparker.com/quotes/on-filmmaking/

[2] I do have some stronger things to say about art in places.

[3] For an extended discussion on the distinctions I make here see Berys Gaut, "Cinematic Art and Technology" in *Current Controversies in Philosophy of Film*, Thomson-Jones, Katherine (ed.) p.21.

[4] Questions of what things *are*, of their deepest nature, are *metaphysical*. If one says of the teapot that it is a material object, for instance, then the metaphysical question arises as to what makes some things count as material objects and other things (rainbows, perhaps) not. Metaphysics is part of philosophy. Hence, the first chapter will be addressing issues of the metaphysics of the cinematic image. Don't be put off by the term. What it amounts to will become clearer in the reading.

[5] Cited in Herrmann, Jorg "From Popular to Arthouse: An Analysis of Love and Nature as Religious Motifs in Recent Cinema", in *Mediating Religion: Studies in Media, Religion, and Culture*, eds., Mitchell, Jolyon P. & Marriage, Sophia p.190.

[6] Interviewed in *Variety*, January 23, 2016. Retrieved from: https://variety.com/2016/film/news/alejandro-inarruitu-diversity-oscars-1201687041/

[7] Though 'ordinary' hardly captures the rich and varied phenomenology of such experiences. It's as demeaning a word to use of perception as it would be to call the whole universe 'Charlie'.

[8] For a scholarly investigation of this thesis, see, D. M. Lopes, 'The Aesthetics of Photographic Transparency', pp. 433-448. For a consideration of transparency in connection with visual imagery more widely see my own *Seeing Things*. The word could apply also to Option 2.

[9] *The Power of Movies*, p.83.

[10] Ralph Waldo Emerson, *Nature*, an essay written in 1836.

[11] Readers eager to follow this up can find an extended discussion of this issue in my book *Seeing Things*, available from Amazon, though that work is hardly introductory.

[12] This was set out in detail by philosopher Kendal Walton. See his 'Transparent Pictures: On the Nature of Photographic Realism', *Critical Inquiry*, Vol. 11, No. 2 (December 1984), pp. 246-277. What I put forward, however, is my own take on the thesis: Film Theorist Andre Bazin also writes of a "transfer of reality from the thing onto its reproduction", this having to do with photography's mechanical means of reproduction.' See, Jeff Fort, 'André Bazin's Eternal Returns: An Ontological Revision', pp.42-61, cited from: https://www.euppublishing.com/doi/full/10.3366/film.2021.0156

[13] I am aware that philosophical complications arise in the case of ordinary perception, too. Again, see my book *Seeing Things* for a fuller but demanding discussion. I do not deny, either, that we may see things imaginatively. These, however, are additional issues.

[14] For scientific readers, I am aware that the word 'now' comes with its own scientific issues here, especially in connection with relativity theory, but I think we can safely ignore those issues in our present context.

[15] A full discussion of this can be found in Fiorelli, Lindsey, *What Movies Show: Realism, Perception and Truth in Film*, Ch.1.

[16] The most extreme case of manipulation I can think of can be seen in the film *Gladiator* (Ridley Scott, US, 2000). The actor Oliver Reed was digitally mixed to look alive *after he had died.* Resurrection clearly goes somewhat beyond the healing arts of photography alone. It may be that digital manipulation is changing the fundamental nature of film.

[17] For a full analysis of the notion of depiction in cinema, with opposing views being discussed, see "Depiction", Hopkins, Robert in in *The Routledge Companion to Philosophy and Film*, Kindle Edition. Ch.6.

[18] I take these thought experiments from a discussion in Kania, Andrew, 'Realism" in *The Routledge Companion to Philosophy and Film*, Ch.22. The first comes from Berys Gaut. On the issue of sufficiency, the counterfactual dependency would have to provide a satisfactory level of detail, though how much remains vague. But this applies also to perception. There is no fine line between seeing and not seeing.

[19] Kania, *op.cit.*

[20] *Ibid.*

[21] For even further subtleties, not all of which matter too much to the purpose of this book, see Hopkins, *op.cit.* Hopkins distinguishes five kinds of Realism but for simplicity's sake I reduce the number to three. The additional subtleties in five do not, I think, matter to us.

[22] For an extended discussion see, Sokolowski, Robert, *Introduction to Phenomenology*, Ch. 9. 'Temporality'. I think it would be philosophically mistaken to regard what we think of as the subjective aspects of time as being less real, too. Indeed, Sokolowski argues that we can only have a concept of time at all on the basis of internal time. More, the very notion of objective time would make no sense were it not for internal time. I think that this puts the lie to a not uncommon scientific attitude that time, at least as we normally think of it, is illusory. Rather, it is *that* attitude that is illusory.

[23] From the internet. URL http://neiloseman.com/barry-lyndon-the-full-story-of-the-famous-f0-7-lenses/

Berys Gaut discusses this in greater detail in Gaut, B, op.cit., pp.21-30.

[24] Gaut, *op.cit*, p.29.

[25] Merleau-Ponty, Maurice, *"The Film and the New Psychology"* (1947) cited by Vivian Sobchackin, "Phenomenology", in *The Routledge Companion to Philosophy and Film*, Kindle Edition. Ch.40

[26] In respect of perception, I am what philosophers call a 'direct realist'. That is, I support the view that in perception we see the world in a direct and visually unmediated way. I am aware of other options - see my book *Philosophical Puzzlement.* In the case of photography, I am an '*in*direct realist'. That is, I support the view that, in photography, we see the world photographed in an indirect and visually mediated way.

[27] https://www.britannica.com/art/motion-picture. Retrieved April 2020

[28] *Cinemascope: Before and After*, p.152.

[29] In respect of the above sub-sections, I acknowledge insight from Dudley Andrew, Robert Sklar, Arthur D. Murphy, Ralph Stephenson & Roger Manvell in their article "Motion Pictures" in *Encyclopaedia Britannica*, 2020.

[30] https://www.britannica.com/art/aesthetic-distance.

[31] Todd AO was named after Michael Todd, a film world entrepreneur, and the American Optical Corporation.

[32] 70mm had been introduced in the 1930s. Indeed wide-screen pictures had been experimented with since the earliest days of cinema just like colour but there was no economic incentive for it to catch on with exhibitors. In the 1930s more people went to cinemas weekly than now do annually.

[33] Only one Cinerama installation still exists in the UK – The Pictureville at Bradford. Each year they have held a 'wide-screen weekend' and such glorious spectacles of cinema can still be seen there. Be aware of ersatz Cinerama, which used 70mm prints on the same curved screen but with reduced picture width.

[34] The history of the technology of cinema is fascinating but it is important to the present book because of its dramatic and aesthetic implications. The fact that it has such implications is, in my view woefully under-acknowledged. However, the history of the development of the wide screen is vastly more complicated than my summary suggests. Those fascinated enough can pass many happy hours studying the websites of 'in 70mm.com' and 'The American Wide Screen Museum'. Both contain a wealth of very careful and thorough research. For those who prefer a book, I recommend Carr & Hayes, *Wide Screen Movies: A History and Filmography of Wide Gauge Filmmaking* (1988) and John Belton's *Widescreen Cinema* (1993).

[35] David Lean in an interview with Barry Norman. BBC TV, *Film 88*, 1988.

[36] In his *The Power of Movies*, p.17. McGinn's book is a very clearly written book on the philosophy and psychology of the film watching experience. It cuts through both the unfortunate, dark, rather obscurantist denseness that typifies much writing on film theory and the rather gymnastic airlessness of conceptual analysis of much analytic philosophy of film (and much Analytic Philosophy in other areas, I would say). I can only dream that my own book leans somewhat McGinn's way. McGinn defends what may be called the 'dream theory' of film watching, it being a major aspect of, as he puts it in the subtitle, the way in which screen and mind interact, and I will be drawing upon his excellent work.

[37] *Op.cit.*, p.197.

[38] Murch, *In The Blink of an Eye*, p.122. McGinn (*op.cit.*, p.19) cites other things that we commonly say we "look into": holes, mirrors, scopes, flames, water, the sky and (more metaphorically) the mind. This is insightful, for all hold a similar kind of fascination and, I would add, can be hugely cinematic phenomena. (In a way, even the mind – see *Being John Malkovich* (Spike Jonze, US, 1999) – can be cinematic.) God is the one from whom "no secrets are hid" but cinema is revealing all the same. McGinn says of the screen that it is "aptly described as a *portal*, which is itself a hole of a certain sort". (*op.cit.*, p.20) My own position is this: we (standardly) look *through* the form of the image on the screen to the events and things photographed but look *into* those events as if they were real. The portal gives the frame *form*, one might say, and one passes through it (that's what portals are for, after all) but the world one passes into is seen through eyes transformed by the form provided by the portal. In the present book I attempt to steer a middle route between 'realism' and 'formalism'. Those who know their film theory may detect here echoes of Jean Mitry, in so far at least as I see differences between seeing things through the cinematic image and just ordinarily seeing things. Despite the fact I hold to realism in holding to the transparency thesis, I do not hold that seeing things through the cinematic

image is a mere re-presentation of the things seen before the camera. (See discussion surrounding this issue in Ch 2 of *Concepts of Film Theory* by Dudley Andrew.)

[39] I am grateful to a helpful article in Wikipedia for the above examples. If further examples and variations on the same point are needed, please consult https://en.wikipedia.org/wiki/Oneiric_(film_theory). Here I simply want to convey the fact that oneiric theory has played a long historic role in our understanding of the film viewing experience.

[40] *Feeling and Form*, p.415.

[41] *Op.cit.*, p.103. McGinn takes matters his own way and while I draw upon his insights, I would not want the reader to take my own ideas as exactly his own.

[42] *Op.cit.*, p.136.

[43] *Ibid.*

[44] McGinn, p.77.

[45] Though I am well aware of the philosophical issues at play concerning the nature of perception. See my *Philosophical Puzzlement*, Chapter 'Seeing Things'.

[46] See McGinn on this, pp.58-59.

[47] See McGinn, op.cit, p.66.

[48] *Op.cit.*, p.78.

[49] This is not entirely what philosophers believed or argued for prior to Descartes. Their position was far more nuanced. (See my *Philosophical Puzzlement.*).

[50] Susanne K. Langer, 1953, p. 413.

[51] McGinn, *op.cit.*, p.79.

[52] Here McGinn (*ibid.*) relates cinema to the Church.

[53] *Op.cit.*, p.159.

[54] *Op.cit.*, p.161.

[55] *Op.cit.*, pp.172-3.

[56] See McGinn, *op.cit.*, Chapters 4 – 7 for further considerations.

[57] *Op.cit.*, p.173

[58] Hopkins, Robert, "Realism in Film (and Other Representation)" in *Current Controversies in Philosophy of Film*, Ch 4, Kindle Edition.

[59] https://www2.bfi.org.uk/sites/bfi.org.uk/files/downloads/bfi-media-conference-2017-teaching-language-mise-en-scene-grace-eardley-into-film.pdf.

[60] Lopes, *op.cit.*, pp. 433-448.

[61] Hopkins, *op.cit*, pp.79 and on.

[62] *Ibid.*

[63] Mark de Valk, *The Film Handbook*, p. 120.

[64] The original source here is Scruton's, "Photography and Representation".

[65] Dominic McIver Lopes. *Four Arts of Photography (New Directions in Aesthetics)* p.6. Wiley. Kindle Edition.

[66] Dawn M Phillips, "Photography and Causation: Responding to Scruton's Scepticism".

[67] McGinn, *op.cit.*, p.47

[68] *How To Read a Film: Movies, Media, and Beyond*, pp. 447-448.

[69] *Faith and Beauty*, p.1. Hans Urs Von Balthasar was a highly influential twentieth century Swiss Roman Catholic theologian. The work cited is his *The Glory of the Lord*, p. 18.

[70] *Ibid.* An extended quote may be in place: "Our situation today shows that beauty demands for itself at least as much courage and decision as do truth and goodness, and she will not allow herself to be separated and banned from her two sisters without taking them along with herself in an act of mysterious vengeance. We can be sure that whoever sneers at her name as if she were the ornament of a bourgeois past -- whether he admits it or not -- can no longer pray and soon will no longer be able to love."

[71] *Beauty: A Very Short Introduction*, p. 197.

[72] http://www.film-intel.com/2016/11/wes-andersons-aesthetic-distance-in.html

[73] Isaacs, Bruce. *The Orientation of Future Cinema: Technology, Aesthetics, Spectacle,* pp. 4&10.

[74] *Op.cit.*, pp. 14-15.

[75] Ralph Stephenson and J. R. Debrix, *The Cinema as Art*, p.236.

[76] *Op. cit.*, p.17

[77] Anthony Kenny, *The Metaphysics of Mind*, p.121

[78] Mary Warnock, *Imagination & Time*, p.21

[79] It is sometimes called "The Vertigo Effect". The 'Film IQ' YouTube website (a useful source for various matters of interest concerned with cinema) has a demonstration on how it is done. See:

https://www.youtube.com/watch?v=Amj6RiGiTOE.

[80] 30 fps may be the acceptable upper limit. This rate was used for the film *Oklahoma* (Fred Zinnemann, US, 1955) the first film in a 65/70mm process called Todd-AO. It was claimed that the higher rate eliminated flicker on the bigger screens used. Having seen many huge films on many huge screens at 24fps, and *Oklahoma* once at 30 fps, I am unconvinced. The Todd-AO process soon gave up the 30 fps standard.

[81] I often wonder whether, say, a tree would really perceive its surrounding world as three dimensional, even if it were magically equipped with two eyes and a visual cortex, for it would still not be able to move around in its environment and see the other sides of things.

[82] In western Christendom there exists a traditional monastic practice of reading scripture called *Lectio Divina* (Divine Reading): one reads (*lectio*) meditates (meditatio) prays (oratio) and then contemplates (*contemplatio*). Cinema offers a similar opportunity, as does any art. The finest of far eastern cinema seems to recognise something of this.

[83] William of Occam (or Ockham) was a mediaeval philosopher who framed a methodological principle of parsimony, namely that in devising any hypothesis one should not multiply one's entities beyond necessity.

[84] McGinn, *op.cit.*, p.77

[85] John Beasley in http://not-critical.com/2010/08/red-desert/

[86] H. Perry Horton https://filmschoolrejects.com/vertigo-color-and-identity-32a2f013616c/

[87] *Op.cit.*, p.156

[88] For our purposes I simplify matters in this section, but they can get rather technical. A useful on-line source that goes into more details with respect to historic colour processes is 'The American Widescreen Museum'. On YouTube you can also find some George Eastman Museum animated videos on old Technicolor. See: https://www.youtube.com/watch?v=g9S76vtk4Ro, and https://www.youtube.com/watch?v=N-T8MVrw1L0.

[89] Again, I simplify. The three strip 'dye-transfer' process as it was called was used for making superior cinema prints until the mid-1970s.

[90] Citation from Jeff Smith in 'Music' in *The Routledge Companion to Film and Philosophy*, p.184

[91] *ibid.*

[92] For a fuller description of the role of music in film see Kathryn Kalinak's *Film Music: A Very Short Introduction.*

[93] See, Jeff Smith, *op.cit*, p.191.

[94] Davison, Andrew, *Music and What Matters Most.* Kindle Ed.

[95] Ibid.

[96] Taken from, https://en.wikipedia.org/wiki/Dogme_95

[97] *Emotion*, p.183.

[98] See Justin Oakley, *Morality and the Emotions* p.7.

[99] John Deigh is cited in Mark Wynn, 'Religion and The Revelation of Value: The Emotions as Sources for Religious Understanding', pp.45-6.

[100] Baxter was a 17th Century Christian writer. This quotation is from his, *The Saints' Everlasting Rest*, a treatise on the joys of the promise to faithful Christians.

[101] At any rate this should be the viewer's default position. Of course, one may bring one's own attention to particular features that one thinks are sinful or admirable, and one can certainly reflect upon each feature afterwards. But while watching a film it can be a dangerous practice. One has to keep as best one can in touch with the whole because it is the whole that does the essential work.

[102] Tim Gray, "Sound Is 50% of the Movie, but Hollywood is Often Tone-Deaf", *Variety*, February 22, 2018.

[103] For a more detailed consideration of this interchange, see: https://www.legacy.com/news/the-quotable-laurence-olivier/.

[104] See Parker Tyler, *Magic and Myth of the Movies*, p.31

[105] Stanley Cavell, 'The World Viewed' in *Philosophy of Film and Motion Pictures,* p.72

[106] Noel Carroll, 'Defining The Moving Image' in *Philosophy of Film and Motion Pictures,* p.127

[107] Arthur C. Danto, 'Moving Pictures' in *Philosophy of Film and Motion Pictures,* p.107

[108] Noel Carroll, 'Introduction to Part II' in *Philosophy of Film and Motion Pictures,* p.55

[109] Cavell, *ibid.*

[110] Quoted in McGinn, *op.cit*, pp.51-52

[111] Steven Roberts, 'High Fidelity Widescreen Cinema: VistaVision Film Production and Style in Britain and the USA', p.123.

[112] Quotes from Andrew Russell, "Slow cinema: what it is and why it's on a fast track to the mainstream in a frenetic world".

[113] *Ibid.*

[114] Film Style and Technology: History and Analysis, p.164.

[115] Welles and Coppola quotes from internet.

[116] Walter Murch, *In The Blink of an Eye*, p.5

[117] Murch, *op.cit*, p.16

[118] Edward Dmytryk, *On Film Editing*, Chapters 5-7

[119] Colin Marshall, *Film*, September 3, 2019 (Retrieved from the openculture.com website).

[120] For more on these and other examples, see the article in Wikipedia on 'Match Cut'. I am grateful to its anonymous authors.

[121] Mike Bedard, 'What is a Jump Cut? 5 Ways to Use Jump Cuts in Film', on the studiobinder.com website.

[122] Of course, almost any series of events that constitutes a film may be regarded as its 'story' in some stretched sense of the word. Here, though, I use the word in the way that indicates a series of related events that we would more naturally be inclined to call a 'story'. I appreciate that the edges are blurry.

[123] Hart, David Bentley. *Theological Territories*, p. 6. I wouldn't like to leave the reader with the impression that I capture all the subtleties of Hart's thoughts on such matters, I just rather liked the line I cite as a standalone quote. I take some general inspiration here from Hart's book.

[124] As reported in 'Rotten Tomatoes', a film reviewing website: https://www.rottentomatoes.com/m/belfast , though to be fair, the reviewer, Deborah Ross adds that she found it "sincere and affectionate".

[125] McGinn, *op.cit.*, pp.55-57.

[126] See his *An Intelligent Person's Guide to Philosophy*, Ch 10, p.127 on for a fuller discussion.

[127] I provide a much fuller discussion of this issue in my book *Philosophical Puzzlement*, Chapter 'The Soul and the Zombie'.

[128] Scruton, *op.cit.*, p.131.

[129] I do mean to imply that these are absent in the non-human world. If we evolved from earlier species and judge that we are *basically animals*, then we must allow that these earlier animal species were *nascently us*. This two-way-ness of evolution seems never to be allowed a foothold in more naïve discussions of the subject (and that includes many discussions that consider themselves scientifically sophisticated). Evolution is more sighted than we tend to think. It is scientific biology, useful as it is to our understanding, that is visually impaired. All science is – necessarily – because it restricts its own possible conceptions to the strictly measurable. (See again my book *Philosophical Puzzlement* for a fuller discussion.) Anyway, if there is no reason to deny simpler, nascent forms of such activities from earlier animal species, there is also no reason to deny it of other modern animal species.

[130] It stems from the Latin word *intentio*, used in mediaeval philosophy. In ordinary English we have lost the wider sense and retained the word only for the special case of mental directedness found in *doing* something intentionally.

[131] For interested readers I recommend Dudley Andrew's, *Concepts in Film Theory*, Ch. 4. "Every artwork demands that we come to terms with its status as a sign before adopting a strategy of interpretation", we are told. This issue plays also into authorial intent and, hence auteur theory, too. However, such considerations of interpretation go beyond the primary interests of the present book, which are more concerned with just what the nature of a cinematic image is, and the implications of this, rather than how we might interpret product in terms of significations.

[132] Historically it is the celebrated writer on cinema Pauline Kael who is known for what I am calling a mistake. In her "Raising Kane", *The New Yorker*, 1971, she points out that cinematographer Gregg Toland has as much right to be called the auteur of *Citizen Kane* as Welles. I have already pointed out why I think that is a mistake. However, it is also misplaced, for the existence of joint auteurs who act as one is hardly a refutation of auteur theory. It is a simple modification of it.

[133] I recall listening on the radio many years ago to Leonard Bernstein's rendering of this piece. He played it with such painful slowness that the BBC announcer was moved to say, "You have just been listening to *The Enigma Variations* by Leonard Bernstein." He was no 'young pup' by this time, I hasten to add, merely an ageing genius giving himself undue warrant – but similar principles of pretention apply.

[134] It was introduced by W.K. Wimsatt, Jr., and Monroe C. Beardsley in *The Verbal Icon* (1954).

[135] https://arnolfini.org.uk/whatson/the-act-of-killing-directors-cut/

[136] Iris Murdoch, 1959, p.215.

[137] See his *Summa Contra Gentiles*, 'The function of the wise man' Book 1, Chapter 2.

[138] I am immensely grateful hereabouts to the teaching and various writings of one of my philosophy teachers, Simon Oliver, now the Van Mildert Professor of Divinity at the University of Durham. It is good to owe such educational debt. Any philosophical or theological error or inadequacy, however, would be entirely my own.

[139] Elliot, T.S., 'Poetry & Truth', in *Theories of Art and Beauty*.

[140] Isenberg, A., in Hursthouse, R., 'Truth and representation' in *Philosophical Aesthetic*, p.91. I owe hereabouts a debt of gratitude to this book.

[141] I would not deny that there are some significant asymmetries between belief and make-belief. (See Elisa Galgut for a fuller consideration of this.) I would maintain only that the two are also significantly related.

[142] Philosopher Suzanne Langer explores such issues in 'Philosophy in a new key'.

[143] This is not to deny strong differences between the arts. Film, for example, does not, *qua* film, consist in syntactic elements that match those of written language, despite attempts by many film theorists to render the idea of 'a language of the cinema' quite literally. See, for example, Gregory Currie, *Image & Mind* on this. Nevertheless, films do tell stories and their essential narrative structure can be related to truth-tellingness in the way that literature can.

[144] For further discussion on these issues see Mary Deveraux, "Beauty and Evil: The Case of Leni Riefenstahl's The Triumph of the Will", in *Philosophy Film & Motion Picture*, Ch. 23.

[145] I employ the word 'appearance' here, and throughout examples will be prejudiced towards the *visual*. However, this is simply a harmless bias, since the context allows us to

take the word to cover the way things are delivered to the other senses. Things I say about the visual can, I believe, be applied *mutatis mutandis* across the senses.

146 It often seems thought that beauty is mind-dependent in the sense that mass isn't. Objects which have beauty, given that minds (of the appropriate kind) exist, would continue to exist *as objects* upon the extinction of such minds but their beauty would not.

147 Even if a picture is of something horrific – a crucifixion – say, we may still distinguish the event represented in the painting and the representation (or mode of representation) itself. It would be in the latter that we take our delight.

148 In saying this one is not denying that a thing's existence is necessary to our coming to judge it as beautiful. After all, if a thing didn't exist, it could hardly have an appearance? (Though we can construct purely imaginary scenes in our mind's eyes.) However, all this would be beside the point. All that matters is that we are simply not *interested* in the thing's existence, only its appearance.

149 The crucial passage in Kant is in *Critique of Judgement* p.43.

150 I may wish, of course, to own, say, a painting, but even if I wish to own it because of its aesthetic value, that wish itself is no part of my aesthetic appreciation of it but just belongs to some more possessive aspect of my psychology.

151 See Kant, *op.cit.*, p.48.

152 *Op.cit.*, p.50.

153 The capital letters are deliberate and allude to the special role each of these notions play in Kantian metaphysics.

154 In Kant, therefore, Imagination goes well beyond (but includes) what we ordinarily think of as being included by the term.

155 Perhaps one may also think here of small children or even babies in this context. Perhaps their fascination with forms is a primitive kind of unarticulated judgement of taste, taking the high ground because they have not yet mastered an adult conceptual scheme. Notice also how all this goes against what I said about the cinematic image in Chapter 1 – that one has to know what such an image *is* in order to judge its aesthetic worth.

156 See Kant, *op.cit.*, pp.62-63.

157 Care must be taken hereabouts. First, the form of a flower may indeed have a purpose – to attract insects for pollination, to produce seeds for the next generation, and so on. (Teleology is respectable in biology nowadays.) Secondly, a picture may well have been produced with the purpose of producing something beautiful. However, all this misses the point, which is that the beauty *itself* has no purpose but seems to have.

158 Kant, *op.cit.*, p.83

159 Thomas Aquinas, *Summa Theologiae*.

160 *Integritas, Consonantia, Claritas*, November 1, 2015, https://onartandaesthetics.com/2015/11/01/integritas-consonantia-claritas/

161 I am thinking here of photographically realistic cinematic images. In abstract cinematic imagery this does not seem to apply. Think of the zooming colour arrays near the end of Kubrick's *2001*. Here, the cinematic image just is the abstract arrangement of colour and light.

[162] For more on this point see Ayfre, Amédée (1895-1963), a student of Merleau-Ponty, cited in "Philosophy of Film: Continental Perspectives", Botz-Bornstein, Thorsten, in the *Internet Encyclopaedia of Philosophy*. No date given.

[163] Simon Oliver, p.6

[164] *Op.cit.*, p.17

[165] David Bordwell, *The Poetics of Cinema*, p.14

[166] McGinn, *op.cit.*, p.130.

[167] The 'British Board of Film Classification', previously the 'British Board of Film Censors', is the British body responsible for classifying films according to suitability for different age ranges and offers brief warnings pertaining to such issues as a film's depiction of sex, drug misuse and violence.

[168] Sayers, a great Christian writer, said this in the context of Christian dogma.

[169] Wayne in interview in https://www.youtube.com/watch?v=YkAPfqK0AZo

[170] The reader may care to look up the webpage mentioned and ask how far its author is really talking about subverting genre in the classical sense and how far filmmakers just like having fun with much looser classifications of films.

Lightning Source UK Ltd.
Milton Keynes UK
UKHW020631050822
406897UK00005B/489

9 781845 497989